IMPOSSIBLE RECOVERY

GENDER, THEORY, AND RELIGION

GENDER, THEORY, AND RELIGION

AMY HOLLYWOOD, EDITOR

The Gender, Theory, and Religion series provides a forum for interdisciplinary scholarship at the intersection of the study of gender, sexuality, and religion.

Martyrdom and Memory: Early Christian Culture Making, Elizabeth A. Castelli

When Heroes Love: The Ambiguity of Eros in the Stories of Gilgamesh and David, Susan Ackerman

Abandoned to Lust: Sexual Slander and Ancient Christianity, Jennifer Wright Knust

Bodily Citations: Religion and Judith Butler, Ellen T. Armour and Susan M. St. Ville, editors

Naming the Witch: Magic, Ideology, and Stereotype in the Ancient World, Kimberly B. Stratton

Dying to Be Men: Gender and Language in Early Christian Martyr Texts, L. Stephanie Cobb

Tracing the Sign of the Cross: Sexuality, Mourning, and the Future of American Catholicism, Marian Ronan

Between a Man and a Woman? Why Conservatives Oppose Same-Sex Marriage, Ludger H. Viefhues-Bailey

Promised Bodies: Time, Language, and Corporeality in Medieval Women's Mystical Texts, Patricia Dailey

Christ Without Adam: Subjectivity and Difference in the Philosophers' Paul, Benjamin H. Dunning

Electric Santería: Racial and Sexual Assemblages of Transnational Religion, Aisha M. Beliso-De Jesús

Acute Melancholia and Other Essays: Mysticism, History, and the Study of Religion, Amy Hollywood

Archives of Conjure: Stories of the Dead in Afrolatinx Cultures, Solimar Otero

IMPOSSIBLE RECOVERY

JULIAN OF NORWICH AND THE PHENOMENOLOGY OF WELL-BEING

HANNAH LUCAS

Columbia University Press *New York*

Columbia University Press
Publishers Since 1893
New York   Chichester, West Sussex
cup.columbia.edu

Library of Congress Cataloging-in-Publication Data

Names: Lucas, Hannah, author.
Title: Impossible recovery : Julian of Norwich and the
phenomenology of well-being / Hannah Lucas.
Description: New York : Columbia University Press, [2024] | Series: Gender,
theory, and religion | Includes bibliographical references and index.
Identifiers: LCCN 2024033241 (print) | LCCN 2024033242 (ebook) |
ISBN 9780231218672 (hardback) | ISBN 9780231218689 (trade paperback) |
ISBN 9780231562409 (ebook)
Subjects: LCSH: Julian, of Norwich, 1343– Revelations of divine love. |
Well-being—Philosophy. | Phenomenology.
Classification: LCC BV4831.J83 L83 2024 (print) | LCC BV4831.J83 (ebook) |
DDC 242—dc23/eng/20240904
LC record available at https://lccn.loc.gov/2024033241
LC ebook record available at https://lccn.loc.gov/2024033242

Printed and bound by CPI Group (UK) Ltd, Croydon, CR0 4YY

Cover design: Milenda Nan Ok Lee
Cover art: Bryan Nash Gill, *Ash* (2003). Copyright © 2012 Bryan Nash Gill.
Used by permission of Bryan Nash Gill Ltd.

For my family

CONTENTS

ACKNOWLEDGMENTS

It is a pleasure to acknowledge the many people and communities that have supported this book. The book began as a doctoral project at the University of Oxford under the supervision of Vincent Gillespie, whom I thank sincerely for his continued guidance, encouragement, and insights. The project was funded by the Arts and Humanities Research Council, without which this book would not have been possible. The dissertation was examined in the summer of 2020, a memorable year on many counts: I thank Nicholas Watson and Mishtooni Bose for their tremendous generosity as assessors and as mentors as I have navigated the early stages of my career. Their support has been invaluable. My thanks also to Annie Sutherland for her helpful feedback on the dissertation in its early form.

The first stages of the book's development began while I was teaching at Corpus Christi College and St Peter's College, Oxford. It was a privilege to discuss medieval literature with my undergraduate and graduate students, and I thank them for their thoughtful work and shared enthusiasm for Julian of Norwich. I owe a great deal to my colleagues during this time: in particular, Helen Moore, who first introduced me to medieval literature during my undergraduate days and has continued to encourage me in the years following, Ben Higgins, Francis Leneghan, Esther Osorio Whewell, and David Russell. I am grateful to Daniel McCann and Phil Knox, who together with Vincent Gillespie helped to cultivate my early interest in medieval literature and medicine at Oxford. Heartfelt thanks also go to my academic siblings: Peter Buchanan, Antje Chan, Tim Glover, and Raphaela Rohrhofer. Last—but by no means least—my love and thanks to Lucy Brookes and Hattie Soper.

I completed the book during a Research Fellowship at Newnham College, Cambridge, funded by the Newby Trust. Thank you to the Trust for facilitating this work. In the Cambridge English Faculty, I have benefited from the kindness of many colleagues and friends: Alex Da Costa, who supervised me during my master's degree and has supported me since, Orietta Da Rold, Becky Field, Elly Myerson, Millie Newis, Alicia Smith, Alexis Statz, Georgina Wilson, Barry Windeatt, and Nicky Zeeman. It has been a pleasure to be a part of "Newnham English" together with May Hawas, Bonnie Lander-Johnson, and Amy Morris. I am also happy to have had such inspiring contemporaries in the other early postdoctoral researchers at Newnham—especially Abbie Bradshaw, Laura Caponetto, Diala Ltief, Kat Mizrokhi, and Fadia Panosetti—and elsewhere in Cambridge, Tanya Kundu and Siddharth Soni.

Encouragement and guidance has come from many places in the wider medievalist community. I am deeply indebted to Liz Herbert McAvoy, who has been an inspiring role model and advocate for many years, and enormously kind in providing feedback on this book. Together with Liz, I am thankful to the community of scholars working variously on medieval gender and mysticism who have made me feel so welcome in the field: Lucy Allen-Goss, Claire Gilbert, Eve Johnson,

Laura Kalas, Ayoush Lazikani, Roberta Magnani, Louise Nelstrop, Godelinde Gertrude Perk, Hannah Piercy, Laura Varnam, and Naoë Kukita Yoshikawa, to name just a few.

The beautiful print on the cover, *Ash*, is reproduced with the kind permission of Gina Kiss Gill, on behalf of Bryan Nash Gill. The rings of the tree trunk capture, for me, the inward spiral of the contemplative life and the multiplicity of time. Unfortunately, ash trees across Europe are being destroyed by the fungal disease Ash Dieback, from which they have little chance of recovery and which will have a devastating impact on biodiversity. In this way, the cover image serves as a poignant reminder that human well-being is deeply interconnected to ecological well-being—an idea also borne out Julian's ecological poetic, as is explored in the later chapters of this book. Thank you to the Faculty of English at the University of Cambridge for supporting the acquisition of this permission.

The extract of prose by Oliver Sacks used as an epigraph for chapter 2 is reproduced with permission from the *New York Times*. The lines of T. S. Eliot that form the epigraph of chapter 3 are reproduced with the permission of Faber & Faber and HarperCollins. The extract by Clarissa Pinkola Estés is reproduced with the permission of Penguin Random House. The extract by Norman Fischer that forms the epigraph of chapter 6 is reproduced with the permission of Simon & Schuster. Thanks to Newnham College for supporting me in acquiring these permissions.

I would also like to sincerely thank Amy Hollywood (as series editor), Wendy Lochner, and Alyssa Napier at Columbia University Press, who have seen the book through from manuscript to production, as well as the book's anonymous readers, whose careful feedback has been vital in getting the book to its present form.

For their continued reassurances that *all shall be well* throughout the development of this book, my love and thanks goes to my family: Ruth, Andy, and Rory Lucas; and also to Harry Begg, Joe Brown, Joel Casey, Isobel Fyson, Nuzha Nuseibeh, Nayana Prakash, and Mary Trend. Finally, thank you to Paul Röttger, for everything.

ABBREVIATIONS

DMLBS	*Dictionary of Medieval Latin from British Sources*
EETS	Early English Text Society
e.s.	extra series
MED	*Middle English Dictionary*
MS	manuscript
MSS	manuscripts
n.s.	new series
OED	*Oxford English Dictionary*
o.s.	original series

NOTE ON EDITIONS AND TRANSLATIONS

The edition of Julian used throughout is *Revelations of Divine Love*, ed. Barry Windeatt (Oxford: Oxford University Press, 2016). Quotations are cited in endnotes as "[L: long text/S: short text].[chapter number].[line number]."

The translation of Martin Heidegger's *Being and Time* (1927) used is Joan Stambaugh's, revised and with a foreword by Dennis J. Schmidt (Albany: State University of New York Press, 2010). Marginal numbers are cited rather than page numbers, as per convention. Original German is cross-referenced from Martin Heidegger, *Sein und Zeit*, 17th ed. (1927; Niemeyer: Tübingen, 1993).

All bible quotations are taken from the 1899 Douay-Rheims edition with the Latin cross-referenced from the Vulgate where necessary.

Unless otherwise stated, all Middle English translations (and errors) are my own.

IMPOSSIBLE RECOVERY

INTRODUCTION

Then and Now: Recovering Julian of Norwich

Syn I recouered was / haue I ful ofte
Cause had of anger / and inpacience,
Where I born haue it / esily and softe,
Suffryng wrong be doon / to me and offense
And nat answerd ageyn / but kept silence,
Lest þat men of me / deeme wolde and seyn
"See how this man / is fallen in ageyn."

Since I have recovered, I have very often
had cause to be angry and impatient, at times
where I have borne it gently and patiently,
suffering wrong and offence to be done to me
but not answering back and keeping quiet,
in case that people would judge me and say,
"See how this man has become afflicted once more."

—Thomas Hoccleve, "Complaint," from the *Series*

An impossible problem connects visionary literature about encountering God with accounts of extreme illness. Both genres deal with the unsayable, with the outermost edges of human experience. In texts where these accounts are personal, very often the author reports their perspective on life to be dramatically changed. They see differently what it means to be alive and what it means to be (and live) well; they have looked through the glass darkly that divides living and dying, human and divine, and what they have witnessed has been a revelation. This book is about what happens when a person comes up against this glass and lives to tell the tale. It thinks about the entanglement of illness and revelation, asking how and why these phenomena seem to share so many characteristics. But most of all, the book considers the aftermath of these fracturing events: their impact on a person as well as the textual artifacts that emerge from them—how they are theorized, interpreted, and put into language. This is a book about what it means to come back from the edge of experience and the possibilities of recovery afforded by the written word.

Few accounts of illness in the Middle Ages evidence the difficulty of recovery so clearly as that of the poet and clerk Thomas Hoccleve (d. 1426), and so he serves as a particularly productive exemplar with which to begin this book. Hoccleve's *Series* is a troubled narrative of thwarted recovery, commonly read as an autobiographical account of the author's own struggles with mental illness.[1] The first half of the poem, "Complaint," recounts this malady: an episode of insanity—"wylde infirmitee" (wild infirmity)—which he claims to have suffered five years prior to the poetic present.[2] This is Hoccleve's first sorrow: an event of illness that "cast and threew" him "oute of [himself]" (threw and hurled [him] out of [his] own self).[3] The reader then learns of a second, additional affliction that seems to weigh equally heavily upon the clerk as his initial illness. He describes this subsequent tribulation in the stanza quoted above, which details the force of judgment by those around him, who he fears will never see beyond his infirmity.[4] In this account of his double sorrow, Hoccleve laments the elusiveness of well-being, a condition he describes as contingent on both his own interior experience and his interactions with the world. For though Hoccleve himself narrativizes his illness in the past tense, he claims repeatedly that people do not trust he is better: "many" around him identify malign weather or "passynge hete" as inevitable triggers for relapse—"quod they / 'trustith this, / Assaile him wole ageyn / þat maladie'" ("when it is extremely hot," they said, "you can be sure that disease will attack him again").[5] Such an amorphous *they* are conceived as an external force with the power to shape and erode the poet-narrator's subjectivity, powerful enough to speak into being the failure of Hoccleve's recovery and give rise to the very "anger and inpacience" that might evidence their claims.

Hoccleve's bid to resolve this relational rupture is to recruit the reader into the interpretive conversation. Writing becomes an opportunity for repair, the text serving as both a personal testimony to his recovery and a cathartic expression of his woe. His poetry gives name to his sorrow and so can be conceived as a remedy against the "silence" he must keep in front of the doubting masses. Just as Hoccleve's body becomes a site of troubled signification, then, the text becomes an equally thorny hermeneutic artifact. Hoccleve's recovery hinges upon this diffusive obscurity, upon the contingency of body and text, and the protocols of interpretation that govern both. But whether Hoccleve's catharsis is successful remains unclear. At the poem's close, Hoccleve writes of the need to bear one's suffering with patience and gives thanks to God, the "salue . . . to al heuynesse" (medicine . . . for all misfortune), for both his well-being and his adversity.[6] His pains, his double sorrow, however, have not been evacuated; the last line of the "Complaint" even calls out for God's mercy and grace. At this point, a friend enters Hoccleve's chamber and requests the complaint be read to him, thus beginning the second poem of the series, the "Dialogue," which now relocates the introspective Hoccleve in conversation. The friend's incredulous response further complicates the reader's knowledge of Hoccleve's situation: he pleads that Hoccleve keep his words to himself because his sickness is "out of mynde" (out of mind); it has already been forgotten by all who know him. What's more, it seems to the friend that Hoccleve's intense and isolated work has thrown him back "into the plyt" (into the plight) he was in before, suggesting that his solipsism has not helped but exacerbated his malady. The external voice of the friend, brought now into the inner chamber of Hoccleve's contemplations, unsettles the reader's trust in the poet-narrator's reliability. Is Hoccleve indeed recovered and seen as such by those at court? If so, what do we make of his paranoia and his own account of his sorrows? Whose version of events do we believe? As the "Dialogue" moves on, the reader is left to deliberate these questions, with the sense that we have been imbricated in the very dance of interpretation described and enacted by the poem.[7]

The deferral of resolution in Hoccleve's text therefore works to illustrate not only the elusiveness of any enduring condition of well-being but also the many intersections of physical, mental, and spiritual forms of health attendant to recovery. As such, it also reflects the central concern of this book: that recovery is an ever-ongoing project, effected through the engagement of self and world. This is a book about recovering well-being—about the health of mind and body—but it is also about the phenomenology of recovery as process, its temporality, and interpretive possibilities. In its most literal definition, *recovery* implies a restoration of something formerly lost; that recovery is spoken of as a journey out of illness and toward health evinces this progressive function. Recovery is, put simply, commonly located on a linear timeline. This book seeks to disrupt this narrative, by examining two theoretical approaches that each conceptualize the search for well-being as occupying multiple temporal frames: the visionary writings of Hoccleve's contemporary Julian of Norwich (1342–after 1416) and the Heideggerian tradition of phenomenological hermeneutics. By considering these bodies of work together, I aim to shed light on a genealogical branch between medieval theology and modern phenomenology, as well as to highlight the tensions and irreconcilabilities between them. The term *recovery* is therefore applied in two ways: first, as it relates to health; and, second, as a reference to historiography and the critical recovery of the past.

Julian of Norwich is this book's primary witness, a writer whose work positions her as not only the first known woman to author a book in the English language but also one of the foremost theologians of the English Middle Ages. Like Hoccleve, Julian similarly underwent a life-altering experience of illness. Compared with Hoccleve's autobiographical text, however, Julian's writing tells us very little about her as a person. Surviving historical information about her is also scant, limited to a small number of wills and bequests from the period.[8] It is known that Julian was born in late 1342 and was enclosed as an anchorite, a medieval recluse attached to a church in Norwich, at some point later that century. When exactly she entered enclosure is not clear: she only writes that she was thirty years old at the time of her illness. In place of Hoccleve's intensely personal torments, Julian's account of her illness focuses predominantly on the divine revelation that accompanied it: over the three days in which her illness blazed in her mind and body, Julian reports that she received a series of sixteen "shewings" that revealed a number of profound insights, including Christ's dying on the cross, God's love for humanity, and the nature of sin. In her texts, Julian meditates on these showings as a unified revelation of love, attempting to describe and interpret their meaning. The product of a lifetime of contemplative work, Julian's visionary writings remain a deeply existential meditation on what it means to be, live, and die well in the world, in anticipation of a heavenly reunion with God.

Julian's work survives in two versions, a shorter and a longer text, commonly known together as the *Revelations of Divine Love*. The short text recounts the showings with relatively sparse exegesis and is now assumed to have been written quite soon after the illness-revelation event.[9] It survives in one mid-fifteenth-century manuscript witness: London, British Library MS Additional 37790 (also known as the Amherst manuscript). The long text is generally taken to be a later revision of Julian's earlier account, adding considerable commentary to the showings as well as two apparently new revelations from 1388 and 1393: first, the revelation that love was the meaning of the revelation as a whole; and, second, the showing of a lord and his servant (or perhaps a new insight into the significance of the showing). This text survives in multiple witnesses, though only one is medieval: London, Westminster Cathedral Treasury MS 4, which only includes the longer text in excerpts. The others are later: Paris, Bibliothèque nationale MS Fonds Anglais 40 and London, British Library MS Sloane 2499 both date to the seventeenth century, while British Library MS Sloane 3705 is thought to be a later copy of the other Sloane MS, dating to the eighteenth century. Finally, several fragments of the *Revelations* survive in MS St. Joseph's College, Upholland, also a seventeenth-century compilation. This lack of an authoritative version has left editors with what Barry Windeatt calls a "moving target" of witnesses, and most editions choose between Paris, BN MS Fonds Anglais 40 and London, BL MS Sloane 2499 for their base text. This book follows Windeatt's recent edition and its use of Sloane, though I seek to highlight differences to the Paris witness where significant.[10]

The foundational premise of this book is that Julian's *Revelations* offer a hermeneutic model of recovery, occurring both in and beyond worldly time. This assertion rests, first and foremost, on her understanding that human existence is a penultimate project, preceding the full salvation of heavenly union. Second, that it is participatory: that part of the existential task of humanity is to understand better their relationship to the divine and seek to deepen this relationship. In light of this, Julian develops a soteriology for how and why humanity suffers, and how to live with this existential knowledge. *Impossible Recovery* subsequently argues that Julian's hermeneutic—her attentiveness to the ways that humans participate in, and even coproduce their experience of the world—finds a comparable expression centuries later in the philosophical method of phenomenology. By exploring the resemblances and dissonances between Julian's theology and post-Heideggerian philosophy—specifically, phenomenologies of health and medicine—the book seeks to provide both a fresh reading of Julian's texts and a contribution to the history of phenomenology's medieval roots. As such, its readings are at once theological, philosophical, and literary-historical, all effected by a close methodological attention to Julian's representational and interpretive strategies. These intersecting aims are driven by the following questions: How do Julian's theological paradigm and post-Heideggerian phenomenologies respectively theorize the recovery of well-being? Where do these models align, and where does the historical and theological inaccessibility of the medieval text forestall recovery for phenomenology's secular mode? And what does it mean for a medieval text to be read as a precursor to modern theories of well-being?

This final question has already been initiated by studies identifying the Middle Ages as a paradigm for modern or postmodern theoretical models. Such attention has been broadly conceived as the "medieval turn" in critical theory, though this turn has since been identified by Andrew Cole and D. Vance Smith as itself bound up with the " 'project of modernity'—specifically, the secularization of medieval philosophical, religious, literary, and economic modes."[11] Cole and Smith explore how the medieval origins of modern theory have, in a modernizing move, all too often accepted a sublimation of their medievalness into secular models. Their recent volume, *The Legitimacy of the Middle Ages: On the Unwritten History of Theory*, puts forward a persuasive counternarrative, attesting to the necessary attention to medieval thought in any theory of modernity, especially modern theory. The inspiration for this volume, and its title, is taken from Hans Blumenberg's *Legitimacy of the Modern Age*, which argued for a model of *dis*continuity between the Middle Ages and modernity; that modernity can only be defined on its own terms, not as a secularized continuation of the medieval. Contra Blumenberg, Cole and Smith instead contend that the Middle Ages must not—and cannot—be broken with for a cohesive theory of modernity, asserting "not only that these aforementioned medieval modes are sustained within modernity, but also that no theory of modernity can be complete or legitimate without a constant reckoning with 'the medieval.' "[12] Put another way, they seek to show, in a riff on Bruno Latour's *We Have Never Been Modern*, that "We Have Always Been Medieval."[13] This book presses further into this seam, to investigate the deep entanglement of medieval and modern theories of recovery.

THE SECULARIZATION THESIS

The aforementioned secularization thesis that Blumenberg so strenuously disavowed has been part of a long-standing and wide-ranging debate around how to theorize the inception and character of modernity. For scholars like Karl Marx, Max Weber, and Émile Durkheim, the secularization of the formerly "enchanted" premodern world was a necessary and predictable decline in religiosity as a result of modernization; these thinkers understood modernity to have cleared a way through the superstitions of religion. More recent studies have sought to complicate this narrative, arguing that a straightforward binary between premodern and modern, secular and religious, is neither helpful nor accurate in the writing of history.[14] For Talal Asad, for example, modernity is not a verifiable object but an "aim" or project toward which certain societies project themselves. Nor, Asad argues, should "the secular" be thought of as "the space in which *real* human life gradually emancipates itself from the controlling power of 'religion' and thus achieves the latter's relocation."[15] Instead, Asad distinguishes "the secular" from "secularism," where the former denotes an epistemic category but the latter "a political doctrine [which] arose in modern Euro-America."[16] One of Asad's primary interlocutors is the philosopher Charles Taylor, who articulates secularization as "a move from a society where belief in God is unchallenged and indeed, unproblematic, to one in which it is understood to be one option among others, and frequently not the easiest to embrace."[17] Rather than a straightforward "subtraction" of religion and belief from society, then, Taylor understands secularization as the production of *new* options for constructing meaning and significance, without reference to the divine or to transcendence. In fact, Taylor inverts the subtraction story entirely, suggesting that the way moderns construe themselves—"the construal we just live in"—instead makes room for unbelief, or removes obstacles to the possibility.[18] He goes on to argue for the vital place of the sacred, or enchantment, in modernity's secular age, and though he differs from Asad in how he believes this can manifest in pluralist societies, both thinkers offer important disruptions to the straightforwardly linear secularization thesis and its attendant binaries.[19]

Where Asad and Taylor are concerned with the cross-pressures of modernity, Cole and Smith focus primarily on its medieval genealogy. However one understands the process of secularization, Cole and Smith argue, Blumenberg's theory of discontinuity fails precisely because "without secularization, and without the Middle Ages, Blumenberg lacks a language with which to describe the various modern hermeneutics of suspicion *as modern*."[20] They explain this dialectic as analogy, the structure of likeness, where historiography requires an attention to something that can only be accessed indirectly: "In discovering the medieval as the object of our contemplation, we discover that it exists in a world that does not fully contain us; yet it remains a world that presupposes our awareness of it."[21] This is a problem of alterity, though not of the "hard-edged" kind; instead, the past is positioned as an absent presence, a precondition for our imagining of both it and other times.[22] Cole and Smith here invoke medievalist Paul Zumthor's description of the medieval past as a "circular, turning-and-returning image" that "transmits the future and brings it back again"—or in Zumthor's own words, "akin to a turntable [*une plaque tournante*, a train hub] . . . both a point of departure and a goal, an exemplary sector, in which traits and tensions proper to medieval civilization take on the intensity of a revelation."[23] Zumthor here describes a distinctly phenomenological temporality, where texts are situated in an "all-embracing present that simultaneously remembers, contemplates, and anticipates."[24] In this view, temporality is more elastic than straightforward periodization allows—even while "'the medieval' and 'the premodern' appear as necessary anachronisms in modernist and postmodern frameworks."[25] Cole and Smith conclude that "all that is designated by 'the medieval' is never overcome and rarely superseded but rather continuously posited as that necessary anachronism that paradoxically generates 'the modern' as we know it."[26]

The possibility of multiple frames of temporality is therefore introduced, where the historian may think of the past, present, and future as having various contemporary expressions. Scholarship in medieval studies has explored this possibility in different ways: while Cole and Smith cite Zumthor as "among the first to posit a futural Middle Ages (or a futural past, in more general terms)," they note more recent work in critical temporal studies that thinks of time similarly expansively.[27] Dipesh Chakrabarty's *Provincializing Europe* is one of these, which takes Martin Heidegger as one of its two framing figures (the other being Marx).[28] Chakrabarty's study thus also exemplifies the efficacy of the phenomenological model in studies of history and time, and so speaks closely to my own approach in this book. Indeed, part of *Impossible Recovery*'s investigation into the mysticism of post-Heideggerian philosophy—and the proto-phenomenology of Julian—is similarly focused on the multiple temporalities at play in these respective projects, especially the (im)possibilities conferred by their respective teleologies. But these models do not only occupy this book's subject matter; they also inform its methodology. Just as, for example, Carolyn Dinshaw finds in the elastic temporalities of the Middle Ages a productive wellspring for theorizing the writing of history, my reading of well-being and recovery, as thought through by Julian and post-Heideggerian philosophers alike, seeks to provide corresponding insights into the recovery of the medieval in the present day.[29]

The book's two definitions of recovery—first as an operation of well-being, and second as an operation of historiography—therefore both rely on the idea of temporality as a multiple and expansive construct. Louise D'Arcens's concept of the *paramodern* is particularly helpful here, a term she coins in a review of Bruce Holsinger's *The Premodern Condition* to describe "a premodern existing not before the modern, but alongside it and within it as a trace, a simultaneous presence and an absence."[30] In this figuration, she explains, the medieval is "neither simply mobilized as a pernicious point of origin for the ills of modernity nor a romanticized, curative alternative, but becomes, to adapt a term finessed by Derrida in *Plato's Pharmacy*, a historical *Pharmakon*: that is, simultaneously, paradoxically and inseparably both poison and remedy to the modern."[31] The Middle Ages become, in D'Arcens's words, "simultaneously cause, symptom and a remedy to the disease of post-Enlightenment rationalism." This diagnostic expression in turn highlights the dual applications of the term *recovery* that this book takes up, where medical discourse becomes more than simply metaphor for historiography, signifying instead an intersecting hermeneutic project. Holsinger's study, too, like Cole and Smith's volume, seeks to identify the indebtedness of modern theory to medieval ideas, a kind of "theoretic medievalism" that he sees as pervading modern thought. The avant-garde philosophers Holsinger addresses find in the Middle Ages "productive sacraments of creative ingenuity, partial remains from an unknowable past invested nevertheless with a transformative capacity in the critical present."[32] This present absence, or absent presence, will be a recurring theme in the following discussion, closely tied as the idea is to mysticism. For now, this overlapping and paradoxical expression serves to make space for the above understanding of recovery as a nonlinear construct. Just as the aforementioned thinkers have problematized a straightforward line from the medieval to modernity, religion to secularism, this book identifies recovery as both possibility and impossibility, where what is gone is, as Cole and Smith put it, "never overcome and rarely superseded" but still remains to generate the present and even, possibly, the future.

THE POLITICS OF RECOVERY

Heideggerian phenomenology is heavily implicated by the above discussions of modernization and serves as a particularly pernicious example of the ways that a desire for the past can poison the present. Martin Heidegger's associations with Nazism are now widely acknowledged, and it has been persuasively shown that this ideology both infuses and shapes his work—a mire that any study invoking his philosophy, even critically, must wade through.[33] A closer look at this connection sheds light on the philosopher's relationship to the Middle Ages and the ways that he adopts and adapts medieval theological ideas for his secularized philosophy.[34] It also, in turn, demonstrates the politics of a kind of recovery driven by nostalgia: a species of "pastism" that seeks to recuperate something historically inaccessible, relying instead on fantasy.

Heidegger's theory and use of language are central to both his philosophical insights and to a critique of his ideology. As Cole and Smith have identified, Heidegger's philosophy "depends largely on modistic grammar (at least in his early work) for his version of medieval scholasticism"—grammar underpinned by a philosophy of language that "insists not only upon the usefulness of analogy as a way to transcendence, but upon its reality."[35] The first chapter of this book explores Heidegger's philosophy of language in more detail, but suffice it to say here that for the phenomenologist, language and experience are ontologically inseparable; that phenomenologically speaking, understanding, being, and signifying are all mutually constitutive. Given this premise, Heidegger's notoriously jargonistic language becomes particularly fraught. Of particular interest to the present discussion is his vocabulary of *authenticity*, which he uses to describe the existential project of human being, *Dasein* (literally, "being-there"). For Heidegger, an authentic understanding of the world and its place in it fulfills Dasein's ontic possibilities, where to understand fully one's own existence in time is, for Heidegger, to live authentically. This idea already gestures toward a far-right interest in purity, since it implies an epistemological return to a more primordial condition of existence.[36] The path to this ideology is marked by signs pointing backward, to the past, where authenticity is so commonly located. Today, this manifests in the widespread populist narratives of nostalgia in Euro-American politics, like the red cap–clad Trumpian cry "Make America Great Again!"—where greatness is defined only by the past tense. Precisely what *was* great is not clear; the far-right gesture is to an amorphous time gone by, held up as somehow closer to humanity's originary nature than any direct experience of the present.

These ideological pulses resonate through the discipline of medieval studies, too, which has in recent years proved itself to be highly susceptible to political appropriation. Among many other scholars working on this important intersection, Jennifer Schuessler has shown how the weaponization of the Middle Ages comes in many forms, "whether it's white nationalist marchers in Charlottesville, Va., displaying medieval symbols or the white terrorist who murdered 50 people at two mosques in Christchurch, New Zealand, using weapons inscribed with references to the Crusades."[37] Medieval studies cannot, then, afford to ignore the nostalgic impulse that threatens historiography—especially in those projects concerned with reading and interpreting the body. As Françoise Meltzer writes in her study of why postmodern theorists are so drawn to the figure of Joan of Arc, there is a "prelapsarian" fantasy at the heart of many of these secular projects.[38] Central to this nostalgia, Meltzer argues, is the materialist desire for a perceived pre-Cartesian holism of body and mind, an impulse of the kind Holsinger also attributes to some of his avant-garde theorists. Meltzer compares this postmodern "attempt at restoration" to the Augustinian desire to restore unity to postlapsarian man, citing the Cartesian mind-body separation as the secular "Fall," for "if knowledge is distance, as interpreters of the Fall have frequently noted, the modern Cartesian subject imposes a fall and a distance of its own: mind from body; thought from being; speculation from materiality."[39] A yearning for the recovery of existential wholeness characterizes this postlapsarian impulse, a project of retrieval that ventriloquizes the Christian story with a secular voice. Meltzer's study of bodily nostalgia therefore extends the secularization thesis, identifying the modernizing desire to recruit categories and structures of the religious past for a secular present.

Heidegger's philosophy may be read as one such iteration of this process, adapting as he does many ideas and concepts from medieval theology. Indeed, Heidegger planned to dedicate his academic life to medieval theology: as Holsinger states, "Had he not been denied a vacant chair in the history of Catholic philosophy at the University of Freiberg, it is likely we would know Heidegger today as one of the great twentieth-century exponents of medieval thought."[40] Following his break with Catholicism, Heidegger proceeded to develop a model of phenomenological hermeneutics after his tutor, Edmund Husserl, which could alternatively theorize the experience of suffering at the heart of human finitude. This personal history has been illuminated by the recent publication of Heidegger's earliest letters and lectures, leading scholars like Ryan Coyne to state that "it is no longer controversial or novel to suggest that Heidegger appropriated certain concepts or structures from texts that are thoroughly embedded within the Christian theological tradition."[41] As Heidegger himself wrote in 1937/38, "Who should fail to recognize that my entire path so far has been accompanied by a silent engagement with Christianity: an engagement that has never taken the form of an explicitly raised 'problem,' but was rather *at once* the preservation of my ownmost provenance—the childhood house, home, and youth—and a painful emancipation from it."[42] Heidegger himself saw Christianity as an early memory—a place of origin—imprinted onto his later work.

These undercurrents find expression in what has been called Heidegger's *detheologized* philosophy, which Judith Wolfe describes as "the emancipation of philosophy from theology as an independent mediatrix of authentic existence."[43] Heidegger's dealings with theology have long been the subject of scholarly study, and it is not the intention of this book to rehearse this wide-ranging field.[44] It is, however, important to assert that a theological basis for Heidegger's philosophy is by no means a radical or original claim. Laurence Paul Hemming, for example, argues quite forcefully that Heidegger's silence is an eloquent way of speaking about the ineffable and also identifies a mystical thread running through his work: a continuity with St. Gregory of Nyssa, Catherine of Siena, and Meister Eckhart.[45] Opting for a narrative of concealment rather than of continuity, Sean J.

McGrath meanwhile writes that "the Godless phenomenology of *Sein und Zeit* (in fact, a phenomenology *for* the Godforsaken) *covers over* an essential ontological structure: religiousness."[46] Some of Heidegger's terminology might even be resonant for the reader of mystical texts: phrases like "letting be" (*Gelassenheit*), "detachment" (*Abgeschiedenheit*), and "devotion" (*Hingabe*).[47] More than this, though, Heideggerian phenomenology theorizes the very structure of human existence in ways that bracket its theological foundation. This culminates in his early—and perhaps most famous—existential account, *Being and Time* (*Sein und Zeit*) (1927), where he theorizes human being as always "being-toward-death," in a perpetual extension outward toward annihilation. This is not, importantly, the teleological end of the Christian narrative, but rather an extension into a groundless *nothing* (*Nichts*). Wolfe calls this the creation of an "eschatology without an eschaton."[48]

This process of secularization closely intersects with both the pastism of nostalgia and the futurist desire for a utopian state. Wolfe argues that it is precisely this detheologized eschatology that "began to intersect with an eschatological consciousness that had shaped German self-understanding since the Romantic era, and was also being appropriated by Nazi leaders and intellectuals"—that is, the identification of an imagined, future nation with the eschatological kingdom of Christ.[49] Nevertheless, she contends that while Heidegger "temporarily thought to be finding in Nazism a spiritual ally—a movement bold enough to realize the intellectual ambition he was projecting—he was soon disappointed by the crass, militant apocalypticism into which the eschatological tradition of Fichte, Hegel and Hölderlin was here being shaped, and disassociated himself from the party programme in favour of an *apophatic eschatology* centered on a very different reading of Hölderlin."[50] Wolfe's measured critique thus builds a picture of a Heidegger that finds inspiration not in the gaze forward toward a nationalist utopia, but in the irrepressible traces of a theology that grounded his early life and thought. More recent work by Richard Wolin has argued that Heidegger's dissatisfaction with the Nazi project was not due to its ambitions but, rather, that it was not ambitious enough. One choice quote among many stark instances of Heidegger's Nazism in Wolin's book reports Heidegger saying in 1936, "National Socialism is the right way for Germany; one must merely 'hold out' long enough."[51]

This book therefore engages with Heidegger's work critically, by highlighting where it falls short and foregrounding new, pioneering voices in the post-Heideggerian tradition of medical philosophy. Front and center to this discussion are the philosophers Fredrik Svenaeus and Havi Carel, as well as other important thinkers like S. Kay Toombs, Kevin Aho, and James Aho. These scholars have variously demonstrated the ways that phenomenological approaches can be productively used to theorize illness, inform medical ethics, and develop new health interventions. Both Svenaeus and Carel, moreover, identify the flaws in Heidegger's phenomenology and press firmly into its ideological risks, like the slippage into totalitarian thinking. These are politically engaged voices that do not shy away from the uglinesses of Heideggerian thought, and which are therefore vital in considering how phenomenology struggles to articulate the Christian eschatology as well as the ways it can productively illuminate the same existential issues as are addressed by medieval texts.[52] By the conclusion of this book, Heidegger's specific phenomenological vision is proved to have failed because he was unable to sustain the irresolution and openness of human existence as it is framed in the Christian eschatology. Yet by engaging these more recent phenomenologists, this book shows that such failure does not have to be universal; that with careful work and thought, phenomenology and theology may still be engaged in edifying conversation about what it means to live and die well in the world.

A PARAMODERN JULIAN OF NORWICH

By taking up the *paramodern* as its methodological north star, this book seeks to unsettle any straightforward pastist or presentist reading of Julian's theology. In so doing, it responds to a wealth of work that has asked after the connections between the medieval and (post)modern in Julian's writing. Central to this project is the feminist scholarship of the last four decades that pioneered the use of theory in the reading of medieval mystical texts, finding Julian to be a powerful interlocutor in discussions of gender and the body. The so-called bodily turn engaged the vocabularies of French feminist theorists like Julia Kristeva and Luce Irigaray to interpret the female mystical body as a site of *jouissance*, producing what Barbara Newman calls "a vast outpouring of scholarship, figuratively written in blood or milk instead of ink."[53] This is best exemplified by the work of Caroline Walker Bynum, Elizabeth Robertson, Alexandra Barratt, and Grace M. Jantzen, to name but a few important thinkers in this area.[54] Jantzen's research is particularly informative for the present study: she identifies in Julian's *Revelations* a hermeneutic of flourishing and natality, an idea that has since informed the work of Liz Herbert McAvoy.[55] Such scholarship locates Julian (in varying degrees) as a proto-feminist thinker who "offers a glimpse of a gendered divine horizon for our becoming," as Jantzen puts it.[56] It has also paved the way for recent scholarship identifying connections between women writers from different cultures, geographies, and temporalities, and so has made room for a Julian who, despite her solitary vocation, can be read as firmly embedded within both local and global communities of religious women.[57]

But perhaps most significantly, these strands of research have identified embodiment—the experience of having and being a body—as the site of generative possibility for the woman visionary, which when enfolded into the Christian doctrine of the incarnation opens up new opportunities for insight, flourishing, and well-being. To situate *Impossible Recovery* in this context, it is therefore important to note the gendered implications of a post-Heideggerian reading of Julian. For despite the gender-neutral emphasis of Heidegger's existential philosophy of human being, his work has been the subject of a good deal of debate as to its usefulness to feminist causes. An early contributor to this discussion, Sandra Lee Bartky, suggested that Heidegger's work was too abstract to be a productive site of feminist interpretation.[58] This view was later challenged by scholars like Jean Graybeal and Patricia J. Huntington, who have variously identified more positive opportunities in Heidegger's phenomenology.[59] First, Graybeal highlights Heidegger's rejection of God the father and subsequent turn toward a feminine hermeneutics of care, locating a parallel to Kristevan *jouissance* in his depictions of authenticity as ecstatic subjectivity.[60] Huntington complicates this view, showing how Heidegger's "powerful embrace of the rampant masculine ethos" of National Socialism renders *Being and Time* "shot through with an ethos of stoic resolve reminiscent of the masculinist posture of impartiality."[61] In the face of these problems, Huntington seeks to show how his ontology might be recombined with Irigaray's thought to produce a philosophy for social change.

It is not much of a stretch to close the circle, as it were, between the Kristevan and Irigarayan readings of mystical texts mentioned above and their connections with Heidegger identified here. Indeed, *Impossible Recovery* is in some ways a reinsertion of the historical "ecstatic subject" into the phenomenological conversation. Just as this book uses the paramodern to challenge Heidegger's appropriation of the medieval, it also highlights his complicated relationship to a species of female mysticism deeply enwrapped—and enraptured—by the feminized body of Christ, the motherhood of God, and the ecstatic co-wounding of the woman visionary. This book does not presume to answer the questions raised by the above scholars about the possibility of a feminist Heideggerian phenomenology; while this is an important and pressing subject, it is unfortunately beyond the scope of the present study. Nevertheless, throughout the book I address the ways post-Heideggerian phenomenologies chime with Julian's *Revelations* and the ways they disagree, constituting chords and discords that also resonate through these conversations about gender. In line with Huntington's view, this book's conclusion finds that Heidegger's embrace of Nazi ideology "issues from his view of human existence as immanent not transcendent"—meaning that humans are responsible for their own realization.[62] Huntington calls this Heidegger's "mystical view of National Socialism," where "the feminine (destiny), who continues to secure even the finite and immediate telos of man's being, is but his projection of what he needs to conquer."[63] I disagree with Huntington's colloquial application of "mystical," here used to describe Heidegger's "metaphysical desire to conquer reality," and which thus equates mysticism with his species of immanent utopianism.[64] The conclusion of this book alternatively locates Heidegger's embrace of the "masculine ethos" of Nazi ideology in his *failure* to sustain the mystical horizon of theology, rather than in the mystical desire itself. This interpretation in fact reaffirms Huntington's project, because it relocates mysticism as a possible node of triangulation between Heidegger and the feminist philosophy of Irigaray. In this way, Heidegger's philosophy is shown to in some ways support but ultimately fail to enact the revelatory potential of mystical theology—a conclusion that reconfirms the mystical text as a paramodern object, existing as absent presence in and beyond this phenomenological mode.

Furthermore, this book engages the paramodern to challenge potential misreadings of Julian that would idealize her emphasis on embodied well-being at the expense of a serious interrogation of her writings on tribulation. As Jantzen has shown in her Irigarayan feminist philosophy of religion, to identify the mystical text as concerned with flourishing is not to ignore its preoccupations with pain and death, but rather to focus on a person's "full humanity" (a category from which women should not be excluded).[65] Readings of Julian's theology that do not acknowledge her writing on pain, suffering, and despair therefore threaten to reduce her *Revelations* to one shallow dimension. And, in doing so, they revert to the kinds of nostalgic desire and prelapsarian fantasy that are so appealing to the far right. Kenneth Leech's essay on Julian's "hazelnut theology" anticipates these concerns, warning against attendant dangers to the otherwise "positive, creative, and abiding contributions" Julian makes to her reader's theological understanding.[66] First is the simplicity of her theology, which Leech argues can be misread as a "spiritual pseudo-innocence which cannot, and therefore does not, face those areas of reality which threaten and disturb it."[67] Second, her optimism can again easily become "pseudo-optimism:" "an optimism which refuses to face the depths of evil in persons and in structures."[68] Finally, her "earthiness" can be rendered as "a green spirituality that bypasses the need for redemption"—in other words, a theology that risks romanticizing nature, "[finding] God in the natural order."[69] Reflected in this last concern is the same purism that motivates right-wing groups: "the folk traditions of race and nature [and] the rich culture of the *Volk*," which "[end] up as a spiritual reinforcement for the dominant order."[70] These are, Leech notes, "essentially forms of retreat," part of the anti-urban tradition that also finds expression in Heidegger's critique of the current technological epoch and its *Gestell* subject as well as his subsequent emphasis on demechanization.

The pseudo-innocence and pseudo-optimism Leech refers to here characterizes the disposition of the nostalgic who, in yearning for a place they never were, imagines it without flaw. In modern spiritual parlance, this posture is called *spiritual bypassing*—a term coined and defined by psychotherapist and Buddhist practitioner John Welwood as "a widespread tendency to use spiritual ideas and practices to sidestep or avoid facing unresolved emotional issues, psychological wounds, and unfinished developmental tasks."[71] To read Julian's optimistic "all shall be well" theology as a universalist sublimation of sin, punishment, pain, and suffering would be to enact this kind of bypassing. It would also be to disregard the very trauma she underwent in her experience of illness and to overlook her continued insistence on spiritual perseverance in the face of sin and its accompanying tribulation, which she understands to be certainties of life. As I show, Julian conceives of pain as akin to sin, the fall into the ditch in the parable of the lord and the servant: a difficult obstacle to navigate but also an inevitable part of worldly living. She subsequently places equal stress on the hard and cruel sides of life as on joy—on "wele and wo" (well-being and suffering)—acknowledging nature red in tooth and claw.[72] Nonetheless, it cannot be overstated that Julian does not advocate asceticism, or what I explore in chapter 5 as *the purgative way*, as a means to access God. For though her revelation is bound up with her suffering, she has experienced for herself the potentially destructive power of pain. In place of ascesis, then, I argue that Julian offers an alternative, contemplative way, where the act of seeking God is presented as a route to existential recovery. This is a theology of transfiguration, "a narrative about changed perspective," as theologian Maggie Ross describes it.[73] In this story, the person is not changed, since they have always possessed the capacity for receiving God; rather, they change the way they figure things out. This new perspective includes rather than denies the multiplicity of human experience, integrating both well-being and pain into new ways of being-in-the-world—all driven by faith in the possibility of change.

This question of change brings to bear the nonclosing aspect of the paramodern. Just as Hoccleve's text leaves the interpretation of his recovery to the reader, Julian defers hermeneutic closure to her "even cristen," her fellow Christians: she writes that her book is "begunne . . . but it is not yet performid" (begun . . . but it is not yet complete), suggesting that meaning is always in the process of being created anew by each reader.[74] I understand this dialogic quality as akin to a hermeneutic circle, a phenomenological concept that usually refers to the idea that an understanding of the text as a whole requires an understanding of its component parts and vice versa. But Julian's circular hermeneutic is rather more literal: throughout her texts, her writing spirals in on itself, returning to and enriching key words and concepts in original and enlivening ways. The result is that one single interpretation is never finalized. This strategy can also be compared to the pseudo-Dionysian spiral, the interpretive movement inward into ever-deeper degrees of understanding. Throughout *Impossible Recovery*, I, too, aim to follow this spiraling rhythm, entering into gradually deeper readings of

Julian's theology. In this way, the book seeks to animate the paramodern "trace" of Julian's texts (to again quote D'Arcens), showing how her writing continues to find different expressions in new conversations and contexts.

Impossible Recovery is structured in six chapters, each of which brings together in varying configurations the book's concern with health and hermeneutics. The chapters broadly trace the arc of Julian's recovery from her lived experience of illness into a condition of well-being, a journey effected by contemplative understanding and revelation. This is a superficially linear timeline, but as the book traverses Julian's account its perspective grows wider, expanding out of the earthly and on to a more eschatological plane. This is a shift from the historical and the subjective to the theological and the universal—a move intended to reflect the indwelling of Julian's own experience amid her wider existential reflections and exegesis. In line with this arc, the weighting of the book's focus (on phenomenology, well-being, and Julian) also changes, beginning with greater phenomenological emphasis and ending in a deeper engagement with Julian's theology. By the book's close, recovery is rigorously theorized as an ongoing hermeneutic process occupying multiple temporalities at once.

Chapter 1 contextualizes the existential project of Julian's texts through an exploration of both medieval and phenomenological accounts of illness and health. It thematizes both approaches under the concept that structures the book's understanding of what it means to be well: the existential phenomenon of *being-at-home*, which I position alongside Julian's own homely theology. By examining homeliness in the context of well-being, this chapter provides a thoroughgoing entry into its paramodern philosophy of recovery, offering a story of health as a continuous rebalancing of the way humans dwell in the world. On account of the hermeneutic emphasis of this model, the chapter also explores the ways narrative and language structure existential experience, thus introducing the idea of the text as a hermeneutic tool in effecting recovery.

Chapter 2 attends to dying as a structuring existential phenomenon, showing how living well relates to dying well in both phenomenological and medieval models. Taking the ars moriendi or "craft of dying" tradition as its core hermeneutic, the chapter explores the potentially revelatory effect that a confrontation with death might incur, which is then theorized in light of the phenomenological concepts of *anxiety* and *authentic understanding* initiated by Heidegger and later developed by Svenaeus and Carel. The discussion concludes by bringing this existential model to bear on Julian's *Revelations*, through a detailed reading of her account of illness and her brush with death. The chapter comes to a close at the moment of slippage between Julian's illness and showings, thus laying the ground for a subsequent reading of her showings themselves.

Chapter 3 investigates the contingency between Julian's sickness and divine revelation. Following Julian's own exegesis, the chapter makes an important distinction between physical and spiritual pains, a theory of penance that will later function as a keystone for understanding Julian's wider theology. I here show how for Julian personally, her illness is deeply transfigurative, appearing to catalyze her encounter with divinity and revelation. However, the lessons she gleans from this event do not translate to a universal model of purgation in her texts. Instead, the existential resoluteness she learns from her illness is alchemized into a spiritual practice of contemplative seeking, an epistemological approach that grounds the discussion of chapter 4, which focuses on the role of the text in this model of recovery.

Chapter 4 marks a shift from a focus on the illness-revelation event to a more macrocosmic perspective of recovery as a universal existential phenomenon, initiated and sustained through a contemplative hermeneutic. The chapter begins by addressing the representational challenges of Julian's illness-revelation event and how she navigates these in language and text: what it means for Julian to experience revelation, and to what extent her texts can fully communicate this phenomenon. Close attention to the epistemological processes at work in her *Revelations* reiterates understanding as the ingredient linking revelation, writing, and recovery. I here compare William Langland's concept of *kynde knowyng* to Julian's epistemological paradigm of *beseking*, which I interpret as a spiritual way of being-in-the-world, an existential mode. A reading follows of the visionary text as part of this existential process, investigating the disclosive capacity of the *Revelations*' language and textuality, which I call Julian's *mystical poetic*, a representational strategy which, the chapter proposes, works on account of the ways language fails as much as how it succeeds.

Chapter 5 is concerned with what Philip Sheldrake calls the "practical-pastoral" element of Julian's writing—that is, the therapeutic framework that Julian offers her "even cristen" (fellow Christian) reader to pursue their own recovery.[75] Continuing the discussion of the disclosive power of the revelatory text, the chapter examines Julian's insistence on contemplation—what I call the *contemplative way*—as the more fruitful road to recovery than that effected by the potentially destructive path of pain or illness. Spiraling down into Julian's soteriology, the chapter then explores how Julian represents this process as a narrative of coming home, crafting and adapting a Middle English vocabulary of homeliness to interpret and describe the recovery journey.

The chapter ends by proposing Julian's paradigm of *beseking* as a mode of prayer which fulfills this existential process, offering a phenomenology of prayer to shed light on its disruptive potential. This practice is, I suggest, a lifelong project, which Julian calls the "wey" of Christ.

The sixth chapter performs a final zoom-out of the critical lens to consider how Julian's eschatology collides with Heidegger's detheologized phenomenology. Julian uses various earthy and domestic topoi to describe the process of *beseking*, which the chapter unpacks for their unique theological applications as well as their metaphorical expressions. I subsequently propose a reading of her anthropology as ecological, in terms of its emphasis on being-at-home and the interconnectedness of self and world. Comparing this homely emphasis with Heidegger's "eschatology without an eschaton," the chapter identifies in Julian's *Revelations* a possibility of recovering a home on earth, as well as the necessity for seeking beyond it. This is a model of attentiveness and action, an integration of philosophy with a Christian ethics not present in Heidegger's philosophy. The chapter ends with a reading of Julian's iteration of the *Christus medicus* motif against phenomenological work on the physician-patient encounter to explore the role of each of these therapeutic actors in Julian's theology, which I read as highly participatory.

The book's conclusion reflects on how successful any secularized reading of Julian can be in the present day and the accessibility of her writing to an audience beyond her assumed medieval reader. This discussion considers the possibility of multiple Julians, whose voices variously resonate with different readers over time. Nevertheless, *Impossible Recovery* ends with an acknowledgment of its titular expression: of the historical and theological inaccessibility of Julian's texts for a Heideggerian project. Julian's medievalism and religiosity are invoked once more as paramodern, absently present, irreconcilable with modernity, and yet inseparably linked. With this, I follow Cole and Smith in their statement that, "in modern theoretical terms, to grasp this temporal project is not to modernize the Middle Ages or to thematize medieval being, nor is it to project nostalgia onto the past. Rather, it is to assign *the productive category of impossibility to medieval language itself* and loosen the restrictive bonds that analogy places on language, being, and time that would discipline and contain the Middle Ages both to its own time (or 'age') and presumed mode of temporality."[76] This book dwells with this impossibility, in the hope that it opens up new modes of inquiry about Julian's particular category of medievalism, which might in turn disrupt the aforementioned operations of discipline and containment.

1

MAPPING THE JOURNEY HOME

A Phenomenology of Well-Being

"Now up the hed, for al ys wel;
Seynt Julyan, loo, bon hostel!"

("Now look up ahead, for all is well;
Saint Julian, lo, good lodging!")

—Geoffrey Chaucer, *The House of Fame*

Jesus and Sayn Gilyan, þat gentyle ar boþe,
Þat cortaysly hade hym kydde and his cry herkened.
"Now bone hostel," coþe þe burne, "I beseche yow ȝette!"

(Jesus and Saint Julian, who are both noble,
Had shown him courtesy, and heard his cry.
"Now good lodging," said the knight, "I beseech you grant!")

—*Sir Gawain and the Green Knight*

Ha i-findeth i-wis Sein Julienes in, the wei-fearinde men yeornliche bisecheth.

(They indeed find Saint Julian's house, which wayfaring men earnestly seek.)

—*Ancrene Wisse*

In these lines from Geoffrey Chaucer's dream-vision poem, *The House of Fame* (c. 1374–1385), the guiding character of the Eagle repeats a standard invocation to St. Julian the Hospitaller, patron saint of hospitality and travelers, to grant good lodging for him and his companion, the poet-narrator Geoffrey.[1] The Eagle's petition attests to the continued popularity of the legend of St. Julian in the fourteenth century, a tale describing a nobleman who fled his home after receiving a prophecy that he would kill his own parents. Like Oedipus, Julian mistakenly fulfills the prophecy when, unbeknownst to him, his wife welcomes his parents into their castle. Following the fated parenticide, Julian then takes up a life of penitential solitude and service to the poor and the sick, establishes a hospice, and is later forgiven when he accommodates a dying leper, a disguised divine messenger, in his own bed.[2] St. Julian's story is told in two very popular texts in the medieval period, Jacobus de Voragine's *Legenda aurea* and Giovanni Boccaccio's *Decameron*. Prayers to St. Julian are meanwhile reported in the late medieval hagiographic collection *The South English Legendary*, to be performed by medieval travelers hoping for a hospitable journey—specifically "Iulianes *Pater Noster*," a Paternoster for Julian's parents that the saint enjoins on travelers who ask for his help.[3]

The cry of Gawain for "bone hostel" is an entreaty of this kind, uttered as he approaches a castle on his quest for the mysterious green knight.[4] *Sir Gawain and the Green Knight* is an anonymous Middle English romance thought to have been written in the late fourteenth century, and so is contemporary to both Chaucer and the other Julian who is this book's subject: Julian of Norwich. In the poem, the inexperienced hero Gawain must find the green knight after agreeing to a duel with him the year prior. He must complete this knightly task by the new year, and so sets out from Camelot into the hoary winter to seek his challenger. Upon nearing an unknown castle, Gawain appeals to St. Julian for a hospitable reception, as evidenced in the above quotation. In my translation, I have glossed the Middle English term *ȝette* as "grant," which is the word's first meaning (as in "get").[5] But it can also be read another way: as *yette* or *yet*. This homonymic slippage inflects the line with an interesting doubleness, for if Gawain beseeches the saint "yette," this implies he has already beseeched him once (perhaps when he performed his prayers en route) and will continue to do so until "bone hostel" is firmly granted. In this way, the construction serves to extend the suspense of the quest, with the reader left wondering if Gawain will find what he's looking for. Ironically, the hospitality Gawain does find turns out not to be so hospitable after all, as he is lured into yet more testing games by his hosts, Lord Bertilak and his wife, who are revealed by the end of the poem to be in league with the villainous Morgan Le Fay, and Lord Bertilak is unmasked as the green knight himself.

There is a kind of penultimacy in Gawain's invocation to St. Julian, then, with his prayer for good lodging depending on the "ȝette" of its receipt. This is arguably true of all prayers to the saint, where to ask for St. Julian's help necessarily locates a person in a state of itinerancy, with hospitality always "up the hed," as Chaucer's Eagle puts it. The thirteenth-century rule for anchorites, *Ancrene Wisse* (c. 1225–1240), further evidences this petitionary protractedness in its instructions on enclosed religious living. The above quotation is taken from part 6 of the rule, "On Penance," a passage based on a sermon by the Cistercian monk Bernard of Clairvaux (d. 1153), which delineates three possible models the anchorite can follow: that of the pilgrim, the dead, or the sufferer on the cross.[6] The invocation to St. Julian is added to the first category of persons, who "thah ha beon i the world, ha beoth th'rin as pilegrimes ant gath with god lif-lade toward te riche of heovene" (though they live in the world, live in it as pilgrims, and travel with a good way of life toward the kingdom of heaven).[7] Passing through the world as "weifearinde men" (wayfaring men), they seek a final lodging-place at St. Julian's house. The "bisecheth" of this passage can, then, be translated as both a prayer to the saint (like the Eagle's and Gawain's), as well as the *act of seeking* the place of rest that has occupied the span of their worldly peregrinations: their true home in heaven.

In this way, St. Julian can be seen as an intercessor between two conditions of being: the peripatetic state of seeking and the hospitable state of homely abiding. As the above examples illustrate, achieving the latter is a challenging undertaking, with a secure sense of hospitality frequently eluding the earthly traveler: *Ancrene Wisse*'s pilgrim must wait until heaven to reach the comfort of St. Julian's house, while Gawain's hospitality in Bertilak's castle is part of a wider deception and the knight's welcome home to Camelot is colored by his "schame" (shame) that he has failed in his task.[8] Even the Eagle's optimistic assertion that "al ys wel" as they arrive at the House of Fame is ironically undermined by the house's mistress, the goddess Fame, who oversees the status and infamy of those residing on earth; whether Geoffrey will be received hospitably remains unclear. And yet, the intercessory powers of St. Julian provide the speaker with faith that finding refuge is possible, even if it seems to be out of reach.

The connection between the legendary St. Julian and the subject of this study, Julian of Norwich, is indirect. Nevertheless, the myth of the former provides a striking poetic antecedent for the latter's life and work. Julian of Norwich was an anchorite of the kind addressed by *Ancrene Wisse*: an enclosed religious who took vows to live her remaining years in a cell attached to a church, a contemplative occupation she entered into some time after the age of thirty. The exact date of Julian's enclosure remains unknown, as is her birth name: it is generally assumed that she took the name of the saint to whom her church was dedicated, and it is uncertain whether this was Julian the Hospitaller or Julian of Toledo.[9] Julian is best known today for her visionary text, *Revelations of Divine Love*, which as I describe in this book's introduction, survives in two versions: one shorter and more autobiographical, and one longer and more exegetical. These are prose writings of accomplished theology, recording and interpreting Julian's so-called revelations of love that she received while on her sickbed in May 1373. Over the course of three days and three nights, Julian witnessed a series of sixteen "shewings" originating from a crucifix held before her—of Christ's passion, his love for humanity, human sin, and much more. Julian's account of these showings is a compassionate and careful negotiation of difficult theological issues, especially those relating to human pain and tribulation, all set against the stark reality of her own near-fatal illness. The result is a deeply existential, clear-sighted, and yet remarkably hopeful account of the possibility of recovery—of things *being well*.

Julian's *Revelations* are therefore grounded in the same concern with homeliness and well-being as the above invocations to St. Julian the Hospitaller, with the Eagle's chirpy "al ys wel" uncannily echoed in perhaps the most widely quoted line from Julian's work today: "al shal be wel" (all shall be well).[10] The latter iteration, however, while capturing the penultimacy discussed above, at once invites an optimism regarding its fulfillment: Julian does not write "all *is* well" or even "all *will* be well," but "all *shall* be well." "Shall" derives from the Old English *sculen* or *sceal*, with a base meaning "to owe."[11] A modal auxiliary expressing futurity, the term indicates a potentiality, even a necessity, for all to be well. Indeed, the full quote, "al shal be wel, and al shal be wel, and al manner of thyng shal be wele" (all shall be well, and all shall be well, and all manner of things shall be well), is expanded later in Julian's work in the voice of Christ, who says: "I may makyn al thing wele; I can make al thing wele, and I wil make al thyng wele, and I shall make al thyng wele" (I may make all things well; I can make all things well, and I will make all things well, and I shall make all things well).[12] The shifting triptych of modals here serves to highlight the power of the Trinity, with the final "shall" denoting the unity of the former three.[13] Julian's "al shal be wel" expression thus refers to the divine *intention* of things being well, the realization of which, she explains elsewhere in the *Revelations*, depends upon human participation.[14]

As in the opening examples, then, for Julian of Norwich things being well—*well-being*—is contingent upon the human action of beseeching, or as she puts it, "beseking."[15] But Julian is acutely aware of the difficulties of this project—of finding hospitality, a safe place to abide, in the face of the trials and tribulations of earthly living. Her writing is driven by the interrogative existentialism of an individual who survived a pandemic and a near-fatal illness, not to mention the everyday trials of fourteenth- and fifteenth-century living. Nevertheless, her *Revelations* are famously optimistic. While Julian acknowledges that true well-being may at times seem elusive, her revelation of God's "homely loveing" (homely love) offers a new way of looking at the penultimacy of worldly living, reminding the reader of the eternal and mutual indwelling of divinity within the soul.[16] In this way, Julian of Norwich is perhaps more closely related to her potential namesake than has been previously recognized: just as St. Julian promises "bone hostel" for the wayfaring traveler, the anchorite's meditations also guide her reader toward well-being and homeliness. For Julian, though, the hospitable home she offers is neither physical nor exclusively heavenly; it resides within the soul, an inner state of spiritual well-being marking a life lived in Christ.

The narrative of recovery offered by Julian's *Revelations of Divine Love* is therefore effected through the incarnation and sacrifice of Christ on the cross. In this postlapsarian story, recovery refers to a paradise regained, an opportunity for humanity to be redeemed for their sins and to find a home in heaven. The above rhetorical pairing of "Sayn Gilyan" with Jesus in *Sir Gawain and the Green Knight* gestures toward this equivalency: just as St. Julian guides the pilgrim or wayfarer toward hospitable accommodation, Christ leads postlapsarian humanity out of the wilderness of sin and toward salvation. To speak of spiritual recovery as a journey home, then, is not for Julian mere metaphor: to receive "bone hostel" is to arrive at an existential condition of homeliness. From the human perspective, this journey happens on a linear timeline; as Julian tells us, human beings may spend their entire lives seeking the way home. From the omniscient viewpoint of the divine, meanwhile, this narrative is rather more atemporal—a predetermined story occurring beyond worldly time.

The present chapter is concerned with the former, human perspective, taking the concept of homeliness—or the journey home—as its hermeneutic north star. Ahead of the book's full reading of Julian's homely theology, however, this chapter considers the concept as it is borne out in the work of phenomenological thinkers after Heidegger. As will become clear, the above story (of humankind as having lost their original home and seeking it ever-after) is absently present, or presently absent, throughout the Heideggerian philosophical tradition. But why is homeliness such a productive concept for Heidegger and for subsequent theorists of well-being and recovery? Answering this question requires a thorough consideration of what it means to be well, what it means to recover, and what it means to be at home in the world. It also requires an investigation into the way language figures into these experiences—why expressions about the home (whether metaphorical, existential, or both) are so generative for written accounts of illness and recovery. This is true for both of *Impossible Recovery*'s primary interlocutors: Julian of Norwich and Martin Heidegger (and medical phenomenologists after him), so that in Julian's case, her experiences of illness and revelation are deeply entangled in her ability to express them in language, and likewise in Heidegger's, language and experience are understood as inextricably linked. Post-Heideggerian phenomenology therefore provides a particularly constructive technical vocabulary for this book's subsequent reading of Julian's *Revelations*, with both paradigms deploying a lexis of homeliness to theorize the hermeneutic character of existence and recovery.

This chapter aims to provide a conceptual map for the journey home, as it were, through the landscape of the phenomenological model. First, I examine Heidegger's phenomenological use of language, briefly comparing the multiplicity of meaning that inheres in phenomenological expressions to that of the mystical text. I then consider the phenomenological view of language and experience as mutually constitutive as well as the implications of this perspective for criticism focused on written accounts of illness. Next, the discussion turns to the category of homeliness, exploring how and why this can be a more helpful classifier of well-being than that of health. I here attend to the psychoanalytic concept of the *Heimlich*—and its negative, the *Unheimlich*—exploring the specific uses of these terms in Heidegger's work and post-Heideggerian approaches to well-being. Finally, I conclude with a phenomenological account of the home: how experiences of the home can be theorized and thought through. The chapter therefore lays the foundation for the book's subsequent reading of Julian's *Revelations* by mapping out what it means, in existential terms, to seek a home in the world.

LANGUAGE IS THE HOUSE OF BEING

The phenomenological method is particularly helpful in understanding figurative expressions of well-being because it theorizes language as part of experience itself: "Language is the house of being. In its home man dwells," declares Heidegger in his 1946 essay, "Letter on Humanism."[17] With this statement, Heidegger suggests that language is the very basis of human ontology, the background against and in which being-in-the-world is contextualized and injected with meaning: "The human being shows itself as a being who speaks," he writes in his foundational phenomenological text, *Being and Time*.[18] In this way, Heidegger sees language as internested with experience. Being-in-the-world is created in part through linguistic articulation: it is, quite literally, a *poetic* act, from the Greek *poiesis*, creation. Figurative expressions like metaphors are therefore central to the Heideggerian model, taking on an ontological inflection absent in many other uses of metaphor throughout history. Aristotle (d. 322 BCE), for instance, held that metaphor is an ornamental add-on to language: an aesthetic category of rhetoric, not ontology.[19] This aesthetic position persisted into the medieval period, finding its way into the didactic manuals of poetry, or *artes poetriae*, such as medieval grammarian Geoffrey of Vinsauf's *Poetria Nova* (c. 1208–1213).[20] Throughout this text, Geoffrey deploys the very features of poetry he describes, using metaphor to denote figurative language and so on. For example, Geoffrey compares poetic composition to the construction of a house: "If anyone is to lay the foundation of a house," he writes, "his impetuous hand does not leap into action: the inner design of the heart measures out the work beforehand."[21] Intended to encourage the writing of a plan before engaging in writing poetry, this analogy speaks to the applicability of the metaphor of the home for speech and language. Yet unlike Heidegger's statement that "language is the house of being," Geoffrey's construction is ultimately an aesthetic one: while Geoffrey finds in the home a productive metaphor *for* the writing of metaphor, for Heidegger language *is* existence and existence *is* language.

Since the twentieth century, linguists and philosophers have broadly agreed that metaphor is a fundamental component of language, perception, and cognition. Friedrich Nietzsche observed that almost every word we utter derives from an image, betraying its metaphoricity, a position echoed by phenomenologists like Hans-Georg Gadamer, who maintained that "Being that can be understood is language" and language contains a "fundamental metaphoricity."[22] Clearly drawing on the Heideggerian model, Paul Ricoeur also made a case for the narrative and linguistic nature of all human life; the Ricoeurian mode of hermeneutics regards all experience and actions as "texts" that require interpretative analysis.[23] Literary critic I. A. Richards similarly claimed that metaphor is an omnipresent principle of language, conceptualizing this process with his model for each half of the double unit of metaphor: "tenor" and "vehicle."[24] *Vehicle* refers to the word that carries the meaning or attributes, and *tenor* the subject to which those attributes are ascribed. Rhetoricians have since substituted the terms *tenor* and *vehicle* for *ground* and *figure*, or in cognitive linguistics *target* and *source*, respectively. These terms provide a useful schema for thinking about the figurative power of language and the layers of interpretation required in the experiential process.

In line with the phenomenological emphasis on metaphor, Heidegger's writings often do not precisely define or narrow down one sense of a word, gesturing instead toward many—at times confusingly diffuse—meanings. Small wonder, then, that Heideggerian scholars have grappled with his language, his jargon one of the most widely criticized features of his work.[25] In his own defense, Heidegger wrote in *Being and Time* that "we must guard against uninhibited word-mysticism"—"nevertheless," he continues, "in the end it is the business of philosophy to protect the *power of the most elemental words*."[26] With this statement, Heidegger is closer to the Middle English sense of the term *mystik* than he appears to recognize. Mystical, in the medieval sense, denotes literally an openness to "symbolical or spiritual interpretation," a *figurative* locution.[27] In other words, medieval mystical language relies on figurative expressions as essential, rather than ornamental, to the expression of meaning. I examine this mystical poetic more fully in chapter 4, but it is important to note here that Heidegger's own dissatisfaction with the scholastic and analytic traditions, such as Geoffrey of Vinsauf's above, appears to have given rise to a species of mystical poetic in his own work—one which similarly understands figurative language not simply as a matter of style but as an ontological expression.

Rather than uninhibited word-mysticism, then, Heidegger's use of language might be called an *intentional* word-mysticism—or even an *inhabited* word-mysticism, whereby his reader is asked to dwell a while in the house of language, pressing into its foundations to coax out meaning. Scholars have identified various instances of this in Heidegger's work, asking whether what has previously been conceived as metaphor can even be called metaphor at all. Giuseppe Stellardi, for example, distinguishes between Heideggerian metaphors that make an "intervention in extraordinary contexts" in order to "make certain otherwise incongruous occurrences interpretable" and "open metaphors" that "[open] up a possibility of meaning and [leave] it in suspense."[28] David Nowell Smith meanwhile argues that "the terms *metaphor* and *metaphoricity*, be they explicitly of a non-metaphysical or a cognitively creative kind, sit uneasily with the aporetic reflexivity of Heidegger's own 'text.'"[29] Smith refers to Jacques Derrida's description of Heidegger's text as "more 'metaphoric' or *quasi*-metaphoric than ever"—a statement that recognizes, with regard to Heidegger's "house of being" concept, that "we are . . . no longer dealing with metaphor in the usual sense."[30] Smith then quotes Heidegger's self-description in the years after *Being and Time*, when he was brought to "abandon [his] own path of thinking to namelessness [*im Namenlosen zu lassen*]," where such "namelessness" becomes the very condition for naming.[31] This is a rhetorical paradox, where the act of examining Heidegger's "namelessness" (the way he replaces or destabilizes concrete concepts with figurative language) results in a necessary construction of rhetorical categories for naming. As Smith writes, if "naming is to trace, and thereby 'bring to language,' something that otherwise remains unnameable, then the attempt to identify a rhetorical category for this bringing-to-language would end up imposing a homogeneity upon a writing that thinks precisely through its verbal and stylistic diversity."[32]

According to this phenomenological model, language and experience are mutually dependent, and so particular uses of language—especially metaphor—are central to the very experiences they presume to signify. This theoretical background greatly informs my own reading of Julian of Norwich's *Revelations*, because it suggests, in line with what I argue about mystical texts more generally, that experiences of sickness are tightly interwoven with the language, narratives, and stories used to describe said experiences. From the phenomenological perspective, metaphorizing illness (and I will suggest, the mystical event) is not only a descriptive act but an enactive process of meaning-creation that gives shape to otherwise nebulous phenomena.

DUAL CITIZENSHIP

Given these insights into the interrelation of language and being, phenomenology is revealed to be a productive lens through which to interpret literature about health and illness. Anita Wohlmann has recently shown that accounts of illness often use and reuse common metaphors, such as the *fight* or *battle* with disease.[33] But what of the notion of *well-being as a journey home*, as is found in the supplications to St. Julian above? How does the locution of health as a place—a geography—help to theorize recovery? Susan Sontag, in her now canonical essay *Illness as Metaphor*, invokes a particularly interesting use of the term that captures the coincidence of opposites that inheres in any expression of habitation. Her essay begins with the statement, "Illness is the night-side of life, a more onerous citizenship"—"everyone," Sontag continues, "who is born holds dual citizenship, in the kingdom of the well and in the kingdom of the sick. Although we all prefer to use only the good passport, sooner or later each of us is obliged, at least for a spell, to identify ourselves as citizens of that other place."[34] Sontag here describes a story of dwelling, or the possibility of inhabiting two places: one a familiar kingdom that feels like home; the other an uncanny place, the familiarity of which is uncomfortable to acknowledge. Though this essay was written in the light of Sontag's own experience with illness—she was suffering at the time from breast cancer and the attendant trials of chemotherapy—the text is *not*, she writes, a description of "what it is really like to emigrate to the kingdom of the ill and live there," but rather an account of "the punitive or sentimental fantasies concocted about that situation: not *real geography*, but stereotypes of national character."[35] Sontag therefore rejects certain metaphors of illness, even while she herself finds habitation a productive metaphor for her own discussion. As Wolhmann has also argued, "While [Sontag] dismisses the harmful uses of metaphors in her essays, she also experiences their empowering and nourishing potential in her own illness experiences and in her reflections on writing, style and interpretation."[36] Sontag demonstrates the ways by which metaphorical language is equal parts essential, social, and political in writings about illness.

Recent work in medical phenomenology has similarly challenged the mystification of illness that Sontag attributes to metaphor, offering new ways of seeing beyond these "punitive or sentimental fantasies" to the multiplicity of illness experiences. But while Sontag avoids mapping out "what it is really like" to dwell in this kingdom, the post-Heideggerian approach demands that the phenomenologist address both experience and language, since to examine the language used to represent illness is also, from a Heideggerian perspective, to chart the very "real" geography of what it means to be unwell. This is the case for philosopher Havi Carel, who in *Phenomenology of Illness* describes her intention to seek toward a "comprehensive, systematic—and distinctly philosophical—account of illness," to walk its "complex topography" with a conceptual map in hand, and "to bring this philosophically uncharted territory into clearer view."[37] To do so, Carel incorporates a first-person phenomenological account of her own respiratory disorder, thus supplying a geography of the lived experience of illness, which she defines as quite distinct from the objective, physiological disorder of disease: invoking a typical phenomenological distinction between the lived body (*Leib*) and the objective body (*Körper*), she writes of how "disease is to illness what our physical body is to our body as it is lived and experienced by us."[38] With this integration of lived experience into the philosophical view, Carel follows in the footsteps of the pioneering work of phenomenologist S. Kay Toombs, whose *Meaning of Illness* was one of the first books to effect a shift in medical philosophy's center of gravity from a focus on illnesses as "evidence" or "clues" to inform theory to an emphasis on the voice of the sick person. Drawing on her own experience of multiple sclerosis, Toombs intended her work to bridge the gap not only between theory and praxis but also between physician and patient: "To bypass the patient's voice," Toombs writes, "is to bypass the illness itself."[39] Together with works like Fredrik Svenaeus's *Hermeneutics of Medicine and the Phenomenology of Illness*, and Kevin Aho and James Aho's *Body Matters: A Phenomenology of Sickness, Disease, and Illness*, among others, such post-Heideggerian scholarship has pushed philosophy to better understand the phenomena that constitute sickness, and to better theorize "what it is really like to emigrate to the kingdom of the ill and live there," by making room for the subjective testimony of the sick person.[40]

By mapping out the effects of illness on the person themselves, this phenomenological work also provides an ethical imperative for modern theorists to disrupt certain socially constructed stories about illness. As Sontag's *Illness as Metaphor* so clearly shows, sickness has long been represented through a negative lens, as a transgressive phenomenon that is inherently *at odds* with the sick person; illness is a fight against death, a war to be fought on the battleground of the body. Michel Foucault famously observed the way deviance was medicalized as sickness by the modern institution of the hospital, but the inverse has also been true: sickness was conceived of as deviant long before the advent of modern medicine. This connection has been traced back to the premodern medical imaginary, where sickness was etiologically tied to sin, the body and soul interlinked in a psychosomatic matrix of health. Aho and Aho have unpacked this trajectory at the level of the word, identifying that "unwell is an adverbial form of the noun phrase 'not good.' But to be 'not good' is tantamount to being bad which, at least in extreme cases, is evil. The Latin term for evil is *crimen*. In sum, then, while crime and sickness are distinguishable, they are far from separable."[41] Of course, what Aho and Aho don't allow is that being "not good" does not always mean "bad"—sometimes it can mean indifference. Just so, illness was not always associated with badness in the medieval imaginary. This is best illustrated by another etymological link: between *penance* and *punishment*, terms that derive from the same root, Latin *poena* (pain): a common ground that indicates a spiritual framework wherein the patient bearing of pain—*patientia*, suffering—is both punishment and remedy. To *re-pent* is to return to pain or hurt; to revisit old wounds in order to come to terms with and heal them. Penance therefore indicates the possibility of a productive aspect of pain, one that in turn lends experiences of tribulation a potentially edifying quality.

The phenomenological thinkers introduced above have opened up similarly generative possibilities in their theories of illness and well-being. By returning to illness as it is experienced, these phenomenologies have reconceived of sickness as not inherently bad or evil, but as a web of phenomena that is simultaneously created and interpreted through a person's being-in-the-world: "No illness," Svenaeus writes, "is entirely somatic or entirely mental," a statement that dispels any lingering dualist sentiment of the spirit's resistance against unruly flesh.[42] The result is a phenomenological corpus that demonstrates the sheer multiplicity of ways illness can be experienced: as painful and destructive, neutral, positive and edifying—or all of these at once. As such, this phenomenological work goes hand in hand with recent developments in well-being and disability studies, which have both placed new emphasis on the possibility of *health within illness*—a phrase coined by nursing literature of the 1990s to express the diversity of sickness experiences and which has made its way into more recent empirical work showing that illness does not necessarily mean a lack of well-being.[43] As this phrase suggests, such work considers a degree of well-being to be possible independent of physiological or psychological cure.

The notion of health within illness provides a productive entry point for theorizing homeliness as a condition of well-being, because it allows for the mutual existence of positive and negative experiences—and so for being at home even in unlikely places. For Carel, well-being within illness can emerge via two paths. The first is the route of *post-traumatic growth*, which describes the way those who have experienced trauma or illness might find themselves positively transformed. Carel charts this growth across three improved areas of life, specifically the revelation of hidden abilities such as coping and resilience; the improvement of relationships; and the shifting of priorities in such a way that provides focus and peace of mind.[44] The second path identifies an adaptive *recession of illness experienced as suffering* for the individual: illness "can . . .—and often does—recede into the background in a way unimaginable to the healthy outsider."[45] Carel here appeals to the theory of hedonic adaptation, writing that "we adapt to—and therefore cease to feel the impact of—changes to things that affect our hedonic state (e.g., the car we drive, the size of our house, and even marital status)."[46] This adaptation also occurs with negative change, including the change to one's being-in-the-world that constitutes illness.

It is important to highlight here that such conceptions of well-being within illness do not necessarily infer *happiness*. As Carel explains, "I am not claiming that a life with illness or impairment is necessarily happy, only that it need not be substantially less happy than a life of a healthy person. In other words, health is neither necessary nor sufficient for happiness."[47] In place of a focus on positive affect—happiness—both Carel and Svenaeus subsequently reconceive of well-being as a condition of *homelikeness*. This is an existential rather than affective phenomenon, which refers to whether a person can meaningfully engage with the world, instead of how they *feel* about it. Homelike being-in-the-world, in these post-Heideggerian models, is defined as a kind of *mood* or *attunement*, a term which explains how a person "finds themselves" in the world—how the world is experienced by them. Heidegger speaks of this phenomenon in the *Zollikon Seminars*: "We find ourselves in different situations by having a broken arm, a buzzing in our ears, a stomachache, and anxiety"—each time, he says, the "attunement" is different.[48] Feelings and emotions are thus entangled in attunement, but they do not necessarily determine it. For example, pain can be an attunement, but how a person feels about the pain is not.

A *homelike* attunement can be described phenomenologically as a kind of equilibrium that maintains itself imperceptibly in the background of everyday living, and that can be thrown out of tune by the arrival of illness. Hans-Georg Gadamer was the first phenomenologist to theorize health in this way, arguing that a "conscious awareness of health conceals itself": "Despite its hidden character," Gadamer continues, "health nonetheless manifests itself in a kind of feeling of well-being. It shows itself above all where such a feeling of well-being means that we are open to new things, ready to embark on new enterprises and, forgetful of ourselves, scarcely notice the demands and strains which are put upon us. This is what health is."[49] Gadamer cites "breathing, digesting, and sleeping" as part of this "rhythm of life, a permanent process in which equilibrium re-establishes itself."[50] In this notion of health as equilibrium Niall Keane has identified echoes of Plato, "for whom the production of health is the establishment of the component parts of the body 'in a natural relation of control and being controlled.'"[51] Recognizable, too, in medieval medical theory as the balancing of humors, and in modern nosology in the biological process of homeostasis, Gadamer's interpretation of health as rhythm articulates a process common to the "order" of natural life.[52]

This perspective therefore also explains the disruption of illness as a breakdown of the equilibrium of health. In a moving account of her own illness, Carel describes this disruption and its effects on her everyday movements and capabilities:

> In illness things grow heavier and further away. A distance I would once call "near" or "a day's walk in the countryside" is now "far" or "impossible." Small tasks like carrying groceries home or lifting a child require preparation, pauses, rest, and cause fatigue. Everything is hard. Everything is far. Everything is strenuous. My world, and the world of those who are close to me, has shrunk. For me, the trap is permanent. There is no release from it. Every movement requires oxygen. This fundamental fact about human biology, known to us all in the abstract, is experienced in everything I do.[53]

Carel's experience here shows the interruption of homelike attunement at work: due to her illness, her ordinary engagement with the world becomes impossible, her routines and actions halted in their tracks. This disruption operates on a universal level, with her entire embodied experience thrown into disarray. From a Heideggerian perspective, this disruption can be understood as a failure of *intentionality*: a failure of how a person understands themselves in the world, and of their ability to direct their actions accordingly. This idea is extended in Maurice Merleau-Ponty's *Phenomenology of Perception*, which further theorizes the doubleness of embodied experience referred to above (the distinction between the *lived* body and *objective* body).[54] According to Merleau-Ponty, a person *is* and *has* their body at the same time, meaning that they can be understood as a body-subject whose very being-in-the-world is sustained through their ability to engage with it: for Merleau-Ponty, being is not a question of "I think" but "I can."[55] To *intend* into the world is, then, to project the self toward possibilities and actions, a process Merleau-Ponty calls the "intentional arc," a ceaseless flow that "projects round about us our past, our future, our human setting, our physical, ideological and moral situation, or rather which results in our being situated in all these respects."[56] When afflicted with disease, the unwell person's ability to intend toward everyday goals is interrupted, as described so poignantly by Carel above; their intentional arc "goes limp," as Merleau-Ponty has it, and they are projected into a condition of *unhomelikeness*: "es ist dem Kranken unheimlich" (the sick person is unhomelike), Svenaeus writes.[57]

THE *UNHEIMLICH*

The phenomenological picture of homeliness as a marker of well-being therefore finds its inverse in the *un*homelike, or *unheimlich* in Heidegger's original German. The *unheimlich* has been variously theorized over time and across different schools of thought. Here, I examine its origins in the work of Sigmund Freud and its later appropriation by Heidegger, before arriving at Carel's and Svenaeus's translations of the concept in their own phenomenologies. This recent work introduces a far more nuanced perspective on well-being within illness than Heidegger himself provides, and has important implications for my own reading of the (un)homely in Julian's *Revelations*, offering an account of the embodied phenomena of homeliness as they are experienced in health and in illness.

Before it was taken up by Heidegger, the *unheimlich* was originally coined as a psychoanalytic concept, commonly translated as the *uncanny* and broadly signifying a sense of *unfamiliarity* or *hiddenness*. In his famous essay "The Uncanny," Freud writes that the feeling of uncanniness is generated by an involuntary return to something hidden or repressed: he writes of uncanniness as the "involuntary return to the same situation" (*unbeabsichtige Widerkehr*).[58] According to Freud, the discomfort of uncanniness arises from the obtrusive compulsiveness of the repetition: from the loss of control or the feeling of being controlled by another. To prove this point, Freud offers a reading of the uncanniness of E.T.A. Hoffman's short story "The Sandman," a tale of "a wicked man, who comes to children when they won't go to bed, and throws a handful of sand into their eyes, so that they start out bleeding from their heads," as the character of the nanny tells the protagonist.[59] In this story, Freud contends that uncanniness rests on this fear of being "robbed of one's eyes," which he argues derives from an Oedipal fear of castration (*Kastrationsangst*).[60] Freud's uncanny is, then, greatly tied up with seeing and knowing, which Svenaeus summarizes thus: that "to know is to see with the eye of the mind," and so Oedipus blinds himself because he "did not even know *himself*."[61]

The common translation of *unheimlich* as *uncanny* preserves this sense of hiddenness or unfamiliarity, deriving as it does from "can" (to know how, to be able to), the Indo-Germanic root of which—*ken*—is retained in the modern words *kin* and *kindred*. But with the erasure of the *Heim* from the *unheimlich*, the term *uncanny* also removes the sense of unbelonging, and the associated longing for a home that inheres within the Heideggerian usage. Furthermore, Marc Falkenberg has noted that Freud's use of *Das unheimliche* "overlooks that the prefix '-un' in German, apart from the negating function that it shares with its English counterpart, has an older, pejorative function that still survives into New High German. 'Unheimlich' thus has connotations, in German, of primal or prehistoric awe, of a fear of all that is unknown to man, that points to fears existing long before the Enlightenment."[62] *Unheimlich* evokes a kind of originary fear of the unknown, or moments that reveal the background of meaninglessness, or homelessness, that exists behind human being. For this reason, the translation Carel and Svenaeus both choose (of *unheimlich* as *unhomelike*) is, I think, a more accurate rendition of this phenomenon. By recentering the *Heim*, Carel and Svenaeus reinvigorate the concept of the uncanny with all the associated significations of the *home*.

In Heidegger's work, the experience of the *unheimlich* is theorized as a clearing or breakdown of everyday meaning. An unhomelike or *unheimlich* attunement arises, as modern understandings of the uncanny suggest, when the familiar is made unfamiliar, when that which is homely is revealed as not a home at all. Heidegger describes these moments of disclosure as moments of *anxiety* or *Angst*:

> In anxiety one has an *"uncanny"* [*"unheimlich"*] feeling. Here, with anxiety, the peculiar indefiniteness of that which Dasein

> finds itself involved in anxiety initially finds expression: the nothing and nowhere. But uncanniness means at the same time not-being-at-home . . . Anxiety . . . fetches Dasein back out of its entangled absorption in the "world." Everyday familiarity collapses. Dasein is individualized [vereinzelt], but *as* being-in-the-world. Being-in enters the existential "mode" of *not-being-at-home* [*Un-zuhause*]. The talk about "uncanniness" ["Unheimlichkeit"] means nothing other than this.[63]

In Heidegger's view, with the collapse of everyday familiarity—the collapse of homelikeness—the world is revealed *as it really is.* Svenaeus explains this more clearly, writing that "the world is revealed in anxiety, not as a collection of things with different characteristics, but as a meaning-structure of human understanding which has no meaning *in itself.*"[64] That is to say, humans inhabit a world that is made meaningful through their interaction with it, and behind that exists a void of nothingness. Dasein is, as Heidegger put it, inherently homeless: " *'Not-being-at-home' must be conceived existentially and ontologically as the more primordial phenomenon.*"[65] So the term *unhomelikeness* describes the revelation of this primordial state; that one is never truly at home in the world. As noted above, this is experienced by the ill person as a kind of attunement: an attunement arising out of a moment, or a series of moments, that reminds the person of their illness and the accompanying inability to engage with their world. Whether from the difficulty entailed by carrying groceries, or lifting a child, or the impossibility of a day's walk in the countryside, the ill person's world is no longer a world in which they feel at home. The "mineness" of the world is lost, and they no longer feel that they belong.

With this focus on homelike attunement rather than physiology, post-Heideggerian phenomenologies locate self-understanding as the cornerstone of well-being. To feel well, a person has to be able to live meaningfully rather than simply be able to perform certain bodily functions. To this end, Svenaeus concludes that *homelikeness* should be the aim of clinical practice, rather than physical cure alone: "to bring the patient back to homelikeness—that is, to health—or, if this is not possible, as far in the direction of homelike being-in-the-world as possible."[66] Moreover, he writes that this clinical goal should not be conceived along linear lines: Svenaeus qualifies that "back" does not mean "backwards," but is often a move *forward* "to a new and different form of being-in-the-world than the one present before the onset of illness."[67] Mitigating and curing physiological disorders might constitute significant aspects of this process, but this phenomenological objective prioritizes how these disorders affect the individual in their everyday life: "Doctors . . . are of course still able to do a great deal for chronically ill patients to make their lives better—their being-in-the-world more homelike—although they cannot cure them," Svenaeus writes.[68] Carel notes this shift as a reorientation of the medical imperative " 'from cure to care,' moving away from a model of disease and cure, to a model of care which promotes health and healing for people with chronic illness and disability."[69] Space is made for experiences of ill health to be accommodated, accepted, and affirmed—to acknowledge "*inability to be* as a way of being."[70]

This phenomenological move marks a sharp turn away from Heidegger's model of human being as active and goal-pursuing, which was also borne out in Merleau-Ponty's "I can" body-subject. For Heidegger, a wholeness of being relies on a person engaging with the world with ease and autonomy. Carel explicitly highlights this as a shortcoming of his work: "In illness, as well as in other situations of dependency, insufficiency, and incapacitation, understanding the human being as 'ability to be' does not seem as useful or descriptive. In fact, one's first and final years are usually periods in which one's 'ability to be' (in the Heideggerian sense) is restricted and dependent on the facilitation of others . . . We begin and end in insufficiency and dependence."[71] Carel takes issue with three main points in Heidegger's model, noting first that "it only captures the middle part of the trajectory of a human life, excluding infancy and aspects of childhood and old age"; second, that "it only captures the paradigmatic cases of healthy, autonomous adulthood;" and third, that "it overlooks the important ways in which our existence depends on other people and is saturated by a background sense of trust." She argues that by definition "inability is implied by ability," since ability is a *process of becoming*.[72] Consequently, Carel suggests that the notion of " 'being able to be' can be broadened to include radically differing abilities," which would be more successful should "being unable to be" be understood "as a form of existence that is worthwhile, challenging, and, most importantly, unavoidable."[73] She therefore proposes a more inclusive replacement of Heidegger's dichotomy of "being able to be" and "being unable to be" with a *spectrum* of abilities-to-be, which is a continuum that allows a change in perspective "from seeing ability as positive and desirable to seeing it as part of a broader, more varied flux of life."[74]

Conceptualizing health and illness in these terms makes space for a model of recovery that resists the dualist and positivist assumptions about what it means to be (un)well; one that allows for the possibility for a person to reattune to homelikeness independently of the restoration of bodily or physiological function. By identifying the ways that the ill person can *feel well* even amid sickness, Carel and Svenaeus have respectively shed light on the capacity for being-at-home in unhomely places—in places of extreme pain, tribulation, and even in the places nearest death. In critiquing and adapting Heidegger's work, they have shown how a failure to recover physiological health does not necessarily equate to a failure to recover well-being, and that a person may make a home even in the kingdom of the sick. Where Sontag was concerned with dispelling the stereotypes of this kingdom, these phenomenological approaches bring this territory of sickness into clearer view, charting its geography through close attention to the phenomena that constitute lived experience.

A LIVING SHELL

Despite the phenomenological interest in homelike being-in-the-world, the nature or essence of the home—the "whatness" of a home—has not been investigated by these medical phenomenologists. Perhaps this is because the home is a phenomenon that is hard to pin down: both deeply familiar to all and yet hard to describe. Frank Buckley has suggested as much: that this hermeneutic challenge derives from the originary—and so perhaps taken-for-granted—quality of the condition.[75] Buckley equates the search for at-homeness with the search to understand human embodiment, comparing the "concurrent *nearness* and *remoteness*" of both phenomena: "'never so far away as when so near' can as truly be spoken of the central human search for the experience of being at home as may be spoken of the deeper awareness of the meaning of my flesh and bones which are so close to me."[76] It is almost, Buckley writes, "as though that which is first for us, as certainly body and home, are the last to be described and thought through."[77] Certainly, phenomenologists like Carel and Svenaeus, who both invoke the (un)homelike as central to their respective theories of ill health, do not unpack this phenomenon at the level of the word—as a phenomenological metaphor (or metaphor-beyond-metaphor). In what follows, I extend their cartographies of illness and health into this semantic domain, asking what *being-at-home* connotes in existential terms. The result is a phenomenology of the home that tracks its linguistic, spatial, and temporal features to better understand its application to the issue of recovery. This discussion also begins to identify the multiple temporal frames which, as will be seen, both structure and limit recovery's possibility.

To begin with, the home must be understood as both created and occupied by the embodied subject. Embodiment is every-*body*'s first experience: that with which everyone is most familiar or most at home. As philosopher Martha C. Nussbaum comments, our bodies "are our homes, so to speak, opening certain options and denying others, giving us certain needs and also certain possibilities for excellence."[78] My earlier discussion has already identified some phenomenological perspectives on how embodiment facilitates being. Merleau-Ponty is a key thinker in such phenomenologies of the body: he writes that the body displays its own kinesthetic wisdom or *praktognosia*, the ability to seamlessly and pre-reflectively maneuver itself through, and orient itself within lived space.[79] According to Merleau-Ponty, the world and the body-subject "intersect and engage each other like gears."[80] In this way, if body and world exist in well-oiled coaction, then by extension the individual's attunement is also more easeful. When a person is in this homelike mood, Svenaeus elaborates, "everything 'flows'"; homelike embodiment is transparent, inconspicuous, and fluid.[81] This is quite different to the *ability-to-be* that structures Heidegger's existential model, since as has been shown above, homelike attunement can be restored even if a person is not able to act in the way they did before illness. To fluidly inhabit space might therefore require an adaptive integration of the ill person's *inability*, acknowledging this difference by finding new ways of inhabiting space and perhaps modifying the space to accommodate these new needs.

Building a home—and recovering homelikeness—may also, therefore, take time. As geographer David Seamon explains, the rootedness of being-at-home requires time spent establishing routines: "The person who lives in the same place his entire life establishes rootedness in the first few months and years of childhood; the person who changes places must re-establish rootedness each time he moves."[82] Seamon gives the example of a particular subject's mother, who "knows the exact location of everything in [the] house" and so can "[go] to it automatically."[83] Routines are necessary to establish this kind of familiarity; a repetitive engagement with space and the things within it. Gradually, as time passes, these spaces and things transform from objective phenomena—like a house—into the subjective—the home. Geographical studies offers a useful way of conceptualizing this shift, with the vocabulary of *location* and *position*: as Neil Smith and Cindi Katz explain, "in geographical terms, 'location' fixes a point in space, usually by reference to some abstract co-ordinate system such as latitude and longitude," while " 'position,' by contrast, implies location vis-à-vis other locations and incorporates a *sense of perspective* on other places."[84] This can be compared to the phenomenological distinction referred to above between the objective phenomenon of disease and the lived experience of illness (and that of the objective body and the lived body), a distinction which rests on the act of living, or *habitation*. Or, further, to Merleau-Ponty's distinction between the *habitual* body (of general and pre-reflexive existence) from the *actual* (of subjective and reflexive existence), which also finds its way into Pierre Bourdieu's concept of the *habitus*.[85]

As the above definition suggests, such habitation depends on a person's orientation or positioning to their environment—a phenomenon of perception that Henri Lefebvre has described as a " 'sense:' an organ that perceives, a direction that may be conceived, and a directly lived movement progressing towards the horizon."[86] People sense and perceive their environment and orient themselves toward it. In her queer phenomenology of orientation and space, Sara Ahmed has since argued that this positionality constructs identity, since "bodies do not dwell in spaces that are exterior but rather are shaped by their dwellings and take shape by dwelling."[87] She also points to the self-contained negative in "orientation"—*disorientation*—since in a way, "we learn what home means, or how we occupy space at home and as home, when we *leave* home."[88] Ahmed refers, by way of example, to the experience of migration, which "could be described as a process of disorientation and reorientation": "bodies 'move away' as well as 'arrive,' as they reinhabit spaces."[89] She observes the supportive interaction of body and environment as the migrating person moves into space, reaching for an identity: "If orientation is about making the strange familiar through the extension of bodies into space, then disorientation occurs when that extension fails."[90]

When these kinds of extension fail in illness, a person's experience of lived-time can undergo a transformation: "lived time, time *as it is for me*, shrinks," as Aho and Aho put it.[91] This "shrinkage" can also affect the body-subject in space: the body can "freeze" or "tighten," psychiatrist and philosopher Thomas Fuchs writes of the depressed patient, who undergoes a "rigidity" of the lived body that can localize in a specific organ, "a feeling of an armor vest or tire around the chest, lump in the throat, or pressure in the head."[92] Fuchs even describes a patient who "felt that her inner body, her stomach and bowels had been contracted so that there was no hollow space left."[93] The lived body "contracts to its own skin," and then to Ahmed's "second skin" of its environment, which "unfolds in the folds of the body."[94] Aho and Aho identify a similar gesture of restriction in Heidegger's term *Angst*, which comes from the Latin *anguistiae*, from *ango*, "to bind" or "press together," "to choke," "throttle," "strangle," "to cause pain."[95] When anxiety strikes, the body is disclosed as less like a home and more like a prison; it might feel constricted to the point of solid matter, but in terms of at-homeness the vessel of the body has become hollow. It ceases to be a home, like a shell without an inhabitant. The philosopher Gaston Bachelard deploys the same metaphor in his *Poetics of Space*, where he quotes Paul Valéry's *Les Coquillages*, in which Valéry praises the geometrical formation of the shell, which "remains mysterious" even though the object itself is "highly intelligible."[96] Bachelard observes that "life begins less by reaching upward, than by turning upon itself," in a "coiling vital principle."[97] There is a difference, though, between a "living" shell and a shell devoid of life: "an empty shell," Bachelard writes, "like an empty nest, invites daydreams of refuge."[98] The hollow space, in its emptiness, conjures a fantasy of making it a home: a longing for rootedness and a longing for freedom.

The home can therefore be described as a place claimed through habitation: home belongs to a person just as they enjoy a sense of belonging when they feel at home. Hence why the body can be called unhomelike when illness occurs: the disengagement of body from self means that the body is no longer experienced as "belonging to me"; what was "mine" becomes "other."[99] Seamon calls this phenomenon of habitation "appropriation," which involves "a sense of possession and control: the person who is at home holds a space over which he is in charge."[100] The resident controls passage in and out of the home, rendering it cut off from the public sphere: "A place to be alone," according to

Seamon, "is part of at-homeness, and the person whose home does not provide such a place feels a certain degree of upset."[101] This occupation is self-constructed, whereby the subject carves out a world for themselves in both space and time. Phenomenologist Otto F. Bollnow, too, describes the construction of a home as world-creating, calling it the foundation of "a cosmos in a chaos." He cites the Dutch philosopher Gerard van der Leeuw, for whom "house and temple are essentially one," since *templum* means something "cut out," an apt expression of a settlement for dwelling: "house building signifies a world creating, world sustaining activity which calls for sacred rites."[102] This expression resonates with Heidegger's 1951 lecture, "Building Dwelling Thinking," in which he shows that "to build is in itself already to dwell": *bauen* comes from "the Old English and High German word for building, *buan* [which] means to dwell."[103] Home-building, or establishing at-homeness, is predicated upon the constructive act of dwelling: "The way in which you are and I am, the manner in which we humans are on the earth, is *Buan*, dwelling."[104]

These principles help to formulate the relationship of being-at-home to being itself. In Bollnow's terms, to construct the cosmos of a home amid the chaos of the outside world means to anchor oneself in time and space—a kind of anchoring that supplies the subject with a zero-point reference so that they will not "be dragged along helplessly by the stream of time."[105] This is a reference point from which all lived movement is conceived as "a going away or a coming back."[106] When homesickness strikes, for example, Anne Winning writes that people must " 'antibody' the old space of [their] lived experience of home and acquaint [their] bodies with the new place."[107] Coming home therefore refers to a place in the past—of first experiences, such as being-at-home in the body—but also to the future, to final destinations. This might be likened to a continual process of reorientation, of rooting and finding one's way back to one's roots. But as this discussion shows, finding one's way "back" to health is not necessarily a return trip: just so, remembering one's origins also involves a quality of distance from one's home; it involves taking the road to faraway places, venturing forward into the unknown. In this way, the human being can be described in the terms of Gabriel Marcel: as "*homo viator*," the pilgrim or itinerant man.[108] Or, in the words of medical phenomenologist Wim Dekkers, "the life of human beings is like an odyssey that comes to an end when one finds one's way home."[109]

In this chapter, my objective has been to establish a theoretical picture of phenomenological perspectives on illness and well-being, identifying in particular those works that have critiqued and revised Heidegger's writings on what it means to be well. To this end, I have highlighted the importance of language and metaphor in phenomenological discussions of well-being, focusing on the expression of homelikeness or the *heimlich*. This term has been revealed to not only describe well-being in the linguistic sense of signification, but also to operate as a complex ontological container, a metaphor-beyond-metaphor that houses being itself. I have also examined the effects of a loss of homelikeness in situations like illness, and further, the implications a theoretical separation of homelikeness from health has for the possibility of well-being *within* illness. Precisely what the *homelike* means phenomenologically has not been previously considered by my two primary interlocutors, Havi Carel and Fredrik Svenaeus, and I have here expanded upon their work to incorporate other phenomenological voices on the nature of the home. This final discussion has shown how homelikeness can be understood phenomenologically as a kind of orientation to one's environment, predicated upon familiarity, reiterative action, routine, a resulting ease of movement within the space, and a sense of belonging or possession.

The overarching claim of the chapter is that well-being should not be conceived as the Heideggerian *ability-to-be* but as *ability-to-be-at-home*: a capacity to repeatedly and dynamically rehabituate oneself to one's environment. Most importantly, I have shown how this capacity to adapt is one that supersedes physiological function or ability—that it is instead a dynamic process of balancing and rebalancing one's relationship with the world. This is not to say that such efforts are straightforward, however, or always available to every person. First-person accounts of illness ("patients' voices") reveal this very clearly, such as those quoted above of Carel and S. Kay Toombs. Equally, historical accounts provide important perspectives on this existential journey, as demonstrated by those medieval texts with which I opened the chapter. These examples show just how arduous it can be to establish well-being in the face of inhospitable circumstances—for things to *be well*. Small wonder that the *Ancrene Wisse*'s pilgrim earnestly beseeches St. Julian, or that Gawain is careful to appeal to the saint before entering Bertilak's castle: it is cold out in the wilderness, with no certainty of well-being "up the hed." Still, this chapter has sought to provide a conceptual map for navigating these uncertainties—a map that incorporates, rather than denies, the multiplicity of experiences of well-being and illness, and so also makes room for the possibilities of revelation and recovery.

2

LEARNING TO LIVE

Julian's Illness and the Craft of Dying

I have been able to see my life as from a great altitude, as a sort of landscape, and with a deepening sense of the connection of all its parts. This does not mean I am finished with life.

—Oliver Sacks, "My Own Life"

As with Susan Sontag's "kingdom of the sick," the neurologist and writer Oliver Sacks here engages geographical metaphor to describe the new perspective which accompanied his terminal diagnosis of metastatic cancer.[1] The inspiration for this piece of writing and the documentary film that followed, *His Own Life*, is the short autobiography of the philosopher David Hume, penned when he, too, learned he was terminally ill. In this text, Hume writes of a curious sense of distance from his life after his diagnosis, despite having "never suffered a moment's abatement of [his] spirits."[2] Sacks's contemplative response, quoted above, articulates his own experience with this dissociative phenomenon, which he characterizes as "not indifference but detachment" and describes as similarly accompanied by the feeling of being "intensely alive." Life and death, as well as fear and gratitude, coexist in both of these accounts, a seemingly contradictory nexus that hints at the possibilities of insight that might be found in even the most earth-shattering encounters with illness. Each of them speaks to an intimacy between facing death and facing the sublime panorama of life—a profound new perspective that might also be called revelation.

These texts therefore provide a striking parallel to Julian of Norwich's account of near-fatal illness, which also shattered her existential outlook and changed the course of her life to come. Yet the revelatory quality of Julian's account is rather more literal than those above, describing the divine "shewings" she received while on her sickbed. In this way, the vista she confronts is framed by a divine horizon absent in the picture painted by Sacks; her perspective is illuminated by the light of God. This chapter pulls focus on the diverging horizons between such religious and secular approaches to illness and revelation, as they are borne out in both Julian's writing and the post-Heideggerian phenomenological writings *Impossible Recovery* has been addressing so far. By examining the deep contingency between Julian's brush with death and her revelation, I consider how the former may have set the stage, as it were, for the latter to occur. Medical phenomenologies provide a productive technical vocabulary for understanding this intersection, but a plunge into Julian's writing throws up striking divergences between these two paradigms. As I show, both Julian and post-Heideggerian phenomenologists tentatively navigate the generative possibilities (and dangers) of illness, but when it comes to addressing the limit-situation of existence—death—they come to very different teleological conclusions.

To triangulate this dialogue between Julian's writing and the particular phenomenologists it engages, the chapter takes as its focus the medieval ars moriendi, or craft of dying—a tradition that was later appropriated by Heidegger for his own philosophical project. To highlight the revelatory potential of the ars moriendi genre and shed light on the Heideggerian connection, I want to begin by setting this tradition against its sister-project: *ars medicina*, the art of healing or medicine. The *ars* appellation indicates these siblings' shared genome, in that they occupy two sides of one coin in the medieval imaginary: *ars moriendi* teaches the living how to die, while *ars medicina* teaches how the sick and dying might live. Yet throughout this chapter, these expressions are shown to be rather more permeable than such a dichotomy allows, with each revealed as equally generative in its capacity to curate well-being of body and soul. Furthermore, despite their theoretical underpinnings, it will become clear that both projects are realized only through sustained practice: they succeed by the implementation of learned technical skills—technical in the sense of the Greek *technē*, craft. Which is to say, they are both forms of craft-work: sites of creative and generative possibility.

Heidegger's appropriation of the term *technē* evidences his interest in these premodern practices and also reiterates the generative associations of the term. He uses the word to theorize, among other things, the human relationship to the earth's resources and to technology: he defines *technē* as an act of *revealing* things or "bringing-[things]-forth," as a sculptor or farmer might who helps to release the potential held within the land.[3] Instead of compelling, "setting upon," or "enframing" (in German, *Gestell*) these materials or objects, Heidegger understands the process of *technē* as that of the craftsman enacting a "letting be" of the natural order.[4] His use of the term in his work is, however, deeply imbricated in his interest in demechanization, which as I describe in the introduction, is also linked to his fascist ideology. There are, moreover, aspects of Heidegger's writing on dying that rely on similarly purist ideas about bodily wholeness and physical ability. This chapter seeks to address some of these problems with Heidegger's philosophy and to show how these issues might be avoided in new phenomenological approaches to well-being.

By examining Julian of Norwich's *Revelations* alongside Heidegger's writings and phenomenologists who have critiqued them, the chapter is therefore interested in identifying the connections between medieval and modern treatments of dying, as well as attending to the sharp edges of the Heideggerian model. To this end, it begins with a brief overview of the medieval craft of dying, drawing in particular on Amy Appleford's work on the death culture of medieval England to explore how this is borne out in Julian's texts. I then examine how dying is conceived in Heidegger's writings as a structuring component of being-in-the-world—a discussion which unpacks some of the problematic elements of Heidegger's work and introduces alternative suggestions by post-Heideggerian phenomenologists Havi Carel and Fredrik Svenaeus. I also investigate the problems of subjectivity that attend to texts about death, as explored previously by D. Vance Smith, and consider how these influence my reading of Julian. Finally, the chapter offers my own phenomenological interpretation of Julian's account of illness, a close reading that illuminates the resonances between these phenomenological approaches and Julian's texts even while it throws into relief their divergent secular and sacred horizons.

THE CRAFT OF DYING

Julian of Norwich's *Revelations of Divine Love* recounts the visionary's experience with a "bodely sekeness" (bodily sickness) that afflicted her so extremely that she knew, irrefutably, that she was dying. Julian's sickness lasts the length of "iii dayes and iii nights" (three days and three nights), during which time she experiences a series of diverse symptoms, which manifest variously on her body and in her "feleing" (her senses or awareness).[5] Despite the relatively sparse detail given by Julian about her illness, its cause and character have been the subject of a good deal of scholarly attention, with a number of studies across the twentieth century attempting to retroactively diagnose this event.[6] Early studies of this kind make manifest the psychoanalytic (and implicitly misogynist) tendency to designate female visionaries as hysterics—a modern rendering of the medieval *discretio spirituum*, or *discernment of spirits* discourse, which sought to ascertain whether the experiences reported were genuinely divine or disordered.[7] The first book-length study to be focused exclusively on Julian offered just such a positivist reading of her illness and mental state: while Paul Molinari ultimately finds Julian both compos mentis and orthodox in her spirituality, his analysis is nevertheless weighed down by lingering designations of female mysticism as an expression of psychological deprivation or pathology.[8] Later scholarship takes a slightly more historicist leaning, though as late as 1984 James T. McIlwain deemed Julian's illness as most likely a case of botulism.[9] These studies evidence the wealth of modernizing analyses of illness that have persisted over the years in Julian studies and that do not satisfactorily account for the intersection of Julian's illness and revelation along theological or phenomenological lines.[10]

To avoid such positivism, I am interested in the language Julian herself uses to report her illness and how this can be contextualized within a wider hermeneutic that structures medieval accounts of dying: the ars moriendi tradition. For despite the sparsity of description of Julian's own illness in her texts, she does offer striking fragments that can be read against contemporary literature about death and dying, and can therefore be used to inform how she herself experiences her near-fatal illness. The longer version of her *Revelations* describes, for example, the procession of the crucifix to her bedside and her receipt of the last rites by a curate, an account that closely echoes the rituals of medieval death culture:

> My curate was sent for to be at my endeing, and by than he cam I had sett my eyen and might not speke. He sett the cross before my face and seid, "I have browte thee the image of thy maker and saviour. Louke thereupon and comfort thee therewith."[11]

> My curate was sent for to be there when I died, and by the time he came I had fixed my gaze and could not speak. He put the cross before my face and said: "I have brought to you the image of your maker and savior. Look upon him and take comfort from it."

The shorter version of Julian's text supplies more detail of this scene, writing of how "he come, and a childe with hym, and brought a crosse" ([the curate] came with a child with him, and brought a cross).[12] This account follows the rubric found in a typical *Visitacio Infirmorum* text—a treatise about visiting the sick that had begun to appear in Middle English translations and devotional compilations in Julian's lifetime. The treatise acts as a guide for both the ill person and their attendants as they move through disease and prepare for death. Such visitations would involve a procession to the home of the sick, as are described by Amy Appleford in her detailed history of death culture in this period. The priest, Appleford writes, "carries the reserved host in a pyx . . . walking behind two altar boys, one of whom holds a cross while the other rings a bell to tell passers-by that they must either join the procession or, as John Mirk instructs, 'knele-a-downe' 'wyth grete devocyone,' as 'Goddes body' is borne by."[13] She describes what this might have looked like in Julian's case: how during this procession the priest would sing the seven penitential psalms, arriving at the house to "join those already there to form the community of 'even-cristen' presupposed in what follows."[14] For Julian, the significance of this performance is felt in the priest's holding of the crucifix before her face, the image of which will function as the entry point for her first showing.

While the *Visitacio* offers a rubric for onlookers, contemporary texts in the ars moriendi tradition tend to provide step-by-step instruction for a first-person preparation for death. Heinrich Suso's *Horologium Sapientiae* (c. 1333–1337) and its vernacular translations (such as the Middle English *Seven Points of True Wisdom*) were particularly influential in this period, as was Jean Gerson's adaptation of Suso's *De Scientia* as *De meditatione mortis* and his own *Ars bene moriendi*.[15] These texts paved the way for the Latin death treatise, *Tractatus de arte bene moriendi*, which was sanctioned by the church after the Council of Constance (1414–1418) and subsequently translated into English as *The Book of the Craft of Dying*.[16] The longer version of this text offers explicit remedy for the "uncunning" (ignorance) of dying, comforting the reader as to the good and necessary parts of the end of life while also addressing numerous temptations that may lead the dying person into sin before death (various diabolic creatures are featured on the woodcuts of the shorter version). With its insistence on the reader's resilience in the face of spiritual difficulty, *The Book of the Craft of Dying* also exemplifies a degree of spiritual perfectionism that was beginning to enter mainstream lay piety in this period, characterized by an emphasis on purity of will. Appleford identifies an anticipatory expression of this in Suso's death writings, which insist that intention trumps contrition and compassion in approaches to dying.[17] She writes that *Craft of Dying* is "not an affective text but a consciously rationalist one," presenting the reader with material "to aid in the mental projection of the self forward in time to the moment of death" through a program of edification and advance preparation.[18] This can be seen in the way the text insists on spiritual practice ahead of time—on getting in the right frame of mind "whyle he is in hele" (while healthy)—because once sickness hits "devocyon passith oute fro the" (devotion passes away from you).[19] *Craft of Dying* subsequently offers various hypothetical deathbed scenes into which the reader is encouraged to imagine themselves, so as to be well practiced in directing their responses toward God when the time comes. The text therefore functions as a particularly striking example of the struggle between acceptance and resistance, as well as virtue and sin, that characterized craft-of-dying literature—and which can also be identified in Julian's *Revelations.*

While such perfectionist programs no doubt encouraged a degree of pious anxiety and what Appleford calls "fits of scrupulosity," this genre of texts nonetheless offered opportunities for the naming and theorizing of an otherwise unnameable and untheorizable phenomenon.[20] This is a closely related problem to that with which I open the introduction to this book: the impossible problem of describing experiences of illness and revelation. D. Vance Smith takes up this question of ineffability in his work on medieval dying, in which he explains that on a philosophical level "people in the Middle Ages were unable to talk about death," in the sense that being *dead* itself cannot be signified. "Literature," Smith argues, "fills the impossible space between the two convictions, between the faith that language reached the dead, and the logic that denied it could.

Literature can talk about something that is not, strictly speaking, logically possible. It is neither a prayer nor a proposition. It is the dream of a possible impossibility."[21] This position disrupts the now outdated notion—as claimed by Johan Huizinga and disputed by Appleford—that medieval culture was rooted in a morbid fascination and "deep psychological strata of fear" of death, and further, that "Renaissance or Reformation modernity was born from a repudiation of [this] death 'fixation.'"[22] Instead, written accounts of dying—like both the ars moriendi tradition and Julian's own *Revelations*—can be read as attempts to describe the possible impossibility of death, to better understand how to live in relation to this phenomenon. Rather than a death "fixation," then, *resoluteness* in the face of death might be posited as an alternative response, a concept drawn from the field of post-Heideggerian phenomenology. Carel calls such an approach "pathophilia," an understanding of sickness as potentially edifying, purifying, or instructive: "Such [pathophilic] attitudes can be found in the premodern world, where illness was unavoidable and thus best tackled with acceptance and preparation."[23] She contrasts this with the "pathophobia" of the present day, where "we can still think that we might learn from bodily aberration, even if we abhor it." Importantly, Carel does not recommend a recuperation of the premodern attitude as a remedy to modernity, but rather argues that "we need to find a middle ground between the two positions. We ought to be prudentially pathophobic, but also to acknowledge that the experience of illness is surprisingly rich and diverse and can sometimes yield unexpected positive results."[24] My discussion of dying in this chapter seeks to find such a middle way, initiating a reading of post-Heideggerian phenomenologies together with Julian's *Revelations* in order to evidence the breadth of destructive and generative possibilities that may be born of facing one's own death.

BEING-TOWARD-DEATH

In a phenomenological recuperation of the ars moriendi tradition, Heidegger called for an approach to living that retains an awareness of death, which he styled as *being-toward-death.* This idea has since been revised by thinkers in the field of medical phenomenology, who have variously identified the problems and possibilities of the Heideggerian approach. Such work asks whether it is possible (or advisable) to live with death always in mind and whether such an awareness can be integrated into a condition of well-being. These queries have major ramifications for this book's understanding of Julian's recovery, because they consider what it might be like phenomenologically to think you are going to die, to come back from this brink, and to go on living. Through a close examination of Heidegger's theory of being-toward-death, especially his concepts of *anxiety* and *authenticity*, the present discussion therefore extends the book's theory of well-being to include the possibility of being well even when facing death.

For Heidegger, being-toward-death rests upon a sustained knowledge of human finitude: that human living is always structured in relation to its mortal limit. In the previous chapter, I touched on the phenomenological theory of how such knowledge might be obtained, outlining the condition of existential disclosure Heidegger calls anxiety or *Angst.* These are moments when the "nothingness" at the ground of human existence is made clear; when a person becomes aware of their own existence and the nullity that exists behind their everyday actions. Anxiety, says Heidegger, "reveals the nothing" (*das Nichts*): "[It] leaves us hanging because it induces the slipping away of *beings as a whole.*"[25] He describes this as a return to the most primordial state of being, where behind his term for the human being,

Da-sein (Being-there), lies the more primitive "being-held-out-into-the-nothing."[26] Anxiety is, for Heidegger, a state of dissociation from everyday existence and a concern about that same state of existence—it *is* and is *about* the same thing. As he writes in *Being and Time*,

> When anxiety has subsided, in our everyday way of talking we are accustomed to say "it was really nothing." This way of talking, indeed, gets at *what* it was ontically. Everyday discourse aims at taking care of things at hand and talking about them. That about which anxiety is anxious is not [nichts] innerworldly things at hand. But this not [Nichts] any thing at hand, which is all that everyday, circumspect discourse understands, is not completely nothing [Nichts]. The nothing of handiness is grounded in the primordial "something" ["Etwas"], in the *world*. The world, however, ontologically belongs essentially to the being of Dasein as being-in-the-world. So if what anxiety is about exposes nothing, that is, the world as such, this means that *that about which anxiety is anxious is being-in-the-world itself*.[27]

The effect of this disclosure is that the continuity of experience and purposeful action that characterizes being-in-the-world is disrupted, and the person no longer feels that their life has meaning. Such awareness of their own existence is, for Heidegger, the key ingredient in being-toward-death. The person is required, in this view, to see things *as they really are* and to move forward in life with this new frame of mind.

This disclosive phenomenon of anxiety seems on its surface to arise as a disturbance of the mind—a specifically mental condition. Indeed, the disruption of meaning, the feeling of nothingness, and the dissolution of purpose are all common symptoms of certain mental disorders and illnesses. But can the same disclosure occur in cases of somatic illness, too? Carel seeks to answer this question with a detailed investigation of the way anxiety manifests *in* and *on* the body. She describes, for example, instances where an individual may retain meaning and purpose, but may physically be unable to realize these goals: "she might still want those things but find them no longer within reach."[28] Carel calls this "bodily doubt," which she configures in relation to the Merleau-Pontian bodily certainty of "I can." In normal conditions, bodily failure might simply frustrate one's actions, but when the body's essential precariousness and unpredictability is disclosed in somatic illness, this "casts us out of immersion and into suspension" as "the familiar world is replaced by an uncanny one."[29] This could be argued to be akin to the *unhomelike attunement* described in the previous chapter, but while anxiety does seem to effect unhomelike attunement, the two are not quite the same—a distinction that rests on the ability to be *at home* even in the face of experiences of dying.

To arrive at the possibility of being-at-home with death, then, some further specification as to these terms (*anxiety* and *unhomelikeness*) is needed. Importantly, Carel distinguishes her concept of bodily doubt from mental anxiety by the physical nature of the disruption: "bodily doubt is experienced as *anxiety on a physical level*, hesitation with respect to movement and action, and a deep disturbance of existential feeling."[30] Carel makes the case of the respiratory patient who fears they will be unable to breathe, an experience that concretizes the effect Heidegger describes in anxiety: "What is threatening cannot come closer from a definite direction within nearness, it is already 'there'—and yet nowhere. It is so near *that it is oppressive and takes away one's breath*—and yet it is nowhere."[31] Once again, Carel takes this further than Heidegger allows, to suggest that anxiety can result from very rational and embodied disruptions as well as those confined to the mind. Being unable to breathe for a respiratory patient, for instance, is a rational fear grounded in knowledge of their body's dysfunctional state.[32] As such, the individual might be able to retain their sense of meaningful engagement in the world even while their continuity of purposeful action is disrupted: "There is not the actual 'sinking away' from 'everyday familiarity' of coping absorption" in these instances, Carel writes.[33] A person might still *desire* to pursue certain activities or actions—indicating a meaningful absorption in the world—but these activities may be out of reach. Even so, bodily doubt still forces the individual to renegotiate their relationship to their world; they may find their being-in-the-world is no longer compatible with the everyday activities of their former life. Since Carel's account of bodily doubt understands the ill person as forced to renegotiate their life in this existential way, she concludes that "Heidegger's account of *Angst* does apply in somatic illness, as well as in mental disorder."[34]

Whether due to a mental or embodied dysfunction, then, anxiety compels the person to focus on their own being-in-the-world, such that the lived world becomes objective and material. Put another way, the focus changes from entities and actions *in* the world to the world itself as a structure: "The world has the character of complete insignificance [*Unbedeutsamkeit*]," Heidegger writes.[35] Heidegger calls this disclosure "authentic anxiety" or "authentic understanding": *authentic*, because the breakdown reveals the world as it really is. *Authentic* has the archaic meaning of "belonging to," "own," or "proper": Taylor Carman comments that one could accordingly translate *Eigentlichkeit* (authenticity) as "ownedness."[36] In this way, authenticity might be understood as a state where a person's *own* being is at issue for them; where they stand in a directly first-person relation to themselves, with an understanding of the ontological structure of their "mineness."[37] I note in the introduction to this book that Heidegger's language of authenticity presents a danger to any theory of recovery that inherits his language: a danger of its interpretation as a call to return to something more primordial, purer, or more originary. This kind of authenticity would (implicitly or explicitly) reject ordinary experience, or inauthentic experience, as insufficient or somehow impure—such as when Heidegger describes inauthenticity in *Being and Time* as being "lost in the publicness of the they," which he calls *das Man*; a "falling prey" to the world in a kind of unconscious way of living.[38] Heidegger does defend himself against such criticism, claiming that inauthentic living is decidedly not a fall *from* a "purer and higher 'primordial condition,'" but rather an existential "entanglement" *in* the everyday flow of the world and of others.[39] Indeed, he vocally objected to a moral or value judgment between living authentically or inauthentically, writing that "the ontological-existential structure of falling prey would . . . be misunderstood if we wanted to attribute to it the meaning of a bad and deplorable ontic quality which could perhaps be removed in the advanced stages of human culture."[40] Nevertheless, his defense has raised more than a few suspicious eyebrows, given that his entire philosophical imperative is directed toward living with an awareness of death. It would seem strange that he would not then privilege one mode over the other.

Heidegger's concept of authenticity has also been criticized on account of its temporal framing, a critique that in turn helps to theorize the temporal expansiveness of Julian's *Revelations*. If, for instance, Heidegger's idea of authentic understanding (as in anxiety) is understood as a momentary leap out of inauthenticity, there is an argument to be made that actually living with lasting anxiety is impossible—and surely not advisable.[41] In response to this, Svenaeus carefully delineates *authentic anxiety* from *unhomelike attunement*. Although he acknowledges that both "offer new perspectives on the worldiness of human being," Svenaeus differentiates the "lasting" quality of unhomelikeness from the brief "moment" (*Augenblick*) of authenticity.[42] Carel meanwhile considers authenticity as not necessarily a fleeting state: *anxiety* lasts only for a moment, she writes, but the *authentic understanding* that follows is "a return to the everyday, to the full thrust of thrown projection and worldly life."[43] Carel supports her reconfiguring of authenticity here with a reference to Heidegger's distinction between "genuine" and "nongenuine" understanding, where *genuine* indicates being-in-the-world as a whole, while *nongenuine* understanding is partial or reductive. Anxiety, Carel concludes, qualifies as *authentic* but *nongenuine*, whereby a person is equipped with authentic understanding but unable to act in the world. *Genuine* understanding, on the other hand, is a condition where a person is able to reenter the world and act within it—as might occur in instances of posttraumatic growth.

Carel's phenomenological revision of Heideggerian authenticity does not, then, require a person to isolate themselves, to cut themselves off from their world, or to live a life dedicated to thinking about death. Instead, she emphasizes the necessity for communal and relational involvement: "In order to face illness authentically, Dasein does not need to sever its links to the world. An authentic attitude to illness may include resolutely facing illness, refusing to repress its impact, and accepting its presence."[44] She subsequently argues for the deconstruction of *authentic* and *inauthentic* as poles of existential possibility, "rejecting the claim that the distinction between authenticity and inauthenticity is clear-cut."[45] With her insistence on the potentially *genuine* or *nongenuine* character of authenticity, Carel configures these two states as "internally related"—namely, that the move to authenticity does not involve abandoning everydayness and being-with-others. Authenticity hence becomes the "full disclosure of the horizon of the everyday, fully retaining Dasein's relationship to other Dasein and to the world."[46] In this reconfigured model, the everyday is allowed a disclosive function, and falling prey to the world, to use Heidegger's phrase, is decidedly not a descent from authentic existence to an inferior state, but "a ground in itself." Authenticity, meanwhile, is viewed as an expansion of a person's ability to view themselves and their world as a whole, occasioning "a structural shift," as Carel puts it.

This revised phenomenological model therefore denotes authenticity as a more specific condition of homelikeness—one that includes the retention of an awareness of one's existence in everyday life. Just as with the transition to homelikeness from states of unhomelike attunement, the individual reestablishes a sense of wholeness in their engagement with their world. The difference lies in the sustained apprehension of one's own existence, which has not been a feature of at-homeness as discussed so far. To achieve this continued awareness, as Carel writes, a person must proceed with *resoluteness*. From the German *Entschlossenheit*, this term literally means "decisiveness" or "resolve," but also has the meaning of "unclosing" or "disclosing."[47] For Heidegger, to be resolute is to face up to the situation in which one finds oneself, as opposed to assimilating it as a "general state of affairs."[48] There is a parallel here with the Aristotelian concept of inspiration, namely an ability to simply see the right ethical rules to make without subsuming them under general rules (*phronêsis*).[49] Similarly, Heidegger's resoluteness consists of a kind of focused engagement that allows a person to act with a "sight which is primarily and as a whole related to existence *transparency*," or "perspicuity" (from *Durchsichtigkeit*, literally "through-sightedness").[50] In her revision of Heidegger, Carel inflects the term with a more optimistic sense by connecting it to the possibility of well-being while dying.

And so my discussion circles back to the subject of dying or being-toward-death, since what is disclosed to the dying person—made transparent—in experiences of anxiety or authenticity is the full constitution of life, which includes its ending. As shown above, Heidegger understood this mortal finitude as humanity's ultimate limit-situation, a view that is inextricable from his understanding of the human being as a *being-there*: eventually, there will come a point where Dasein *can no longer be*. Heidegger calls this "demise," a term which refers to the objective ceasing of consciousness from a third-person perspective—i.e., the death of another, or the transformation of a lived body into a corpse. This is not to be confused with his notion of "perishing" (*Verenden*, literally "the ending of what is only alive")—a biological concept indicating the cessation of an objective organism's life-maintaining functions without their awareness of this happening.[51] *Demise* meanwhile refers to the narrative completion of another's life, or their death *as a person*. And since a person cannot experience their own demise, Heidegger comes up with another term entirely to describe the first-person experience of death: "dying." Dying precedes biographical demise, indicating instead "the *mode of being* in which Dasein is *toward* its death."[52] Carman summarizes the distinction thus: "What Heidegger's existential phenomenology of death discloses, then, is the first-person dimension of death insofar as the death is my own, the death into which I constantly project myself, without ever being able to step out of it, live through it, and stand over against it as I do the deaths of others."[53] Death is, in this view, a determining aspect of being: as Heidegger puts it, "only in dying can I to some extent say absolutely 'I am.'"[54]

The relationship between authenticity and dying is therefore contingent, in that an awareness of one discloses the other. William Blattner goes so far as to argue that Heidegger's concept of death *is* anxiety; that the experience of death is directly equivalent to the existential crisis of *Angst*.[55] Carel has since reintegrated Blattner's view with Heidegger's concept of resoluteness, arguing that the idea of dying as anxiety is helpful in that it shows us how Heidegger's "death" is a way of being, but that it lacks the notion of temporal finitude so crucial to his ideas.[56] For Heidegger, human being exists as the "between" of birth and death.[57] He uses the term *care* to denote the unity of this temporal projection, where a person's "facticity" characterizes their past and their "falling" characterizes the inauthentic present. A person living inauthentically brackets death as irrelevant to life: they tranquilize themselves in a "constant *flight from death*."[58] To face death authentically, they must free themselves from this tranquilization by actively projecting themselves forward into their own finitude. They must, in other words, be authentically "there," "in the moment" (the *Augenblick* referred to above). This is what Heidegger means by resoluteness: the awareness that one's death is a fundamental structure of being, an "expecting" of this limit-situation that then allows the person a "*freedom toward death which is free of the illusions of the they, factical, and certain of itself.*"[59] Just as no one can live my life, "*no one can take* [*my own dying*] *away from* [*me*]."[60]

With resolute anticipation, then, the human being recognizes its death as its own. Death "belongs" to them; it is their "ownmost." This belonging may individuate the person, experienced as the cutting off from their lifeworld described above as anxiety. But as Carel makes very clear, this is only the first stage in her phenomenological ars moriendi: "that of non-genuine authenticity."[61] The same revelation of their existential condition must then be held while a person is engaged in their world and with others. Indeed, in Carel's view, this is the more genuinely authentic way of dying and thus the more genuinely authentic way of living. As the intimacy between the *ars moriendi* and *ars medicina* suggests, learning to die well also means learning to *live well*—*ars bene vivendi*—and learning to live *with others*: a rendering of the existential condition that underscores the entire project of human living as intersubjective, created and sustained through relationship.[62] Such a phenomenological reinvigoration of the craft of dying has major implications for the project of recovery, because it rethinks a prevailing perspective of modern medicine: that the last stages of life are a defeat. The phenomenological ars moriendi instead demands they are viewed as life's fulfillment—or, to use the phenomenological indicator of well-being, as a going/coming home. To confront death with genuine authenticity is not, then, a return *back* to a prelapsarian state of knowledge about living and dying, but rather a move *forward* into a new way of being—one in which a person can retain a bird's eye view of their existence and can appreciate their own finitude as they move through the world with others. This is ultimately a narrative of hope, promising the ever-present possibility of being-at-home even at times when recovery seems impossible.

I UNDERSTOOD . . . THAT I SHOULD DYE

Julian of Norwich's *Revelations of Divine Love* provide an account of dying that both exemplifies and enriches this phenomenological narrative. As noted above, Julian's texts can be contextualized against the turbulent political climate of the fourteenth century, and of course, the Black Death, the mortality rate for which is estimated to be approximately one third of the population of England.[63] Phenomenologically speaking, it could be argued that such a context might have provided more opportunities for the kind of existential disclosure Heidegger deems necessary for good living—for a deep existential awareness of human finitude. But as the *Craft of Dying*'s rationalist approach might suggest, much of the death literature in post-1348 England is programmatic. Dying in the Middle Ages, Smith states, was not "the ultimate expression of the irreplaceability of the individual subject" but a scripted, "internalized protocol."[64] Internalization of the process mostly occurred, Smith argues, for the observer, for whom the death text functions as a didactic structure. He gives the example of the narrator of Chaucer's *Book of the Duchess* (and of the *Canterbury Tales*, too), who "cannot understand it because it can't be put into language, and the gap between what he ought to know and what he is capable of knowing represents the gap between the impulse to narrate death and our ability to understand it."[65] Dying, like finitude, is a paradox that cannot be understood unless you are outside it, and when you are outside of it, it cannot be accurately narrated. Of both the Man in Black and the Old Man of "The Pardoner's Tale," Smith writes: "In seeking death (especially a 'pure' one), both figures will continue to fall into language and being: 'Alway deynge and be not ded.'"[66]

This distinction—between the narrator's third-person incomprehension and knowing death firsthand—finds expression in the above Heideggerian dichotomy of *demise*, the completion of another's life, and *dying*, an orientation toward one's own death. These terms can be helpful in negotiating the challenges faced by texts that try to orient their reader toward their own death, like medieval texts of affective devotion such as passion meditations, which involve a problem of linguistic and hermeneutic participation to which I will return in subsequent chapters. And while Julian claims her account as a subjective artifact—as an account of dying *as she experienced it*—the text also sits astride the instructive corpus referred to above in its self-conscious presentation as a literary artifact. That is, the *Revelations* are written by Julian to work through her own experience of nearly dying, as well as for her "even-cristen" audience to glean something from it themselves, just as the *Craft of Dying* writes with the reader in mind. Importantly, at numerous stages throughout the text Julian flattens certain subjective expressions, humbly rejecting the role of author, "techere," or final interpreter of the event: in a reference to her gender absent from the longer version of the text, for instance, she writes in section 6 of the short text, "Botte God forbede that ye schulde saye or take it so that I am a techere, for I meene nought soo, no I mente nevere so. For I am a woman, leued, febille, and freylle" (but God forbid that you should say or believe that I am a teacher, for I do not mean that, no I never meant that. For I am a woman, unlearned, feeble, and frail).[67] The degree to which this flattening of subjectivity is only a conventional expression-of-humility *topos*, particularly necessary for a woman writing in a time when women were forbidden from preaching, remains unclear. Nevertheless, this strategy of self-negation also arguably makes space for the reader to enter into the text of the *Revelations*, in a manner not dissimilar to the "intimate scripts" of affective devotion Sarah McNamer describes in this period.[68] Julian's writing is not a script for her reader to rehearse dying as is the *Craft*, but by contemplating her nearly-dying and the accompanying revelation, I suggest that she does offer an opportunity for an attendant change of perspective in the reader. I explore this suggestion more fully in chapter 4, but my point here is that Julian appears to integrate subjective artifact with literary artifact, offering insights into her experience of *dying* (the first-person experience) and also of her *demise* (the third-person perspective). For now, I focus on the former: on the account as it is relayed in the first-person.

Julian's account begins with a description of the symptoms of her illness, which appear to intensify both in physical severity and in the severity of the existential disruption they enact. At the onset of her sickness, she reports an affliction of such severe pains that she believes they will be fatal: "And I understood by my reason and by my feleing of my peynes that I should dye" (And I understood through my reason and through the pains I felt that I was going to die).[69] This statement implies that Julian retains in this moment a level of lucidity that allows her to rationally engage both thought and feeling as well as mind and body. Moreover, it expresses her understanding of body and soul as a unified seat of experience, an approach also taken up in post-Heideggerian phenomenology's secularized framework of a *gestalt* body-subject. Svenaeus defines this existential seat by a number of processes, of which I suggest that Julian's "reason" and "feleing" broadly correspond to his categories of "understanding" and "attunement." The former (understanding) differs from straightforward cognition in that it relates specifically to action: as Svenaeus explains, "understanding can include the active and incarnated sides of life."[70] The latter (attunement) denotes the mood in which a person finds themselves in the world of intersubjective meaning: the mood as they experience certain actions and events. Reading Julian's description in these terms suggests that her attunement at this stage of her illness remains meaningful, that she has not yet experienced the total disruption described above. For though Julian says that by the time the curate has come she physically "might not speke" (might not speak), she is still able to act out the ars moriendi discourse as she hears and understands the words of the curate: "I have browte thee the image of thy maker and saviour. Louke thereupon and comfort thee therewith" (I have brought to you the image of your maker and savior. Look upon him and take comfort from it).[71] In response, Julian fixes her gaze on the crucifix before her—an act which demonstrates her continued awareness of her situation and its attendant rituals, or in phenomenological terms, the retention of these existential capacities.

On this third night of her illness, Julian recounts her belief that she would die: "I wened oftentymes to have passyd" (I believed often that I would die).[72] While this may seem like a moment of surrender, I want to suggest that this expression is nonetheless a conditional one—that her assent remains at this stage of her account a *performance* in the craft-of-dying tradition—that is, not a first-person subjective artifact. Julian's description of the prayer for a sickness made when she was young helps to contextualize this description: "In this sikenesse I desired to have all manier peynes bodily and ghostly that I should have if I should dye" (In this sickness I desired to have all manner of pains, bodily and spiritual, such as I would have if I were to die).[73] Her use of modals here—"should" and "if"—expresses the contingency of her request, referring also to her wish to perform a compassionate *imitatio* of the suffering of the martyred St. Cecilia described in the short text, who "hadde thre woundys with a swerde in the nekke" (had three wounds from a sword to the neck).[74] With this prayer to St. Cecilia in mind, Julian's initial desire for death may yet be described as imitative rather than subjective, still inflected with the same performativity of this earlier petition. Indeed, this is more explicit in the short text than the long, when she writes:

> Botte in this I was ryght sarye and lothe thought for to dye, botte for nothynge that was in erthe that me lykede to lyeve fore, nor for nothynge that I was aferde fore, for I tristyd in God. Botte it was fore I walde hafe lyevede to have lovede God better and lange tyme, that I myght, be the grace of that lyevynge, have the more knowynge and lovynge of God in the blysse of hevene.[75]

> But in this I was truly sorry and loth to die, despite the fact there was nothing on earth that I wanted to live for, nor nothing that I was afraid of, because I trusted in God. But still, I wanted to have lived to love God better and longer, so I might by the grace of that same living have had more knowledge and love of God in the bliss of heaven.

Julian desires to remain on earth so she can love God the longer, a sustained devotional focus that correlates with her ability to stay in the room and away from anxiety. She feels no fear: "no peyne that I was aferd of" (no pain that I was afraid of).[76] Rather, "Methought I was wele," she writes, "for my eyen were sett uprightward into hevyn" (I thought I was well, for my eyes were fixed upward toward heaven).[77] "Wele" is an important word for Julian, here and in her wider exegesis of the revelations—a term indicating a species of spiritual well-being that extends far beyond physical or mental function.[78] Her use of it here is no different, indicating the sustaining power of participation in the ars moriendi rites and focused attention on the cross. On account of her ability to continue with these devotional practices, she is able to remain, while not free of pain, at least *at home* with her situation.

In these opening stages of her account, Julian's approach to dying cannot then be described phenomenologically as an *authentic* acceptance of death, since the question whether she will die remains predicated upon her desire to *live*, forestalling the requirement of resoluteness in Carel's genuine authenticity. Instead, the contingency of Julian's attunement to death places her at a remove from it. Conceived of or understood by a person living inauthentically, this approach to death might be called one of *demise* in yet another Heideggerian inflection of the term: demise is used by Heidegger as a term to describe not only a third-person understanding of death (i.e., the death of another) but also an "inauthentic death," that is, the condition by which a person "inauthentically understands (i.e., disowns) [their] death," as Blattner explains.[79] Their death is viewed as though it is another's. As a result, "inauthentic Dasein misunderstands death as being demise," and "hence does not come face to face with death, and thereby evades anxiety about death."[80] The evidence of this is in Julian's own words, in her description of how she is able to remain engaged with her surroundings and companions. She has not yet encountered *dying*, in the sense of a first-person event, and it soon becomes apparent that when this does occur it threatens a much greater disruption to her subjectivity and her ability to remain focused on God.

This breakdown begins with the steady failure of Julian's bodily function, the first instance of which occurs in chapter 3 of the longer text. After assenting to God's will, Julian writes: "Thus I durid till day, and be than my body was dede fro the middis downewards, as to my feleing" (So I lived until daybreak, and by then my body was dead from the middle downward, as far as I could feel), a state of apparent lower-body paralysis that disables her from self-motivated movement.[81] Pressing into this moment phenomenologically sheds further light on how Julian is experiencing her decline. Her description of the illness so far has been reported using the subjective "I," but with this onset of paralysis her body becomes an object—"my body"—which she describes as "dede." Phenomenological accounts of embodiment can help to unpack this shift as Julian experiences it, explaining the body-subject's capacity to occupy the position of both perceiving subject and object of perception. Merleau-Ponty gives the example of his right hand touching his left: "If I can, with my left hand, feel my right hand as it touches an object, the right hand as an object is not the right hand as it touches: the first is a system of bones, muscles and flesh brought down at a point in space, the second shoots through space like a rocket to reveal the external object in its place."[82] The revelation of this body part as an external object corresponds with Julian's description of her "dede" torso, which "as to [her] feleing" becomes corpse-like. Philosopher Herbert Plügge writes of just such a phenomenon, explaining that when a body part either feels dead or dies it "takes on many characteristics of objective thinglikeness, such as an importunate heaviness, burden, weight, with the quality of a substance that feels essentially strange, wooden, like plaster of paris, in any event as largely space-filling and hence not altogether as a part of ourselves."[83] S. Kay Toombs similarly observes that this sense of alienation is "particularly pronounced in pathological disturbances such as paresis," arguing that "the loss of tactual and kinesthetic sensation is experienced as a radical disengagement of body from self."[84] She cites Edmund Husserl's notion of kinesthetic sensations giving the body an "interior," clearly defining it as "mine": "To lose this sense is to become dissociated from one's body. It is 'the' arm, rather than 'my' arm which moves."[85]

In extreme cases, this kind of objectification can lead to total bodily disownership or denial, called *somotoparaphrenia* in modern medicine. In his study of body disownership in post-traumatic stress disorder, Yochai Ataria writes that this condition "can be defined in terms of neglect on both the visual and the sensorimotor levels."[86] Ataria describes how "the neglected limb or, in more severe cases, half of the body is experienced as heavy, dead, or lifeless."[87] He describes this as a loss of bodily *ownership* (SBO), giving the example of a patient, "GA," who suffers from somatoparaphrenic symptoms, and describes his hand and arm as "dead."[88] The limb is identified as "not mine," indicating a lack of SBO, but more precisely, Ataria notes, "the *dead hand* is no longer both subject and object. It is no longer a tool like the blind man's cane, allowing GA to perceive the world, but rather a thing, an object that cannot touch or be touched."[89] Here, GA neither feels agency or ownership over his hand.[90] And while Julian's account of her paralysis does not appear to indicate a full loss of SBO (her body remains "my [*her*] body," and she continues to use "I" intermittently), her description does seem to signify a shift from the body as subjective to objective, and with it a dissolution of agency—as evidenced by the following passage in chapter 3, recounting her companions maneuvering her into an upright position: "Then was I stered to be sett upright, underlenand with helpe, for to have more fredam of my herte to be at Gods will" (Then I was steered to be set upright, propped up with support so I would have more freedom of my heart to be at God's will).[91] This detail suggests that Julian's own bodily agency has been compromised and she is now physically reliant on those around her.

Furthermore, Julian reports that she wishes to relieve the involuntary constriction of her body so that she can "[thinke] on God while [her] life would lest" ([think] on God while [her] life would last), a description that indicates the contingent effects of her paralysis on her cognition—as emphasized by the modal "would."[92] James T. McIlwain and Richard Lawes have separately suggested biomedical etiologies for the relief that accompanies Julian's move upright, but a phenomenological approach understands differently the upright posture, conceiving of it as a gestural indicator of healthful or homelike embodiment.[93] "Freedom," as Julian has it here, arises after a state of oppression or constraint such as that which accompanies paresis, which from the Greek πάρεσις (*paresis*, a letting go) and παρίημι (*pariémi*, to pass by or over) denotes a loss of voluntary movement (literally, a letting go of control of the body). Maintaining an upright posture is therefore a maintenance of bodily control, which requires agency in terms of motor, sensory, and cognitive communication. As phenomenologist Erwin W. Straus shows, the upright posture "remains a task" for the lived body, which must "oppose the forces of gravity" in a counteraction which literally "with-stands" its environment.[94] "The natural stance of man," Straus writes, "is, therefore, 'resistance.'"[95] An essential paradox of homelikeness thus comes to the fore: that homelike embodiment means *exertion* but also *freedom*, and *resistance* but also *non-constraint.* For Julian, this freedom or agency is facilitated "with helpe" from her companions, who are acting as caregivers while she is incapacitated. By "stereing" Julian to set her upright, they paradoxically take and restore control of her bodily movement, relieving the oppressive weight of her abject body. In turn, this interference maintains Julian's homelike attunement, helping her to adapt to her new dysfunction—a moment that serves to reiterate the importance of intersubjectivity, or *being-with* in

Heideggerian terminology, in the cultivation of well-being. A whole or homelike self is revealed here to also be a relational self, a notion of communality that will be foundational for Julian's later soteriology.

From this point on, however, Julian's illness begins to worsen. She describes how her sight deteriorates, leaving her in the dark, and her breathing becomes difficult:

> After this my sight began to failen, and it was all derke about me in the chamber as it had be night, save in the image of the cross, wherein I beheld a comon light, and I wiste not how. All that was beside the crosse was uggely to me, as if it had be mekil occupyed with the fends. After this the over party of my body began to dyen so ferforth that onethys I had ony feleing. My most payne was shortnes of onde and failyng of life.[96]

> After this my sight began to fail, and it was all dark around me in the room as if it were night, except in the image of the cross where I beheld a general light, and I knew not how. All that was beside the cross was ugly to me as if it had been greatly occupied by devils. After this the other parts of my body began to die to such an extent that I hardly had any feeling. My greatest pain was a shortness of breath and feeling of passing away.

The short text adds more detail to this scene, describing a bodily posture that seems to mimic Christ's on the cross, her head lolling to one side: "Myne handdys felle downe on aythere syde, and also for unpowere my heede satylde downe on syde" (My hands fell down on either side, and also for lack of strength my head settled down on one side).[97] Julian's description of breathlessness as the "most pain" that she feels is corroborated by the work of Carel, who cites recent research on dyspnea that shows that the same brain pathways are activated in breathlessness as in pain, hunger, and thirst.[98] This suggests, Carel writes, the possibility that "breathlessness bears a family resemblance to pain," since it is "acutely distressing in other ways."[99] So, while Julian's paralysis has spread upward on her body and sensation receded with it, she remains in a state of suffering, if not "pain" as such. At this stage in her account, Julian's body remains objective and her attunement to the feelings in her body shifts to an attunement to their dying: "my body began to dyen."[100] And, while her companions have helped her to maintain a seated position until this point, they cannot assist with her breathlessness. Accompanied by the failure of her sight, Julian becomes completely cut off from the sickroom: all that surrounds her becomes strange, "as if it had be mekil occupyed with the fends."[101] It becomes, in other words, *unhomelike*.[102] In the prior chapter, I explored how unhomelikeness discloses one's world as "other" to the self: how the unhomelike, or the uncanny, denotes something unfamiliar, an involuntary disclosure of a primordial unknown. But Julian here conceives of this attunement in terms that are both historically and theologically charged: the world becomes dark, as though the agents of the devil who first tempted humanity into original sin have been revealed.

It is here, then, that the divergences between Julian's account and the secularized phenomenological approach come into sharp focus. In Heidegger's phenomenology, the primordial "homelessness" he speaks of very clearly draws on the Augustinian notion of the postlapsarian world as *regio dissimilitudinis*, a region of unlikeness into which humanity was exiled in consequence of the fall.[103] Describing both a geography and a temporality, this idea constitutes the worldly condition of original sin into which all postlapsarian humanity is born. It is, moreover, a condition ontologically defined by analogy—the region is *unlike* a prelapsarian state, an unlikeness which is the very foundation of its existence. I explore this complex temporality further in chapter 6, but here I want to stress how in removing the divine horizon from his account of worldly homelessness Heidegger elides the ontologically analogous nature of Augustine's model. Just as Andrew Cole and D. Vance Smith write that Hans Blumenberg ignores the ontological necessity for "the medieval" in his theory of modernity *as* modern (as I discuss in my introduction to this book), Heidegger similarly evacuates the *likeness* to God which determines the foundation of Augustine's region of *un*likeness. The consequence of this secularization is that a Heideggerian reading of Julian's experience of unhomelikeness equally fails to account for the eschatological nature of her existential disruption. Where this moment of inbreaking does appear to reveal to Julian the reality of her world as in Heidegger's account of anxiety, then, the reality of *her* world is that it is a postlapsarian one, created and held by God.

It is only within this theological frame that the disruption of Julian's illness can be sufficiently theorized, since as the above discussion makes clear, her experience is structured by an engagement with medieval Christian rites and symbols. This is most apparent, however, at the moment when Julian's revelation begins: when without feeling in her body, without sight, and without breath, she finally desires "to have passid," to die. But instead of this prayer being granted, Julian's pains are taken from her, and she experiences a sense of renewed wholeness:

> And, in this, sodenly all my peyne was taken fro me and I was as hole, and namely in the over party of my body, as ever I was aforn. I mervalid at this soden change, for methought it was a privy workeing of God and not of kinde.[104]

> And in this, suddenly all my pain was taken from me and I was whole again, as healthy in my body as I was before. I marveled at this sudden change, because I thought it was a secret working of God and not of nature.

From this state of renewed health, Julian is then struck with the renewed desire for the second wound of compassion: "Than came *suddenly* to my minde that I should desyre the secounde wounde, of our Lords gifte and of his grace, that my body might be fulfilled with minde and felyng of his blissid passion as I had before praied" (Then came *suddenly* to my mind that I might desire the second wound of our lord's gracious gift, that my body might be filled with knowledge and feeling of his blessed passion, as I had prayed for before).[105] Vincent Gillespie and Maggie Ross have observed that the adverb "sodenly" is one of Julian's most common descriptors, repeated three times in seven lines in this passage to signal "the suspension of 'ordinary' time."[106] The signal here is that Julian has slipped out of the everyday and into a more capacious, expansive plane: the plane of revelation. It is in this moment, finally, that she receives her first showing: "In this sodenly I saw the red blode trekelyn downe fro under the garlande" (In this suddenly I saw the red blood trickling down from under the crown of thorns).[107] Thus, my discussion arrives at the slippage between Julian's illness and her revelation. Emptied out by her sickness, Julian is now filled with the sight of Christ.

This chapter has explored the ways an encounter with death can change a person, exposing them to new understanding about what it means to live and be well. It began by considering how the medieval ars moriendi genre of literature invited imaginative encounters with death, investigating how this death culture was borne out in texts and traditions contemporary to Julian of Norwich. Building on the work of Amy Appleford and D. Vance

Smith, I considered the problems of subjectivity that attend to these literary artifacts of dying and their implications for a reading of Julian's own brush with death. I then traced the development of a comparable ars moriendi in the work of Heidegger and subsequent phenomenologists, mapping out the specific characteristics of insight and attunement that may attend to experiences of dying. Of particular importance to my discussion is Havi Carel's reconfiguration of Heidegger's concept of authenticity: as I have shown, Carel revises the concept of authentic understanding as not mutually exclusive to being-with-others. The phenomenological possibility of going on living even with a sustained awareness of one's own mortality was therefore introduced: a possibility that in turn sheds light on the potentially generative aspects of illness and dying.

In the second half of the chapter, I turned to Julian's *Revelations of Divine Love* as an exemplar of such an encounter with the limits of mortality, examining in phenomenological terms how her illness disrupts all aspects of her body and mind. I sought to identify the moments of slippage described in Julian's texts: how she moves from an engagement with her surroundings into a state of genuine existential anxiety. I have shown how, when this happens, she experiences a severance from her surroundings, a suspension in space and time that limits her awareness to the sight of the cross. By the end of this phenomenological reading, the chapter has arrived at the significance of the divine horizon that grounds this existential event. For while Julian's illness has incurred extreme pains—so extreme to entail even a desire for death—this dark night of the soul has also led her to an experiential plane beyond experience itself: an experience of the divine. It is here that the fullest divergence is identified between Julian's texts and the medical phenomenologies this book has been engaging. Given Heideggerian phenomenology's secular roots, such accounts of dying necessarily structure being-toward-death as a stretching out into nothingness, or a revelation of homelessness. Yet Julian's *Revelations* evidence a different kind of revelation altogether, one which discloses the possibility of finding a home again in God. It is this divine horizon to which the next chapter now turns, where I consider the complex intersections of revelation and tribulation.

3

BEARING WITNESS

Revelation, Suffering, and the Fiend

The wounded surgeon plies the steel
That questions the distempered part;
Beneath the bleeding hands we feel
The sharp compassion of the healer's art
Resolving the enigma of the fever chart.

—T. S. Eliot, "East Coker," from *Four Quartets*

Medieval contemplative texts are of such varying genres and offer such varying directives that they pose a complex challenge to the historian seeking to theorize accounts of illness and revelation. The weight placed on penitential or purgative practices against more temperate regimes is one particular point of difference across the literature. Surviving texts from the Continent, for instance, broadly evince a more ascetic focus than those found in England at the time Julian of Norwich was writing. Texts written by and for women, too, demonstrate a keener demand for, or pressure in favor of, ascetic devotional practice.[1] The contemplative milieu of fourteenth-century England is often characterized as less austere, with a renewed emphasis on the incarnation and the passion of Christ felt in literature in the centuries preceding Julian's life. Since Anselm of Canterbury's *Cur Deus Homo* inquiry in 1094–1098, Christ was increasingly centered in the soteriological narrative, a trend reiterated in 1215 by the Fourth Lateran Council's attention to Christ's bodily suffering at the passion, and resulting edicts in favor of eucharistic piety and communion. By Julian's lifetime, this Christological emphasis finds expression in the influence of popular texts like pseudo-Bonaventure's fourteenth-century *Meditationes vitae Christi*—translated by Nicholas Love as *The Mirror of the Life of Jesus Christ* (c. 1400)—which stands as an exemplum of the genre of texts Sarah McNamer calls "affective meditations," defined as such by their emphasis on "the performance of feeling" or compassion.[2]

Christ functions as the theological keystone of this compassionate hermeneutic: the wounded surgeon whose passion provides the promise of recovery for humankind's ills. Together with Mary and other holy exempla offering models of meekness and humility, Christ is the divine paradigm for holy suffering to be emulated and imitated in devotional practice. Julian speaks of such *imitatio* when she writes in chapter 55 of her *Revelations*, "and thus Criste is our wey" (and so Christ is our way), and when she refers, in the shorter version of her text, to the exemplary St. Cecilia and the three mortal wounds that martyred her.[3] Furthermore, Laura Saetveit Miles has recently proposed that the Virgin Mary's reception of the annunciation offers "the primary model" for Julian's (and her contemporary, Margery Kempe's) "own reception of the visionary gift."[4] Such compassionate identification with holy figures could be undertaken via meditation on words or images of their suffering, which were thought to instigate a dissolution of boundaries between the contemplative and the holy person. The meditant would begin to empty out the self, making room for a cowounding with the divine.

The present chapter pulls focus on Julian's own contemplative strategies against this devotional backdrop to investigate the ways her illness both catalyzes and disrupts her revelation, and the resulting distinction she draws between embodied and spiritual suffering. As Julian herself discovers, physical suffering can be generative, but it can also be dangerous, destructive even, leading the ill person away from the realm of the therapeutic and into the realm of despair. Julian negotiates both conditions throughout the *Revelations*, providing a strikingly vulnerable account of the effect of illness on her devotional capacity—and, in turn, the impact of devotion on her recovery. The chapter opens by examining the cognitive and affective protocols of this devotional model, theorized once more in the light of phenomenological thinkers after Martin Heidegger. This reading considers the disruptions to time and space that occur in both illness and revelation, and how one may have instigated the other in Julian's case. Continuing with this phenomenological interpretation, I then consider the effect of pain on Julian's ability to focus on Christ and the threat it subsequently poses to the revelatory event. I compare these with the spiritual pains of despair Julian experiences thereafter, exploring how shame hinders her capacity to reorient herself to God. Finally, the chapter traces Julian's recovery from the sickroom and into the anchorhold, arguing that the events experienced in the former set a precedent of compassionate being-with-others that is also borne out in the anchoritic vocation. The chapter concludes by comparing the Heideggerian hermeneutic of being-toward-death with what I call a *being-toward-God*—a comparison which highlights once more the divergent horizons of these phenomenologies and Julian's theological approach, the background of nothingness of the former now sharply profiled against the latter's divine frame.

ABIDING IN BEHOLDING

When Julian's revelation begins, this change is described as "soden" (sudden); an inbreaking into the experience of her illness.[5] Suddenly Julian wishes for the second wound of compassion; suddenly she sees the cross before her start to bleed; suddenly she understands this is Christ; and suddenly the Trinity fills her heart with joy. These sights and insights happen simultaneously, as Julian slips into what theologian Maggie Ross calls the "boundless present" of beholding. In the Bible, Ross writes, the term *beholding* is used to "[interrupt] the narrative," bringing the reader back to the here and the now, freeing them "from the bondage of time-bound self-consciousness to receive a glimpse of eternity, however fleeting."[6] In just such an extended moment, Julian is lifted out of ordinary time and graced with a new perspective; a brief immersion in the divine view of God-time. By examining this time-space of beholding as it relates to Julian's sickness and comparing it with phenomenological accounts of illness, the below discussion sheds light on the changes to Julian's subjectivity that accompany this event and so lays the groundwork for further investigation of the disruptive power of her pains.

The temporal disruption of beholding bears striking resemblance to phenomenological accounts of illness, which highlight similar changes in the subjective experience of time. In phenomenologist S. Kay Toombs's description of her own sickness, for instance, she writes of "a continuum of discomfort," in which "past and future pains coalesce into a stagnating present."[7] Toombs calls this the "ever-present" of illness, which afflicts the ill person with an enduring preoccupation with "the here and now."[8] John B. Brough also identifies "dilating nows and fractured selves, the conception of time as landscape rather than as beads on a string" as the vivid phenomena of serious illness.[9] As such, the slippage across the marginal boundaries of experience that occurs in revelation seems a smaller leap when originating in the already expansive temporality of illness, which can be read as a kind of disruptive runway to the latter. Vincent Gillespie calls this prerevelatory state of illness a condition of *abject liminality*, wherein "the abject man or woman, reduced to their bare humanity, can achieve a focused attentiveness to matters of life and death, and potentially to matters of spiritual significance."[10] Such a condition can be identified in Julian's *Revelations* when, at the end of the second chapter of the long text, her pains recede and she is occupied with the desire for the second wound of compassion. She longs for her pains to be replaced with the pains of Christ: that her body might be *fulfilled* with "minde and felyng" (knowledge and feeling) of his passion.[11] Julian qualifies that she is not asking for a corporeal vision of the passion; she does not need to *see* the crucifixion, only to know and to feel it. While she has formerly had "mind and feeling" of her *own* pains, then, Julian here opens herself to a complete experience of Christ's suffering. In the short text, her head is even described as lolling to one side, a reflection of iconography of the passion: "Myne handdys felle downe on aythere syde, and also for unpowere my heede satylde downe on syde" (My hands fell down on either side, and also for lack of strength my head settled down on one side).[12] She becomes compassionately porous to the suffering of Christ and to his beholding.

Upon crossing this threshold of revelation, Julian also enters a new condition of "hole" or "hele" (wholeness or health), as the two witnesses to the long text report in chapter 3—terms which both suggest a condition of comfort or at-homeness.[13] Reflecting on the event later in chapter 8, Julian then writes: "And the bodily sight stinted, and the gostly sight dwellid in myne understondyng. And I abode with reverent drede, joyand in that I saw" (And the bodily sight stopped, and the spiritual sight dwelled in my understanding. And I abode with reverent dread, enjoying in what I saw).[14] This moment further stresses the homeliness Julian finds in her revelation, expressed in a chiasmic hermeneutic wherein the showing finds a home in her understanding while she simultaneously finds a home in the space of beholding. In this way, the vision and the visionary dwell in each other, in an expression of mutual indwelling Julian will later develop as the nucleus of her anthropology. Indeed, Julian's choice of language here does some of this theological work already, where in describing how she "*abode* with reverent drede, joyand in that [she] saw" she can draw on both noun and verb forms of "abode" to express both the act of dwelling in the space of the revelation as well as the revelation *as* a space, a topography in its own right.[15] As a result, the sickroom becomes something of a proto-topography for the spiritual otherworld of the revelation; an uncanny space between ordinary life and the extraordinary divine. But this parallelism can be extended in another direction, too, to include the space Julian will enter later: the anchorhold. As Liz Herbert McAvoy writes, "The sickroom becomes [Julian's] figurative anchorhold; the inert body which houses her soul echoes its tomb-like walls and the only visible animation is that which emanates from the suspended crucifix before her."[16] Laura Saetveit Miles has also identified the anchorhold as a space beyond the world: "a site for heaven on earth as well as a site of visionary (re-)experience that achieved an intimacy with God otherwise unreachable in this world."[17] Miles emphasizes the temporal disruption of this site, which brings the anchorite "out of marketplace time into her own 'heterochrony' of God-time: a mélange of liturgical schedule, personal time of life and death, and universal eschatological time."[18] Both

McAvoy and Miles here speak to the unusual ways time and space work in the anchorhold, noting the similarities with Julian's experience of the sickroom. My reading closes this circle, as it were, with the suggestion that the revelation itself provides a third, intersecting time-space in which Julian finds homeliness, akin to both sickroom and anchorhold.

While my discussion arrives at the anchorhold by the end of this chapter, I wish to remain a while longer with Julian's illness and revelation to consider the challenges these phenomena pose to each other over the course of the *Revelations*. In particular, I focus on how Julian finds a degree of well-being in her beholding and is able to reconnect with her companions in the sickroom. This is by no means a straightforward process, as she is buffeted by an overflow of ambivalent feelings during the revelation. Of these, Julian identifies two crucial modes: "love" and "drede." These feelings, she writes in chapter 74 of the long text, are "brethren, and thei arn rotid in us be the goodnes of our maker" (siblings, and they are rooted in us by the goodness of our maker).[19] With these words, Julian is possibly drawing on a tradition of medieval tribulation literature that theorizes the intersection of positive and negative feelings in events of suffering. This is also borne out, for example, in the later fifteenth-century *Book of the Craft of Dying*, where the author writes that dread of God is "the begynnynge of wisdom so it is the begynnynge of helthe of mannes soule" (the beginning of wisdom, so it is the beginning of health of man's soul).[20] Daniel McCann has glossed this affective process as "a complex emotional experience": "[Drede] is," McCann writes, "as an emotion and the first medicine of the soul, potent and powerful."[21] Put another way, dread is an awe-ful condition of knowledge of God. There are strong echoes of this kind of affect in the Heideggerian moment of anxiety I explored in the previous chapter, where the realization of the nothingness upon which human existence is grounded throws the anxious person into a new way of seeing—except now, of course, the disclosure is not a realization of nothingness but the realization of God's power. In the same chapter, Julian glosses the specific form of "drede" she experiences as that which most fully pleases God, since it is "full soft"—that is, it is always accompanied by love.[22] Julian thus colors the therapeutic tenor of "drede" as found in contemporary tribulation literature with her characteristic emphasis on loving compassion, where to be "full soft" is to be porously open to the terrible and generative qualities of this species of fear, welcoming it with reverence and wonder.

In short, in Julian's beholding she encounters something more than an ordinary, everyday condition of well-being. She is made aware of her connection to God, and so can attune to his love even while she remains "in drede"—a kind of spiritual "hele" within illness. This condition is further evidenced by Julian's few vocal expressions during her illness, such as when she exclaims in chapter 8, "And as longe as I saw this sight of the plentious bleding of the hede, I might never stinte of these words: 'Benedicite Domine!'" (And as long as I saw this sight of the plenteous bleeding of the head, I might never stop uttering these words: "Benedicite Domine!").[23] Jennifer Bryan observes that this statement closely echoes Mary's own "lo, me, Gods handmaid" in chapter 4, indicating a performative aspect to both expressions.[24] And while I suggested in the previous chapter that an engagement with her surroundings showed that Julian had not yet faced death entirely, the onset of the revelation can be argued to have changed Julian's experience of being-with-others. Now, when paired with the new perspective provided by her beholding, the ability to respond "Benedicite Domine!" can be seen as evidence of a kind of genuine authenticity, to return to

Havi Carel's terminology, with her situation; evidence that she has entered a new kind of relationality with God and her companions. Indeed, Julian confirms that throughout the entire showing she has been able to remain in compassionate awareness of her fellow Christians: "In al this," Julian writes in chapter 8, "I was mekil sterid in charite to mine even-Cristen" (In all this, I was greatly stirred to charity for my fellow Christians).[25] The passage implies that this stirring lasted the duration of the revelation, and when Julian's perception then exits the visionary space to reenter the sickroom, this concern finds expression in her statement, "It is today domys day with me" (It is today doomsday with me).[26] This utterance is intended, Julian writes, to inform her companions of the showing's message: "for to make hem to have mende that this life is shorte, as thei might se in example" (to make them see by example that this life is short) so that they might have "lovid God the better" (loved God the better).[27] Julian here seeks to share her comfort with those around her, soliciting them to also seek the beholding of God, which will extend the "curtes love and endles godenes" (courteous love and endless goodness) she has glimpsed in her own revelation.[28]

Julian's account of her beholding thus incorporates at once the abjection of illness, the homely dwelling she finds in the showings, and the oneness she feels both with God and her fellow Christians. This final element might be read as the phenomenological condition of being-with-others, which Carel identifies as necessary for a person to develop what she calls "resoluteness" in the face of death: "As opposed to anxiety, resolute existence contains both being-alongside and being-with."[29] This phenomenological condition depends on a person's reintegration into the patterns and routines of their world, paired with the sustained understanding they have gleaned from the illness experience. In Julian's case, she reenters the space of her sickroom with a resolved compassion for those around her—a compassion which then extends through her *Revelations* to her reader. Indeed, while Julian uses the phrase "myn even-Cristen" twice in chapter 8 of the long text, she will deploy the term nine more times across the *Revelations* and four more in the variant "*our* even-Cristen."[30] She makes this explicit with a passage closely following her return to the sickroom and her "domys day" statement:

> I sey not this to hem that be wise, for thei wote it wele; but I sey it to yow that be simple, for ese and comfort, for *we arn al one in love*. For sothly it was not shewid me that God lovid me better than the lest soule that is in grace, for I am sekir that there be many that never had shewing ner sight, but of the common techyng of holy church, that loven God better than I. For if I loke singularly to myselfe, I am right nowte; but in general I am in hope, in onehede of charitie with al myn evyn-Cristen. For in this onehede stond the life of all mankinde that shall be savid.[31]

> I say this not to those who are wise, for they know it well, but I say it to you who are unaware, both for ease and comfort, that *we are all one in love*. For truly it was not showed to me that God loved me better than the least soul that is in grace, for I am sure that there are many that never had showing nor sight of him, except in the common teachings of the holy church, who love God better than me. For if I look singularly to myself, I am entirely nothing; but in general I am in hope, in oneness of charity with all my fellow Christians, for in this oneness stands the life of all humankind who shall be saved.

Here, Julian insists with humility that she is no better than anyone who may only have encountered God in the liturgy, a statement that amounts to a denial of her specialness as visionary. But this passage also stresses the indwelling of the singular in the universal—of herself in oneness with her fellow Christians. This serves as an important reminder that Julian does not see the homely dwelling she has found in her beholding as an individual condition; just as she is comforted by those around her in the sickroom and wishes to comfort them in turn, she sees herself as "all one in love" with her readers. In this way, her first-person plural address extends both revelation and recovery beyond the boundaries of her own subjectivity, as the pursuit of well-being for the *we* as well as the *I*.

IS ANY PAYNE LIKE THIS?

In light of the disruption of her illness and her subsequent dwelling in the comfort of beholding, Julian begins to develop a tribulation theology that distinguishes physical pain from spiritual suffering, and which identifies well-being as a condition extending beyond physiological function. It is possible to be "sekir in wo and in wele" (secure in suffering and in well-being), she sees in the seventh showing, if sustained attention is focused on the love of God.[32] This word "sekir," which can also translate to *certain*, *sure*, *safe* (spiritually, in the way of salvation), and even *genuine* (predating Carel's language of genuine authenticity), suggests the fixity of well-being that can be found across these ambivalent states—an idea doubly enacted by its pun on the term *seke* (as in *sick*), which linguistically blurs the boundaries between sickness and well-being.[33] This insight is realized for Julian by an equally fixed attention to the cross, as her request to feel what Christ feels is fulfilled:

> The which shewing of Cristes peynys *fillid* me ful of payne, for I wiste wele he suffryd but onys, but as he wold shewn it me and *fillen* me with mynde, as I had aforn desyryd. And in al this tyme of Cristes presens I felte no payn but for Cristes paynys.[34]

> The which showing of Christ's pains *filled* me full of pain, for I knew well he suffered only once, but as he would show it to me and *fill* me with knowing, as I had desired before. And in all this time of Christ's presence I felt no pain except for Christ's pains.

These pains are so severe they lead Julian to question her own urge to perform *compassio*: "I knew but litil what payne it was that I askyd" (I knew but little of what pain it was that I asked for), she thinks to herself.[35] Yet Julian's faculties remain intact, and she is able to configure her response: "Is any payne in helle like this?" (Is any pain in hell like this?).[36] It is in this moment that Julian lands upon the crucial distinction that will underwrite her tribulation theology, when she is answered "in [her] reason" that there are indeed pains beyond those experienced in the body: "Helle is another payne, for there is despeyr. But of al paynes that leden to salvation, this is the most payne: to se thy love suffir" (Hell is another pain, for there is despair. But of all the pains that lead to salvation, this is the most pain: to see your love suffer).[37]

With this, Julian teases out a crucial distinction between the disruptive suffering of physical pain and the more severely damaging spiritual pains of "despeyr." Omitted from the long text is her qualification that such despair in hell is "*mare*" (*more*) than physical pain, "for that es *gastelye* payne" (for that is *spiritual* pain).[38] Although this expression of hierarchy is only present in the short text, she elaborates on the insight in other ways in chapter 73 of the longer version, where she distinguishes two "manner of sekenes" (two kinds of sickness) that might give rise to a turn away from God and so to despair: "that on is onpatience or slouth, for we bere our traveyl and our peynes hevily; that other is dispeir or doubtfull drede" (the one is impatience or sloth, because we bear our labors and our pains heavily; the other is despair or doubtful dread).[39] The former ("onpatience") implies a breakdown of control, an inability to "bere" pain, from *patientia*, "suffering" or "patience." By associating the heaviness of this "traveyl" with "slouth," the sin of sloth, Julian possibly invokes the condition known in monastic and eremitic contexts as *acedia* (also *accidie* or *accedie*, literally "lack of care"): an affliction thought to derive from the devil leading the individual into despondency and inertia.[40] This "noonday devil" is described by the early Christian theologian John Cassian (d. c. 435) in terms of a physical disease: "like some fever which seizes him at stated times, bringing the burning heat of its attacks on the sick man at usual and regular hours."[41] Such a condition was treacherous, as it would break down the person's will or capacity for devotional practice.[42] Julian seems to refer to an equivalent spiritual disruption in her category of "doubtfull drede," which she describes as afflicting a person such that they turn away from the divine and into themselves: a dread that "dwellith" in the individual and submits them to "the beholding of ourselfe and of our synnes aforn don" (the beholding of ourselves and of our sins done before).[43] This is a dread quite apart from the soft, reverent dread described above. Instead, it is characterized, like impatience, as a severance from God's love, where the person is made "so sorry and so hevy that onethis [they] can finde ony comfort" (so sorry and so heavy that [they] can hardly find any comfort).[44] These "ii manner of sekenes" can thus be classified as two types of spiritual "disese," each leading the afflicted into the realm of total despair.

Julian encounters something like this solipsistic self-beholding in the seventh showing, when she experiences a violent fluctuation between "wo and wele": "I was turnyd and *left to myselfe* in hevynes and werines of my life and irkenes of myselfe, that onethis I coude have patience to leve" (I was turned and *left to myself* in heaviness and weariness of my life and such annoyance with myself that I could hardly endure to live).[45] Oscillating between pain and comfort, her symptoms come and go, but in their acute presence they entirely preclude the alternative state of "ease." It is only when her pain is relieved once more that she is able to tap into "comfort" and "rest in soule," and she then cannot imagine how any dread, sorrow, or bodily pain could disease her.[46] In the short text she adds in this moment of relief, "there was nothynge in erthe that schulde hafe grevyd me" (there was nothing on earth that could have grieved me).[47] She describes these fluctuations using words from Paul and Peter: "And in the same tyme of joy I migte have seid with Seynt Paul: 'Nothing shal depart me fro the charite of Criste.' And in the peyne I migte have seid with Seynt Peter: 'Lord, save me, I perish'" (And in that same time of joy I might have said with Saint Paul: "Nothing shall depart me from the charity of Christ." And in the pain I might have said with Saint Peter: "Lord, save me, I perish").[48] These changing conditions reiterate the sheer focus that pain demands and the perceptual limitations it incurs, which appear to be only a moment away throughout the *Revelations*, lurking at the periphery of Julian's consciousness and threatening to intrude on her beholding.

Attempting to interpret these diverse pains after the fact, Julian begins to theorize how and why such suffering is possible—an account that again, bears striking resemblance to the phenomenological approaches to illness described previously. In her exegesis on this experience in chapter 48 of the long text, she interprets her oscillation of feeling and accompanying self-beholding as a product of the postlapsarian condition, which renders humanity as continually receding back toward sin:

> and anon we fallen into ourself, and than fynde we no felyng of ryth nowte but contrariouste that is in ourselfe, and that of the elder rote of our first synne, with all that followyn of our contrivans. And in this we arn traveylid and tempestid with felyng of synnys and of peynes in many dyvers manner, gostly and bodyly, as it is knowen to us in this lif.[49]

> and at once we fall into ourselves, and there we find no right feeling, nothing but the contrariousness that is in ourselves, and that of the elder root of our first sin, with all that followed of our fall. And in this we are belabored and tempested with feelings of sin and pains in various ways, spiritual and bodily, as it is known to us in this life.

Just as post-Heideggerian phenomenology considers health a rhythm of dynamic balancing and rebalancing, Julian understands the inheritance of original sin as having left humankind in a fragile state, prone to slipping into sin or disease. She also writes in chapter 47:

> I understode this: man is chongeable in this lif, and be frelte and overcummyng fallith into synne. He is onmytye and onwise of hymself, and also his wil is overleyd; and in this tyme he is in tempest and in sorow and wo, and the cause is blindhede, for he seith not God.[50]

> I understood this: man is changeable in this life, and by frailty and pride falls into sin. He is weak and does not know himself, and

> his will is also clouded; and all the while he is in tempest and in sorrow and suffering, and the cause is blindness, because he sees not God.

This rhythmic and self-effacing quality means that "if peyn be taken fro us, it may commen agen" (if pain is taken from us, it may come again), as Julian understands from the fifteenth showing, and that more generally humanity will always slide again into sin: "God browte to my mynd that I shuld synne" (God brought to my mind that I would sin).[51] Just as for the phenomenologist the condition of homelikeness serves to disguise the existential "otherness" of the world, then, Julian understands that health or lack of pain is merely a temporary relief from a more chronic condition, which might be described as homelessness. As discussed in the prior chapter, this species of homelessness is for Julian more akin to the Augustinian *regio dissimilitudinis* than the null void of Heidegger's model, a region of unlikeness that is ontically created and sustained through likeness to God. And while this understanding of postlapsarian existence is distressing, it is not, crucially, an experience of total severance. While her own pains seem intolerable, at this stage of her account Julian therefore maintains that "it is spedeful to some soulis to fele on this wise" (it is profitable for some souls to feel like this).[52] In other words, she attributes her fluctuating pains to the will of God and strives to bear them accordingly.

How Julian can make this statement after undergoing such tribulation is perhaps a testament that she has not yet been visited by the spiritual suffering she describes as "despeyr." In the face of her physical pains, Julian recognizes that they are temporary, or that they will pass. She therefore conveys the lesson of this showing as she understands it: that God "kepyth us even alike sekir in wo and in wele" (keeps us all equally safe in suffering and in well-being).[53] Pain, woe, and suffering must be endured patiently, with a fixity on the love of God: "For it is Godds wil we hold us in comfort with al our migte; for blisse is lestinge withoute ende, and peyne is passand and shal be browte to nougte to hem that shall be savyd" (For it is God's will that we hold ourselves in comfort with all our might; for bliss is everlasting without end, and pain is passing and shall be brought to nothing to them that shall be saved).[54] God's love, which sustains humanity in grace, offers the comfort of homely dwelling even in experiences of pain: "And therefore," Julian concludes her exegesis of the seventh showing, "it is not Godds wil that we folow the felynge of peyne in sorow and mornyng for hem, but sodenly passing over and holden us in endless likyng that is God" (And therefore, it is not God's will that we follow the feeling of pain in sorrow and mourning for them, but quickly pass over it and hold ourselves in the endless consolation that is God).[55] Stoic forbearance is facilitated by faith in this condition of endless love.

SHAME HURTS

As has been shown, Julian's encounter with the physical pains of her illness has already given her great insight into the mutability of well-being and the therapeutic potential of devotion to God. Yet it is only in her account of the more severe pains of spiritual despair—namely, *shame*—that Julian can be seen to truly face up to existential dread. Such despair occurs when, after fifteen showings, her symptoms return in force, disrupting her beholding in turn. Julian sets up this moment in the *Revelations* with a statement in chapter 65, that it is God's will that she and her readers "pass . . . lytely over, and sett we [our pain] at nowte" (pass . . . lightly over, and count [our pain] as nothing), instead focusing their attention on his love so that they "shall have patience and ben in great rest" (shall have patience and be in great rest).[56] Nevertheless, while she acknowledges the mutability of pain, she admits that passing over it may not be an easy task, since when a person is *in* pain, they can "thynke ryte nowte but that we arn in, or that we felyn" (think of nothing else but the state we are in, or what we feel).[57] This notion of the distracting force of pain finds an earlier expression in Aquinas's writing on the soul's capacity for receiving God, the *intentio animae*—a concept Heidegger's tutor Edmund Husserl would later appropriate with his theory of intentionality, which identifies consciousness as an attitude of engagement with the world.[58] As Michael Raby notes in his own phenomenological reading of Julian, Aquinas acknowledges that the soul in pain cannot receive new information, entirely occupied as it is with the sensation: "physical pain, more than anything, absorbs the soul's energies [*intentionem animae*]."[59] Raby observes how Augustine, too, points out how bodily pain "blocks off the internal routes through which the soul's attention [*intentio*] was striving to reach out and sense things through the flesh."[60] As Raby shows, when these routes are sufficiently blocked by pain, it may become difficult—impossible, even—to focus the attention toward God. Pain is passing—but until it does, it can be all-consuming.

Julian encounters such a force when her symptoms return in chapter 66 of the long text and she is left spiritually as well as physically wretched:

> and anon my sekenes cam agen: first in my hede, with a sound and a dynne; and sodenly all my body was fulfillid with sekenes like as it was aforn, and I was as baren and as drye as I never had comfort but litil. And as a wretch I morned and hevyed for felyng of my bodily peynes and for fayling of comfort, gostly and bodily.[61]

> and at once my sickness came again: first in my head, with a sound and a din; and suddenly all my body was filled with sickness as it was before, and I was as barren and dry as if I had never had any comfort except a little. And as a wretch I moaned and heaved for the feeling of my bodily pains and the failing of comfort, spiritual and bodily.

The idea that Julian's suffering is laid bare by a *failure* of comfort, spiritual and bodily, here again preempts the phenomenological idea of health as transparent; an imperceptible rhythm pulsing in the background of life. In this moment, any such rhythm Julian has been feeling is interrupted, and with it so is her beholding of the showings: "al was close and I saw no more" (everything ended and I saw no more).[62] She has, as she writes in chapter 47, "*fallen into* [herself]," a statement that also resonates through the Heideggerian concept of "falling to" the world that characterizes an inauthentic Dasein.[63] In sum, Julian's comfort and divine vision have both been equally muddied—become opaque—as she succumbs to the distracting force of her disease.

In theological terms, however, such a fall into the self is not only an expression of inauthenticity, as in the phenomenological model, but is also tantamount to a rejection of God. This spiritual disruption manifests for Julian upon the following visitation of a "religious person," perhaps a friar or canon, who enters her chamber and asks how she fares.[64] In her reply, Julian deems her visions as just another symptom of her condition, dismissing them as mere ravings: "And I seyd I had ravid today, and he leuhe loud and inderly. And I seyd, 'The cross that stod afor my face, methowte it blode fast'" (And I said I had raved today, and he laughed loudly and inwardly. And I said, "The cross that stood before my face, I thought it bled profusely").[65] Yet with the *discretio* of this person Julian is encouraged to look again, and is "sor ashamid and astonyed for [her] recleshede" (greatly ashamed and stunned by [her] recklessness).[66] The term "recleshede" is an important one here, possibly translating as a lack of prudence or *prudentia* which, equivalent to wisdom, was considered one of the four cardinal virtues in both classical philosophy and medieval theology, denoting an ability to project oneself ahead to preempt the outcome of one's actions.[67] As the sixth-century philosopher Boethius (d. 524) writes, "Prudence must measure up how things will work out in the future."[68] This notion of temporal projection is also crucial to the phenomenological concept of intentionality noted above, which is structured by both an anticipation of the future and an awareness of the recent past. Unlike the liberating boundlessness of beholding, then, the disruption of illness to this sense of projection seems to prevent Julian from recognizing the divine significance of her visions, as her *intentio* is blocked by the tunnel vision of the self-conscious mind.

In this reading, Julian's following desire to be "shrevyn" may be understood as a move to redirect her *intentio* and thus recover her sense of prudence—to turn toward God in openness and care. To be shriven, or to give confession, was considered an act of soul-cleansing in medieval devotion, whereby the priest would usually recommend a program of penance which drew on the purifactory power of pain (bodily or spiritual) to purge the deviant of their sins. The following absolution was thought to render the soul unmarked, emptied, and receptive to the Word; as described in the *Tretis of Discrescyon of Spirites* (c. 1390s), where the soul's divine receptivity is metaphorized as a piece of parchment, which after confession is a "clene paper leef" (clean paper leaf) ready to be inscribed upon.[69] Such purifactory practices required a degree of individual accountability or self-verification; the subject was asked to read the text of their own soul, seeking to erase sin and inscribe the Word upon it. This is especially true in visionary accounts, which are, as Karma Lochrie writes, "engaged in a continual process of self-verification."[70] Such a need for self-verification was reiterated in 1215 at the Fourth Lateran Council, when new emphasis was placed on the sacraments of confession: for the individual to be responsible for their own sins. But in this scene of the *Revelations* Julian struggles with such a requirement, recoiling in horror at the idea that she has fallen into the sin of self-beholding: "This was a gret synne, grete onkindness, that I for foly, of feling of a litill bodily peyne, so onwisely left for the time the comfort of all this blissid shewing of our Lord God" (This was a great sin, a great unkindness, that I for folly, because of feeling a little bodily pain, so unwisely lost for this time the comfort of all these blessed showings of our Lord God).[71] The "onkindness"—or *unnaturalness*—of sin will constitute the basis of Julian's later hamartiology, and I interpret it here as referring to her sin of denial: that she has dismissed her showings as ravings. And so Julian despairs, understanding her error but apparently unable to act upon it due to the paralyzing condition of shame: she "cowde tell it no preist" (could tell no priest), because she is so "ashamid" (ashamed).[72]

In my view, this word "ashamid" does the work of indicating Julian's particular spiritual plight and its relationship to the physical pains she has experienced so far. A brief comparison between Julian's own description of this state and recent work in the field of affect theory throws more light on the nuances of the term—in particular, on the redemptive possibility that the condition appears to forestall. Recent studies have identified links between the neural firing in both pain and shame, suggesting that the emotion can be considered within the same phenomenology as acute pain: as psychologist Patricia A. DeYoung states, "shame hurts. If our shame is exposed, the pain can be unbearable."[73] DeYoung writes specifically of the disconnective effects of shame on intersubjectivity and the therapeutic necessity for a reintegration of the person suffering from shame with both themselves and their world: "Shame in all its forms is relational. Shame is the experience of self-in-relation when 'in-relation' is ruptured and disconnected. A chronic sense of self-in-disconnection becomes a profound sense of isolation."[74] This psychological definition locates shame as the result of a breakdown in an individual's sense of personhood, a belief in an innate worthlessness or lack within or associated with the self.

Sociologists have further theorized the sociohistorical contexts of shame, showing how it variously functions as a force of violence and social control across different periods and cultures.[75] But examining shame in medieval England raises a number of very specific questions about its role in Christian theology. As Peter N. Stearns writes, there was "an obvious problem" for Christian thinkers "which the Greeks and Romans had not faced: Christians had obligations to God, not just to society, and these two duties could clash."[76] Augustine provides one solution to this problem, who as Stearns notes, carefully distinguishes between shame (*pudor*) and guilt (*culpa*), where "guilt . . . addressed sin and governed the individual's relation to God, whereas shame was merely a response to group opinion."[77] In other words, guilt is attached to a perceived fault not in the self but in action, which in the Christian context may always be redeemed. Applying the above Augustinian categories to the medieval practice of penance, it is possible to theorize confession as a disclosure of *guilt* rather than shame, a productive acknowledgment of error in thought or action—a moral failure—but not of personal worthlessness. As Isaiah 59:2 has it, to sin is to *turn the face away from God*, a rejection of him that separates and isolates the self from its creator. It follows that to be absolved is to be welcomed back into communion with him: a restoration of the self-in-relation, or the self-in-relation-with-God.

Echoing Augustine, Julian's *Revelations* also stress that God considers all his servants worthy of love, forgiveness, and absolution; as far as Julian sees it, nobody is inadequate in his eyes. The problem of shame as it manifests for Julian, then, is that the faulty self-perception it incurs prevents her from pursuing this redemption. As she herself writes in chapter 39 of the long text, in this condition a person may "thynkyth hymself he is not worthy but, as it were, to synken in helle" (think themselves not worthy except, as it were, to sink into hell).[78] This is the catch-22 of the shame cycle: that a person needs to think themselves worthy enough of forgiveness to seek recommunion with God, but they will not feel their worth until they are recommuned. Julian's description of sin, contrition, and confession in this chapter further evinces the self-objectifying power of such a feeling. She describes how a person can be led to confession by the Holy Ghost, to show their sins "nakidly and truely, with grete sorow and grete *shame* that he hath defoulyd the fair ymage of God" (nakedly and truly, with great sorrow and great *shame* that they have defouled the fair image of God).[79] Put another way, they have fragmented the soul which is "onyd" (oned) to God. To negotiate this breach between self-perception and action, the person must have faith in God's mercy, in the fact that God considers them deserving no matter how low their opinion of themselves. Only then can they "begynn his woundis to *helyn* and the soule to quickkyn, turnyd into the life of holy chirch" (begin to *heal* their wounds and quicken the soul, turning to the life of holy church) and "underfongyth . . . penance for every synne" (undertake . . . penance for every sin).[80] With its careful elucidation of this penitential process, this passage manifests what Nicholas Watson calls Julian's "Trinitarian hermeneutic," in which the Holy Ghost acts as the dynamic of love and grace that allows the soul to pursue reunification with God.[81] As Julian writes in chapter 48 in her discussion of patient suffering, "the Holy Gost, which is endles lif wonnyng in our soule, ful sekirly kepyth us, and werkyth therin a peas and bryngith it to ese be grace and accordith it to God and makyth it buxum" (the Holy Ghost, which is everlasting life dwelling in our soul, keeps us fully safe, and creates a peace therein and brings it to ease by grace and accords it to God and makes it obedient).[82] In this way, the Holy Ghost, through its facilitation of loving faith, maintains the soul's receptivity to God, allowing the person to intend toward contrition and penance, and to find "ese" from the painful "disese" of shameful sin. This is ultimately an attunement of hope, as Julian writes a little later in the *Revelations*: "in which werkyng the Holy Gost formyth in our feith hope that we shal cum agen up aboven to our substance, into the vertue of Criste, incresid and *fulfillid* throw the Holy Ghost" (through which activity the Holy Ghost forms in our faith the hope that we will rise up again to our substance, into the virtue of Christ, increased and *fulfilled* through the Holy Ghost).[83]

To conclude this reading of shame in the *Revelations*, I want to suggest that if Julian were able to connect with the "touchings" of the Holy Ghost described above, she would be able to realize God's mercy for her mistake. She would, as a result, feel a sense of guilt: the discomfiting dissonance between her actions and values. Combined with a sustained faith in God's love, she might then be able to engage in the healing process of confession, and to reattune to a relational and homelike "onyng" with God. As it stands, however, Julian mentions twice how "ashamid" she is of herself, restating her own unworthiness. The question she utters in this moment of shame—"How should a preist levyn me? I leve not our Lord God" (How could a priest believe me? I didn't believe our Lord God)—rhetorically enacts the contingency between love and belief, playing with the homonymy of "leve" (believe) and "love."[84] By denying her faith ("I leve not"), Julian in turn denies her capacity to love God and be loved by God. Instead, she is paralyzed in a state of shame: she describes herself as "astonyd," a term which translates as "stupefied" or "stunned," as well as the more physiological "insensate," "unconscious," and in reference to the senses or mental faculties specifically, "dulled," "benumbed," or "deadened."[85] So Julian might be read as experiencing a "deadening" of her senses that recapitulates the earlier deadening of her torso in her illness: just as her paralysis affects her "fro the middis downewards" (from the middle downward), revealing her body as an object, Julian's paralyzing shame exposes her *self* in its self-conscious subjectivity. "Here may you sene what I am of myselfe" (Here you may see what I am of myself), she writes, in an expression of plaintive and powerless vulnerability.[86]

THE FIEND'S BUSYNESS

Julian's *Revelations* therefore map out her journey of recovery in two internested parts: first, as she learns to suffer her physical disease, and second, as she endures the spiritual tribulation of despair. Both encounters disclose to Julian her postlapsarian condition of homelessness, the first via the failure of her body (which is mostly tolerable) and the second via her failure of trust in God (which is intolerable). Two final episodes conclude my reading of this second, spiritual tribulation: Julian's visitations by the devil, or devils. The first occurs at the end of chapter 66 in the long text, just after Julian has denied her showings to her visitor. I read this devil as a kind of shame-demon, manifesting and testing the lack of self-belief so central to the condition of shame. The second visitation comes a few chapters later, once Julian has been reassured by Christ that she will not be overcome, even if she may still suffer. Read together, I argue that these scenes not only function as the ultimate trials of Julian's faith and her fixity to God but also as pivotal moments in Julian's recovery, demonstrating the spiritual aspect which must be restored for all to be truly well.[87]

The first of these scenes in which the fiend appears is recounted in chapter 66 and received by Julian as a nightmare: an "oggley shewing" (ugly showing) of a devilish face and then a physical feeling of heat and a smell in the sickroom, a "foule stinke" (foul stink) that she believes to be from smoke coming in the door.[88] Yet she faces the dream with firm resolve, holding fast to the memory of her revelation and meditating on the showings "as to [her] comforte" (for [her] comfort).[89] This leads to the quick recovery of her physical and mental faculties by the end of the chapter: "And anone al vanishid away, and I was browte to gret rest and peas, *withouten sekenes of body or drede of conscience*" (And quickly it all vanished away, and I was brought to great rest and peace, *without sickness of body or dread of conscience*).[90] Such recovery is expedited by Julian's companions who, upon her waking, comfort her with their own tender beholding: "The persons that wer with me beheld me and wet my temples, and my herte began to comforten" (The people that were with me beheld me and wet my temples, and my heart began to be comforted).[91] She then reenters the revelation to be shown the divine indwelling of God in the soul, after which, in chapter 68, Julian writes of Christ's reassurance that her showings are indeed divinely sent: "Wete it now wele that it was no raveing that thou saw today, but take it and leve it, and kepe the therin, and comfort therwith, and troste thou therto, and thou shalt not be overcome" (Know it now well that it was no hallucination that you saw today, but take it and believe it, and keep and comfort yourself with it and trust unto it, and you shall not be overcome).[92] These two moments are proximate to each other in the text; a temptation and a remedy recounted in quick succession. Christ's statement of reassurance can, then, be read as a direct response to the fear that Julian has been raving and also a response to her shame. She has been reassured that she can endure what the devil may throw at her, a statement of encouragement that sets her up to resist the second, more viciously distracting temptation by the devil to follow.

The second and final temptation by the devil is recounted in chapter 69 of the long text, which Julian calls the "second long temptation of the devill to despeir" (second long temptation of the devil to despair).[93] In this scene, Julian reports a more disabling effect on her resolve by the devil's appearance, as his "hete" and "stinke" (heat and stink) return to make her "full besy" (entirely busy).[94] I want to dwell for a moment on Julian's use of the word *besy* here, as an affective term that captures both cognitive and theological aspects of the devil's disruption. Quite literally, Julian is *made busy* by the devil; her attention is completely occupied by him.[95] But this acute condition has wider epistemological implications, too, as evidenced by Julian's use of the term in previous chapters to refer to a state of preoccupation with unanswerable theological questions. In chapter 33, for instance, she writes "the more we *besy* us to knowen his privities in this or any other thyng, the ferther shal we be from the knowing thereof" (the more we *busy* ourselves with knowing his secrets in this or any other thing, the further we shall be from the knowing of it).[96] With this, she describes the mind tying itself in knots in trying to understand, an accretive kind of epistemology that contrasts against the contemplative impulse toward apophasis: a mind *filling* itself with questions rather than emptying and waiting for an answer. Julian has experimented with this dialectic herself in chapter 11, when, deploying the scholastic *quaestio* format, she asks: "What is synne?" (What is sin?).[97] She is then informed that God does "al thing" (everything), but any explanation as to how he does so is shut down with a further question: "I am God . . . How should anything be amysse?" (I am God . . . How should anything be amiss?).[98] Julian—and the reader—are thereby reminded that the human mind cannot and should not be able to grasp some divine truths: as Augustine says, "Si enim comprehendis, non est Deus," or *if you understand it, then it is not God.*[99] As a result, she is left to "assenten with gret reverens, enjoyand in God" (assent with great reverence, enjoying in God), a line which defers once again to the pairing of reverence (as in reverent dread) and joy (as in love) that has underpinned her showings so far.[100]

In line with these examples, I suggest a reading of this vocabulary of problematic "busyness" as signifying human issues with interpretation—namely the various layers of distraction or ignorance that separate the soul from God. These can be of a generally existential character: a related articulation can be found, for instance, in the collocation "bisi dred," which is used by Julian's contemporary, Geoffrey Chaucer, and later by John Lydgate, to denote a state of deep anxiety or worry: "That love is thyng ay ful of bisy drede" (That love is a thing full of busy dread), Chaucer writes in book 4 of his tragic poem, *Troilus and Criseyde* (c. 1380s).[101] This definition of busyness as a kind of anxious, dreadful occupation in turn corresponds with the Heideggerian condition of anxiety I described in chapter 2: the breakdown of meaning that renders the world unrecognizable, plaguing the individual with distraction or "disese." I have been reading Julian's illness as incurring a comparable breakdown, but the visitations from the fiend induce a more acutely spiritual form of distraction. This is best evidenced in the second visitation, reported in chapter 69, when Julian describes how the bodies of these fiendish apparitions jangle as though they are holding "a parlement with a gret bysynes" (a parliament with a great busyness).[102] Importantly, Julian recognizes this busyness is intended to "stirre [her] to dispeir" (stir [her] to despair), a phrase which explicitly connects the devil's busyness to the spiritual affliction of despair, that state which leads to shame and away from God.[103] Indeed, Julian reiterates that this temptation manifests not bodily but spiritually—"Methowte that bysynes myte not be likenyd to no bodily bysynes" (I thought that busyness could not be likened to any bodily busyness)—thus setting up the nexus of spiritual sicknesses or sins she will soon be expounding in chapter 73.[104] Looking backward in the text, too, the passage builds on her earlier claim in chapter 13, where she writes of the devil's evil as "the which of mallice and shrewidnes *bysyen* hem to contriven and to done agens Gods wille" (the malice and shrewdness which occupies him to contrive and go against God's will).[105] Interwoven throughout all these passages is an emphasis on busyness as a potentially sinful business, as it were: a clouded vision of God and an inability to comprehend him.

I suggested above that Christ's reassurance in chapter 68 that Julian will not be overcome sets her up with the faith needed to fend off the fiend again. It remains to examine how she describes this act of forbearance, a reading that rounds out my definition of the term busyness as a distinctly phenomenological state and, in turn, reveals a more positive side to the concept. In the face of the second temptation by the devil, Julian continues to set her eyes on the cross before her, finding comfort with her "tonge with speech of Crists passion and rehersing the feith of holy church, and [her] hert to festen on God with al the trost and the myte that was in [her]" (tongue with speech of Christ's passion and rehearsing the faith of the holy church, and [her] heart to fasten on to God with all the trust and the might that was in [her]).[106] In this way, Julian occupies herself with God, focusing body (tongue), mind (rehearsal of faith), and feeling (heart) as totally as she can onto the divine. In doing so, Julian enacts a counterremedy to the devil's attempts to "bysyn" her, by busying herself in turn with the things of God, or a *good* sort of busyness. She thinks to herself: "Thou hast now grete bysynes to kepe the in the feith, for thou shuldst not be taken of thi enemy. Woldst thou now fro this time ever more be so bysy to kepe the fro synne, this were a good and a soverain occupation" (You now have a great business to keep yourself in the faith, so you should not be taken by the enemy. If you would now, and for this time ever more, be so busy to keep yourself from sin, this would be a good and distinguished occupation).[107] This passage more explicitly puns on the noun form of the term "business," connecting the mode of concentration I have been describing as *busyness* to the more vocational sense of "occupation." A whisper of the anchoritic life might be identified here in the expression of a "good and a soverain occupation," a solitary life so paradoxically unbusy to the outside world that the anchorite can busy herself entirely with God. In this moment in the sickroom, however, Julian enacts busyness as a mode of concentration which reattunes her to the homeliness of God's love. In the face of the devil's occupation—"he occupyed me al that nyte" (he occupied me all that night)—Julian takes her own advice from chapter 10 to "sekyn wilfully and bisily, withouten slauth" (seek wilfully and busily, without sloth), by actively focusing her attention on God.[108]

Following her forsaking of her showings as "ravings" after her bodily pain, these temptations from the devil are a form of spiritual tribulation that threaten to lead Julian further from the beholding of God, tormenting her after she has feared she may be unworthy of his love. After her initial mistake, however, Julian comes to understand that her error is behavioral, not personal—that God still has faith in her and so she must remain faithful to him. So, she does her best to keep herself "besy" in the face of the fiend's own busyness, by refocusing her attention on God and so increasing her capacity for homeliness, even when her perception is almost overwhelmed by her illness. This endeavor is, ultimately, facilitated by the reassuring presence of Christ, who tells her she will not be overcome. As such, these chapters exemplify an arc of recovery that goes well beyond a straightforward recession of disease: one which, Julian learns, is realized by her ability to sustain her attention on God, to strip away solipsistic thoughts and reattune to the soul's "onyng" with him. Just as Julian's sickness discloses her homeless condition, then, it also reveals her capacity for approaching tribulation with equal parts fortitude, patience, and compassion.

INTO THE ANCHORHOLD

The discussion so far has revealed how Julian's recovery from both physical and spiritual affliction depends on a degree of resoluteness on her part—a focused engagement or attentive receptivity to God. I have defined resoluteness phenomenologically as an attitude of openness: as Taylor Carman puts it, "the word *Entschlossenheit* ["resoluteness"] means decisiveness or resolve, but it also literally means unclosing, or disclosing, which is to say, remaining open."[109] In this sense, resoluteness can be understood not as a momentary change but rather a lasting way of being-in-the-world that is taken forward after the event of illness. In Julian's case, continuing in this way means reintegrating herself back into her world and community while still retaining the insights and awareness she has gleaned from the revelation; she must go on living with the knowledge of sin, pain, and God's everlasting love. The final component to be discussed in Julian's recovery from her acute illness is, then, her life lived after the illness-revelation event of May 1373. Of this life very little is known, save her entrance into anchoritism and what survives in her texts. But as I aim to demonstrate, these are fruitful phenomena in themselves. In this final discussion of the chapter, I propose that Julian's decision to enter the anchoritic life and her decision to pen her *Revelations* can each be taken as evidence of her recovery, by the ways they evince the *lasting* quality of Julian's transfiguration, post-illness and post-revelation. This concluding word therefore bears witness to two final expressions of Julian's subjectivity beyond 1373: to the Julian who is writing the text and the Julian of the anchorhold.

This shift of perspective from the event of revelation to the extended process of Julian's authorship broadly maps onto the now well-known distinction drawn by Lynn Staley in her analysis of *The Book of Margery Kempe* (c. 1430s) between Margery-the-subject and Kempe-the-author.[110] Kempe was Julian's contemporary, and she famously reports in her *Book* that she visited Julian in her cell to seek advice on spiritual matters.[111] Yet the two visionary women could not be more different in their approaches both to devotional practice and to authorship. Where Margery's outbursts of affective devotion can be read as attempts to authenticate herself, drawing on the figures of holy women to perform her own religious identity, Julian's contemplative process is self-negating, rejecting any singular, interpretive authority on the showings.[112] Examples of this can be identified in her expressions of humility, where she seeks to negate the authorial *I* in favor of a communal *we*—as in the short text's authorial *apologia* that, revised to an abbreviated version in the longer text, foregrounds Julian's fellow Christians for whom she believes the showings are meant:

> Alle that I saye of myselfe, I meene in the persone of alle myne evyn-Cristene, for I am lernede in the gastelye schewynge of oure Lorde that he meenys so. And therfore I praye yowe alle for Goddys sake, and cownsayles yowe for yowre awne profyt, that ye leve the behaldynge of the wrechid worldes synfulle creature that it was schewyd unto, and that ye myghtlye, wyselye, lovandlye, and mekelye behalde God, that of his curtays love and of his endles goodnes walde schewe generalye this visyon in comforthe of us alle.[113]

> All that I say of myself, I mean for all the people who are my fellow Christians, for the spiritual showing of our Lord taught me he means it so. And therefore I pray to you all for God's sake, and counsel you for your own benefit, that you leave the beholding of the wretched world's sinful creature that it was showed to, and that you mightily, wisely, lovingly, and meekly behold God, who of his courteous love and of his endless goodness would show this vision generally for the comfort of us all.

The passage manifests the transfigurational process of Julian's revelations at large, moving from singular to plural address, incorporating the "I" with "alle myne evyn-Cristene" and "yow" in the inclusive "us alle." Julian goes on to write (and I quote from chapter 9 of the long text): "For if I loke singularly to myselfe, I am right nowte; but in general I am in hope, in onehede of charitie with al myn evyn-Cristen. For in this onehede stond the life of all mankinde that shall be savid" (For if I look singularly to myself I am entirely nothing, but in general I am in hope, in oneness of charity with all my fellow Christians, for in this oneness stands the life of all humankind who shall be saved).[114] As I noted at the start of this chapter, this extract emphasizes not only Julian's humility—that she is no better than those who have not received divine showings—but also her insistence on the oneness of humanity, united by the love of God. Together, these self-negating passages exemplify the insights Julian has herself gleaned from the illness-revelation event, now woven into the fabric of her texts.

This reading of Julian as moving toward a communal subjectivity across the short and long text is supported by studies exploring the autobiographical elements of her writing. Liz Herbert McAvoy, for example, argues that Julian's initial tentativeness in the short text's *apologia* displays an "anxiety about her sex and gender, the purpose and meaning of her showings and, in particular, what she was supposed to do with them."[115] This anxious quality is (seemingly paradoxically) accompanied by greater autobiographical detail in the short text, including aspects of her sickbed experience that are excised from the longer version. Vincent Gillespie has meanwhile proposed that the short text may have been a *probatio* text of the type required of applicants to the anchoritic profession, which might explain what he calls its "theologically cautious, perhaps even defensive" quality.[116] This would account for the marriage of apologetic self-deprecation and autobiographical narrative in the shorter version. In this view, the long text can therefore be read as exemplifying the personal and theological maturation that follows Julian's prolonged contemplation on the second 1388 showing that "love was his mening" and the third 1393 showing of the lord and the servant, leaving behind much of Julian's origin story in favor of exegesis. Or, to put it another way, the texts' shift from a personal to a more universal focus is reflected by Julian's framing of her subjectivity within.

The possibility that Julian was an anchorite at the time of writing the long text also supports this interpretation of a shift toward intersubjectivity, despite the seemingly paradoxical sentiments of this claim. For though anchoritism was a solitary pursuit, walling the enclosed religious off from the outside world, it was nevertheless considered a highly communal vocation. To enter the anchoritic life was to "nought" the self (to use Julian's term): the anchorite was considered to symbolically die upon entering the cell, and hence to be reborn as part of the communal body of Christ. In the reconfiguration of the anchorite's identity, then, the anchorhold becomes a site of both tomb and womb, a doubleness investigated at length by Liz Herbert McAvoy and Mari Hughes-Edwards, who write of the anchorhold as a "communal 'womb' from which would emerge an idealized sense of a community's own reborn potential."[117] They also describe a "heteroglossic interactivity between anchorhold and society," a statement echoed in turn by Gillespie's observation that Julian's writing "has many of the dialogic characteristics of Bakhtinian 'heteroglossia.'"[118] In Bakhtinian terms, heteroglossia refers to a multiplicity of voices within a text, the use of "*another's speech in another's language* . . . a special type of *double-voiced discourse*."[119] This kind of ventriloquism implicitly connects one person with another via the sharing of speech across subjective boundaries. Or, more literally in the case of the anchorite, across the boundaries of window and cell as they would receive visitors and give spiritual advice to the community.

This idea can be taken even further, however, to include in Julian's heteroglossic mode the *language of the body*. As my reading of the phenomenology of Julian's illness has shown, her bodily suffering breaks down the barriers between self and world, opening her up to a more porous engagement with her surroundings and companions. In this sense, Julian's heteroglossia begins with, or at the very least, manifests on the body, before it emerges in her representation of the event in the *Revelations*. This kind of embodied intersubjectivity is enacted first through Julian's connection to Christ on the cross and her compassion for his pains. But it also extends to her connections with those around her, which I suggest lay the foundations for her lifelong occupation of enclosure. For example, Julian recounts in the short text how her "modere" (whether this refers to a biological or religious mother is unclear, though the former is more likely if we take this text to be of the *probatio* type) "behelde" her and reached to close her eyes, believing her dead: "sche wenyd I had bene dede or els I hadde dyede. And this encresyd mekille my sorowe, for noughtwithstandynge alle my paynes, I wolde nought hafe been lettyd for loove that I hadde in hym" (she thought I had been dead or else that I had just died. And this greatly increased my sorrow, for even apart from all my pains, I did not want to be restrained because of the love I had for him).[120] Here, the touch of Julian's mother crosses the boundary of her body in a somewhat uncomfortable way; Julian appears to resist her gesture. And yet, her compassionate touch still anchors Julian to the room and to those around her, showing the same loving care as is present in Julian's own gaze on Christ.

The ambivalence of this moment is borne out in the diverse critical interpretations of its meaning, to which I offer my own phenomenological addition. Nicholas Watson and Jacqueline Jenkins suggest that it "reinforces the parallel between [Julian] and Christ made in Section 2 . . . Julian's mother stands in for Mary, whose grief is described in lines 38–43 and whose presence at the Crucifixion is often said to increase Christ's pains."[121] McAvoy meanwhile comments on Benedicta Ward's "unduly harsh" interpretation of this "maternal reaction," which Ward argues "[shows] no warmth at all in [Julian's] solitary mention of [her mother]; in fact, her own mother totally misunderstood her."[122] This reading, McAvoy writes, "misses the multivalence of the description altogether. . . . Far from lacking in warmth . . . the response of Julian's mother is qualified by this touching display of a heightened concern for her dying daughter, mixed as it is with a poignant misunderstanding." McAvoy instead sees this moment as one of closure, "one of the last bodily acts available to her as a mother."[123] I agree that this scene captures a moment of grief, with Julian's mother performing a final conclusive—indeed, a closure—of the ars moriendi ritual. Further, I want to suggest that the *Revelations* depict a multilayering of compassionate care, or to use Julian's term, *beholding*. This term describes the act of holding gently, "in an ungrasping and self-emptying way," as Maggie Ross puts it—and so applies to both the cognitive-affective processes at work in revelation and more mundane attentional acts of care such as this.[124] In this moment, Julian's mother beholds her just as Julian beholds God, and just as Mary beholds Christ in chapter 4 of the long text.[125] To be *beheld* in this way is to be cared for, to be made to feel at home. And so, the various beholdings that occur between persons in the text extend this homeliness outward, in a series of internested acts of dwelling that connect each of them together in "onyng."

Finally, I propose that the anchorhold offers another space for Julian to cultivate this sense of communality, or being-with-others, paired with a resolute acceptance of death. These two conditions were introduced above as necessary for genuinely authentic being-toward-death, to again invoke Carel's phenomenological vocabulary. I have already suggested that the anchorhold is an apparently paradoxical space, wherein solitariness is intended to transform the individual self into a more porous and open container for receiving God, and for communing with people in need of guidance. The irony of the quiet hermit's life, theoretically speaking, is that it allows them to be busy with God. In this final discussion, I now suggest that the anchorhold, in a manner parallel to Julian's acute experience of illness, in fact stages an extended (indeed, lifelong) practice of being-toward-death—one which, unlike in the Heideggerian model, is framed by the divine horizon of heaven. I call this the practice of *being-toward-God*.[126]

The craft of dying was central to the protocols of anchoritism. First, upon their enclosure in the cell, the anchorite, together with church officials, performed a consecration ritual closely resembling funeral rites.[127] In this way, the cell was to become the tomb of their former identity. But the ars moriendi did not end there: as the thirteenth-century rule for anchorites, *Ancrene Wisse*, details, the anchorite was also instructed to dig their own (symbolic and actual) grave a little every day: "Ha schulden schrapien euche dei the eorthe up of hare put thet ha schu*le*n rotien in" (They should scrape each day the earth up from their grave that they will rot in).[128] By following this instruction, the anchorite was meant to face their own mortality, grasping it with their bare hands and rooting themselves to the earth to which their body would return. This gesture of rootedness is further expressed linguistically in the etymology for *anchor*, which not only refers to a mechanism of fastening or mooring to a place, but is also descriptive of an object itself, from **ang-/*ank-*, "to bend," also as in "angle." To anchor oneself, then, is also to *angle* oneself necessarily both toward and away from something. This is, admittedly, a false etymology for *anchorite*, which derives from the ancient Greek, ἀναχωρεῖν (*anakhōrein*, to retire, retreat).[129] Nevertheless, it provides a striking gloss for the kind of *orientation* I am discussing here: an orientation toward the church—quite literally, as the cell was "anchored" to the church building—toward God and toward death.

This kind of anchoritic orientation is temporally as well as spatially constructed. I have already noted the "heterochrony" of the anchorhold, as discussed by scholars like McAvoy and Miles. But now, to conclude, my discussion moves outside the time warp of the cell to gaze on what lies, as it were, beyond. In Heideggerian terms, the "beyond" of life is straightforwardly negative: a void of homelessness or nothingness that lies behind all human existence. For the medieval theologian, however, the concept of a beyond looks rather different; it is structured instead by the promise of finding a true home in heaven. A glimpse of such a home is given to Julian in her sixth showing, which she reports as lifting her understanding up "into hevyn, where [she sees] our Lord as a lord in his owne house" (into heaven, where [she sees] our Lord as a lord in his own house), and where God "hath clepid al his derworthy servants and freinds to a solemne feste" (had called all his honored servants and friends to a sacred feast).[130] In this merry scene, God is the ultimate host: "I saw him rialy regne in his hous, and fulfillid it with ioy and mirth, hymselfe endlesly to gladen and to solacyn his derworthy frends ful homeley and ful curtesly" (I saw him royally reign in his house, which he filled with joy and merriment, himself endlessly gladdening and comforting his honored friends with fullest homeliness and courtesy).[131] This is a perfect picture of hospitality, of the kind any supplicant to St. Julian might hope for when beseeching him for "bone hostel," as I explored in chapter 1. But Julian understands that this home is ultimately beyond-the-world: she must stand outside herself and outside earthly temporality to get sight of this place. As Christ tells her later in the *Revelations*, this is a place where "thou shal *never* have no maner of peyne, no manner of sycknes, no manner of mislekyng, no wanting of will, but *ever* joye and bliss withouten ende" (you shall *never* have any manner of pain, any manner of sickness, any manner of sorrow, any displeasure, but *ever*lasting joy and bliss without end).[132] It is, in other words, a place of unending well-being, far removed from the human situation on earth. Nevertheless, at the end of the chapter Julian is reminded that "all the peyne and travel" (all the pain and suffering) that one might suffer is surely worth this homely reward.[133]

The task of the living, then, as far as Julian understands it, is the endless seeking of this home with God: a *being-toward-God* enacted through love, devotional practice, and the teachings of the holy church. This expression, which adapts the Heideggerian concept of *being-toward-death*, includes a teleological destination absent in the phenomenological mode, wherein *to be* means to be "held-out-into-the-nothing."[134] In the secular, phenomenological schema, authentic living means recognition of the "nothing" of one's limit-situation: anxiety brings Dasein "face to face with the possibility to be itself."[135] This is an "expecting" of this phenomenon that then allows Dasein a "*freedom toward death, which is free of the illusions of the they, factical, and certain of itself.*"[136] Because death is annihilation, however, it cannot be a totality: "Death," as Carel explains, "is an end, but not a teleological end."[137] Judith Wolfe calls this Heidegger's "eschatology without an eschaton," wherein the "consummation" of Dasein is at the same time its negation.[138] In Christian theology, however, death is but one event in the eschatological timeline. Human living is directed toward a different end—a different *telos*—as determined by the salvation narrative: an existence in "orientation towards an envisioned end as determinative of the present," as Wolfe puts it.[139] As I have been showing, Julian's *Revelations* are oriented toward just such a salvific end. First in the event of her illness, and later in her anchoritic lifestyle, Julian faces up to death: she "expects" it, in that "expecting is not only an occasional looking away from the possible to its possible actualization, but essentially a *waiting for that actualization*," as Heidegger describes in *Being and Time*.[140] This perspective might be described as a resolute "letting be" of this potentiality, which anticipates death as an eventuality out of human control. Just so, Julian's mystical longing for *compassio* with Christ is contingent on the conditional "if" of being-toward-death: she desires to have "all manier peynes bodily and ghostly that I [Julian] should have *if I should dye*" (all manner of pains bodily and spiritually that I should have *if I were to die*).[141] She knows her death is ultimately in God's hands. Nevertheless, the conditional is eternally vouchsafed by the power of Christ's soteriological act. Julian does not, then, consider death her limit-situation, because her being-toward-death has a *theological* end, which will arrive at "domys day." This is the *eschaton* that has been bracketed by Heidegger's phenomenology and that structures Julian's genuinely authentic way of living, which she calls the "wey" of Christ, a submission of one's life to its negation, with the faith that this negation is not the end.

While for Heidegger, then, "we stand before the nothing and recognize that we are not at home in the world," Julian stands before the world and seeks a home in God.[142] This chapter has examined how this process is borne out in Julian's *Revelations*, focusing on the complex entanglement of her physical and spiritual tribulation as they relate to her showings. I have identified the ways these forms of suffering open her up to new insights and the ways they threaten to overwhelm her and draw her away from the revelation: how she encounters the difference between bodily pain and more serious spiritual afflictions like despair and shame. These afflictions have been theorized in light of modern psychology and affect theory, as I considered how Julian's own encounter with shame relates to her subsequent temptations by fiends. The chapter then identified Christ's reassurance to Julian that she will not be overcome as a crucial moment in her forbearance against the devil, which allowed her to reattune to the homeliness of God's love and so to the beholding of him.

In this final section of the chapter, I considered how the phenomenology of Julian's *Revelations* might be extended to include her life beyond the sickroom: in particular, how both the sickroom and the anchorhold initiate a transfiguration into a more porous subjectivity, more connected to others. Moreover, I showed how the anchorhold stages an ars moriendi comparable to that of the sickroom where Julian first learns how to die. By considering the afterlife of Julian's illness and revelation in this way, I extended this book's view of her recovery as not only a recuperation of body and mind following her sickness but also as a lifelong existential project of being-toward-God. In doing so, I have highlighted the theological challenge to the post-Heideggerian phenomenologies of well-being that I have been engaging to theorize Julian's recovery: that of the divine horizon and the possibility of life beyond death. For despite the chronicity of human homelessness, Julian writes that God's loving grace will "hele us ful faire" (heal us so graciously [also: justly, equitably]) in heaven, if she and her readers choose the "wey" of Christ.[143] To make this choice is not a momentary request but a lasting way of being-in-the-world, one which—like the phenomenological understanding of well-being—requires continuous rebalancing and reorientation. For Julian, this resolute and reiterative decision was surely enacted over many years in the anchorhold, as a practice of *becoming* as much as *being* well. The writing of her text might be considered part of this practice, overlaying the processes of vision and re-vision in new and enlivening ways. It is to this textuality which the next chapter turns, thereby shoring up this book's understanding of Julian's hermeneutic of recovery through a close look at her own protocols of language and interpretation.

4

SEEKING UNDERSTANDING

Julian's Mystical Text

Our language can be seen as an ancient city: a maze of little streets and squares, of old and new houses, and of houses with additions from various periods; and this surrounded by a multitude of new boroughs with straight regular streets and uniform houses.

—Ludwig Wittgenstein, *Philosophical Investigations*

Divine revelation, like illness, stretches language to its limits, finding wanting the usual ways of talking about experience. This poses an impossible problem for the scholar trying to interpret the visionary text, just as it poses a problem for the visionary author: how do I write about something that is beyond language itself? So far, I have been referring in this book to Julian of Norwich's *Revelations of Divine Love* as recounting a visionary "experience." But this thorny term has very different implications from the standpoint of Western modernity than it does from the medieval view, tightly bound as it is with post-Cartesian assumptions about the individuated subject and the supremacy of the thinking mind. To claim an experience of something, in the modern context, necessarily creates a subject doing the experiencing and an object being experienced, which in turn gives power to the thinking subject—"I think therefore I am"—and to the senses as sources of knowledge.[1] But in medieval writings like Julian's, theories of experience were framed by a horizon of divine power that precluded any such claims to human omnipotence. Medieval texts dealing with contemplation and revelation, especially those in the apophatic tradition, held that the thinking mind (ruled by the intellect) and even the feeling body (ruled by the affect) could never be capable of understanding God entirely. Moreover, they held that God could not be objectified straightforwardly as some*thing* to be experienced. Theologians and visionaries throughout the Middle Ages debated these ideas at length, and it is against this context that this chapter reads Julian's writings on her own textual process. Put simply, the chapter focuses on how Julian thinks about thinking and writes about writing: how she reflects on the protocols of understanding that govern her revelation and recovery, and how these might be taken up by her reader for their own contemplative benefit.

Pulling focus on the diverging medieval and modern definitions of experience in turn throws up striking resonances between the mystical and the phenomenological. Barbara Newman has already posed the fundamentally phenomenological question of medieval visionary texts, "What did it mean to say 'I saw'?"[2] In the present chapter, I extend this question to ask, What does it mean to receive revelation? And how can such an event ever be rendered into language? It will soon become apparent that how Julian interprets, organizes, and represents her revelation is no straightforward task, in the most literal sense. Now that the discussion has arrived at Julian's theological writing, any perceived linearity of her experience as represented in the prior chapter dissolves, revealing an eschatological perspective that goes well beyond worldly time. As her texts make clear, Julian glimpses this alternative temporality already in the God-time of beholding: the boundless present wherein seeing, knowing, and speaking all merge into one atemporal moment. Following this event, she then constructs a complex ontotheology that captures the contingency of being and knowing. She develops, in other words, a theory of human existence as an ongoing process of seeking understanding: a hermeneutic project. Her *Revelations* manifest a complex map of this project: across her two texts, she builds a textual architecture akin to the winding maze of streets and squares referred to by Ludwig Wittgenstein above, engaging images and words in masterly ways to get as close to the revelation as she can. By entering these mazes and streets, the following discussion therefore continues this book's cartographical project as it was introduced in chapter 1, now charting the web of language and experience that comes together in Julian's visionary texts, to explore the terrain of her distinctly proto-phenomenological theology of recovery.

The chapter begins by situating Julian's contemplative epistemology in its medieval context, interrogating categories of experience as defined by earlier and contemporary theologians. It then examines how Julian's theory of knowledge—her epistemology—also functions as a theory of existence—an ontology. This requires some discussion of Julian's anthropology of the human soul, which she configures as always connected to God in substance, an idea that provides the ground for her subsequent theology of love. Next, the chapter explores Julian's writing on revelation as a moment of divine inbreaking, which I compare with the phenomenological idea of authentic understanding as outlined in previous chapters. I here read Julian's epistemology alongside the writing of her contemporary, William Langland (d. c. 1386), arguing that their shared usage of the term *kynde* functions as a medieval counterpart for the Heideggerian concept of authenticity. Phenomenology is once again invoked in the final two sections of the chapter, which turn from epistemology and ontology to the poetics of Julian's *Revelations*. Heidegger's theory of language is here engaged to theorize the ways meaning is created through linguistic expression in Julian's texts, and further, through what is *not* expressed—that is, through apophasis and silence. The chapter concludes by arguing for the contingency of the revelation and its textual account, a position that sheds light on various opportunities for readerly engagement and participation in Julian's communal theology.

WONDER'S STRANGENESS

As suggested above, the term *experience* is a tricky linguistic problem when it comes to revelation, and this was as true for premodern theorists as it is today. *Experience* was an epistemological axis around which medieval theological schools variously positioned themselves, depending largely on how much epistemic capacity they assigned to human beings, or to what extent they believed they could really know God. Because of this, medieval notions of *experience* are frequently rooted in a sense of the incompleteness of experiential knowledge: in the human lack of knowledge, and whether (and by what means) this lack might be filled. It is only by the later Middle Ages that *experience* is used as an authentication of human authority—as in the *expertus novit* tradition, which was employed by theologians to distinguish themselves as possessing superior knowledge of divine texts. John Duns Scotus (d. 1308), for example, writes "expertus infallibiter novit" (he who has had an experience, has flawless knowledge), echoing the words of Bernard of Clairvaux (d. 1153): "Loquor vobis experimentum meum quod expertus sum" (I tell you my experience because I am experienced).[3] This compares to modern conceptions (from the Renaissance onward) of experience as self-authenticating, born out of the subject-object relationship upon which modern ideas of selfhood and world are modeled.

The medieval Latin terms *experientia* and *experimentum* gesture toward this problem of the human search for divine knowledge. As Sabetei Unguru points out, though the terms "were used almost interchangeably throughout the Middle Ages all the way to the Renaissance, a growing sharpening of conceptual distinctions took place gradually," with various scholars distinguishing between "mere experience, observation" and situations "not occurring normally in nature."[4] *Experientia* might refer, then, to the direct experiencing of spontaneous phenomena, while *experimentum* might denote knowledge acquired by the rational interpretation of phenomena external to the self. By the early modern period, the experimental took on an increasingly methodical and scientific meaning: it was understood to be a kind of experiential venture, defined by the efforts it would take to arrive there. Unguru describes this phenomenon in the form of a balanced equation, whereby "*experientia quaesita = experimentum*."[5] That is, the experimental is a *sought-after experience*. The term even acquired undertones of the occult or diabolic, given Augustine's interpretation of the devil tempting Jesus to jump from the pinnacle of the temple as an experiment: the experimental nature of this event is, Heiko A. Oberman suggests, as much about the temptation as it is about the curiosity, "to see what happens."[6] In this way, *experimentum* came to refer to something hidden, perhaps something forbidden—to be sought out and understood. It referred, in other words, to a desire for knowledge.

The origins of this emergent experientia/experimentum distinction can be seen in Aristotle's sentiment that science and art come to men *through experience*, based on the principle that experience (and so also knowledge) was acquired through the senses.[7] But Aristotle made an important distinction that further complicates the relationship between these two faculties: between knowledge acquired by sense perception (empirical or observational knowledge) and knowledge of causal explanations, which he calls *wisdom*. Wisdom he attributes to artists who "know the wherefore and the cause": "[the senses] do not tell us the reason for anything, as for example why fire is hot, only that it *is* hot," Aristotle writes.[8] To really *know*, then—to achieve wisdom, in the Aristotelian view—is not only to experience but to interrogate the principles and causes of this experience.

This paradigm is later borne out in the medieval scholastic method, which similarly emphasized the requirement of human ratiocination in the epistemological project. But in this model, the Aristotelian conviction in the power of human reason (*ratio*) to deduce genuine knowledge (*epistēmē*) had to be balanced against the ultimate unknowability of God. Augustine had resolved this tension with his theory that holy wisdom (*sapientia*, as opposed to knowledge, *scientia*) was a product of both faith *and* reason, an epistemological program Anselm of Canterbury (d. 1109) would later term "fides quaerens intellectum" (faith seeking understanding). This dual emphasis then made its way into later models of the rational soul and its cognitive faculties, or modes of apprehension. Medieval theologians like Thomas Gallus (d. 1246), Hugh of Balma (c. 1200s), and the anonymous author of the *Cloud of Unknowing* (c. 1375) each offered their own view, variously interpreting the soul's intellect (*intellectus*) or affective capacity or will (*affectus*) as the means by which the contemplative could apprehend or achieve union with God. For

Hugh, loving awareness of God transcends the intellect, while for Thomas, "the unitive experience is . . . achieved through the power of love, in the *apex affectus*," as Rosemary Ann Lees writes, a transintellectual union she calls "knowledge-in-love."[9] The *Cloud*-author, meanwhile, stresses that the intellect—and the imagination—must be abandoned entirely for the contemplative to proceed toward God.[10] These choice examples show the varying emphases placed on the importance of apophasis, the negation of human experience, in texts of contemplative theology in this period. In the journey of ascent to the divine, the contemplative is drawn toward the eternal truth of God and away from the linear temporality of human experience.

Whether enacted through the intellect, the affect, or a recombination of the two, medieval theologians always theorized the contemplative ascent to God as demanding an active and focused devotional practice. Hugh of Balma, for instance, writes that wisdom is achieved "through *practice* in the purgative and illuminative ways and under the inward instruction and direction of God alone."[11] It is on account of this emphasis on practice that monasticism has been called a lived theology; if theology is the contemplation of God, then monastic theology is devoted to the disciplines that nurture that contemplation—disciplines like *lectio divina*, or holy reading.[12] Derived from the Benedictine tradition, *lectio divina* denotes an ascent toward illumination, or wisdom, through a program of attentive reading (*lectio*), reflection (*meditatio*), vocal or mental prayer (*oratio*), and attentive stillness (*contemplatio*). In the first two states, the reader occupies a mode of awareness, *cogitatio*, broadly equivalent to Aristotle's mode of sense perception, in which they are preoccupied with curiosity, restless mental activity, and passions. At this level, the mind processes images that become abstract, free-floating thoughts. When the mind wants to ascend, it concentrates on these thoughts, an act which Richard of St. Victor (d. 1173) defines as "the eager exertion of the mind which affectionately tries to investigate something."[13] Finally, *contemplatio* engages the mind in a free gazing on to divine manifestations, with a kind of astonishment or admiration—*admiratio*, in Richard's terms—which, as Karl Baier writes, "expands the established horizon of understanding (it is *supra aestimationem* as Richard says)."[14]

The term *admiratio* again derives from Aristotle, who in his *Metaphysics* argues that the state of *wonder* is the root cause of all epistemological inquiry: "it is through *wonder* [Greek: *thaumazein*] that men now begin and originally began to philosophize."[15] The state of wonder is contingent upon the wonderer's acknowledgment of their lack of knowledge: "he who wonders and is perplexed feels that he is ignorant (thus the myth-lover is in a sense a philosopher, since myths are composed of wonders)," writes Aristotle.[16] But while for Aristotle wonder is the maternal agent of thought, a mystification which, through its natural coupling with critical inquiry, labors and gives birth to knowledge or the *epistēmē*, wonder as understood by the apophatic tradition is transfigurative in its capacity to reach beyond such positivist realms. Mary-Jane Rubenstein writes on this difference, noting that "Aristotelian thaumazein [wonder], one might say, seeks the very resolution that Socratic thaumazein struggles to resist; for, all the way up the ontological chain, causal knowledge gradually replaces the very wonder that sets it in motion. In the words of the early seventeenth-century mechanician Simon Stevinus, '*Wonder en is gheen wonder*'—(the) wonder is no longer (a) wonder."[17] This is not to say, Rubenstein clarifies, that wonder precludes investigative thinking, but rather that there is an "irreducible difference between a rigorous, investigative thinking that sustains wonder's strangeness and a rigorous, investigative thinking that endeavors to assimilate that strangeness."[18] She continues: "To the extent that thinking remains with wonder, it is not inimical to all propositions, but rather keeps propositions *provisional, open-ended, and incomplete*": "Wonder," Rubenstein argues, "wonders at wonder."[19] This is a kind of "groundless awe," or apophatic indeterminacy which, for Rubenstein, "can either be inquisitively endured or it can be covered over with unquestionable premises and conclusions that obstruct further inquiry."[20]

In the last chapter, I touched upon the effect of this *admiratio* or wonder on the visionary, in terms of the wounding or emptying of the subject that occurs in instances of revelation and sometimes in illness. This process does not, crucially, obstruct or close off the individual to further wonder, but instead perpetuates the condition of *admiratio.* It is, as the post-Heideggerian phenomenologist would have it, a leap out of inauthenticity and into the perspective of *authentic understanding.* In response, the person can attempt to assimilate this situation, driven by a desire to "get back" to the everyday, or they can try to sustain this state of authenticity, to "[sustain] wonder's strangeness," as Rubenstein puts it. This is not to say that the fear, dissociation, or unhomelikeness of the encounter must be sustained, but rather that the authentic understanding that has accompanied it must be. That is, after the initial disruption, the contemplative must reenter their thinking mind and world with a continued awareness and interrogation of their own existence, such that they don't slip again into the comfort of not-seeing. I previously defined this kind of sustained awe using Havi Carel's term *genuine authenticity*, as a process that does not purport to reveal epistemological truth or certitude, but rather offers an engaged and understanding way of living.

Julian's contemplative epistemology similarly understands human logic or rational interpretation as constrained by its earthly bounds, but with a rather different end goal to the phenomenological approach. In Julian's theological context, humanity's postlapsarian ignorance—or "blindhede," as she puts it—means that the wonderer must continue to wonder, to attempt to sustain *admiratio* until the beatific vision itself.[21] From this perspective, the contemplative project is theorized as fundamentally experimental, if experimentum is defined as *experientia quaesita*, a seeking out of further knowledge, or the Anselmian *fides quaerens intellectum*, faith seeking understanding. In such an epistemological model, experientia and experimentum are therefore not in opposition; one does not provide closure on the other. Rather, they operate in a circular and mutually generative relationship, where the tantalizing ineffability of the divine revelation leads the visionary into further inquiry—a lifelong project that is never complete, "begunne" but "not yet performid" (begun . . . but not yet complete).[22]

A HERMENEUTIC CIRCLE

Despite the divergence of sacred and secular horizons that I have been stressing throughout this book, the phenomenological language of disclosure nevertheless resonates strongly with the above theological vocabulary of wonder or *admiratio*, offering a comparable description of the inbreaking that can occur in moments of illness—or via practices of contemplation. A closer look at Julian's own hermeneutic lexis will enrich this picture, highlighting the resonances and divergences between these two paradigms. I here focus on two of Julian's most significant hermeneutic markers: *beseking* and *beholding*, which I suggest come together in her *Revelations* in an internested relationship, expressing a similar circularity to that described above between experientia and experimentum. Theorizing this hermeneutic then sets up an ensuing discussion of Julian's wider epistemology—that is, her account of what knowledge is, what knowledge of God can be achieved on earth, and how the soul's faculties structure and define said knowledge. By unpacking Julian's own hermeneutic against the backdrop of medieval contemplation and, in turn, the phenomenological model, new aspects of her strikingly optimistic theology of recovery are brought into clearer view.

In the previous chapter of this book, I introduced the term *beholding* as an experiential tipping point where grasping and ungrasping, knowing and unknowing meet in the single, unbounded moment of revelation. To gloss this phenomenon, I drew on the work of theologian Maggie Ross, who has theorized beholding using two intersecting epistemologies of contemplation. Ross writes of these epistemologies as working across what she calls the *self-conscious mind* and *the deep mind*, the former of which is where experiences are interpreted (as experimental), while the latter is where revelation irrupts as continual *excessus mentis*.[23] The deep mind, Ross writes, is not directly accessible but can be influenced by "intention, paradox, and resonance."[24] In the moment of beholding, "the self-conscious mind stops analysing and becomes attentively receptive, open in an ungrasping and self-emptying way to irruption from the deep mind."[25] Beholding bridges the epistemological chasm between these two aspects, a bridge built by the force of faith. The contemplative is required to open themselves to God, reaching to feel God with what René Tixier calls the "groping hand of a trusting love."[26]

In this view, beholding can be considered *experiential* only in apophatic terms: an engagement with divinity that is beyond the principles of earthbound knowledge or ratiocination. It arises out of the fissure, the "between" of ordinary and extraordinary perception, at the point of coincidence between willing and unwilling, desire and the giving up of desire. In this sense, beholding displaces experience—it stands in opposition to experience—because such engagement with the activity of the divine spirit is only *experienced* retrospectively, when the revelatory activities are processed as effects in the self-conscious mind, which assimilates these irruptions as *experimental* knowledge.[27] Ross argues that this experimental interpretation is how the brain interprets the world, rendering it "good and necessary," but that is also "always distorted": "experience is *always* interpretation, and as such it must *always* be provisional."[28] It is the "enigmatic mirror" through which one perceives phenomena, while in beholding one "sees face to face."[29] Importantly, these two epistemologies work together, with the deep mind always infusing the self-conscious mind, "so that ordinary daily life draws on its wellspring of silence and trans-figuration," as Ross puts it.[30] This schema of epistemologies therefore works to theorize the supra-experiential phenomena of beholding, and the way they are incorporated into thinking and language.

These terms are helpful for reading Julian's *Revelations* because her texts also combine different ways of knowing and interpreting God. First, during the revelation itself, Julian learns that she must relinquish her desire for ratiocinative thinking in favor of the more capacious epistemology of beholding. Only then can she begin to integrate this knowledge and seek further into its meaning—a hermeneutic project that will occupy her for the rest of her life.[31] Beginning with this initial process (of surrender), I address here the epistemological requirements beholding demands of Julian. Repeatedly, she finds yielding to her beholding and to God's will a difficult task. The showings pose impossible theological problems which she simply can't comprehend—how, then, is she meant to proceed? Her impulse is to turn to God for answers; in chapter 11, for instance, at the start of the third showing, she asks: "What is synne?" (What is sin?).[32] This passage has a distinctly scholastic feel, as Julian deploys the *quaestio* and *disputatio* of scholastic inquiry, following her question with qualifications of what she knows to be true: "I saw treuly that God doth al thing, be it never so litil. And I saw truly that nothing is done be happe ne be aventure, but al thing be the foreseing wisedome of God" (I saw truly that God does all things, no matter how small. And I saw truly that nothing is done by accident or luck, but all by the providential wisdom of God).[33] She navigates conditionals—"If it be happe or adventure" (If it is by accident or luck)—and deduces a firm conclusion: "Wherefore me behovith nedes to grant" (Why then I must concede).[34] Just as with the scholastics, when *disputatio* would take place as philosophical dialogue between master and student, this dialectic examines a statement based on reason and authority.[35] But for Julian, her question concerning the nature of sin has no rational solution; she must defer to faith in her beholding. This is evident in chapter 50, too, where upon asking God after the blameworthiness of sinners ("How may this be?") Julian receives the answer that he assigns "no more blame than if we were as clene and as holy as angelys be in hevyn" (no more blame than if we were as pure and holy as angels are in heaven).[36] The response perplexes Julian, and she describes her reason as "gretly traveylid by [her] blyndhede" (greatly troubled by [her] ignorance), giving her "no rest."[37] So, she remains "in onknowyng" (in unknowing), just as the servant—as Adam—is described in the following chapter as "blinded in his reason and stonyed in his mend" (blinded in his reason and astonished in his mind) after the fall.[38] In this moment of revelation, Julian is not being asked to understand; she is being asked to trust.

One final example reiterates God's demand that Julian relinquish her solipsistic need to know and instead accept his omnipotent love. In chapter 35, Julian takes the opportunity of the revelation to ask after someone she cares for, inquiring into their well-being: "I desired to wetyn of a certeyn creature that I lovid if it shuld continu in good lyvyng" (I desired to know whether a certain creature who I loved would continue to be well).[39] Julian is swiftly told she will not be receiving an answer, and is instructed instead to "take it generally, and behold the curtesy of the Lord God as he shewith to the; for it is mor worship to God to behold hym in al than in any special thyng" (think generally, and behold the courtesy of the Lord God as he shows it to you; for it is more worshipful to God to behold him in all than in any particular thing).[40] Julian is instructed to *behold* the totality of God—to enter into the self-forgetting contemplative mode—rather than to dwell in the singular preoccupations of her self-conscious, worldly perspective.

Julian must therefore learn for herself, through trial and error, the openness required to sustain beholding. Any insights she gleans into these ways of knowing are interspersed with her own struggle to sustain them, as evidenced by the examples above. Yet it is particularly striking that just before her question, "what is sin?," Julian has already been theorizing epistemological methods for herself: in chapter 10, at the close of her account of the second revelation, she witnesses two modes of knowing: "two werkyng . . . : that on is sekyng, the other is beholdyng" (two workings . . . : one is seeking, the other is beholding).[41] She describes how these workings intersect, writing of seeking as a faithful directedness of the person toward God, which makes them receptive to the beholding of him: "It is Gods wille that we seke into the beholdyng of him" (It is God's will that we seek into the beholding of him).[42] Denys Turner defines these two terms as "prayer" and "contemplation," respectively, which he writes differ from and relate to one another in ways that parallel the relationship between the "temporality of our historical condition" and the "timelessness of vision."[43] *Seeking* and *beholding* are here positioned in line with time and eternity, the eschatological "not yet" and the eschatological "now."[44] In this view, moving from one to the other—*seeking toward beholding*—is therefore a process of distillation, where the soul is continually focused and redirected until beholding, when it is concentrated entirely on God.

Upon the opening of the third showing, in chapter 11, Julian appears to have entered this mode for herself, as she writes: "And after this I saw God in a poynte—that is to sey, in myn understonding—be which sight I saw that he is in al things" (And after this I saw God in a point—that is to say, in my understanding—by which sight I saw he is in all things).[45] This term "poynte" is a multivalent one, capturing the sense of both a focal point and a point in time—an instant.[46] With this doubleness, Julian suggests that she has reached some kind of divine center: she has found God in the unbounded moment of beholding, which is also at the center of the contemplative spiral inward. It is worth noting that this image of "God in a poynte" is not original to the *Revelations*: Anna Maria Reynolds argues for a source in the pseudo-Dionysian tradition, where God is conceptualized as the center of a circle where all the radii meet.[47] Wolfgang Riehle meanwhile writes that this concept for expressing God's infiniteness dates back to antiquity and makes its way into other mystical writings: he quotes Meister Eckhart, who says that the soul that has left all things behind it throws itself "in das punt des zirkels" (into the point of the circle).[48] Possibly drawing on this spiraling tradition, Julian characteristically puns on both spatial and temporal senses of the term to describe this moment of deepening into beholding. However, in the lines immediately following this "poynte" locution, Julian reverts to the "what is sin?" mode of questioning—a collapse back into ratiocination which serves to reiterate the cyclicality of her own epistemological process. Her arrival at the "poynte" is not, then, her final destination; this moment of insight is followed by a moment of uncertainty, which is then followed by the desire for further insight. This cycle brings to bear her earlier statement in chapter 10: "And thus I saw him and sowte him, and I had him and I wantid hym" (And thus I saw him and sought him, and I had him and I wanted him).[49] Beholding will always, it seems, drive further seeking.

With this in mind, I propose that the *Revelations*' hermeneutic mode is comparable to the phenomenological hermeneutic circle—a principle that traditionally refers to the interpretive interdependence within any meaningful structure between parts of that structure and its whole.[50] For Heidegger, however, this circular structure is part of the existential constitution of Dasein, which he understood to be both presuppositional and projective: "This circle of understanding is . . . the expression of the existential *fore-structure* of Dasein itself."[51] This ontological specification clears up one of the major criticisms leveled at the concept: of epistemological closure, or holism. Judith N. Shklar argues that the interpretive "movement back and forth" between parts and whole need not have a center: "The hermeneutic circle makes sense only if there is a known closed whole."[52] Shklar cites the Bible as the only text "which can be understood in terms of its own parts and which has as its core God, who is its anchor and creator . . . It is the only possibly wholly self-sufficient text."[53] In Julian's case, her circular epistemology does locate God as the zero-point reference of the circle, as her "poynte" locution shows, but crucially, Julian does not insist on the *known*ness of this whole. For Julian, the "point" of this circle of contemplation is not so much to reach the center—to reach the point—as the dynamic revolutions effected by the process itself, which (in its very nature as cyclical) is never complete, because of the human, postlapsarian condition. Even beholding relies entirely on God's grace, as Julian writes in chapter 10: "It is Gods wille that we seke into the beholdyng of him, for be that he shall shew us himselfe of his special grace whan he wil" (It is God's will that we seek into the beholding of him, because that is how he will show us himself when by his special grace he wills it).[54] Julian therefore reminds her reader of their epistemological limitations; that all they can do is seek God. But by prefacing this with the statement that "sekyng is *as good as* beholdyng," Julian reiterates that God values contemplative seeking *as much as* he values the insights of beholding, a quite remarkable statement that positions both modes as equally important in this epistemological process.[55]

As such, I suggest a reading of Julian's circle of contemplation as ontological as much as epistemological, where to engage in seeking is framed as an *existential* aspect of the soul's being. This idea dates back to Aristotle, who viewed the soul *as* its capacity: to be capable of something, in Aristotle's theory, is to actively strive toward it, finding being in this striving.[56] Edmund Husserl then appropriated this idea in his phenomenology of intentionality, suggesting that to be living is to be directed toward the world in "acts."[57] He called this the "natural attitude," an unconscious way of moving through the world. When the phenomenological mode of analysis (traditionally called *reduction*) is engaged, what is otherwise transparent is revealed; by paying attention to it, the natural attitude is made conscious. For the phenomenologist, this hermeneutic practice reveals the self-createdness of being, showing how existence sustains itself through engagement with the world. In the same way, for Julian the contemplative practice of seeking reveals something about human ontology, but this revelation is about the soul's natural (as in primordial) directedness toward, and ontological union with, God. The contemplative circle facilitates this disclosure: when the contemplative engages in seeking, they are drawn out of linear time and into the boundlessness of the present (and possibly into beholding). Essentially, in seeking toward beholding the contemplative becomes aware of the mode of their own existence—of their existence qua existence. Seeking toward beholding can, then, be understood in a similar way to the phenomenological aspiration toward *authentic understanding*, but one in which being-toward-death is replaced by the condition of being-toward-God. In this sense, beseking is a kind of phenomenological reduction, which doesn't so much *reduce* the soul as expand it, thereby fulfilling its ontological capacity.

Julian takes up the idea of the soul's capacity in a particularly knotty passage of the *Revelations*, the meaning of which remains a point of contention among scholars. The passage occurs in chapter 6 of the long text, where Julian writes: "A man goyth uppe ryght, and the soule of his body is sparyde as a purse fulle feyer" (Mankind walks upright, and the soul of his body is closed like a very splendid purse).[58] This passage is common to only two witnesses of Julian's long text: Paris, Bibliothèque nationale MS Fonds Anglais 40 and London, Westminster Cathedral Treasury MS 4, but curiously does not appear in London, British Library Sloane MS 2499. Cristina Maria Cervone calls this excerpt the "'soule' crux," on account of the scholarly disagreement about the interpretation of Julian's use of the term "soule."[59] Cervone points out that Julian's editors Edmund Colledge and James Walsh established a critical tradition of translating "soule" as "cooked, digested food," and thus as a description of excretion.[60] Julian's later editors Nicholas Watson and Jacqueline Jenkins agree, writing that "'soule' is probably a spelling of 'saule'/'sawlee' (French *saulee*), food or meal, a common word in late Middle English. The 'purse' is then the bowel, and 'nescessery' excretion."[61] This is in turn supported by Barry Windeatt's edition, where he notes that "Isidore of Seville's influential seventh-century encyclopaedia, the *Etymologies*, explains that 'the human stands erect and looks towards heaven so as to seek God, rather than look at the earth, as do the beasts that nature has made bent over and attentive to their bellies.'"[62]

These readings of Julian as invoking the lowly, "bestial" nature of the human condition are supported by another passage later in the *Revelations*, in chapter 64, where she discusses the relationship between the body and soul in more detail. Here, Julian describes "a body lyand on the erth, which body shewid hevy and oggley, withoute shappe and forme, as it were a bolned quave of styngand myre" (a body lying on the earth, which looked bulky and ugly, without shape and form, like the swelling convulsion of a stinking bog).[63] Suddenly, from this body springs "a *ful fair* creature, a little childe full shapen and formid" (a *very splendid* creature, a little child fully shaped and formed), an image Julian interprets as signifying the purity of the soul against the "wretchidnes of our dedly flesh" (wretchedness of our mortal flesh).[64] Cervone makes a connection between these two chapters, leading her to read "soule" in the purse passage in the more traditional sense of "spirit," and the "purse" as the fleshly body, which is opened and closed again to let out the soul at the moment of death, as in the "little childe" passage.[65] This reading makes a lot of sense, providing a broadly dualist interpretation of the body-soul dynamic that aligns with Julian's emphasis on enclosure in both sections: in the former, the purse encloses the soul, and in the latter the body encloses the creature. This is important to Julian's subsequent statement in chapter 64, that the soul can be relieved of the pain of earthly living but pain will always "commen agen" (come again) to the body.[66]

To this interpretation, I want to add another potential layer of meaning—one which complicates any straightforward body-soul dualism, by thinking of the "soul" as not only a separate "spirit" but as a more integrated, embodied phenomenon. For despite Julian's insistence on the wretchedness of the human body, she also writes in chapter 6 (the location of the purse passage) that God does not spurn these "lower" aspects of humankind. God, she writes, "comith downe to us to the lowest party of our nede" to "quickyth our soule and bringith it on life, and makyth it for to waxen in grace and vertue" (comes down to us to the lowest part of our need . . . enlivening our soul and bringing it to life, and making it grow in grace and virtue).[67] Once again, the thing being enlivened here might be either the lowest aspect of the spirit, the lowest part of the body, or as I am suggesting, a multilayering of the two. This idea—that "soul" could refer to the unified experience of body *and* soul—is in turn supported by Julian's reuse of the exact term "ful fair" across both the purse passage and the "little childe" passage, applied respectively to the "soul" of the body and then the "creature" of the soul that leaves the body. By reapplying the phrase in the two contexts, I see Julian as carefully linking together the physical and the spiritual, even while she witnesses the subtleties of their distinction. This interrelation is later borne out in Julian's writing on "substance" and "sensualite," the two aspects of the soul, which I address below.

Returning to the purse passage, then, I find it hard to imagine that Julian would not have been alive to the pun of "soul" as referring to both physicality and spirit. If this is the case, then the opening and closing she describes can be read as not only of the body, but as also referring to the soul's capacity to receive God too, as in the Augustinian expression of *capax Dei*.[68] Strikingly, Augustine also compares the soul's capacity to receive God to a leather purse: as Michael Raby notes, this purse is "stretched by desire when God withholds what he wants to see. Augustine urges his audience to stretch their own purses so that they might increase their capacity to receive God."[69] To this end, Raby writes, Augustine cites Paul: "I have forgotten what is behind, I have stretched out [*extentus*] to what is ahead; in accord with the plan [*secundum intentionem*] I pursue the victory of my lofty calling."[70] Raby is here discussing Julian's writing on prayer and how it makes the soul receptive to God, rendering it "supple and buxom" (flexible and obedient) to receiving him.[71] He does not, however, comment on Julian's own purse passage and its resonances to Augustine. Closing the circle here, I extend Raby's reading of Julian's proto-phenomenological rendering of the soul as made ready for God through prayer, with the suggestion that she linguistically folds in physicality with spirituality to comment on the human capacity for encountering God; just as the stomach takes in food, the implication is that the soul has a similarly enclosing quality, opening to receive the divine.

KNOWING AS BEING

By considering Julian's writing on the body-soul connection, the ways she configures beseking as an existential mode also become more readily apparent. The process of seeking God is rendered an innate part of the Christian experience, or as I describe it in phenomenological terms, a being-toward-God. For despite her insights into heaven as humanity's future home, the incarnational emphasis of Julian's epistemology pulls focus on the possibilities available for knowing God on earth, *in this life*. With this, she rejects the Neoplatonic spirituality of ascent in favor of an incarnational spirituality wherein "redemption is a redemption *of* this life, not a redemption *from* it," as Simon Tugwell has put it.[72] Hers is, therefore, a holistic epistemology which integrates rather than denies the parts of human being that are limited or flawed. For Julian, the fragmented human soul retains the potential for reunification and healing, even while it is constrained by its postlapsarian condition. This process is, Julian understands, not only one of seeking salvation but also a process of realizing the true existential potential of humanity. It is an ontological sine qua non.

The grounding tenet of this anthropology is the principle of mutual indwelling: that the soul resides in God and God resides in the soul. Accordingly, it stands that knowledge of God may be achieved by the means of *self*-knowledge and vice versa. Knowing God, Julian writes in chapter 56 of the long text, is in fact easier than knowing the self, since God is closer even than the created soul:

> And thus I saw full sekirly that it is redyer to us and more esy to cum to the knowyng of God than to knowen our owne soule. For our soule is so deepe groundid in God, and so endlesly tresorid, that we may not cum to the knowing therof till we have first knowing of God, which is the maker to whom it is onyd.[73]

> And so I saw for certain that it is more convenient for us and easier to arrive at the knowing of God than it is to know our own soul. For our soul is so deeply grounded in God, and so endlessly treasured, that we may not arrive at the knowing of it until we first have knowing of God, the maker to whom it is joined.

Regarding self-knowledge, Julian also writes in chapter 46 that "we may never full know ourselfe into the laste poynte, in which poynte this passend life and alle manner of peyne and wo shall have an end" (we may never fully know ourselves in [possibly: until] the last point, at which point this life ends and all manners of pain and woe shall have an end).[74] Julian's invocation of the "poynte" image here can again be read for a double meaning: first, referring to time in the sense of "moment," and second to a thing, in the sense of an "iota." The line can be understood, then, as referring to the inherent itinerancy of the human soul, which cannot know every bit of itself even until its last moment on earth, possibly even until the last judgment. Nevertheless, this passage also puts a positive spin on this state of seeking, emphasizing that some degree of knowledge can indeed be reached on earth: "We may have knowing of ourselfe in this life be continuant helpe and vertue of our hey kynd, in which knowing we may encrecin and wexen be forthering and speding of mercy and grace" (We may have knowing of ourselves in this life with the continuing help and virtue of our higher nature, in which knowing we might increase and expand with the support and assistance of mercy and grace).[75] With this, Julian suggests that even while the contemplative movement inward will never be complete—will never reach its conclusion—by virtue of the soul's groundedness in God it is possible to increase its capacity for knowledge of him, and self-knowledge in turn, by attuning to this higher part.

Seeking God, as Julian has it, therefore means reconfiguring the self-conscious mind away from solipsistic self-beholding "of ourselfe and of our synnes" (of ourself and of our sins): "ourselfe" as in the self as it is experienced in the everyday, which stands objectively over and against the world.[76] Heidegger theorizes a similar self when he writes of the individual who has fallen prey to the world of *the They*: the individual who proceeds inauthentically.[77] Conceived theologically, however, this self has instead fallen prey to sin, a condition which has warped the soul and led humanity into "blindhede." This is what Julian means when she says that "ourselfe" is further away than its true, divine nature. The paradox is that this cultured self is, itself, self-concealing: it distorts the subjective view of the world, leading the individual away from divine truth or knowledge. To know God fully, then, the contemplative must look past the stories and narratives humans construct for themselves and toward a less time-bound awareness of existence. Julian exhorts her reader to look to a more experiential kind of knowledge—that is, experiential in the sense of *existential*, as in *ontological*. She asks them to inquire into the nature of their being.

This concept of knowledge through existential inquiry, which I will here call *knowing as being*, is dependent on Julian's incarnational anthropology, which is in turn grounded in the atemporality of the eschatological timeline. At the point of creation, Julian sees the soul in two parts: "our kynde substance" (our essential [also: natural] substance), which is overseen by God, who keeps it "in hym, hoole and save without end" (in him, whole and safe without end), and the "changeabil sensualyte" (changeable sensuality), which is judged by "man," and which "shewyth outward" (is outwardly expressed).[78] This "substance"/"sensualite" distinction does not, importantly, conflate to a simple spirit/body dichotomy. Rather, Julian understands the "substance" as the "heyer parte" of the soul which is always in God. The "sensualite," meanwhile, refers to the specifically human, time-bound experience of the world, which limits the perception of God's loving nature and eschatological plan.[79] Julian writes that humankind is "made sensual" when the soul is "inspirid into our body," a "knitting" of these two parts together.[80] This fragmentariness puts the soul in constant danger of turning back into itself ("beholding of ourselfe"), toward sin and away from God: "And thus in our substance we arn full, and in our sensualite we faylyn" (And so our substance makes us whole, and our sensuality is the part by which we fail), Julian writes.[81] The "sensualite" is, however, redeemed and reunited with the "substance" by the grace and goodness of God, which fulfills his nature through the incarnation of Christ on earth. As Julian puts it, "The heyer part was on in peace with God in full joy and bliss; the lower partie, which is sensualite, suffrid for the salvation of mankynd" (The higher part was at one in peace with God with full joy and bliss; the lower part, which is the sensuality, suffered for the salvation of humankind).[82] The incarnation grounds and roots the earthly experience of the divine, leading the soul to be restored by grace: "for he [God] is ground in whom our soule stondith, and he is mene that kepith the substance and the sensualite togeder so that thai shall never departyn" (for he is the ground in which our soul resides, and he is the means by which the substance and sensuality are kept together so that they shall never separate).[83] Julian's final showing, recounted in chapter 67 of the long text, concludes this ontological schema, as she witnesses with her "gostly eye" (spiritual eye) Jesus sitting within her soul, which is "so large as it were an endles world, and as it were a blisfull kyngdom" (so large as if it were an endless world, and as if it were a blissful kingdom).[84] This kingdom, she perceives, is the site of humanity's "endles wonyng" (endless union) with the Trinity—"wonyng" as in *oneing* but also "wonen," *to dwell*.[85] The showing thus reiterates her conception of the Trinity as "our moder, in whom we arn al beclosid" (our mother, in whom we are all enclosed), an enclosure which is paralleled by God's enclosure within humanity.[86]

Many scholars have pointed out the clear allusions of Julian's indwelling doctrine to the teachings of St. John the Evangelist, who similarly understood the human relationship with God as one of reciprocal dwelling: "Whoever confesses Jesus to be the Son of God, God dwells in him."[87] In her explication of this model of indwelling, Grace M. Jantzen cites the paradox from John's Gospel, "abide in me and I in you," which she observes also occupies an important place in Pauline writings, with their emphasis on "Christ in you" and "you in Christ."[88] Julian renders this chiastic structure in a similarly reflective syntactical triad of "beclosings": "We arn beclosid in the Fadir, and we arn beclosid in the Son, and we arn beclosid in the Holy Gost; and the Fader is beclosid in us, and the Son is beclosid in us, and the Holy Gost is beclosid in us" (We are enclosed in the Father, and we are enclosed in the Son, and we are enclosed in the Holy Ghost; and the Father is enclosed in us, and the Son is enclosed in us, and the Holy Ghost is enclosed in us), she writes in chapter 54 of the long text.[89] This doctrine of indwelling does not describe the momentary irruption of visionary beholding, but a constant and abiding presence: a "lasting oneness-of-being," as Wolfgang Riehle describes it.[90] "From this," writes Riehle, "stems Julian's view that epistemological knowledge is strongly rooted in the corporeal, and indeed starts from the body, if not entirely, then to a considerable degree."[91] That is to say, this ontological structure provides the basis for the contemplative epistemology outlined above: for the human ability to direct the self toward God on earth. Framing the soul and body as a unified seat of divine indwelling, Julian's ontological framework uplifts lived experience as the foundation of the human connection to the Trinity.

This anthropological schema in turn gives rise to Julian's theodical conclusions about the nature of sin and suffering, for it is on account of her ontological understanding of the soul that she determines the possibility for *choosing* a life of love—for choosing God—over sin. Julian outlines the nature of this free choice in her account of the thirteenth revelation, where she sees that all shall be well, and in which she explains the nature of the will in the souls of the elect. According to Julian, the will is made up of two parts: the "godly will" and the "beastly will," which can be translated respectively as "godly" or "goodly" (as in noble) and "beast-like," "sensual," or referring to the animal nature of humanity.[92] These terms denote the human inability to choose anything *but* goodness and love, and the tendency to bury this connection to God beneath failings of love, or sins:

> For in every soule that shal be savid is a godly wil that never assentid to synne ne never shal. Ryth as there is a bestly will in the lower party that may willen no good, ryth so ther is a godly will in the heyer party, which will is so good that it may never willen yll but ever good.[93]

> For in every soul that shall be saved there is a godly will that never gave in to sin and never shall. Just as there is a beastly will in the lower part that may will no good, there is accordingly a godly will in the higher part, which is so good that it may never will that which is ill but always that which is good.

Denise N. Baker notes various theological precedents for Julian's "godly will," writing of it as "the nexus between Julian's theodicy and her anthropology," the mechanism with which she develops her optimistic theology of predestination.[94] Baker makes a particularly productive comparison between Julian's schema and the Bernardian framework of free will.[95] Bernard, Baker writes, moves the *imago Dei* from the mind (as in Augustinian theology) to the will "in order to indicate, as Bernard McGinn explains, that 'freedom, understood in its most general form as the absence of external coercion, is the inalienable characteristic of the human person as human.'"[96] Baker compares Julian's beastly and godly wills with Bernard's "*liberum arbitrium* (free choice)," which is "freedom from necessity, the essential condition of humankind both before and after the Fall" and "*liberum consilium* (free counsel), lost by Adam but restored by Christ," which "enables the elect to refrain from sin."[97] For Bernard, the grace of God "acts as the intermediary between these two parts of the will for the elect": "True, we cannot be completely without sin or sorrow here on earth," he writes, "but we can, with the help of grace, avoid being overcome either by sin or sorrow."[98] This is the nature of prevenient grace, that illumination of the Holy Spirit that is endlessly available, and which precedes the free determination of the will.

Both Bernard's and Julian's models thus enable the soul to refrain from sin and pursue beholding in this life. However, Baker (quoting Bernard McGinn) rightly distinguishes between Bernard's "affective, operational union of willing and loving" and Julian's "essential or ontological union between God and the soul."[99] For Julian, humans are only separate from God in terms of the difference between creator and created: an *ontological*, rather than moral distinction. Julian describes this separation in terms of analogy—"likeness" and "unlikeness"—since her theology of mutual indwelling understands the "substance" as remaining always within God (and God within it), and so to redirect the soul toward the "substance" is to redirect it toward the divine. Julian writes, for example, of how prayer "onyth the soule to God," since "thow the soule be *ever lyke to God in kynde and substance*, restorid be grace, it is often *onlyke* in condition be synne on mannys partye" (unites the soul to God . . .

though the soul is always like God in substance, and restored by his grace, its condition is often unlike him due to humanity's sin).[100] Julian here presents prayer as part of the mode of seeking, the intentional being-toward-God that will enact this reunion of "sensualite" and "kindly substance," redeeming unlikeness to likeness. By consistently configuring God and substance as *alike* "in kynde"—as "kindly"—Julian suggests that this part of the self is innately or naturally divine. Indeed, Julian's use of "kindly" might be read as denoting the ontology of the soul, its essential nature that is never separate from God: Julian sees no difference between God and the substance ("And I saw no difference atwix God and our substance, but as it were al God"; And I saw no distinction between God and our essential substance, but it seemed as if it were all God), equating this part of the soul with the divine, who is its "kindly ground."[101]

This is not, however, an ontology of indistinction. Julian remains committed to the Augustinian tradition and is careful to distinguish between creator and created: "and yet myn understondyng toke that our substance is in God: that is to sey, that God is God, and our substance is a creture in God" (and yet my understanding took it to mean that our substance is in God: that is to say, that God is God, and our substance is a creation within God).[102] The soul is *made* of substance but from *nothing made*, united to God who is *unmade* ("substancial kynd onmade"; substantial nature unmade) in its creation.[103] The body, meanwhile, is not "like" God in its creation because it is *made* from the already created earth:

> And thus I understond that mannys soule is made of nought, that is to sey, it is made, but of nought that is made, as thus: whan God shuld make mans body he tooke the slyppe of erth, which is a matter medlid and gaderid of all bodily things, and therof he

> made mannys bodye. But to the makyng of mannys soule he wold take ryte nought, but made it.[104]
>
> And so I understood that man's soul is made of nothing, that is to say, it is made, but of nothing that is made, as such: when God went to make man's body he took the mud of earth, which is something mixed and made up of all physical things, and from this he made man's body. But to make man's soul he would take precisely nothing, but made it.

So, the human experience of the body—known via the "sensualite"—is only united to God through Christ's incarnation, and is more likely to lead a person away from God and into sin.

In this way, Julian's ontology positions all aspects of the soul as integral to the contemplative process of beseking and beholding. Since Christ has redeemed the "sensualite," nothing need be suppressed within the soul for it to reunite with God, only *reoriented* away from sin and toward the "substance." A similar process is described by Maggie Ross's two contemplative epistemologies, where she writes of a "turning away from the distractions of experience and their noise . . . continually choosing to 'seke [him] to the beholding.'"[105] Importantly, this is a holistic enterprise engaging all aspects of the mind, which are fused together in a transactional and mutually affecting process: Julian refers to "reason *and* grace" as the motivational forces that exhort a person to prayer.[106] By attaching the one to the other, she reiterates the requirement of the intellect in this cyclical epistemology: indeed, for Julian, "our reason is *in God*."[107] In this sense, the exercise of seeking can be understood to strip the soul's capacity of its worldly excesses, paring back its epistemological capabilities to a more intuitive kind of knowing. This is enacted using what Julian calls "kindly reason" or "mannys reason naturall" (man's natural reason), a ratiocinative capability that stands in contrast to a person's everyday postlapsarian reason, which has been rendered "so blynd, so low, and so symple" (so blind, so low, and so blameless) after the fall.[108] Julian does not, then, define humanity's fallen state as hopeless. Instead, blindness or unknowing are simply points of departure for loving faith, with which a person can commit to the redirection of attention and action toward God.

This language of reorientation is slightly more explicit in the Sloane manuscript than in the Paris witness and the shorter version of Julian's text. In the latter two witnesses to what is chapter 47 in the long text, Julian describes the soul as frail or "vnkunnyng," a term that appears to relate not just to knowing but also to action—just like the Heideggerian "existential" of *understanding* I discussed in chapter 1.[109] By the time the Old English *cennan* (to know, to understand) and *cunnan* (to be able or to have power to) converge in the Middle English *conne-*, the word refers to both possession of knowledge and of skill in an action, as in *can*.[110] In this way, "vnkunnyng" can refer to the defective state of fallen transcendence; that state of "effortful striving" that makes it that much harder for humanity to reattune to homeliness on earth. It recalls humanity's inherited, originary homelessness: the primordial *loss* of "kunnyng" caused by the devil, who made use of his own cunning to induce humankind to sin.[111] The term also rings through Freud's "uncanny," the "involuntary return to the same situation"—in this case, the situation being sin.[112] While "vnkunnyng" recalls the fall, however, the Sloane version directs attention to the possibility of change, with "overcummyng" in its place.[113] This variance agrees with Sloane's abundant use of the *over-* prefix elsewhere (twenty-nine times in total). Meaning "to pass over," "to overturn," or to "upset" something, "overcummyng" could also denote the damage to humanity's natural condition.[114] But instead of a simple negation, "overcummyng" reads as an overlaying or *distortion* of the soul's essential goodness: just as Christ's dying face is "*over*rede with drie blode," the will is "*over*leyd" with worldly accretions.[115] Sloane's variance therefore resonates with the turning and re-turning structure of Julian's epistemology, and with it Christ's redemptive words "thou shalt not be overcome."[116] To seek the beholding of him is, in this model, a seeking of humanity's innately divine capacity, a coming back (which is also a going forward) to the self with a genuinely authentic understanding of its own nature and its relation to God. Humankind has been brought low by the fall, but it remains in *imago Dei*, in the image of God.

KYNDE KNOWYNG

Julian's contemplative mode therefore focuses on the human potential for knowing and reuniting with God on earth—an epistemology similar to that of Heidegger's phenomenological model, which describes Dasein's potential for authentic understanding and homelike being-in-the-world. Phenomenologically speaking, these conditions converge to effect a life of *genuine authenticity*, whereby the individual sees clearly and is able to reenter the world and act within it. It is worth reiterating at this point that the phenomenological use of the term *authenticity* is not a literal one; the term does not carry the same associations as in everyday speech today. Heidegger's term *Eigentlichkeit*, commonly translated as authenticity, in fact literally translates as *ownedness*, from *eigen*, "own" or "proper." So, to pursue authenticity is to pursue the becoming of *one's own self*—or, as Søren

Kierkegaard puts it, to "become what one is."[117] As in the above collocation, Heidegger links this concept with *understanding*, the German for which, *Verstehen*, derives from the idea of "taking a stand": for Heidegger, humans concretize their identity by taking a stand, enacting their roles, choosing how they present themselves in the world. In doing so, they *understand* it.

In this section of the chapter, I explore how Julian's own proto-phenomenological epistemology is constructed, by examining the collocation *kynde knowyng* as a medieval counterpart to the phenomenological concept of authentic understanding. The term is used in medieval texts to refer to a specific form of experiential knowledge, drawing on the various associations of "kynde" with nature and creation. More specifically, though, the collocation denotes the entire cognitive and precognitive process of knowing something by experience, not just in terms of affective knowledge—through loving—but knowledge gleaned through the act of *living*. And while Julian does not explicitly use the phrase *kynde knowyng* in her *Revelations*, she does use the term "kynde" or variations thereof almost eighty times throughout the long text. The word features most markedly in her anthropological schema, governing her understanding of the relationship between created and creator: for instance, since God is "[Paris: vnmade] kynd," and humans are "grounded in kynde," the act of seeking God is to seek "kynde," and so also to seek to know their divine nature.[118] In this model, seeking that which is "kynde" is therefore equivalent to *seeking toward beholding*, as defined above. As such, *kynde knowyng* functions as a particularly useful hermeneutic for understanding Julian's contemplative epistemology, especially the ways in which Julian grounds human knowledge of God in lived experience, as both a return to humanity's originary nature and a move forward into redemption.

Kynde, or *kind*, in medieval usage broadly refers to nature or that which is natural.[119] The term was widely used in the English Middle Ages to denote both the natural order of the universe as well as the natural disposition of human*kind*, with the etymological associations of *kind* with *kin* and *kindred* invoking a sense of the species as a collective. The one definition informs the other, with *kynde* in terms of the literal earth (nature) also invoking the animating *logos* of Genesis, which spoke human nature into existence. In his ecomaterialist study of earth in the Middle Ages, Alfred Kentigern Siewers points out: "Earth to the ancients meant a realm including land and sea, ultimately planet *and* soil, native country *and* the dust of Genesis, from which humans were energized by God's breath, *pneuma*," which "entwined the *logoi* of the speaking-into-being of Creation, in which *logos* could mean at once harmony, word, discourse, story, reason, and purpose."[120] Rebecca M. Douglass also writes of the medieval concept of *kind* as "character," "type," and also as "everything"—"the amorphous mass of all matter"—which Neil Evernden states was "not simply a physical entity but a record of the will of God."[121] These double meanings, of nature as object and as generative force—created and force of creation—are rooted in the Greek notion of *phusis* (Latin: *natura*), literally meaning "beginning, coming to be," and which came to mean "everything," as in the "conceptual container for the universe."[122] Classically, *phusis* denoted the principle of change, set against the immovable gods or mathematics, paving the way for the creator/created distinction that saw, in the Christian tradition, God as distinct from nature as an artist from their work or parent from their child—a relationship also borne out in Julian's distinction between "unmade" God and the human soul, which is in its "kynde substance" made of that which is "unmade."

Julian's use of *kynde* might conceivably be understood as referring to the prelapsarian condition of humanity: its original state as it was created, prior to the intervention of humankind. As Douglass writes, the "natural" generally refers to "something untouched by the human."[123] Julian's usage certainly invokes this kind of originary "nature," her ontology describing the soul at the point of creation: "the blissed Trinite made mankinde to his image and to his likenes" (the blessed Trinity made humankind in his image and likeness), "knitt to God in the makyng" (united to God in its creation).[124] But since Julian's interpretation of the fall is that humanity has distorted, not destroyed, the image of God in the soul, she understands its nature as fundamentally unchanged by the lapse into sin. This is not to say that Julian's theodicy is Pelagian—that position that held that humans have free will to restore themselves to perfection.[125] Instead, for Julian, the soul's "substance" remains in God, but she acknowledges that humans are dependent on Christ to redeem their "sensualite," he who is, as the author of the fourteenth-century religious manual *Pore Caitif* writes, both God and man, "perfiȝtli double *kynde*" (perfectly double in *nature*).[126] Indeed, Julian is explicit that "the redemption and the ageyn-byeng of mankynd is nedefull and spedefull in everything" (the redemption and the being-again [also possibly: buying-again] of mankind is necessary and profitable in everything).[127] The corollary is that while Julian's contemplative schema offers a reattunement of the soul to its natural or authentic state, this is not a return to prelapsarianism, since she acknowledges humans will always sin. Instead, she describes a commitment to the transcending-returning cycle of contemplative seeking, of expanding the soul in its divine capacity. She offers a commitment to the "wey" of Christ, because Christ is the archetype of "kindness"—"*our kinde Lord*"[128]—in whom is contained all the potential humans possess for redemption. Julian's pursuit of "kynde" is not a mystical ascent *out* of the world but a reimmersion of the self *within* its own divine creatureliness.

This theological vocabulary corresponds in many ways to William Langland's use of the collocation *kynde knowyng* in *Piers Plowman* (c. 1370–1390), an epistemological echo which sheds light both on Julian's application of the term and its usage in the literary-devotional milieu of England at this time. The phrase has been glossed by some critics as "natural knowledge," the Thomistic type of knowledge deriving from sensation and intellection (the other type being revelatory knowledge).[129] Others read the term as a variant of divine wisdom, experiential knowledge, *sapientia*, or the Pauline concept of gnosis: Mary Clemente Davlin, for example, observes that wisdom or *sapientia* had "no fixed English name" in the late fourteenth century, citing biblical translations of the term as "knowyng" and similar variants.[130] *Kynde knowyng* can feasibly be understood as a kind of affective knowledge, experienced through the will rather than the intellect: in Langland's allegory, Will (as in human will) seeks a more direct knowledge of God, who is repeatedly figured as "Kynde." But throughout the poem *kynde knowyng* remains elusive, and is repeatedly inflected with both positive and negative connotations. Nicolette Zeeman examines these nuances at length, arguing that *kynde knowyng* suggests "both a 'good' and yet also a site of potential deprivation, a place of 'having' and 'not having.'"[131] D. Vance Smith presses into this negative view even further, suggesting that Langland's use of "Kynde" evokes "the great subject of negative theology: the unknowability of the ultimate causes of things."[132] Certainly, *Piers Plowman* frequently refers to *kynde knowyng* as a negative, to describe what Will does not know: "Yet haue I no kynde knowyng," he says in passus 1.[133] This knowledge extends to the poetic project of the text itself, which explores variously the ways language cannot capture the divine. But just as negative theology depends on its opposite—for something to be negated—there are striking moments in the poem where Will does get a glimpse of *kynde knowyng*: for instance, in passus 16 at the Tree of Charity, where Will pulls down the sapiential knowledge of its fruit, "to assaien what sauour it hadde" (to test [also: taste] what taste it had).[134] In this scene, Will literally and figuratively samples *sapientia* (from *sapere*, to taste).

A now conventional reading of *Piers Plowman* is that Will journeys from *scientia* to *sapientia*, or "from reason to affective knowledge," as James Simpson puts it.[135] But a path of linear ascent does not fully capture the positive and negative slippages of the term: as the above readings suggest, *kynde knowyng* seems to integrate knowings of many kinds, operating simultaneously. Hugh White articulates this polyvalency, writing that *kynde knowyng* is not *sapientia*, which is solely a theological form of knowledge, nor *scientia*, factual knowledge, but is "a manner of knowing *various* things."[136] According to White, this is indeed a kind of "experiential knowledge" (as Davlin has it), but that which is not confined to the experience of the *object* of knowledge.[137] It apprehends rather the experience of the thing *and* the experience of its opposite. This is the same logic which governs the circular epistemology outlined above: in Julian's understanding, it is the nature of a Christian life that a person will experience both love and suffering as well as well-being and woe. Similarly for Langland, the progress of society circles from promise to decay.[138] With each rotation or turn of the spiral, humanity is granted a deeper understanding of their nature—of the self, both personal and collective.

With its logic of opposition, the phrase *kynde knowyng* seems therefore to capture the idea that life contains both suffering and bliss, and that each depends on the other. This is borne out in the conclusion of Will's personal journey: as White comments, "perhaps it is because Will is now, as he has not always been, actually suffering, evidently deeply immersed in the flow of natural experience, rather than merely looking on, that the lesson which presents itself carries conviction—it has been learnt on the pulses."[139] White describes this as a "sense of authenticity" that is the "quintessence of wisdom," resulting from Will's confrontation of death: "the emergence of the teaching *ex extremis*."[140] This description is of a kind with the knowledge I have been identifying as emerging from Julian's experience in extremis: a distinctly phenomenological kind of knowing, or authentic understanding. As Will learns from Piers, *kynde knowyng* is an earthly goal, based on effortful seeking over many years. Piers serves Truth with commitment and fortitude: "I haue ben his folwere al þis [fourty] wynter" (I have been his follower all these forty winters).[141] Such an epistemology depends "upon grace and upon loving effort (for Piers, to 'sowe and sette')," and is only achieved after a lifetime of experience.[142] The same can be said of Julian, for whom knowing is contingent upon both her suffering and her committed seeking—an epistemology sharply allegorized in her showing of the lord and the servant, which demonstrates the necessity for digging and delving in the search for authentic understanding, cultivating the soil of the soul and "sekyn the depnes" ([seeking] the deepness), just as Piers sows and sets the earth.[143]

Finally, I want to show how the definition of *kynde* as type or character can illuminate Julian's ontological schema of "likeness" and "unlikeness." If *kynde* is understood to be nature, as in the essence of all created things, then to focus on humanity's divine likeness, on its "kynde substance," is to concentrate on part of the "*thisness*" of its existence. The scholastic approach might call this *haecceitas* (the "thisness" specific to human being) or *quiddity* (the "whatness" of this being): in other words, the pretheoretical essence of factical life. Yet this term risks slippage into the objectivity of scientific or materialist thought. For Julian, knowledge of the "thisness" of human being emerges not from objective interrogation or inquiry, but from humans' active engagement with the world: their being-toward-God. I return to this question of *haecceitas* in chapter 6, but my point here is that Julian's ontology is distinctly phenomenological, in the way she also uses the term "kynde" as something to be sought after, cultivated, and engaged repeatedly, by attending to the "kynde substance" of the soul which has its likeness in the "kinde Lord" of Christ. This is an active project, and it frames the nature of human being (in terms of its salvific fulfillment) as deeply enmeshed with its search for understanding. Just as Heidegger wrote, "I must see away from the what-content [*Wasgehalt*] and attend only to the fact that the object is a given, attitudinally grasped one," I understand Julian's position to be that the nature of human existence is always situated by their worldly, temporal experience, which is hermeneutically structured and sustained.[144]

Julian's foundation for this position lies in her differentiation between the "workings" or energies of God, which can be known, and the being or essence of God, which cannot be known. To get to know its divine aspect, the soul must know it through *God's being in the soul.* Julian is shown that Christ partakes of human "sensualite" through the incarnation, thus providing the means (or "mene," in Julian's terms) for redemption through his sacrifice at the passion. This redemptive fulfillment goes beyond the mechanics of causality, operating as part of God's simultaneously occurring narrative. Humanity cannot comprehend this narrative fully from their position on the eschatological timeline, since the human experience is to be always in the process of being fulfilled. For the Christian, then, they must seek to reorient to the "kynde substance" by searching for understanding, continuously turning and re-turning toward Christ even when their "changeabil" nature leads them away from him. In this sense, the dynamism of the post-Heideggerian definition of health has a parallel in the Christian way of life, where the search for salvation is also a rhythmic rebalancing or reorientation toward the homeliness of Christ, who dwells always in the soul. And so, the search for "kynde" in Julian's *Revelations* is similarly one that incorporates positive and negative, knowing and not-knowing, but which is grounded always by the possibility of savoring some taste of understanding through an active pursuit of God's love.

PERFORMING THE TEXT

Julian's contemplative epistemology has been theorized so far as an existential mode, a way of being-in-the-world. I suggest that the cyclicality of this process renders it inevitably non-closing, a feature Heidegger similarly deems to be part of the human condition: "A *constant unfinished quality [Unabgeschlossenheit]* thus lies in the essence of the basic constitution of Dasein."[145] But where Heidegger understands this incompletion as set against the nothingness of the world, Julian theorizes it theologically as an inevitable product of God's ineffability: that since humanity can never fully reach divine wisdom on earth, the interpretive products of the self-conscious mind will always be experimental. This is the same principle of epistemological limitation that shapes René Tixier's description of the *Cloud of Unknowing* as an "experiment in love," and is also borne out in Julian's own declaration that her text is "begunne" but "not yet performid" (begun . . . but not yet complete).[146] From this discussion of Julian's contemplative epistemology, then, the chapter now arrives at the question of textual performance—that is, the phenomenological and linguistic mechanics of the visionary text. In her account of Julian's *Revelations* and *Piers Plowman*, Barbara Newman describes the complicated relationship of "*visio*" to "*vita*," using these Langlandian terms to describe "the moments of seeing and the span of living."[147] As the above circular epistemology makes clear, the very open-endedness of Julian's writing rejects any neat chronology between the two. Newman acknowledges this, writing of how Julian "[refuses] a schematic elegance that would have unduly privileged *visio* over *vita*."[148] Instead insisting on the provisionality of her interpretation of the visions, Julian defers to the ineffability of the divine revelation. The result is a text in which even the categories of Julian's own interpretive triad—"bodily sight," "words formed in mine understanding," and "ghostly sight"—are continually slipping their definitions. Interweaving her own musings about the meaning of the revelation into her account of the revelation itself, Julian embraces fluidity between her showings and their interpretation, enacting textually her understanding of human being as a hermeneutic process.

This narrative strategy serves to construct what might be called a porous or wounded text, wherein the showings and Julian's interpretation leak into one another.[149] Julian's voice drops into the text intermittently, like the drops of blood that fall from the garland of thorns, "spredeing" (spreading) and dissolving into the showings themselves such that the reader is not always aware of any distinction between them.[150] The author makes herself transparent so that the revelation can flow through her and to the reader, for the communal body of her "even cristen." And, with this, Julian positions herself not as interpreter—"God forbede that . . . I am a techere" (God forbid that . . . I am a teacher), she writes in the short text—but as a communicator of the Word as she receives it, for her reader to take and interpret in turn.[151] Given the difficulties of visionary interpretation outlined above, however, the question remains of how successful this representation can ever be. Until now, my discussion has been limited to Julian's own recovery journey precipitated by her sickness and revelation. This is a subjective, firsthand transfiguration, whereby her death is revealed as her *ownmost*. But as D. Vance Smith shows, literature about death will always struggle to put into language this subjective epistemological shift.[152] Such texts can only hope to lead the reader to the edge of their own knowing, to prescribe a preparation and cultivation for when their own revelation may strike. Julian does not presume to do otherwise: she acknowledges that beholding may never occur even for her fellow Christians. Hence her emphasis on beseking, on the preparatory work of directed and focused attention. Yet the phenomenological model of illness can nevertheless be helpful here in understanding the possibility of transference between Julian and her reader, the possibility that her reader may glean something of Julian's own insights or experience for themselves. As the phenomenologist Havi Carel argues, firsthand experiences with existential anxiety are not the only possibilities for the disclosure of authentic understanding: in fact, "grief and mourning *for others* can also intimate mortality and thus have an edifying role."[153] Carel subsequently proposes that the death or pain *of another* can effect a secondhand, sympathetic response, predicated upon interrelational participation. She here argues for the disclosive power of compassion. In these final sections of the chapter, I suggest that a comparable interrelationality can be identified in Julian's *Revelations*, in terms of the texts' affective and didactic qualities, but most of all in terms of their revelatory potential. I explore, in other words, the compassionate text as a tool for the reader's own journey of seeking understanding.

What does it mean to call Julian's a compassionate text? Recent work in medieval studies has helpfully negotiated the subtleties of the term as it is used in devotional literature of this period. A. S. Lazikani marks an important distinction between *compassion* and *empathy* in religious texts, calling the former "co-feeling," a term she borrows from Milan Kundera.[154] The latter, meanwhile, might be defined as "*in*-feeling," from the Greek *empatheia*: *in* + *pathos*. To be *in*-feeling means to be drawn into pain in a self-reflexive way, such that the pain may be overwhelming. Traumatological studies show that individuals can suffer from empathetic overload or fatigue, which in the literature is often referred to as "compassion fatigue" or "secondary traumatic stress"—a definition that does not allow for the compassion/empathy distinction, using compassion to denote both states.[155] More recent work in neurophysiology has drawn out this difference, finding empathy to be more taxing than compassion and providing fewer positive effects.[156] Empathy is, in this context, characterized as a focus on the person-in-pain's experiences, while compassion invites feelings of loving kindness and care for the person themselves. That is to say, empathy identifies with the *pain*, while compassion identifies with the *person-in-pain*, with different brain pathways activated in these respective experiences of self-feeling and socially connected feeling.[157] Compassion is a relational encounter, wherein the person's pain doesn't become *my* pain; their pain remains *theirs*, but invites a sympathetic connection between me and them.

In the medieval imaginary, the power of participatory emotion underpinned the rubrics of many devotional texts, particularly those focused on the life and death of Christ. Affective meditations of this kind have been called "scripts," on account of their schematic methodologies: as Sarah McNamer writes, these are "quite literally scripts for the performance of feeling—scripts that often explicitly aspire to performative efficacy."[158] To enhance affective efficacy, these scripts were often highly self-reflexive, using first-person, present-tense utterances to direct the reader's response toward the passion. They are not, as McNamer has pointed out, always "altruistic," in that they certainly do not always seek to relieve the suffering of the individual in question; they are, in fact, often "self-interested."[159] That is to say, they are invested in the positive potential of compassionate suffering-*with* Christ. This reflects the cooperative aspect of the soteriological enterprise, where part is undertaken by Christ through his labor on the cross, and part is undertaken by humanity, who must remember his pain and perform their own compassionate labor in kind. This is an epistemology of love, whereby Christ's death on the cross symbolizes God's eternal love of humankind, and meditating on this event would elicit compassionate love in turn: *passio* leads to *compassio*. Poetic concepts such as the "wound of love" or "love languor" articulate this pathetic framework in physical terms, particularly in anchoritic texts, where as Lazikani observes, "love and compassion are coupled together as joint efforts."[160] This is, then, a medieval model of participatory compassion, based on an integration of intellect and will, thought and feeling.

In tracing elements of this participatory project, Julian's own compassionate text comes into clearer view, as does the extent to which her revelatory insights can be received by her "even cristen" reader. Just as affective meditation invites readerly participation, Julian's texts defer hermeneutic closure to her reader: "For the shewing I am not goode, but if I love God the better; and in as much as ye love God the better, it is more to you than to me"

(I am not good just because I received the showing, only if it makes me love God better; and inasmuch as it will help you love God better, it is more worthwhile to you than to me), she writes in chapter 9 of the long text, encouraging an affective response in her reader.[161] By recruiting the reader into the interpretive conversation in this way, Julian appears to claim that they, too, can be changed by the text, just as she has been changed by her revelation. Moreover, this transfiguration can be argued to change the text itself: as the concept of the hermeneutic circle suggests, fore-structures of understanding (experience) allow phenomena to be interpreted in a preliminary way, which then leads to an understanding of the whole (the text)—a new interpretation that can be understood as a new experience in itself. When applied to the visionary text, this means that each reader of the revelation (including the initial visionary) contributes an interpretation to the text of the showings: in the case of the visionary, this means translating the revelation into the language of the visionary text; in the case of the reader, this means adding their perspective to this hermeneutic circle. The text is shaped by each reader, just as each reader is shaped by the text, but interpretation of the showings is continually deferred: from showing to visionary to text to reader, the hermeneutic chain is never complete.

The interchange between these vehicles might be described as constructing a *shared* or *fluid text*—a concept rooted in enactivist theory, which, derived in part from phenomenology, describes meaning as performatively created. The act of conversation, for example, is interpreted by the enactivist approach as a process of mutual sense-making, in which each conversation partner is engaged in creating something new.[162] In her writing on Julian's ecological sensibility, Claire Gilbert draws on these enactivist principles to argue that the Julian texts have a "visceral, material effect that can call their reader into a performative response."[163] Gilbert writes that there is a "vast mysterious store" of meaning "behind what we show each other and are aware of ourselves," which is revealed "by participative performance and not by cognitive reasoning."[164] In this interpretation, the reader's compassion is contingent on their relating to the suffering described within the text, which involves operations of memory or imagination. Medieval faculty psychology explains such operations with the term "vertu imaginatif" (*vis imaginativa*), which refers to the ability to form and retain images and impressions in the mind, and "covers both memory and our 'imagination' (in both the creative and speculative/anticipatory senses)."[165]

As in the medieval model, phenomenological accounts of shared meaning-making combine both intellect and affect, a pairing which can also be mapped onto Julian's contemplative epistemology. As Maggie Ross writes, "For the mind to function optimally, it must be recentred in the deep mind . . . restoring the circulation between the two epistemologies so that ordinary daily life draws on its wellspring."[166] This seems to apply not only to the individual who receives the showings—to the state of beholding itself—but also to the mind that is nourished by participatory performance of compassion. Both visionary and reader can be changed by the hermeneutic circle of the shared text, which functions as a channel for the "wellspring" of beholding. This is further borne out in the relationship between beseking and beholding in Julian's writing, a hermeneutic she offers for her reader's edification as much as her own. The participatory, performative nature of this process is captured in the Sloane manuscript of the long text, where in chapter 10 Julian claims that "we" (both she and her "even cristen") must "seke him *to* [Paris: into] the beholdyng of him" (seek him *to* the beholding of him).[167] The preposition in Sloane's version of this statement might be compared to the Latin *ut* or the Heideggerian *um zu*: to seek him *in order to, for the purpose of* beholding, or indeed, *until* the beholding is reached. Seeking is, to use another favorite phrase of Julian's, the "mene" by which beholding might be realized.

Julian is careful, however, to assert that beholding may not be directly available for all who seek God; that revelation is a rare occurrence. Nevertheless, even if divine revelation may not appear, she reminds her reader that "sekyng is as good as beholdyng" (seeking is as good as beholding).[168] With this extraordinary statement, Julian says that it is enough to pursue compassion, to live with a directedness toward Christ, and to live with faith. In her concept of beseking, then, Julian offers a secondary means by which the reader might enter into the divine relationship, quite apart from her own entrance via the abjection of illness. This is an equivalent cowounding since it is a relational act—it is *com*passionate: a withness, not a mineness. The recognition is of an interpersonal connection that lies at the very heart of the human being: through Julian's identification with Christ and the reader's identification with both, the reader might reattune to their own divine aspect, their "kynde substance."

By engaging the reader in this way, Julian's text can therefore be conceived as its own disclosive tool, which the reader can use to assist in their spiritual seeking. As this phrase makes clear, the responsibility of this cocreation lies with the reader as much as the visionary: to interpret the ineffable is a necessarily experimental project, and these epistemological limitations prevent direct communication of Julian's revelation. Just as the devoted Christian is required to perform their part of the compassionate labor of salvation in response to Christ's dying, then, the reader is required to perform their own labor via the act of reading. The text cannot *do* the seeking for them; it merely opens up space, raises questions, and gestures toward answers. It leads the reader to the edge of the revelation, holding a light so that they might peer into its apophatic depths.[169] And so, a crucial part of Julian's task is to find a language that can deliver her reader to this experiential brink: her text must preserve the Derridean "play of signification"—of absence and presence—which Vincent Gillespie and Ross together argue characterizes "the human experience of engagement with the ineffable."[170] In the final section of this chapter, I describe this strategy as it is borne out in Julian's writing as a *mystical poetic*—a strategy that leads the reader into the realm of signification and hints at what might be accessible to those searching in its depths.

MYSTICAL POETICS

In the first chapter of this book, I explored the phenomenological idea of existence as a web of intersubjective meaning. In phenomenological terms, this web is constructed using a shared system of signs known as language: to again quote Heidegger, "Language is the house of being. In its home man dwells."[171] It follows that all lived experience is a text that requires interpretive analysis, as the means through which humans can understand their own being. I have since been arguing for the contemplative epistemology itself as an existential model, wherein Julian's showings "dwell" in her "understondyng," a self-conscious act of interpretation that integrates them into a shared system of language, and which she must then attempt to represent in the visionary text. However, if beholding is not *experience* as such, but a prediscursive *relinquishing* of claims to experience, what kind of language is most suitable for this apophatic project? I have already touched upon the various strategies with which late medieval theologians sought to cross the channel between the prediscursive mind and the realm of discourse. Scholasticism, for example, offered a route to wisdom through reason: language of questioning and debate, which would produce knowledge through logic and ratiocination. The visionary, by contrast, was required to find language that preserved the negative quality of the apophatic experience—the play of signification that leads them beyond intellect and into the unknown.

In the Christian story, language and ontology are connected at the first word: God doesn't think, he *speaks* creation into being. With the arrival of the Word-made-flesh, he then partakes in human being, including language, through the incarnation. Language is also an essential part of the medieval contemplative epistemology, providing an access point to understanding. To further theorize this relationship between language and visionary experience, I here turn to Wolfgang Riehle's writing on mysticism, where he distinguishes mystical language as part of the revelation itself: "If the mystics now frequently use the language of earthly sense perceptions in a spiritual meaning when relating their personal experiences, then it would be wrong . . . to understand and assess this language simply as the use of metaphor in the normal sense of the term, for this is no mere makeshift language but rather one in which the mystical experience itself takes place."[172] This statement supposes that the spiritual senses reveal a supernatural object "as if it were present in some concrete manner," and so Riehle claims that "the language which expresses such experiences is something rather different than mere metaphor."[173] Riehle is here arguing for an internesting of supernatural experience and language, where cognition and language both organize and inform the preconceptual phenomena of visionary experience. In her writing on the poetics of the incarnation, Cristina Maria Cervone summarizes Riehle's argument thus: that "individuals can experience mystical union with God *as metaphorical language*."[174]

On its surface, this idea appears to echo Heidegger's conception of human being's existential discursiveness. For Heidegger, humans exist as discursive beings, which is to say that the meaning of being is disclosed to the person through their participation in what he calls *discourse*. Discourse is one of Heidegger's "existentials," which I mentioned in chapter 1: "*The existential-ontological foundation of language [Sprache] is discourse [Rede]*," he writes in *Being and Time*.[175] It is the primordial "articulation of intelligibility" which "lies at the basis of interpretation and statement" and, moreover, at the basis of meaning. What is articulated in discourse is, in Heidegger's words, "the totality of significations," and the human "attuned intelligibility of being-in-the-world *expresses itself as discourse*."[176] He identifies this expression of discourse as an objective presence in nature and culture, which he calls "*existential language*."[177] This is a seemingly contradictory term that blurs the distinction between discourse as an "existential" and language itself, which Heidegger defines separately. Language is, emphatically, not an existential, even though it is constitutive of the fluency with which humans understand their being-in-the-world. Rather, it is a tool with which this disclosure can be effected. In explaining this, Heidegger cites the Greek definition of human being as *zoon logon echon*, which has been interpreted as the *animal rationale*, the rational being, an unfortunate translation which, Heidegger argues, "covers over the phenomenal basis from which this definition of Dasein is taken": "The human being shows itself as a being who speaks."[178]

Heidegger subsequently distinguishes between discourse itself and the "fundamental structures of the forms and constituents of discourse" that have been developed "following the guideline of *this logos*": linguistics.[179] Grammar, Heidegger writes, "searched for its foundation in the 'logic' of this *logos*," but this logic is "based on the ontology of what is present."[180] He advocates the *freeing* of grammar from logic—that is, the return to discourse as an existential mode. Language, on the other hand, he writes of as "expression" or "what is expressed" (*Ausgesprochenheit*: literally, "spoken-out-ness"): "discourse expresses itself and has always already expressed itself. It is language," he writes.[181] In this sense, language discloses, unconceals, or discovers the discursive meaning—truth—that constitutes being. This is, as Matthew King points out, what Heidegger means when he says that "language is the house of being": "language is being's home, the place where being is allowed to be."[182] As a disclosive tool, then, language can be encountered as something transparent, something to be used without thinking—a phenomenon Heidegger calls *ready-to-handedness*.[183] The inverse, *unready-to-handedness*, defines objects that are no longer phenomenologically transparent, or those things which reveal themselves *as* objects.[184] Perhaps the most famous example of unready-to-handedness is Heidegger's hammer, which is revealed as a hammer only when it breaks: the brokenness of the hammer reveals that the user's experience of the hammer is defined by their everyday engagement with it. The inobtrusiveness of language works in a similar way, facilitating the everyday performance of what Heidegger calls "idle talk," the mode of discourse common to the inauthentic Dasein, who is entangled in, or fallen to, the world.[185] When language becomes an object of analysis—to the literary historian, for example—it is then made obtrusive, as word-things. Language is the means by which discourse is expressed, and like any tool, this expression can fail.

With this in mind, Riehle's notion that mystical experience *is* metaphorical language might be revised in more precise terms. Glossed phenomenologically, the visionary event is disclosed by Julian's discourse, in that she reveals, interprets, or makes intelligible the experience in her self-conscious mind. From the phenomenological perspective, then, mystical experience might be understood as *discourse* rather than language (as spoken discourse). This is a necessary distinction to make, since "*listening* and *silence* are possibilities belonging to discoursing speech," Heidegger writes—possibilities that are not components of language, which in his view is solely speech.[186] Silence can be defined only in relation to its opposite, just as an encounter with the divine can only be expressed in apophatic language: "Authentic silence is possible only in genuine discourse."[187] "One who never says anything is . . . unable to keep silent," Heidegger concludes: "In order to be silent, Dasein must have something to say."[188] Heidegger's assertion that being calls for *saying* also finds expression in Ross's work on contemplation and silence, though she does not make the same distinction as Heidegger between discourse and language: referring only to the latter, she writes that "language feeds silence and silence is a wellspring for language."[189] This is borne out in the interchange between her contemplative epistemologies of the deep mind and the self-conscious mind, where the act of beholding is ultimately an act that restores what Ross calls the "flow" between the two, "*finding the balance between silence and speech.*"[190] This is the nature of spiritual being-in-the-world: an energetic balancing act.

Though Ross's and Riehle's readings of mystical language do integrate the ineffable, the Heideggerian model helps to articulate the negative space that exists beyond or behind language, and which is brought to bear in mystical experience. In these terms, I suggest that genuine mystical discourse can be conceived as the iridescent web of meaning in which all people share, defined by the gaps between each thread as much as the threads themselves.[191] Language, meanwhile, is akin to the material used for each thread, which can be understood either through its production or its use or in terms of its metaphysical qualities. It is only in relation to discourse that language can be understood; meaning emerges at the point of intersection of these graticular crosshairs. Therefore, since this web of discourse encompasses both thread and space—speech and silence—the mystical *poetic*, the linguistic tool or *mene* with which the visionary articulates this discourse, must engage all this multidimensional zone of positive and negative material. Ross writes that "poetry is often the conduit" to this exchange, "because it draws on both ways of knowing simultaneously."[192] Hence the mystical poetic is able to perform the mystical text of the showings by drawing simultaneously on silence and speech—through strategies of apophasis, metaphor, and other figurative expressions. Put another way, the mystical poetic draws attention to its own limitations, speaking about God by acknowledging its incapacity *to* speak about God. This apophatic strategy is inherited from the pseudo-Dionysius, who wrote: "we must not dare to apply words or conceptions to this hidden transcendent God," and yet in the act of worship still "praise it by every name," names which are "fittingly derived from the sum total of creation."[193] Or, in the words of Augustine, "Have I spoken of God, or uttered His praise, in any worthy way? Nay . . . God is not even to be called 'unspeakable,' because to say even this is to speak of Him. Thus there arises a curious contradiction of words, because if the unspeakable is what cannot be spoken of, it is not unspeakable if it can be called unspeakable. *And this opposition of words is rather to be avoided by silence than to be explained away by speech.*"[194] This topos of inexpressibility is borne out, for example, in Julian's account of the pains of the dying Christ that "may not be told."[195] Just as Julian's bodily intentionality ceases to function transparently in sickness, so, too, does language become a stumbling block in her encounter with these pains: language as ready-to-hand becomes unready-to-hand, objectively experienced in its incapacity to serve its purpose.

In the mystical poetic, then, the very unready-to-handedness of language that might otherwise be considered a *disruption* of the existential mode in fact functions as part of its *disclosive* capacity. This reiterates the creative project of the visionary text as one of performance rather than exegesis: a sounding out of the remnants of the revelation in the realm of earthly signs, in which one can only perceive such phenomena through a glass darkly. In this pseudo-Dionysian model, cataphatic and apophatic language act in a mutual relationship, with affirmative statements or descriptions of God collapsing into negation. In linguistic terms, this cataphatic-apophatic dialectic can be described as the disruption of linear or literal sign-signification relations, with truth emerging from the deferral of signification rather than from a closed dyadic sequence. Metaphorical or figurative language facilitates this deferral, with signifying vehicles gesturing beyond their literal meaning to any number of abstract signifieds. Gillespie and Ross call this a "poetics of effacement," which through the interweaving of likeness with otherness, "[offers] mystical writers a means of counteracting the pull of referentiality."[196] With this effacement, the mystical poetic also engages what Cervone describes as "a sort of supereffability," which she defines as "an understanding of sacred fullness enacted through form."[197] Supereffability points, Cervone writes, "to something beyond itself," "[encoding] the expectation that the sought thing cannot be comprehended fully at once in its own nature but must be understood by means of something-it-isn't, expressed in language-it-isn't—perhaps in and through time as a series of something-it-isn'ts."[198] This series of "something-it-isn'ts" then comes together to produce an "eddying back of sense," which Cervone characterizes as an "*Incarnational poetic*," that is, "a vernacular poetics of metaphor triggered by the issue of Incarnation."[199]

This notion of an incarnational poetic serves as a striking point of comparison for what I am calling Julian's mystical poetic, which is similarly rooted in dynamic images which gesture beyond language. Cervone goes on to explain how the incarnational poetic works, showing how by focusing on the moment of connection of human and divine—the hypostatic union—it emphasizes the middle term of the incarnational narrative: the verbal enactment of "the Word *made* flesh."[200] The incarnational poetic, as Cervone understands it, seeks to express this dynamism in language, invoking images and allegories that are verbal and kinetic: "It is no coincidence," Cervone points out, "that these writers incline toward thought experiments that portray emanative activity or organic growth rather than stasis or passivity," since the incarnational poetic complements the "willed, kenotic leaping of love" of the incarnation.[201] She gives the examples of Christ represented as a book or as language; as cloth, clothing, or enwrapment; and as a plant, growth, or life force.[202] All of these images "momentarily reverse 'the Word made flesh' to render Christ's body in figure as something *other than* a human body," a fleeting reversal that in turn "calls attention to the cognitive shift involved in understanding the metaphor."[203] Cervone describes this as a strategy of "making the abstract concrete in order to highlight the abstract."[204]

Similarly, in Julian's mystical poetic, her use of metaphor serves not only to intimate the presence of divinity on earth but also to elevate and redeem experiences of earthly things, while continually deferring interpretation into further abstractions—spiraling ever inward to new understanding. This poetic strategy creates a distinct circling or eddying feel in Julian's prose, which Denys Turner relates to the pseudo-Dionysian spiral, which "moves forward, as one does along a straight line" but "constantly returns to the same point, as one does around a circle."[205] The repetition, Turner writes, "is therefore never identical, for it has always moved on—it has a progressive trajectory, up or down, into higher reaches or greater depth."[206] Julian's showing of the lord and the servant exemplifies this visual hermeneutic, with its tangle of image and typology overlaying creation, fall, and incarnation in a transtemporal tableau. In this lively scene, Julian's circling poetic reifies the Trinity as earthly things: the earth, the plants, the gardener, and so on. The various objects and roles ascribed to each person prevent the reader's interpretation from settling, instead shifting between perspectives and between signifieds. These formal choices draw attention not so much to the objects themselves as their enactive functions: all are located within action-based contexts, with transformational, dynamic purposes of planting, emanative growth, cultivation, and flourishing. Yet each movement is never complete; instead, the earthiness of Julian's language gestures onward toward the next layer of meaning. With this mystical poetic, Julian expresses in language the hermeneutic nonclosure of the showings' discourse: language, the thread of spoken discourse, continually expands the web of meaning without ever reaching completion, drawing the reader into the endless existential cycle of seeking and seeing, beseking and beholding. As Julian writes of her own encounter with Christ: "And thus I saw him and sowte him, and I had him and I wantid hym" (And thus I saw him and sought him, and I had him and I wanted him).[207] Just so, the language of the text draws the reader in, deferring resolution and so sustaining their own desire for understanding.

In this way, Julian's mystical poetic surely evinces Heidegger's argument that language both conceals and reveals.[208] For Heidegger, language should be an unobtrusive medium for communicating discourse, and human dominion over it "merely conceals the uncanniness of language," "holding him [humankind] out of his essence": "How far," Heidegger writes, "man is from *being at home in his own essence* is revealed by his opinion of himself as he who invented and could have invented language and understanding, building and poetry."[209] In this violence of "taming and ordering," Heidegger's human being is "always thrown back on the paths that he himself has laid out . . . He turns round and round in his own circle."[210] This violence "shatters against *one* thing. That is death," the "strange and alien <un-heimlich> thing," which "banishes us once and for all from everything in which we are at home."[211] Mystical language, however, does not presume to have invented the meaning that emerges, nor does it claim dominion over such language: meaning-making in visionary texts is instead the communication of meaning from a divine source. The visionary does so by finding the most appropriate *mene* to gesture toward this divine truth, the elusive point of meaning Jacques Derrida once theorized as the "Transcendental Signified."[212] The hermeneutic circling of the visionary text is not, moreover, broken by the annihilating force of death as in Heidegger's philosophy. Julian's circling, eddying, mystical poetic does not bar humanity from their essence, but asks them to journey inward toward it, reorienting to their "kynde substance." To create this kind of text, the visionary author must themselves negotiate the limitations of language and understanding, for it is these very limitations that will drive the project of contemplation onward.

To conclude, this chapter has examined the protocols of interpretation and representation of Julian's *Revelations*, locating her contemplative epistemology against a backdrop of medieval mystical theology to explore how she herself theorizes "understondyng." To do this, I have carefully navigated Julian's own existential theology, exploring how her theory of knowledge also functions as a theory of human existence, wherein the search for understanding structures human ontology. I identified Julian's hermeneutic markers *beseking* and *beholding* as signifying her internested epistemology of contemplation and revelation. The discussion then compared this cyclical, transcending-returning structure to that of the hermeneutic circle in Heidegger's phenomenology, which he similarly viewed as a fore-structure of human being. Julian's anthropology of the soul and theory of the wills was then introduced to explain how the process of seeking enacts a reorientation to the soul's substance or divine likeness. I here staged a comparison with Langland's *Piers Plowman*, invoking the phrase *kynde knowyng* as an illuminating counterpart to Julian's own use of the term *kynde*, and further to the elusive authentic understanding that is borne out in Heidegger's phenomenology.

In the final two sections of the chapter, I turned to the poetics of Julian's *Revelations*, asking to what extent her texts can successfully communicate the understanding she gleans from the showings to her "even cristen" reader. The concluding discussion invoked Heidegger once more to theorize the poetic and representational challenges of the visionary text. In this last word, I have suggested that Heidegger's theory of language and discourse can help to illuminate the negative protocols of apophatic literature, but that it also insinuates a violence over language that is at odds with Christian mysticism. In this context, death is not the annihilating force of language that Heidegger presumes it to be, and obtrusiveness in language does not necessarily signify a failure of representation. Julian's *Revelations* evidence this clearly: she does not strive for ready-to-hand transparency in her language, instead constructing a mystical poetic that acknowledges the speech/silence paradox of discourse by its very obtrusiveness. In this way, her language provides an access point to divine meaning, constructing threads which may slip from the reader's grasp even while they are drawn further into its web. Julian's mystical poetic therefore both enacts and represents her showings, but does not presume to complete them—a project of interpretation that is deferred to each new reader of her compassionate text.

5

THE CONTEMPLATIVE WAY

The Performance of Prayer and *Homlyhede*

There are many ways to go home; many are mundane, some are divine. My clients tell me these mundane endeavors constitute a return home for them . . . although I caution you, the exact placement of the aperture to home changes from time to time, so its location may be different this month than last. Rereading passages of books and single poems that have touched them. Spending even a few minutes near a river, a stream, a creek. Lying on the ground in dappled light. Being with a loved one without kids around. Sitting on the porch shelling something, knitting something, peeling something. Walking or driving for an hour, any direction, then returning. Boarding any bus, destination unknown. Making drums while listening to music. Greeting sunrise. Driving out to where the city lights do not interfere with the night sky. Praying. A special friend. Sitting on a bridge with legs dangling over. Holding an infant. Sitting by a window in a café and writing. Sitting in a circle of trees. Drying hair in the sun. Putting hands in a rain barrel. Potting plants, being sure to get hands very muddy. Beholding beauty, grace, the touching frailty of human beings.

—Clarissa Pinkola Estés, *Women Who Run with The Wolves*

Reading, rereading, sitting, walking, driving, boarding, making, greeting, praying, holding, drying, putting, potting, *beholding*. This passage by Jungian psychoanalyst and writer Clarissa Pinkola Estés tells of many ways to return home, mundane and divine; there appears to be no quantitative limit to the paths available to the home-seeker.[1] Estés suggests, moreover, that home is not found in the completion of any one project, but in the doing, in the verbal suspension of the now. In this way, these vignettes in motion serve as a reminder: there is a grammar to coming home. This chapter explores how Julian of Norwich suggests her reader might find their way home and the language she uses to describe the journey; it attends to the grammar of homecoming in her *Revelations of Divine Love*. The book's discussion has already shown how homeliness emerges via the act of habitation or dwelling: as Heidegger wrote, "Language is the house of being, in its home man dwells," a statement that tells of both the containing force of language and the transformative power of dwelling.[2] The present chapter now asks: how does Julian's Middle English vernacular contain her existential theology? And how is her reader invited to enter in? I seek to answer these questions by dwelling a while in the house of Julian's language, so to speak, in order to witness the emergence of the home—by considering the ways her lexical, grammatical, and syntactical constructions enact and express her theology of recovery.

To do so, the chapter begins with a close lexicological reading of Julian writing, focusing on her use of the word *homely* and its variations. I first trace the rhetorical amplification of this term throughout Julian's texts—from *homely* to *more homely* to *homeliest*—which I read as subtly charting the contemplative movement inward, into the self and toward God. The discussion then lands on *homlyhede* as a final manifestation of this important term, which I suggest captures grammatically the processual aspect of Julian's existential theology, signifying a homeliness enacted and fulfilled by the human relationship to God. I here reflect on Julian's use of the vernacular of Middle English and the particular lexical opportunities it affords her in developing her theology. Next, the chapter considers how Julian suggests her "even cristen" reader might enact homlyhede through the performance of prayer, a specific form of contemplative seeking which I theorize in phenomenological terms. By again invoking phenomenological thinkers to read Julian's writing on prayer, I delve deeper into the phenomena of spiritual and physical suffering already introduced in chapter 3, now exploring whether prayer can transform a person's subjectivity in ways comparable to experiences of illness. The embodiment of prayer is a significant point of discussion here, and I conclude that the crux of difference between the bodily disruptions of prayer and illness resides in the engagement of the will. With this attention to embodied contemplative practice, the overarching focus of the chapter is on what Philip Sheldrake has called the "practical-pastoral" element of Julian's writing: the suggestions she makes as to how her "even cristen" reader might themselves effect their own recovery or how they might begin their journey home.[3]

HOMELY, HOMELIER, HOMELIEST

The degree to which Julian's text successfully communicates her homely theology is governed by her mystical poetic, which I described in the prior chapter as the discursive expression of visionary experience. But one aspect of Julian's language remains yet unexplored: the system of signs within which she undertakes this representational project, Middle English. Whether Julian had the capacity to write in Latin is uncertain, and so any discussion of Julian's linguistic "choices" is necessarily limited.[4] Nevertheless, the vernacular text has many important features of representation and expression worth investigation. While Germanic in phonology, morphology, and syntax, Middle English has a hybrid vocabulary rich in borrowings and loanwords. In the Heideggerian understanding of language as a tool, this hybridity may be understood as *instrumental* to the disclosive properties of the language at hand, where numerous instruments from multiple linguistic systems and traditions are gathered in one place—constructing in Julian's case what Vincent Gillespie calls her "vast echo chamber of allusion and imitation."[5] This is a chamber in which the speaker is at home: *vernaculus*, meaning "domestic," "indigenous," or "native."[6] But this home is also connected to many other languages, in contact with other vernaculars: while one nation's vernacular may not be the same as another's, it might be argued that the bond of being-at-home presides over both.

The phenomenological view helps to elucidate this condition of linguistic habitation, offering conditions against which the homeliness of the vernacular can be investigated. Phenomenologically speaking, the sense that a language (or indeed anything) is "natural" is only constructed by virtue of it being well-known or conventional to the speaker, characteristics that stem from a process of repetition or reiterative performance. The root of both "native" and "natural," Latin *nātus* (born, made), gestures toward this generative meaning. Julian's vernacular poetics is therefore already grounded in the phenomenological features of the home as defined in chapter 1 of this book: it has a quality of *fluidity*, in the sense of one's primary language requiring no additional degree of cognitive processing with which to access the meaning. The shared dwelling of this language is inhabited *easefully*, allowing for the establishment of a "time-space routine" within it: just as a person extends themselves into the geography of the home, they negotiate the web of discourse, establishing a lived realm or dwelling out of this residence. And by this occupation or habitation, they are made intimately *familiar* with the topography of the language, an orientation that establishes both an affinity and sense of identity with the dwelling. This itself is a kind of mutual indwelling, whereby the speaker *belongs* to the language just as the language *belongs* to them.

In fourteenth-century England, however, vernacularity did not just pertain to linguistic signification; it brought with it a host of historically specific and political concerns. Written English was emerging in this period as a form of theological expression, in the face of increasingly heated political debates about the legitimacy of this medium. The vernacular was thought to be a corruptible vehicle, which would allow old women (*vetula*) to become teachers, and women (*mulierculae*) to talk philosophy and dare to instruct men (as Richard Ullerston reported his opponents arguing during the Oxford translation debates).[7] In his landmark work on vernacular theology, Nicholas Watson has pointed out that "Julian's book provides the most striking confirmation of the worst fears of Ullerston's opponent (and of Hoccleve) over the effects of religious education on women . . . Here is a text in which a woman indeed teaches (and teaches men, among others) and advances, if not heresy, then unusual religious teaching."[8] Indeed, while scholars have highlighted Julian's careful and deliberate distancing of herself from this conversation, others have noted Julian's imaginative approaches to questions of eschatology and soteriology. Justin M. Byron-Davies has, for example, recently suggested that while Julian remains orthodox, her texts do display confluence with Lollard writings around their approach to the apocalypse and in their vernacularity: he concludes that "Julian's decision to write a vernacular, biblically-based text for her evenchristen bears comparison with Wyclif's desire for the Bible to reach the laity."[9] This echoes earlier Protestant readings of Julian that found in her text an affirmation of the Reformation before it happened: as Nancy Bradley Warren observes, the Anglican priest George Hargreaves Parker, who reissued Serenus Cressy's 1670 edition of the *Revelations* in 1843, "does not go so far as to say, as John Foxe does of Chaucer, that Julian was a Wycliffite," but he does suggest "a connection between the two figures," arguing that they "manifest the same truth as Wycliffe's writings." In Parker's words: "The Authoress, a pious recluse of the name of Juliana, was contemporary with Wiclif; it does not however appear that she had any connection with his party; the work before us bears independent witness to the truth."[10]

While Julian's *Revelations* are not of the self-consciously political kind such as those by Bridget of Sweden (d. 1373), Margery Kempe (d. c. 1440), or Elisabeth Barton (d. 1534), by dint of her vernacularity Julian must be positioned if not alongside, then at least proximate to such works. This vernacularity perhaps finds clearest expression in what might be called her theological *communality*—that is, her emphasis on an inclusive readership, extending to "all mankinde that shall be savid," or all Christians who will be redeemed.[11] As Philip Sheldrake writes, Julian is a vernacular theologian "not simply because she used Middle English prose rather than Latin but also because her vision and projected audience is democratic rather than limited to a spiritual or theological elite."[12] Denys Turner, too, ascribes to Julian the role of vernacular, or *demotic*, theologian—a term suggested by Alastair Minnis and deriving from the Greek *dēmotikos*, "popular," from *dēmotēs*, "one of the people."[13] These terms emphasize the communality which lies at the heart of Julian's theological—and linguistic—project. Nevertheless, readings of Julian's vernacular as an explicit or implicit rebellion against clerical or Latinate hegemony must also be approached with caution, for they are dangerously close to those narratives which would romanticize the "Englishness" of Julian's text, and so lay the foundation for a vernacular nostalgia of the kind Sarah Stanbury has warned against.[14] The following discussion seeks to intercept any misrepresentation of Julian's communal language as exalted or politically inflected. Instead, it extends the prior chapter's interpretation of Julian's vernacular as an instrument or tool for her mystical poetic, which she engages for both its limitations and its representational potential.

One distinct feature of this vernacular style is Julian's repeated return to certain key words and syllables, a dwelling-with particular words to expand and disrupt their signification. A similar kind of attentional strategy is described in the *Cloud of Unknowing* (c. 1375), where the author asks the reader to

> take thee bot a litil worde of o silable; for so it is betir then of two, for ever the schorter it is, the betir it acordeth with the werk of the spirite. And soche a worde is this worde *God* or this worde *love*. Cheese thee whether thou wilt, or another as thee list: whiche that thee liketh best of o silable. And fasten this worde to thin herte, so that it never go thens for thing that bifalleth.[15]

> take for yourself just a little word of one syllable; this is better than two, because the shorter it is the better it agrees with the work of the spirit. And just such a word is the word "*God*" or this word "*love*." Choose however you will, or another as you like: whichever you like best of one syllable. And fasten this word to your heart, so that it will never go from it for any reason.

With single-pointed meditation on this one-syllable word, the chosen word will paradoxically break apart and its associated meanings will begin to dissolve. The seed syllable is dilated both phonetically and semantically, so as to draw the contemplative into its truest expression of divinity: a pseudo-Dionysian spiraling back to the "poynte." Then, as the *Cloud*-author describes, language may begin to fall away, leaving the contemplative in a state of blind gazing on the being of God. Textually, this monosyllabic repetition is not, as Eleanor Johnson points out, available in many Latin constructions.[16] Johnson argues that the "atomic style" of the *Cloud*-author—the expressions "God, God, God" and "love, love, love"—would be "ruined" if the poem were composed in Latin.[17] The same might be argued for Julian, whose statement on God's meaning would lose its one-pointedness if rendered in Latin: "Wete it wele: love was his mening. Who shewid it the? Love. What shewid he the? Love. Wherfore shewid it he? For love" (Know it well: love was his meaning. Who showed it to you? Love. What did he show you? Love. Why did he show it to you? For love).[18] Who, what, wherefore: all is for *love*, the word driving the syntax onward even as it recapitulates the point of the passage.

To turn to the particular word that is the focus of this chapter: Julian uses the term *home* and its grammatical variations nearly thirty times in the long text (compared with six in the short text), adapting and expanding this seed syllable in new and unexpected ways. A brief etymological analysis of the word will shed light on these innovations as they relate to both the mystical event and Julian's wider theology, the latter of which I will then explore in further detail. The core meaning of the term has not changed a great deal between medieval and modern usage: the headword *hōm** derives from the Old English *hām* and refers to a geographical place of dwelling. The various forms the word takes, however, express a number of historically specific meanings: Julian's favored adjectival form *hōmlī*, for example, is glossed by the *MED* as follows:

> 1. (a) used at home; characteristic of a home; ~medicine, household remedy; (b) pertaining or belonging to a household, domestic; ~chirche, a church in one's house; ~fo, an enemy in one's own house; ~heue (hine, man), a household servant; ~meinee, members of one's family or household; *fig.* God's servants; ~womman, a female servant; *fig.* an anchorite; (c) as a noun: members of one's family or household; *fig.* the disciples of Christ; (d) native, indigenous; (e) of sections of anatomical parts or bodily organs: inner, interior.[19]

While the term indicates a variety of uses in both secular and religious contexts, this adjective locates the quality of homeliness as emerging from a relationship between subject and object: a servant is homely with God, with the master of the house, or, as a disciple, with Christ. Furthermore (and the last sense here alludes to this most clearly), the homely is implicitly connected to that which is *bodily*, or *of the flesh*: that which is *closest* or *most interior* to a person. Homeliness is defined as a condition that arises through interrelation, dialogue, and embodiment—distinctly phenomenological qualities of being-in-the-world.

The attestations offered in the *MED* demonstrate the fairly standard usage of the term in texts contemporary to Julian, which may have influenced her own vocabulary. Notable instances from or after the turn of the fifteenth century include the Middle English rule for anchorites *Ancrene Riwle* (a. 1400), which uses the term to describe an anchoritic woman: "Þe fende scheteþ mo querels to homelich wymmen þan to an hundreþ leuedies in þe werlde" (The devil thrusts more complaints onto homely women [i.e., anchorites] than to a hundred laypeople in the world).[20] The anonymous Middle English poem, *Pearl* (c. 1400), meanwhile describes how "he gef uus to be His homly hyne" (he [God] gives [also: grants] us to be [also: gives to us] His homely household), while *The Chastising of God's Children* (c. 1390s) also has "þe cause of chaungyng of suche affeccioun is to moche famuliarite, as for to be to homly" (the cause of the changing of such affection is too much familiarity, as when being too homely).[21] In a secular context, Thomas Hoccleve's *Series* (c. 1420), quoted in the introduction to this book, offers a resonant use of the home as a psycho-spiritual metaphor for his recovery, describing the peregrinations of his itinerant wits during his mental illness and their subsequent return home to him: "my wit / wer hoom come ageyn" (my wits had come home again).[22]

Prior to 1400, however, fewer instances of the term survive. Richard Rolle's *Psalter* (roughly dated to the decades before his death in 1349) features it a handful of times, though more examples can be found in Wycliffite texts, particularly in the variant "homelynesse."[23] The later version of the Middle English Bible (c. 1395) in Oxford, New College MS 66 (a. 1450), for example, has "hooly homelynesse in byleeue profitith to him silf aloone" (holy homeliness in belief is a profit to himself alone), where "homelynesse" replaces "cherlhed" (Latin: *rusticitas*) in the earlier version.[24] Whether or not Julian would have had access to such texts remains unclear. Regarding a Middle English Bible, Georgia Ronan Crampton, editor for the TEAMS edition of Julian's *Shewings*, is doubtful: "Though she [Julian] might have used a Wycliffite translation, her wording is not close to the only ones known to have been in circulation in her time. Other possibilities are a Wycliffite Bible unknown to us or an Anglo-French translation."[25] Crampton cites Colledge and Walsh's conclusion that "her own translating is most probable," arguing that Julian's work is "consistent with Biblical familiarity through hearing and quotation from memory."[26] Annie Sutherland also points out that "Julian's words do not *exactly reproduce* those of the Vulgate" and there is no evidence of her accessing a biblical translation.[27] Nevertheless, the above instances do indicate a lively vernacular poetics of the home in the late fourteenth-century imaginary, against which Julian's own unique rendering of this lexis can be located.

Pressing into this vernacular context also sheds light on the ways the homely poetic functions as a grammatical map for a genre of progressive piety common to contemplative texts of this period. One strategy of this genre is that of rhetorical amplification or *amplificatio*, where a condition or task is given in degrees or stages through which the contemplative could move, ascending the figurative ladder of devotion. A triadic progression of this kind can be identified in part 6 of the *Ancrene Wisse*, quoted in chapter 1, which describes three models for the anchorite to follow: the pilgrim, the dead, and the sufferer on the cross.[28] St. Julian is invoked in relation to the first state: the pilgrim, the home-seeker who traverses the earthly realm in pursuit of true rest.[29] In this text, each state functions as a stage in this life of seeking: as Rosanne Gasse writes, these degrees function as "a set of stairs the anchorite climbs, each step upward being a move toward perfection."[30] Other such amplifications can be found across the writings of Richard Rolle, Walter Hilton, and the *Cloud*-author—texts often positioned as conversation partners with Julian in modern readings of the English contemplative canon.

Perhaps the most famous contemporary grammatical triad of this sort, however, can be found in William Langland's late fourteenth-century dream-vision poem, *Piers Plowman* (c. 1370–1390). Here, the dreamer Will seeks, as well as the mysterious

Piers, the allegorical characters "Dowel," "Dobet," and "Dobest," the precise meaning of which has frequently eluded critical consensus. One reading by John A. Alford conceives of this allegorical schema as its own progressive ascent, where Will is driven by a desire to obtain "more kynde knowynge" of Dowel.[31] This sequence represents, Alford writes, "that of the learning process," whereby "Wit (native intelligence)" is joined with "Study (*studium*, application)," which leads to "Clergy (learning)," which "resides with Scripture (books, writing)," and all of these contribute to "Imaginatif (prudential judgment)."[32] As Alford points out, however, Will becomes more confused the further he proceeds, and "neither learning nor Dowel appears to be crucial to salvation."[33] After the abrupt end of the poem's A-version, Alford observes that the "dream-within-a-dream" of the B-continuation suspends the main action to allow for the resolution of this conundrum: "Up to this point," Alford writes, "he [Will] has conducted the search for Dowel as if it could be known without being lived."[34] Will's journey "has been marked repeatedly by conflict between the intellect and the will, by the dreamer's refusal to accept what his reason was telling him."[35] I discussed this progression in the previous chapter, where I examined *kynde knowyng* as encompassing knowledge of an experience and its opposite, or the full spectrum of lived experience. The same distinction might be made here: as the inner dream of *Piers Plowman* shows with its emphasis on fear and shame, the affective part of the soul is "an essential partner in the intellect's search for Dowel."[36] Indeed, the affect may supersede the intellect: as Ralph Hanna argues, "the insistent association of Piers with 'kynde knowyng' presupposes the non-institutional power of the individual to access, understand, and actuate God's law," situating learned knowledge as "potentially unnecessary to Christian action or salvation, open to all."[37] Will has to *live* Dowel, not simply *know* it.

Julian's contemplative path to recovery follows a similar route, progressing into and through the showings with an accompanying amplification of homeliness, from a "ghostly sight of his *homely* loveing" (spiritual vision of his *homely* love) in chapter 5, to one which is "*more homley*" in chapter 6, and finally in chapter 67, the soul finds a dwelling in "his *homliest* home."[38] Beginning with the first form of this grammatical triad, it is worth noting the shifting of gravity between the worldly and the heavenly that revolve around this rhetorical axis. In chapter 4, for instance, Julian tells of her astonishment that God would be "*so homely* with a synfull creture liveing in wretched flesh" (*so homely* with a sinful creature living in wretched flesh).[39] This observation appears amid Julian's description of the "bodily" part of the first showing: the crown of thorns. "In this same time," however, she is shown a "ghostly sight of his homely loveing": the showing of the "littil thing, the quantitye of a hesil nutt" (little thing, the quantity of a hazelnut).[40] This shift from bodily to ghostly showing is made more explicit in the longer version of the text than in the short: where in the shorter version the pseudo-hazelnut showing is accompanied by the annunciation sequence, a pairing that lends weight to the "erthelye besynes" (earthly business) and immanence of God's love, the longer version shifts the image of the annunciation to the previous chapter.[41] In place of this, Julian emphasizes the spiritual relationship between the soul and God: removing the opening reference to the former "bodily sight" of the garland of thorns, she inserts more phrases of comprehension—she looks "with eye of [her] understondyng" (with the eye of [her] understanding), and she is "answered in

[her] understondyng"—thereby drawing the focus toward her spiritual exegesis of the anthropological schema of indwelling.[42] Indeed, after her ensuing description of the "iii properties" of the soul ("that God made it," "that God loveth it," and "that God kepith it"), she then expounds upon the proximity of the soul to God: "For, till I am substantially onyd to him, I may never have full rest ne very blisse; that is to sey, that I be so festined to him that there is right nowte that is made betwix my God and me" (For, until I am substantially united to him, I may never have total rest nor total bliss; that is to say, until I am so fastened to him that there is entirely nothing of creation between my God and me).[43] She details how this might be achieved by seeking knowing of God, "for he is the very rest": only when the soul noughts "all things that is made" can it receive this "ghostly rest."[44] Finally, Julian adds that "it is full gret plesance to him that a sely soule come to him nakedly, and pleynly, and *homely*" (it is a great pleasure to him when a simple soul comes to him nakedly, and plainly, and *homely*), a statement that reiterates the homely progression as a return: a stripping down of the soul of its worldly excesses, to its most natural or "kindly" state.[45]

The long text's version of these two chapters thus performs a movement of "supereffability," to again invoke Cristina Maria Cervone's term, describing "sacred fullness enacted through form."[46] Julian first establishes a sense of God's presence in the physical realm—his *lively* presence, as she puts it—through the images of Christ's garland of thorns and the immaculate conception. Indeed, it is Christ's bleeding head that will provide the most visceral descriptions in the *Revelations*. She then moves from a description of the homely qualities of the flesh to the more abstract, spiritual manifestations of his love, performing a cataphatic-apophatic maneuver where the circular crown of thorns becomes the "littil thing," which, "round as a balle," encompasses all of creation.[47] But Julian goes one step further: just as she holds this "in the palme of [her] hand," God holds creation in his "homely loveing" (homely love), like "clotheing" (clothing) which "wrappith" (wraps), "halsyth" (embraces), and "beclosyth us, hangeth about us for tender love" (encloses us, hanging around us for tender love).[48] In this sequence of internested enclosures, Julian circles from the physical to the abstract, and finally back to the physical, with God's love reified as wrapping cloth. I have already discussed the function of the circle within Julian's hermeneutic strategy: meaningful in the perpetuity of its circumference rather than solely in its signification of "das punt," as Meister Eckhart says. The circling poetic here makes manifest the same contemplative principle: later, in the eighth showing, the garland will be coated with blood, "as it were garland upon garland," constructing another imagined stratification or layering of circles, this time of Christ's lifeblood.[49] The circles are collected one upon the other in an active sequence of layering, emphasizing—as in Cervone's incarnational poetic—the eternal dynamism of the mutual indwelling of God and humanity, via the homely paradox of concurrent stripping and enwrapment.

The second term in Julian's triad of amplification arrives in chapter 6 of the long text, where she integrates both bodily and ghostly showings of God's love in the image of his goodness, which "comith downe to us to the lowest party of our nede" (comes down to us to the lowest part of our need), "quickyth our soule and bringith it on life, and makyth it for to waxen in grace and vertue" (enlivening our soul and bringing it to life, and making it grow in grace and virtue).[50] Julian describes this goodness as "nerest in kind and redyest in grace" (nearest in nature and readiest in grace),

> For as the body is cladde in the cloth, and the flesh in the skyne, and the bonys in the flesh, and the herte in the bouke, so arn we, soule and body, cladde in the goodnes of God and inclosyd. Ya, and more homley, for all these may wasten and weren away. The godenes of God is ever hole . . .[51]

> For as the body is clad in the cloth, and the flesh in the skin, and the bones in the flesh, and the heart in the book, so are we, soul and body, clad in the goodness of God and enclosed. Yes, and more homely, for all of these may waste and wear away. The goodness of God is ever whole . . .

This passage underscores the figurative progression that has played out in the last two chapters of the *Revelations*: from that which is homely in the physical world (the body in relation to clothes, the flesh to skin, the bones to flesh, etc.) to the comparative homeliness of the soul to God, which is *more* homely than these fleshly parallels. The comparison thus serves not only as rhetorical amplification, but as a reminder of the transfiguration and "quickening" the soul must undergo to know God and to fully find rest. With this spiritual or anthropological amplification, Julian shows how God's goodness supplies the soul with a sense of homeliness if it directs itself away from worldly things and comes to him plainly in beseking. Which is to say: while the fugitive, homeless soul is eternally rest*less*, the soul-at-home has attained the condition of rest*ful*ness. Just as with Will and Dowel, the soul must *seek* homeliness, not just know it.

Finally, it is with Julian's description of the sixteenth showing in chapter 67 of the long text, of the soul as the "blisfull kyngdom" (blissful kingdom) of God, that the superlative manifestation of the homely amplification can be located: "his *homliest* home."[52] Here, Julian's "gostly eye" (spiritual eye) is opened, and she witnesses "the soule so large as it were an endles world" (so large as if it were an endless world), a "worshipful syte" (worshipful sight) where Christ sits in the "midds" (middle).[53] The linguistic play on sight/site here reiterates the locative aspect of the passage, at once invoking the homeliness of the showing (the sight) itself—the time and space of her beholding—as well as the visual of a kingdom within the heart (the site). In this way, the sight of Julian's beholding encloses her within a dwelling immense enough to permeate the boundary of heaven and earth, which then creates another level of layered indwelling: the *site* of the soul-kingdom dwells within Julian's ghostly *sight*, while Jesus dwells within the *city*. Here "is his very wonyng; and the heyest lyte and the brightest shynyng of the cite is the glorious love of our Lord, as to my syte" (is his very dwelling; and the highest light and the brightest shining of the city is the glorious love of our Lord, as to my sight), Julian writes.[54] Superlatives litter this chapter, with Christ appearing as "heyest bishopp, solemnest kinge, worshipfulliest lord" (highest bishop, most solemn king, most worshipful lord) who dwells "in the worthyest place" (the worthiest place).[55] Accordingly, Julian concludes the chapter with her statement regarding the perfection of the soul: "For I saw in the same shewing that if the blisfull Trinite myte have made mannys soule ony better, ony fairer, ony noblyer than it was made, he shuld not have be full plesid with the makyng of mannys soule" (For I saw in the same showing that if the blissful Trinity might have made man's soul any better, any fairer, any nobler than it was made, he should not have been full pleased with the making of man's soul).[56] The soul is so perfect in its creation that it is the site of Christ's "*homliest home* and his endles wonyng" (homeliest home and endless union [also: dwelling]).[57]

Chapter 67 therefore reaches a textual climax, both in its conclusion of the sixteen showings and in its showing of the perfection of the soul: its "onyng" (or "wonyng") with Christ. Julian's recent editors, Nicholas Watson and Jacqueline Jenkins, gloss this vision as representative of "the New Jerusalem of Rev. 21:1–27, as represented in contemporary art and poems such as *Pearl* or *The Pricke*, where the vision of God 'es mast joy' of the city of heaven, a city 'so large and wide' it has space for all the saved, all of whom can nonetheless clearly see 'the face of God allemighty.'"[58] Watson and Jenkins also note that this image of heart-dwelling can be found in *Piers Plowman*, in which Piers tells the pilgrims that if they search diligently for Truth, they will find him in their own hearts: "Thou shalt se in thiselve Truth sitte in thin herte, / In a cheyne of charite, as thou a child were . . . , / To suffren him and segge nought ayein thy sires wille" (You shall see in yourselves Truth sitting in your own heart / In a chain of charity, as if you were a child . . . , / To suffer him and say nothing against your lord's will).[59] This parallel highlights how in the progressive poetic, images of interior enclosure or indwelling mark the fulfillment of the soul/pilgrim/dreamer's seeking: the end of the sowing and setting, digging and delving, that effortful process of making the soul a perfect dwelling-place for the divine and finding its perfect dwelling in God.

Finally, the sense of culmination and fulfillment of Julian's *Revelations* comes to a head in an alternative iteration of the homely poetic: "*full homely.*"[60] This expression is found in chapter 12 of the long text, where Julian recounts the sight of the scourging of Jesus and the spilling of his blood:

> And than cam to my minde that God hath made waters plentivous in erthe to our service and to our bodily ease, for tender love that he hath to us, but yet lekyth him better that we take full homely his blissid blode to washe us of synne; for there is no licor that is made that he lekyth so wele to give us; for it is most plentivous as it is most pretious, and that be the vertue of his blissid Godhede.[61]

> And then it came to my mind that God has made plenteous waters on earth for our service and for our bodily ease, for the tender love that he has for us, but yet it pleases him better that we take full homely his blessed blood to wash us of sin; for there is no liquid that is made that pleases him so well to give us; for it is most plenteous as it is most precious, by the virtue of his blessed Godhead.

While the manuscript witnesses do not greatly differ in their representations of Julian's homely poetic, this is one instance of textual *mouvance* where meaning is gently pulled in different directions: where Sloane has "full homely," Paris has "*full holsomly*," which is retained in Watson and Jenkins's edition and expanded from "we take fullye" in the short text.[62] Watson and Jenkins point out that this passage bears similarities to Richard Rolle's meditations on Christ's body as a meadow "ful of swete flouris and *holsum* herbis" (full of sweet flowers and *wholesome* herbs).[63] The "licor" referred to here certainly invokes the liquor of medicine, as well as that of the sacramental wine, both of which—like Rolle's "holsum herbis"—are conducive to good health. Yet considering Julian's extended association of *homeliness* with *wholeness* and indeed *health*, I read the "full homely" of the Sloane manuscript as a similarly therapeutic expression. Moreover, "full homely," in Julian's usage, has the double meaning of taking Christ's blood close to, or indeed *into* the body, and the notion that this act of taking will provide full wholeness, holiness, or health. This soteriological moment is taken further when, two chapters later, Julian describes her lord as hosting his "derworthy frends *ful homeley* and ful curtesly" (deserving friends with *great homeliness* and courteousness).[64] Fullness in these instances suggests a capacity of/for homeliness, in both humanity's dealings with Christ and Christ's dealings with humanity. When the soul reaches its fullness or fulfillment—its "fulhede"—it will finally be "reysid above the depeness of the erth and al vayne sorows, and enjoyen in him" (raised above the deepness of the earth and all vain sorrows, and enjoying in him), the worthiest, brightest, highest, and homeliest home in which God can dwell.[65]

PERFORMING *HOMLYHEDE*

The final variant of the term *home* Julian deploys is *homlyhede* (also: *homlihede*), a word she uses to describe the condition the soul aspires to with its beseking. By examining the specific grammar of this term in this section, I aim to highlight the strikingly phenomenological features of Julian's contemplative theology, which emerge through her use of language as part of her overarching vision of recovery. On its surface, *homlyhede* denotes the intimacy of the soul with God—and in its furthest extension, the ultimate contemplative goal of *unio mystica* or mystical union. This formulation is not entirely Julian's own: contemporary literature also uses the homely lexis as a vernacular translation of the *familiaritas cum Deo* motif, the process of becoming familiar with God, which Wolfgang Riehle observes manifests in Middle English with "the more concrete Germanic words *homli* or *homlihed* and *homlines*."[66] The homely poetic also appears in Walter Hilton's (d. 1396) *Eight Chapters on Perfection* as a direct synonym for mystical union: "whanne his soule is ooned with Crist, and right hoomli with him" (when his soul is united with Christ, and truly homely with him).[67] Such "oneing" or *unio* is the highest point of contemplation following the spiritual ascent of the *Scala paradisi*, at which point the soul meets the divine. But Hilton's schema does not allow for this union of homeliness—for the recovery of the soul's connection to God—while the soul remains on earth. As I will show, Julian's iteration of this poetic meanwhile offers a rather more optimistic picture.

While Hilton describes the process of mystical union as an ascent in line with the rhetorical amplifications above, his homely poetic grounds the process more explicitly as a journey *in* and *through* the world: specifically, as a pilgrimage to New Jerusalem (which, I would note, translates to *place of peace*, from the Western Semitic **uru*, "house," "town," and **salim*, either "peace" or "Shalim"). The itinerancy of this state of seeking recalls Gabriel Marcel's *homo viator* that I quoted in chapter 1: the Odyssean conception of life as a pilgrimage.[68] In Hilton's Augustinian story, however, the perceived difference between God the "unmade" creator and the soul that is still "made" (though made from that which is "unmade") precludes any kind of complete union occurring on earth. This rests on the problem of the soul's fragmentation following the fall, which continually leads the soul away from the divine and toward sin. Humanity has, as John Trevisa's (a. 1387) translation of Ranulf Higden's *Polychronicon* attests, lost its primordial "homlynesse": "Man in his bygynnynge . . . fel . . . out of homlynesse [Higden: familiaritate] into offence and wreþþe" (Man in his beginning . . . fell . . . out of homeliness into offence and wrath).[69] Even Eckhart, whose writing on this point has exposed him to accusations of pantheism, maintains that the soul and God do not completely fuse in *unio mystica*: "God is in the soul, but only in so far as he mirrors himself into it."[70] Consequently, the journey home—the pilgrimage to New Jerusalem, as Hilton, among others, would put it—is never truly fulfilled as long as a person lives; they can be familiar with him in this life, but never entirely "oned" with God.

For Julian, while humanity remains distinct from God, the ontological union of the "substance" with the divine suggests that a degree of homeliness can be achieved in this life. Or rather, she suggests that the soul is *already* at home, or "oned" to God, on account of his grace: a state which can then be fulfilled through the act of beseking.[71] To return to the pilgrimage analogy, homeliness can be found along the pilgrim's road, rather than only at their destination. There is an important distinction to be made, then, in the theoretical lexis of the present study: between the phenomenological concept of home*like*ness derived from Heidegger and Julian's concept of homlyhede. The distinction rests on the figurative and philosophical mechanics of each term. For Heidegger, homelikeness (*heimlichkeit*), emerges as an attunement against a background of nothingness; in this context, Dasein can therefore only ever experience something *like* a home, since its base ontic state is homelessness. This is where the Heideggerian projection ends; there is no affirmative teleology in Heidegger's analogy. Julian's theological frame meanwhile provides a different opportunity for homeliness, since she understands the base human state as always and already at home with God in some degree. In chapter 1, I discussed

Julian's understanding of the postlapsarian state as akin to Augustine's *regio dissimilitudinis*, the region of unlikeness of the fallen world. Theorizing Julian's use of *homlyhede* in these terms highlights a different analogous horizon to the phenomenological model, where the ontic baseline is already affirmative, and home-loss has been incurred through the human fall into sin. Put another way: where for Heidegger humanity creates something like a home against a background of nothing, Julian understands the home to be the originary state of the soul, which has only been distorted by the fall.

Despite the significance of this term, however, *homlyhede* has been frequently transcribed or translated out of existence in versions of Julian's *Revelations*—a scribal and editorial practice of modernization which, as my discussion aims to show, flattens not only the aesthetic expression of Julian's text but its theological meaning, too. Watson and Jenkins observe linguistic variance between the Paris and Sloane witnesses' use of the *-hede* suffix generally: where *-hede* is retained throughout Sloane, they note, Paris typically renders it *-nes(se)*.[72] This is an unfortunate editorial decision that persisted into print: the first printed edition of Julian's text produced by Serenus Cressy in 1670 also transcribes *homlyhede* as "homeliness."[73] Even Watson and Jenkins's synthetic edition, which they justify as a reflection of the diversity of written forms and culture of "textual *mouvance*," does not offer any theological interpretation for Julian's diverse and recurrent use of the *-hede* suffix.[74] Yet a closer look at the dialectical and grammatical features of the suffix reveals that the *homlyhede* construction is essential to Julian's theology—and so, I suggest, likely her own linguistic choice.[75] For one thing, the *-hede* suffix carries with it specific connotations of participation absent in its Middle English alternative, *-nesse*. The latter is commonly attached to an adjective, sometimes to form a noun, and generally signifying, as in modern usage, a quality or condition of a thing.[76] Trevisa, for instance, frames "homlynesse" as a condition of *familiaritate*.[77] This is, of course, retained in modern English: the *OED* glosses *-ness* as a formation of "abstract nouns from adjectives, participles," and so on.[78] Julian's preferred suffix *-hede*, however, is a term which most commonly features in composition with a noun as a simplex, denoting a role, rank, or position.[79] The *OED* offers a similar definition for the modern derivative, *-hood*, glossing the original form as a "distinct noun" meaning "person, personality, sex, condition, quality, rank."[80] While *-nesse* indicates, then, a quality or approximation of a thing, *-hede* suggests a participatory condition: indeed, a communal condition, shared by a collective or group of people.

As such, I read Julian's invocation of *homlyhede* as more specific than the generalized sense of potency which the suffix *-nesse* affords. While *-nesse* denotes a condition of a state of *being*—a characterization of a specific element in a person/thing's ontic state (its *haecceitas* or "thingliness")—the *-hede* variant offers a simplex for a person/thing's *capacity*. This sense of a capacity/role reiterates Julian's performative anthropology: according to Julian's model, human essence or "thisness" emerges out of active engagement with the world; humans discover the "divine likeness" of their "kynde substance" (the "*thisness*" of their existence) through the process of seeking or being-toward-God. Similarly, since God's essential nature or being cannot be known, humanity can only come to some knowledge of him through his workings or energies: through the "Godhede," a perichoretic reference to the work or operations of the Trinity. According to Gregory of Nyssa, this term "Godhead" refers solely to the divine operation of seeing or beholding, as "His nature cannot be named and is ineffable. We say that every name, whether invented by human custom or handed down by the Scriptures, is indicative of our conceptions of the divine nature, but does not signify *what that nature is in itself*."[81] In other words, the Godhead is made known to humanity only via the hypostatic union of the incarnation.[82] As Julian herself articulates, coming to know the soul's divine aspect is a similarly ineffable pursuit and is similarly bound up in the energetic presencing of its nature: just as the "Godhede" is made known by the workings of the Trinity, human homlyhede with God is made known via the lived pursuit, or beseking of him.

Homlyhede denotes, then, a way of living I have been describing phenomenologically as being-toward-God: a recognition and sustained understanding of the human condition, combined with an active directedness toward the divine and so toward wholeness. Consider Julian's use of the suffix elsewhere: *fulhede*, *hardhede*, *roundhede*, *plentioushede*, *lordhede*, *heyhede*, *kinghede*, *faderhede*, and, of course, *moderhede*. These choice instances give an impression of the enactive quality of each term: those used to describe Christ's blood in chapter 7 of the long text, for instance, function as a kind of wordplay on "the plentious bledeing of the *hede*."[83] The dripping of the blood fulfills its *plentioushede*, the spreading its *roundhede*, both of which are reiteratively accreted as she circles around the *forehede*. Each *-hede* word is, significantly, likened by Julian to a domestic image: the *roundhede* of the pellots to "the scale of heryng" (scales of the herring), the *plentioushede* of the spreading on the *forehede* to the "dropys of water that fallen of the evys after a great showre of reyne" (drops of water that fall off the eaves after a great shower of rain).[84] Finally landing on "plentioushede inumerable" (plenteousness innumerable), the spiraling amplification collapses and Julian falls back on paradox: "This shewing was quick and lively, and hidouse and dredfull, swete and lovely" (The showing was swift and vivid, and hideous and frightening, sweet and lovely); and God who is "so reverent and dredefull" (so mighty and awe-inspiring) is also "so homley and curtes" (so familiar and courteous).[85] The dynamic bleeding of the *hede* in this passage acts as an analog to the performance of homlyhede, and offers a *mene* by which the reader might access it, opening them up to their own compassionate, enactive participation in this homely project.

Unlike the phenomenological condition of homelikeness, then, Julian's homlyhede draws together her existential framework with an optimistic model of compassionate recovery through contemplation on Christ. In Julian's theology, humankind remains essentially united to God, and so can reorient toward homeliness by the exercise of redirecting their attention and action to God. By pursuing this way of living—this being-toward-God—they can make themselves receptive to God's gift, which is to redeem, indeed remold, the distorted soul back to its *imago Dei*, which has been warped out of shape by generations of inherited sin. Moreover, for Julian, redirecting the soul to God is a collective vocation: to realize the *kin*ship of human*kind*, so as to heal the communal body of all "even cristen." In this sense, the collective identity of Christians is defined through compassionate withness, a joint project that will facilitate the fulfillment, the *fulhede*, of its very potential. Julian presents a communal way of being-with, or identifying with the world: an opportunity for a collective identity based, fundamentally, on love.

THE POROSITY OF PRAYER

The discussion so far has defined beseking as an existential mode or condition of human nature, characterized by a conscious redirection of intention and worldly living toward God. I have been arguing that *homlyhede* emerges of the same enactive process: that just as Langland's Will must seek Dowel, Julian proposes that the soul must seek homlyhede through their way of living. I therefore position homlyhede and beseking as mutually constitutive conditions of being-toward-God. As with *homlyhede*, however, many modern editions of Julian's *Revelations* translate *beseking* as its modern cognate *beseeching* (to seek after, search for, try to get, to seek to know), an editorial decision that silences not only Julian's dialectal voice but also some of the more subtle theological currents of her writing.[86] To fully theorize Julian's contemplative model then—that is, the framework she offers her reader for their recovery—this term must be equally carefully considered for its linguistic and historical specificity. By doing so, a more thorough distinction can be drawn (already introduced in chapter 3 of this book) between Julian's devotional model of contemplative prayer and the more ascetic model of purgation which makes use of the generative sides of pain.

Beseeching is a prefixed form of the Old English *sēčan* (to seek or inquire about) from around 1200, often used to denote an act of petition or prayer. The *OED* notes that the *seek* in *beseking* displaced the southern *seech* in the simple verb, while in contrast, the modern *beseeching* retains the southern form. A search in the electronic *Linguistic Atlas of Late Mediaeval English* affirms this north/south variance in the *k* and *ch* forms of the verb: a dot-map fit for the *k* forms of *beseking* and *seeking* shows a cluster of matching linguistic profiles in the east and northeast of England, concentrated around the East Anglian and East Midlands border.[87] As such, any translation or glossing of *beseke-* as *beseech* imposes a false dissociation between Julian's two terms, *seke* and *beseking*, both of which are common to her dialect.

But more is lost in modern translations of this term than simple dialectal expression. As with *homlyhede*, Julian uses *beseking* to denote a specific enaction of seeking: the performance, or realization of the soul's capacity to seek God. The prefix *be-*, the *MED* states, is used to form transitive verbs from simple transitives, "usually with intensive, completive, or figurative meaning(s)," with *bisēchen* cited as a form inherited from Old English.[88] Similarly, the *OED* cites the original meaning of *be-* as "about" or "around" in its various senses, such as "bespeak" (speak about), or "beset" (encompass), in which the notion of "all round" naturally intensifies the sense of the verb.[89] So, while the transitive *seek* (i.e., "seke him") denotes the directedness of the soul *toward* God, the intensive be*seking* focuses the act of seeking *around* or *about* God, or specifically *concerning* God. In addition to the usage of *beseking* as a verb, however, what is equally (if not more) significant is Julian's use of the term as a gerund. The *MED* defines the gerund *bisēchinge* as "(a) Entreaty, supplication, prayer, intercession, or an instance of it; (b) *law* a petition or plea."[90] Prefixed in this way, *beseking* functions as a noun, denoting the objective *act* of seeking God. A person doesn't only *beseke* at/toward the grammatical object—"we shuld besekyn mercy and grace" (we should beseek mercy and grace); "thou besekyst it" (you beseek it)—but *beseking* also becomes a verbal noun, and importantly, a collective project: "*our besekyng.*"[91]

The translation of *beseking* as *beseeching* confines the term to the category of petitionary prayer. This is an understandable editorial decision in some ways, given that Julian does use the term in chapters 41 to 43 of the long text to outline the power of prayer and its effect on the soul. Prayer, Julian writes, makes the soul "supple and buxom to God" (flexible and obedient to God), which leads to the union of the soul with the divine.[92] Yet with these grammatical points in mind, Julian's definition of prayer does not seem limited to a sense of supplication or petition, but rather to increased porosity and unification—that is, the catalyzing force of the dynamic balancing and rebalancing of the human relationship to God. Paul Molinari calls this "*unitive* prayer" rather than petitionary prayer, while Philip Sheldrake refers to Julian's treatment of prayer as "fundamentally relational rather than instrumental."[93] In my view, it is both: relational, in that it does indeed describe "our life-long relationship with God and God's relationship with us," and instrumental in that it *discloses* this relationship.[94] It is on account of this linguistic movement that Julian is able to report in chapter 41 that "our besekyng is not cause of the goodnesse and grace that he doyth to us" (our beseeking is not the cause of the goodness and grace that he does to us), but that God himself has proclaimed, "I am ground of thi besekyng" (I am the ground of your beseeking).[95] God is the ontological foundation of the soul, including its capacity for seeking, and so is also the foundation of beseking.

In my reading, Julian's iteration of *beseking* as prayer refers to the dynamic fulfillment of the human relationship with God. This practice is driven by desire, which Julian describes as stemming from the "godly" or "kindly will." Molinari outlines in detail how her understanding of the wills relates to this prayerful project, wherein the "longing" of the soul corresponds to the "good will of God." This leads, Molinari writes, to two movements: "the one of the soul aspiring and tending towards God, and the other of God desiring to have us, [which] are shown by Julian as intrinsically joined, as two aspects of one reality, when she says: 'our kindly Will is to have God, and the Good Will of God is to have us.'"[96] Molinari writes of this union as achieved in degrees, whereby "a certain degree of union . . . is already established" merely by the soul longing for God, an aspiration that must then be developed into full union for it to "become more concrete and exercise its influence on man's life. Therefore from the union of aspiration or of desire, Julian proceeds to the union of the wills by means of prayer."[97] This process is made evident in Julian's discussion of prayer in chapter 41, already mentioned above, where Christ clearly outlines certain stages of beseking: "first it is my wille that thou have it, and sythen I make the to willen it, and sithen I make the to besekyn it and thou besekyst it. How shuld it than be that thou shuld not have thyn besekyng?" (first, it is my will that you have it, and after that I make you will it, and after that I make you beseek it and you beseek it. How should it then be that you should not have your beseeking?).[98] Julian then understands that "besekyng is a trew, gracious, lestyng will of the soule, onyd and festenyd into the will of our Lord be the swete, privy werke of the Holy Gost" (beseeking is a true, gracious, lasting will of the soul, united and fastened into the will of our Lord by the sweet, secret workings of the Holy Ghost).[99] She understands that prayer effects a willed receptivity that leads the individual toward God.

Beseking can therefore be read as a willed disclosure or reunification of the soul to its natural form; to its true state of *wonyng* and *onyng*, dwelling and wholeness. This is, crucially, an intentional act, which Julian describes in chapter 42 as a "turning" of the will toward God: "our wil be turnyd into the will of our Lord, enjoyand; and so menith he whan he seith, 'I mak the to willen it'" (our will is turned into the will of our lord, enjoying: and this is what he means when he says, "I make you will it").[100] Julian's language of turning here also resounds through Heidegger's later description of religious conversion as a "turning-*toward* God and a turning-*away* from idol-images," a connection that again reiterates the proto-phenomenological quality of Julian's account of prayer.[101] And so, with this account of voluntary beseking, Julian offers her reader an alternative to the involuntary disclosive experiences of pain, trauma, or illness. Where her illness functions as an external catalyst for revelation—working from the outside in—Julian's account of beseking begins with an internal movement: "Pray *inderly*" (Pray *inwardly*), says Christ in chapter 41.[102] Indeed, while Julian acknowledges in chapters 39 and 40 that experiences "from withoute" (from the outside)—like bodily sickness—can render a person "clene" (clean) and "redy" (ready) for the higher stages of prayer, she does not dwell on these for long.[103] Molinari attributes this brevity to Julian's understanding that too much purgation might make a soul "spiritually self-centred," which would hinder their progress.[104] Certainly, if we consider Julian's anxious avoidance of the self-beholding I discussed in chapter 2, it is clear that she favors the willed disclosure effected by compassionate reading, learning, and prayer over the involuntary disclosure of pain and purgation. This might be ascribed to a Bernardian prioritizing of the internal over the external—"for, just as the soul is more important than the body, so spiritual practices are more fruitful than material ones"—but it is unlikely that her choice is so schematic.[105] Considering her holistic attitude to the body-soul connection, I think Julian is aware of the difference between these lower degrees of purgative disclosure against the higher degree of willed contemplation and beseking, a difference which lies in the matter of the will.

In phenomenological terms, both routes—the purgative way and the contemplative way—involve practices that disrupt a person's ordinary being-in-the-world and so also potentially open them up to receive the divine. In the purgative way, however, there is an added level of effort or will required, an extra turn in the circular epistemology: in illness, the subject must turn *away* from the potentially distracting force of pain before they can turn *toward* the homeliness of God. More specifically, the will is only engaged once a person is in the condition of pain—which Julian learns for herself when her pain draws her into self-beholding and momentary despair, as described in chapter 66 of the long text. The practice of nonresistance is common to most contemplative traditions, now widely recognized by modern mindfulness and yogic frameworks.[106] Grounding this practice is the idea that suffering emerges out of perceptive response to painful attunement: it is the story the mind tells itself about pain, the mind's judgment of the signals or sensations of the body. The upshot is that the will might be able to hijack the rational thinking mind, and so the subject may be able to *choose* to respond differently to pain. Instead of telling themselves a story about the unbearable nature of pain—i.e., "I will never feel well again," or, as with Julian, "Is any payne in helle like this?" (Is any pain in hell like this?)—the nonresistant individual might seek to replace these beliefs with new thoughts, such as "I have survived pain before, I can survive this too," or, like Julian, "peyne is passand" (pain is passing).[107]

Such secularized theories of suffering as resistance cannot, however, accurately capture the Christological paradigm that grounds all tribulation writings from the English Middle Ages—a paradigm that sees differently the generative possibilities and limitations of worldly suffering, which are always set against God's ultimate sacrifice at the passion. Thomas Aquinas, for example, distinguishes between categories of experience wherein a person retains their ability to choose—to reason, *ratio*—and others where their reason is disrupted. He calls the latter *perfect passions*, and the former *imperfect passions* or *propassions*.[108] Derived from Greek philosophy, *propassion* translates literally as *pro-* (in place of, for, instead of) and *passio* (suffering).[109] For Aquinas, propassions are a quality of the virtuous; the ability to choose one's response to external stimuli means they can incline their reason toward good judgment. Aquinas makes this distinction to clarify the paradox of Christ's exemplary suffering: to explain how Christ functions as the paradigm of nonresistance but also as the paradigm of suffering. He writes that Christ could suffer far more powerful propassions than any human on account of his higher powers—reason—being hypostatically connected to God (indeed, *as* God).[110] As Nicholas Kahm puts it in his study on Aquinas, "untouched by original sin and full of grace, and experiencing the beatific vision, the strength of Christ's higher powers could and did suffer very vehement passions that did not disturb or affect his reason, for example, he could sweat blood for fear of death without it affecting his choice."[111]

With this in mind, a theologian might identify a person's will—or their reason, in Aquinas's terms—as possessing a certain degree of tolerance for the sensual experiences provoked by external stimuli, including pain. Since Christ's tolerance is higher than any human's, he is able to take on the suffering and sin of *all* humanity while remaining nonresistant—until the very last moment, when, at the apex of his kenosis, he cries out, "my God, my God, why hast thou forsaken me?" (Matthew 27:46; Mark 15:34). Perhaps this is the point where Christ's propassions lapse into perfect passions: dying in his humanity, Christ's pains are transformed into suffering. This concludes the "experiment" of God's embodiment in human form: the act of suffering par excellence, the passion. Christ suffers and dies *as* a human *for* humanity, encompassing both the *passionate* "I suffer," the *compassionate* "I suffer with," and the propassionate "I suffer *for*." It is on account of this same paradigm that Julian can write of the "wey" of Christ as the path toward compassionate living. As Aquinas's model acknowledges, however, a person's propassionate capacity, their level of tolerance of the will or reason, may not be enough to choose this path. This resilience is not, importantly, a matter of virtuousness or strength of character. To understand it in this way uses the same faulty reasoning as does language of fighting illness, the logical conclusion being that if a person succumbs to suffering, they have simply not tried hard enough. For most people this is well beyond their control, as Julian experiences for herself when she is overwhelmed with pain. And, even if a person has *willed* pain, as in Julian's earlier request for a bodily sickness, the effect of pain on their perception can be dramatic: a lifetime of contemplative practice may not be enough to endure these experiences as neutral phenomena.

This understanding of the potentially destructive facets of suffering can be argued to account for Julian's skimming of the preparatory, external stages of beseking in favor of the higher practice of prayer; her foregrounding of the *contemplative way* over the *purgative way*. It may also account for the disrupted death sequence in Julian's showing of the passion, when, in chapter 21, Julian anticipates Christ's death but "saw hym not so" (saw him not so).[112] Instead of dying, Christ changes his "chere" (facial expression), an advent of joy which draws focus away from the intensity of his pain.[113] This "dying-but-not-death" serves as a reminder of the duality of God's internal and external countenance: that there are less accessible, inner expressions behind Christ's outward suffering, expressions of love and joy that are not always visible to the human eye.[114] With the moment of his changing "chere," Julian thus avoids bearing witness to the slippage of Christ-in-pain into Christ-in-suffering. In her revelation, Christ remains propassionate until the end, a plot twist which bypasses any equivalent association of ability to endure pain as a virtuous trait, as in the Thomist view.

Instead of emphasizing the need for *patientia* in terms of *suffering*, then, Julian's representation of the passion emphasizes the need for the reader to be patient in their *seeking*. For while the purgative way requires a person to train their will against pain, the contemplative way trains the individual in practising (and practicing) receptivity and attentive nonresistance to all circumstances. The former is driven by the pain event; the latter is a daily, reiterative practice. Indeed, the latter prepares the individual for the former: when the contemplative inevitably does experience pain, they may then be able to engage the will and reattune to the homeliness of God more easefully. By beginning with the contemplative way of beseking, the individual learns how deal with unwilled and discomfiting circumstances—to suffer pain without suffer*ing*.

PRAYER POSTURE

This reading therefore defines Julian's path of beseking, the contemplative way to recovery, as a lived practice of coming home. Like coming into a state of rest, contemplative union or beholding cannot be forced, and so this practice is always anticipatory. All the contemplative can do is create the conditions for beholding: to cultivate the soul's receptivity to the divine. This cultivation can lead them toward beholding, but beholding itself arrives by the grace of God in a moment of release—an ungrasping of that same effort, or willed unwilling. The Gospel of Mark speaks to this in its account of Christ in the Garden of Gethsemane, which describes a similar state of watchfulness for God: "Take ye heed, watch and pray. For ye know not when the time is. Even as a man who going into a far country, left his house; and gave authority to his servants over every work, and commanded the porter to watch. Watch ye therefore, (for you know not when the lord of the house cometh . . .)" (Mark

13:33–35). Phenomenologist Benjamin Crowe quotes this verse with two further passages about the night in the garden, in which Jesus finds the disciples sleeping, saying to them: "Watch ye, and pray that you enter not into temptation" (Mark 14:38).[115] Crowe writes that "*watchful prayer* is an essential response to the message of the imminent kingdom of God. Praying in a spirit of 'watchfulness' means praying with one's eyes peeled and ears opened for the fulfillment of the new creation."[116] It means praying in a spirit of preparation. This is the Christian way of life: such a life, Crowe writes, "is often called a life 'in the Spirit,'" which means "recognizing prayer itself as a *gift*, as a part of the radically altered existential situation of those who have received the gift of the Spirit."[117]

In the final discussion of the chapter, I extend this phenomenological account with a reading of Julian's *Revelations* to explore how she understands the embodied experience of prayer. This concludes, in turn, the chapter's discussion of beseking, reiterating its function as a contemplative methodology for pursuing recovery, and sets the stage for the book's final chapter, which considers this journey on the eschatological plane. First, I want to draw attention to a comparable spirit of watchfulness borne out in Julian's account of beseking, in her emphasis on the cultivation of the soul's receptivity. Prayer, she writes, makes the soul "supple and buxom" to God, a plasticity she describes elsewhere as like a purse, which expands to receive him: "A man goyth uppe ryght, and the soule of his body is sparyde as a purse fulle feyer" (Humankind walks upright, and the soul of his body is closed like a very splendid purse).[118] I already introduced this passage in chapter 4, where I discussed Julian's sensitivity to a unified body-soul dynamic and an Augustinian understanding of the soul as *capax Dei*. But Julian's image of the "uppe ryght" person also supplies a figurative analog to the embodied practice of prayer. Since Julian's understanding of beseking is of a lived practice that must be intended toward in both spiritual and material terms ("sensualite" toward the "substance"), so is prayer an embodied, reiterative act of making oneself receptive to the divine. Phenomenologist Merold Westphal writes, for example, of "prayer as the posture of the decentered self . . . a posture of the soul, of an inner attitude of the self that can appropriately express itself in a variety of outer stances."[119] Such a self "is not its own origin," Westphal writes: "It does not make itself but rather receives itself in receiving what is given to it *by putting itself at the disposal of the gift*."[120] Thinking of prayer in this way—as a posture—is a productive schematic for understanding the ways in which beseking opens up the self to porosity or decenters it. In the passage quoted above, the person is "uppe ryght" when the soul is "sparyde" (closed) like a purse.[121] So, too, is the lived body "upright" in its everyday doings. This posture is, phenomenologically speaking, a kind of *body language*, which serves to indicate healthful or homelike attunement: "Within philosophy," Heidegger writes, "we must not limit the word 'gesture' merely to 'expression' . . . Each movement of my body as a 'gesture' and, therefore, as such and such a comportment does not simply enter into an indifferent space. Rather, comportment is always already in a region [*Gegend*] which is open through the thing to which I am in a relationship, for instance, when I take something into my hand."[122] This notion of the gestural body is taken further by Maurice Merleau-Ponty, who examines how this bodily intentionality facilitates a person's habitation of the world: for Merleau-Ponty, gestural signs are the physical basis for words, fleshly "speech acts" that are part of human psychical self-expression.

Uprightness might, then, be read phenomenologically as the gestural body's natural attitude, in which state it transcends into the world with homelikeness. As the phenomenologist Erwin W. Straus explains in an account of uprightness, this posture suggests a sense of equilibrium, stability, or steadfastness: it is an intentional stance of stability that allows the subject to "[gain] his standing in the world."[123] Uprightness also opposes the forces of gravity, requiring the maintenance of a "character of counteraction": "It calls for our activity and attention."[124] Straus therefore argues that "the natural stance of man is . . . 'resistance,' " a status that "demands endeavor. It is essentially restless. We are committed to an ever-renewed exertion."[125] This aligns with the phenomenological definition of homelikeness as a condition that must be perpetually established and reestablished, on account of the individual's existential home*less*ness. The practice of establishing and reestablishing homelike attunement is never complete, just as uprightness "is not finished with getting up and standing"; a person has to "*with-stand*."[126] Paradoxically, the task of finding rest requires a significant amount of physical toil and labor. It requires the subject to move through the rest*less*ness of their natural attitude, consciously cultivating the conditions, the postures, wherein they might find some ease. Even rest requires resistance.

In this way, the phenomenological account of uprightness parallels Julian's epistemological project, with both always in process. Indeed, Julian's favorite epistemological term—*understanding*—is etymologically linked to the concept of *standing*, through the shared **sta-* root: "to stand, make, or be firm." *Substance*, too, comes from the Latin *substare*, or *substant-* (standing firm), which becomes *substantia* (being, essence). See, for example, the first MED sense of *stōnden*—"To assume or maintain a standing position, *stand upright*; stand in a place"—and the associated phrase "stonden on rōte" (stand upright).[127] Similarly, consider *-stan* as in place names: from Persian "country," "*home of*," literally "place where one *stays*." Straus notes that this latter family of words is kept together by one and the same principal meaning: "They refer to something that is instituted, erected, constructed, and, in its dangerous equilibrium, threatened by fall and collapse."[128] This recalls the instability of homeliness, which is continually threatened by worldly experiences of pain and trauma: as Julian puts it, "if peyn be taken fro us, it may commen agen" (if pain is taken from us, it may come again).[129] Humankind's existential instability is in this way the very foundation of its beseking, with Julian's "uppe ryght" man functioning as a figurative or physical synecdoche for the body-soul unity, which must be perpetually and effortfully redirected toward God: "And whan it is tyme of his nescessery, it is openyde and sparyde ayen fulle honestly" (And when it is the necessary time, it is opened and closed again as is proper) and so God "comyth downe to us to the lowest parte of oure nede" (comes down to us to the lowest part of our need).[130]

Where Heidegger's phenomenology departs from this mystical model is in the ontic background of nothingness that grounds Dasein. As discussed above, Julian's notion of the soul's indwelling in God allows for a more optimistic picture than the Heideggerian framework allows, wherein the substance of the soul remains in some ways always at home in God. Nevertheless, in seeking to reunite the two aspects of the soul to wholeness, the practice of prayer must engage both this divine substance as well as its "lowest parte," the embodied human experience or "sensualite" where the "bestly will" resides.[131] Coming down to this lowest part is not only God's task, then, but the task of the individual beseking him. In true phenomenological fashion, beseking needs to disrupt and redirect the body as much as the mind. In Julian's *Revelations*, she describes prayer as enacting this physically by disrupting the upright body, a phrase used here to denote not only literal uprightness, but in phenomenological terms, the body's natural attitude, too.

Medieval texts contemporary to Julian offer some insights into how this disruption could be effected posturally in prayer. The outstretched *orans* gesture, for instance, came to signify ecstatic prayer, while lying prostrate demonstrated subjection and an awareness of humility, which J. A. Burrow calls "[gestures] of submission."[132] Burrow notes, for example, Langland's Pride, or Pernelle Proud-Heart, who prostrates herself to express contrition: "Pernele proud-herte platte hire to þe erþe / And lay longe er she loked, and 'lord, m*er*cy!' cryde" (Pernelle Proud-Heart prostrated herself to the earth / And lay there long before she looked, and cried "lord, mercy!").[133] John Mirk's *Instructions for Parish Priests* (c. 1400) meanwhile suggests that kneeling and outward-facing hands were encouraged in the laity: "Teche hem eft to knele downe sone, / And whenne they here the belle rynge / To that holy sakerynge, / Teche hem knele downe, both yonge and olde, / And both here hondes up to holde" (Teach them again to kneel down straightaway, / And when they hear the bell ring / For that holy consecration, / Teach them to kneel down, both young and old, / And hold up both their hands).[134] By the mid-sixteenth century, Ignatius of Loyola's *Spiritual Exercises* (c. 1522–1524) suggests a movement toward personal discretion in the adoption of prayer postures, depending on the intention of the practice: "To enter on the contemplation now on my knees, now prostrate on the earth, now lying face upwards, now seated, now standing, always intent on seeking what I want."[135] Ignatius here implies a sense of physical modification, of changing the bodily attitude as the person desires.

All these devotional postures variously engage the visual and gestural field in downward or upward movements, correlating with the sense of "being below what is higher" in the religious attitude—that is, the vertical relationship with the divine is correlated with the vertical motion of the body. Denise N. Baker has discussed this language of elevation in relation to the mystical paradox of the soul: "Because [the] highest point of the soul is also its deepest recess, the metaphors of ascent and depth are interchangeable; the summit or point of the soul is also its foundation or ground."[136] She quotes Denys Turner, who writes that "the two metaphors of inwardness and ascent themselves intersect at the point where God and the self intersect, so that which is most interior to me is also that which is above and beyond me; so that the God who is within me is also the God I am in."[137] By choosing to direct one's kinesthesia downward then, the body necessarily also directs itself upward and inward: "When we lower our heads or kneel in prayer, when we bow or bend our knees in greeting, *the deviation from the vertical reveals the relation to it*."[138] That is to say, the deviation from uprightness reveals the relation to God: it reorients the subject to the divine.

Furthermore, the prayer posture is not confined to a static spatial placement of the body. Although representations of prayer in visual culture from the Middle Ages imply stasis—take the illustrations to Peter the Chanter's prayer manual, for example—these are a kind of "immobile posture of the type captured by artists," as Richard C. Trexler puts it.[139] Kinetic postures offer similar opportunities for reorientation; like the whirling dervishes in the Sufi tradition, or the ecstasies of the Low Country beguines, movement can function as a kind of gestural mantra, a physical display akin to the verbal repetition of spoken prayer.[140] Movement is even perhaps an easier route than stillness, for finding stillness is akin to seeking silence; it requires a great deal of focus. Regardless, I suggest that both possibilities remain examples of *willed unwilling*, since they may be understood as operating according to the same phenomenological principles. Edmund Husserl writes that all bodily intentionality is determined by kinesthetic processes, which have the character "I do," "I move," or even "I hold still," all of which are dynamic events.[141] Dorion Cairns also remarks that "rest is the null value of motion, until there is perceived motion there is no rest."[142] There is, in other words, constant kinesthetic value across this spectrum of movement and stillness. And, importantly, theological writings like Julian's suggest that God is found in the intersection between these kinds of paradoxes: in the moment in which speech collapses into silence, thought into nothingness, seeking into beholding, and the upright, kinesthetic body into downward rest.

What all prayer postures have in common, then, is the intentional surrender of the lived body. This is, in phenomenological terms, where the collapse of the body in prayer diverges from the involuntary collapse instigated by illness or trauma, since the subject is *choosing* to relinquish their body to God. Whether pursued via the contemplative or the purgative way, however, Julian recognizes that such disclosive practices do not guarantee beholding. Most people, she admits, will remain in the state of seeking their entire lives without encountering the same kind of revelation as she has herself. Nevertheless, "sekyng is as good as beholdyng" (seeking is as good as beholding), for it is in the process—rather than the destination—that homlyhede is realized.[143] Snatches of understanding may emerge along the way, and yet still such understanding will always lead to further seeking. It is in this context that prayer can be understood as a necessary component of beseking in Julian's *Revelations*: as an effortful, embodied practice of receptivity to God. This practice is both nonclosing and lifelong, one that requires continued commitment and work. It is a practice of compassion, a labor of love.

My discussion in this chapter has journeyed through the grammar and language of Julian's *Revelations*, exploring her various expressions of homeliness as a precisely curated vocabulary for her theology of recovery. The chapter began by paying close attention to Julian's rhetorical amplification through degrees of homeliness, landing on *homlyhede* as a signifier central to her participatory theology. I here examined the *-hede* suffix as an indicator of a thing's capacity enacted through process. This reading has implications for my interpretation of Julian's contemplative epistemology as it was treated in the previous chapter, especially my reading of how she theorizes beseking as a being-toward-God: I have connected the condition of homlyhede to the practice of beseking or seeking the divine, defining *homlyhede* as a condition that emerges out of this practice of reorienting the soul toward the divine. *Beseking* was also identified as a similarly precise Middle English construction, with a specific processual character lost in the common modern translation, *beseeching*. Phenomenological studies provided a theoretical vocabulary for thinking about how these processes might catalyze divine insights, leading me to elaborate on the differences between the willed practices of contemplation and prayer and involuntary disclosures that might occur in illness. I concluded that Julian's own encounter with sickness may have given her a taste of the destructive force of pain, leading to a reticence in recommending this purgative way to her reader in the *Revelations*. This position was then elaborated through a discussion of the will, which compared the modern practice of nonresistance with Aquinas's discussion of propassions in his account of Christ's death.

In the second half of the chapter, I focused on how Julian suggests homlyhede might be achieved through the practice of prayer. Phenomenological accounts of the body helped to shed light on Julian's difficult description of the soul as a purse, which I interpret as a pun incorporating both physical and spiritual senses of the human receptivity to God. This passage of Julian's "uppe ryght" man was here located alongside contemporary medieval representations of devotional postures, which I consider as variously enacting a willed surrender of the physical body. In this way, the chapter has arrived at a fuller understanding of Julian's concept of beseking as a lived way of being-toward-God, which includes the more specific practices of prayer and contemplation and which is ultimately fueled by an innate condition of homeliness both with and in God. This is the "practical-pastoral" offering of the *Revelations*, to return to Philip Sheldrake's words, which Julian gives to her "even cristen" reader for the purposes of their own recovery—a contemplative way, map, or grammar by which to undertake their journey home.

6

MAKE STRAIGHT THE PATHS

Christ, Providence, and Salvation

We begin at home, we leave home, we return home. Even when it looks like we're going far afield, we're always on our way back. We have what we need, and we are where we are going; the spiritual journey is a journey of return.

How do we make this journey? There are no maps. The path is mysterious, dark. It leads us to the corners, the subtexts, of our lives, the in-between, unconscious, unknowable places. We think we know who we are and what our lives are about. But suppose we don't. Suppose our lives are not what we think they are; suppose something else is going on, deep streams flowing underground that come to the surface only now and again, in little springs or freshets or maybe only in telltale spots of moisture where weeds or scraggly flowers grow. And suppose that the task of our lives is not so much to shape or control our stories so that they will turn out according to our preference or preconception but rather to recognize that our stories, the visible images of our lives, are cover stories, narratives that hide within them deeper, underground narratives, that we can sense and taste now and again but never fully comprehend.

—Norman Fischer, *Sailing Home*

The focus of Julian of Norwich's theology, set out in her *Revelations of Divine Love*, is the recovery of humanity's wholeness or homeliness with God. This is at its heart a soteriological story, where healing is enacted through a pairing of personal development and God's grace. As the previous chapters of this book have shown, the paradoxes that govern this journey are many, with recovery a project of return as well as forward movement, a process of arrival and ever-further pilgrimage. Recovery means venturing into darkness as much as into the light—into the corners, subtexts, and unconscious parts of human living. With the help of phenomenologists after Martin Heidegger, *Impossible Recovery* so far has sought to articulate Julian's experience of this process as she describes it in her texts, negotiating her plunge into illness and the accompanying revelation which followed. It has also examined the devotional model Julian offers to her "even cristen" reader, which advocates a careful and attentive contemplative practice of seeking understanding. This chapter digs deeper into the theological principles that ground this practice, into the complex soteriology Julian develops to understand her own recovery and the potential recovery for all humankind. In doing so, it concludes my reading of Julian together with post-Heideggerian phenomenologies of well-being to show, finally, how the eschatological structure of the *Revelations* is silenced by Heidegger's secularized philosophy, and to explore the implications of this divergence for any philosophical reading of Julian's remarkably hopeful texts.

To unpick this final seam, the chapter begins with one of the key scenes that underpins Julian's *Revelations*: the lengthy allegorical showing of the lord and the servant. Julian reports having received this showing in 1393, two decades after her initial revelations, and it appears to have informed and shaped her exegesis in the long text. My reading of this passage focuses particularly on the showing's earthy aspects, identifying its ecological character as closely bound up with Julian's theology of indwelling and her homely poetic. Comparing the showing with another topographical scene in the *Revelations*, the deep-sea passage, I consider these two ecological sites as hermeneutic keys for understanding Julian's text more widely. The discussion attends to how Julian interprets the labors of the servant as a process of deep personal cultivation, which will prepare the ground for God's grace—an ecological expression of the dynamic of *homlyhede* that I examined in the previous chapter. The chapter then undertakes a final expansion of this book's temporal perspective, widening its interpretive frame to include the atemporal, eschatological timeline of Julian's recovery story. The knot of paradoxes upon which Julian's *Revelations* depend are here shown to collapse in on one another, coming together in a single flashpoint of understanding, wherein the road to recovery is in part undertaken by Christ and in part by humanity. Finally, the Heideggerian model is sharply profiled against Julian's eschatological horizon, highlighting the confines Heidegger put on the theological understanding of being as a participatory phenomenon. While Heidegger rejected any ontology that included a creator on account of the implied objectification of humans as created products, I show how Julian manages to avoid such objectification, by constructing a masterly ontotheology that makes room for free will and for the dynamism of humanity's existence on earth—and so, too, for its redemption. The chapter concludes by examining how the therapeutic power of Christ's passion facilitates this theological schema, reading Julian's Christological focus as a unique rendering of the medieval *Christus medicus* topos. Phenomenological work on the physician-patient encounter helps to articulate the dynamics of this therapeutic relationship, which resonates with the fundamentally interrelational emphasis of Julian's theology. In this way, the chapter ends by restating the communal aspect of recovery as theorized in the *Revelations*, which can only be realized through a compassionate openness to the suffering of others and love for the world.

THE ECOLOGICAL SOUL

Throughout her *Revelations of Divine Love*, Julian invokes the language of homeliness—of dwelling, arriving, abiding—to describe the human relationship to God. Yet this homely poetic is reified through one final figurative landscape that has yet to be examined in this study: the showing of the lord and the servant. Julian received this showing (or at the very least, a new insight into its meaning) in 1393, a full twenty years after her initial illness and showings, and five years following the showing that love was God's meaning. It is very possible that Julian was already enclosed as an anchorite by this time and that she had already completed the shorter version of her text: as Nicholas Watson persuasively argues, the short text's meditation on the nature of sin, which concludes "Amen par charite"—included in section 24 of Nicholas Watson and Jacqueline Jenkins's edition of the short text—may have been intended as a peroration on the showings.[1] According to Watson, the passage that follows "reveals Julian's dissatisfaction" with this emphasis on sin and her subsequent desire to refocus the text toward the revelation that love was his meaning.[2] By the time of the showing of the lord and the servant, then, Julian's thinking may have undergone something of a shift, to align better with this more hopeful revelation about the nature of sin and recovery. Indeed, as the final element concluding the entire revelation of love, the lord and the servant showing is often read as a hermeneutic key for understanding her textual project as a whole. In what follows, I unpack this showing for both its poetic and theological insights, to reveal the showing's function as both a poetic expression of and hermeneutic blueprint for Julian's contemplative theology, which combines representation and interpretation into one energetic picture.

Recounted in chapter 51 of Julian's long text, the lord and the servant showing metaphorizes the various actors of the salvation narrative, constructing a rhetorical exemplum that combines fall and redemption into a single scene. On its surface, the servant can be read as Adam who, eager to fulfil the wishes of his lord, rushes off to do his bidding only to fall, sore and bruised, into a ditch. But on a second, allegorical level, the servant is also Christ, second Adam, who dwells in the wilderness of the human soul, cultivating the ground with tender loving care. As is so often the case in her *Revelations*, however, Julian takes this allegory much further than straightforward exegetical doubling. Through her inclusion of an entire landscape in the eye of the beholder, Julian's account of this story enacts what Cristina Maria Cervone describes as an *incarnational poetic*: a verbal and kinetic representation of the salvation narrative as growth or life force, momentarily reversing the Word-made-flesh to render Christ as something other than flesh.[3] Yet Julian goes even further still: in line with her theology of mutual indwelling, she not only interprets Christ as growth/plant-life/the earth, but incorporates her entire anthropological schema into this allegory. All of humanity is included within her figurative universe, in a blurring of distinction between the material and immaterial, human and world. Through this wide-angle lens, the persons of the story become participants in a much bigger framework of organic and generative signification, a microcosmic mise-en-scène of the rise and fall, "wele and wo," of creation.

In this way, the lord and the servant showing extends Julian's homely poetic into a more universal commentary on human life on earth. Particularly significant to this topography is Julian's configuration of the soul as *kynde*, part of the natural landscape and its cycles, but also nature as God made it. With this descriptor in mind, I want to put forward a reading of Julian's anthropology as *ecological*, an expression of homeliness that insists on the condition of connection. For in its etymological sense, *ecology* derives from *eco*, or the Greek *oîkos*, house—meaning that the ecological can also be thought of in terms of at-homeness, as well as the phenomenological comportment of being-with-others. As the biologist Barry Commoner famously wrote, the "first law of ecology" is that "everything is connected to everything else."[4] So, a healthy ecology means that everything is at home in the world *and* at home with other people and things.[5] Julian's earthy allegory can be read, then, as a reminder of the role of humanity (their *-hede* identity) within a dynamic ecosystem that is constantly shifting and changing, living and dying. Most importantly, this is an ecosystem (or ecology) of salvation that offers the possibility for reunification in and with the earth, for cultivating a home together within this global organism, through a constant labor of seeking and transfiguration.

Throughout the lord and the servant showing, Julian locates the human soul in space, situated amid the earthly terrain. This spatial configuration is always rendered in relation to God, the zero-point reference from which humankind begins and to which it returns: "our homliest home" (our homeliest home), as Julian puts it.[6] The soul is *grounded* and *rooted* to God, terms that are quite theologically commonplace, but which, in typical Julian fashion, she works with in new and surprising ways. Grounding and rooting can, for instance, be traced to the Latin *fundus* or *profundus*, which are often used in theological texts, as Denise N.

Baker writes, "to identify the subsistence of the soul in the deity, the source of all existence."[7] These are Augustinian concepts originally invoked to express the doctrine of participation, wherein ontology is defined not by discrete ontic categories but by participation in the "True Being" of the divine.[8] For Julian, too, creation is a condition of shared ontological existence, dependent upon its connection to God; as in her suggestion that the "substance" or higher part of the soul, which is "knitt to god in the makyng" (united to God in its creation) is a self-evidently spatial construction.[9] When theological texts attempt to describe the immanent divinity of God, however, deixis becomes unstable: above/below, up/down, here/there, left/right all cease to function in straightforward patterns of signification. As Cervone notes, spatiotemporal positioning "has no meaning with regard to an all-encompassing, ever-being God . . . In linguistic terms, God's deictic center, the locational and temporal *origo* for the speaking subject, must be everywhere, always."[10] In prayer, for example, the downward direction of the body might project the subject both upward (toward God) and inward (toward self), while reaching upward might enable them to see the bottommost groundedness of the self in God. Denys Turner articulates this paradox when he writes, "The *intinerarium intus* is also an *ascensio superius.* The two metaphors of inwardness and ascent themselves intersect at the point where God and the self intersect, so that that which is most interior to me is also that which is above and beyond me; so that the God who is within me is also the God I am in."[11]

The same paradox of indwelling can be found in Augustine's Neoplatonic spirituality of ascent, but it is the Rhineland mystics who articulate the most explicit configuration of the soul's ontological union with God as ground. Meister Eckhart (d. c. 1328) regularly invokes the idea of the "ground of the soul" (*grunt der sele*), and Johannes Tauler (d. 1361) uses it even more frequently.[12] Wolfgang Riehle denies any likely (or traceable) influence between the theology of Eckhart or Tauler and Julian: any parallels—such as those pointed out by scholars J. B. Dalgairns, Evelyn Underhill, and Anna Maria Reynolds—he ascribes to common scriptural and scholastic sources, such as the Thomist notion that man is nearer to God than to his own soul; of God as a "fundamentum et basis omnium aliorum entium" (the foundation and basis of all other beings).[13] Julian does share her anthropological lexis with Neoplatonist theology: this is evident, for example, in the terms "substance" and "sensualite," which are common to *De Trinitate*, where Augustine distinguishes between higher and lower reason in the soul. As Cervone rightly notes, however, these terms were "picked up by other theologians and commentators throughout the Middle Ages, including, among others, Hilton, [Julian's] contemporary."[14] It is an enticing possibility that a direct relationship may exist between Julian and the Rhineland mystics, whose work she could have encountered as it made its way into the vibrant port of Norwich from the Continent.[15] Nevertheless, it is perhaps not so important to determine the extent to which Julian is aware of or subscribes to these strands of Neoplatonist anthropology. More pertinent to the present discussion is Julian's linguistic treatment of these terms within her own theological framework: specifically, how Julian instrumentalizes this ecological lexis as a tool of disclosure.

As has been noted at various points throughout this book, metaphor disrupts the literal tenor of a signifying vehicle with a figurative deferral to another (or many other) abstract signifieds. In the case of Julian's anthropological terms, the vehicle *ground* carries the literal sense of "the bottom; the lowest part or downward limit of anything," usually "of the sea, a well, ditch, etc., and of hell; rarely of heaven."[16] Used within a theological context (such as in Augustine's or Eckhart's writing), however, these spatial connotations are in turn reconfigured as abstractly spiritual. That is, the reader's attention is drawn into an imagined, metaphorical space of the soul, a perspective from which they are referred to the ground, the apex, and so on. But the interchangeability of such deictic terms—upward also referring to downward, and vice versa—refuses these metaphors any kind of figurative solidification. The spatial construction within the imagination collapses as soon as it is built; the reader can't get a grasp on the figurative ground beneath their feet. Superficially, Julian's *Revelations* seem to adhere to this particular spatial poetic, expressing her theology of mutual indwelling using the same principles referred to above. Yet Julian's ability to blend abstract thought with her homely language drawn from everyday experience offers a new kind of poetic to her "even cristen" reader. Adding another link in the chain of signification, Julian's implicit invocation of these abstract scholastic terms remakes them, spatially and pictorially, through their figurative rendering.

This ecological representation of the human soul is not limited to the lord and the servant showing: there is another instance of this ecological poetic added to the long text in chapter 10, which I propose should be read in conjunction with the showing of the lord and the servant, on account of strong hermeneutic resonances between the two. Here, Julian gives an account of the second showing, describing how "one tyme mine understondyng was led downe into the see-grounde, and there I saw hill and dalis grene, semand as it were mosse begrowne, with wrekke and with gravel" (one time my understanding was led down into the sea ground, and there I saw green hills and dales, seeming as if they were overgrown with moss, with seaweed and with gravel).[17] When "a man or a woman" is "under the broade watyr" (broad water) of God's enveloping goodness, she writes, they should have "mor solace and comfort than al this world can telle" (more solace and comfort than all this world can tell).[18] Scholarship hasn't agreed on the meaning and significance of this image of the "see-ground," perhaps on account of its sudden imposition among the description of Christ's seeping blood; the singular temporal location ("one tyme") displaces the image apart from the rest of the showing. Juliana Dresvina attempts to locate a scriptural referent here, that the "user of an illustrated Psalter would immediately think of the image of David in water, beginning Psalm 68 (69)," while Watson and Jenkins have suggested an association with the story of Jonah (as in the *Gawain*-poet's late fourteenth-century *Patience*), noting the connection to Julian's earlier reference to herring scales.[19] I wonder, however, if assigning a biblical source here does not draw the focus away from a highly Julian-ish turn: a topographical, ecological rendering of the concept of divine indwelling. The landscape is interpolated into the midst of the second revelation of Christ's discoloring (where Julian notably also introduces her "seek, suffer, trust" triad), just as the more detailed landscape of the lord and the servant allegory will be interpolated later in the text, between showings fourteen and fifteen (that God is the ground of *beseking*).[20] Indeed, both passages are additions to the longer version of the text, suggesting that the sea-ground image is, as with the lord and the servant parable, a visual heuristic for accessing the meaning of the revelation as a whole.

The topographical resonances between the two passages support this theory, with both offering a visual rendering of the soul-as-ground topos. Inadvertently speaking to this parallelism, Amy Appleford remarks on the "crisp detail" of the underwater landscape as "a visual echo of the regular land above the sea."[21]

The verdancy of the sea ground—the green hills and dales, overgrown with moss and seaweed—here anticipates the flourishing brought to bear on the earth by the servant, who "turne the earth upsodowne" ([turns] the earth upside down), making "swete flods to rennen, and noble and plenteous fruits to springen" (sweet floods to run, and noble and plenteous fruits to spring forth).[22] The ground is underwater, overturned, upended, all by the poetic *mene* of this topography topos, which literalizes the otherwise abstract anthropological term as land that can be traversed and travailed: just as Julian's understanding descends onto the sea ground, so the servant falls into the ditch and must work the land, and so did Adam/Christ descend into hell and then "com up into hevyn" (come up into heaven).[23] In *grounding* her anthropological schema of divine indwelling in visual topography, Julian thereby *upends* the metaphor by reverting to the literal tenor of the vehicle *ground*, as in the ground of the earth. Or, if the view is taken that metaphorical meaning is interpreted simultaneously to the literal meaning, as Cervone argues of Julian's text according to recent work in cognitive linguistics, then Julian can be read as layering another semantic stratum onto the textual terrain.[24] In yet another circular maneuver, ground-of-the-earth becomes abstract ground-of-the-soul, which through her figurative imagery is rendered ground-of-the-earth once more.

This linguistic doubling upon doubling allows Julian to navigate a topographical picture of the human relationship to God, at once positioning the reader in time and space, only to collapse the rules of this constructed universe with a paradoxical inversion of ascent and descent. As Turner writes, "Julian can confidently play with formulas little short of Eckhart's in audacity while remaining firmly within the common Neoplatonic tradition."[25] One final example brings this reading full circle, back to Julian's concept of "uprightness" examined in the previous chapter, which can also be compared to the Platonic notion of the rational soul as housed in the uppermost aspect of the body. For Plato, this elevates it to the position "not [of] an earthly but [of] a heavenly plant—up from earth towards our kindred in the heaven."[26] Heidegger also favored this analogy to plant-life, quoting Johann Peter Hebel, who wrote "we are plants which—whether we like to admit it to ourselves or not—must with our roots rise out of the earth in order to bloom in the ether and bear fruit."[27] Heidegger adds: "For a truly joyous and salutary human work to flourish, man must be able to mount *from the depth of his home ground* up into the ether."[28] Plato's heavenly plant, however, has its roots not in the ground of the earth but in the sky, in the eidetic sphere, the realm of ideas which nourishes and sustains the psyche. As philosopher Michael Marder writes, only "when this tie remains intact is the body itself 'upright,' literally and figuratively, spatially and morally, in the sense that the rational soul stays firmly in charge of the animal and vegetal desires in us."[29]

Julian's framework of groundedness is less exclusively rooted to the heavens, instead focusing on the necessity of earthly grounding *within self and world*. This is most insistently borne out in the lord and the servant showing, which reiterates not only the ontological status of the human soul but also her emphasis on spiritual reunion and growth—the means by which homlyhede is performed. In Julian's description of the showing, her multilayering of ecological metaphors expands the architecture of domestic images established in the first half of the text (as in the "see-ground" passage discussed above), moving from the visceral picture of Christ's homeliness as he appears to her in the bedchamber, to a more global—a more *ecological*—sphere of homeliness, thus emphasizing the universality of the eschatological timeline and the participatory nature of her theology. These first fourteen showings, with their focus on Christ's passion, have invited Julian's "even cristen" reader to themselves engage in the porosity, connection, and relation to God described within. The lord and the servant parable then asks them to enact, indeed to fulfill, in their own lives the self-investigative spiritual cultivation and growth—the performance of homlyhede—made possible by the *passio* of the salvation narrative.

CULTIVATING THE EARTH

In line with Julian's theology of mutual indwelling, the ecological soul in the lord and the servant showing becomes both the ground to be tended and the gardener who tends it. Without the cultivating labor of the servant, the lord is "nothing but wildernes," identified *as* the wilderness, just as the human soul is identified with the "barren and desert" abode where the lord sits, which the servant—as Adam or Christ—is required to tend.[30] The fulfillment of the salvation narrative depends on this uncultivated land, with the wilderness typology functioning as the theological zone of unlikeness, the *regio dissimilitudinis* of postlapsarian living. As contemporary renderings of this topos suggest, the wilderness is a wild land not yet brought under human control, and possibly also not under God's control. In the *Gawain*-poet's description of the "wyldrenesse of Wyrale" (wilderness of Wirral), for instance, this is a region in which there lived "bot lyte / Þat auþer God oþer gome wyth goud hert louied" (but few / That loved God or man with a good heart).[31] Rebecca M. Douglass describes the point of this passage in *Gawain* as "not so much that the land is uninhabited as that the inhabitants, human and otherwise, are not part of the court world . . . they are not Christian"—a reading that stresses the duality of *kynde* and *unkynde*, the natural or unnatural, or the familiar and the unfamiliar.[32] Yet since Julian's anthropology understands human nature as fundamentally unchanged by its original lapse into sin, her use of the wilderness motif does not fit so neatly into this dichotomy. Julian's incarnational theology does not envisage the uncultivated soul—that which is *unkynde*—as evil or irretrievably broken. As the parable illustrates, the servant is not held culpable for their fall. Rather, they are simply figured as in need of being helped to their feet and righted—in need of dutiful care and loving attention.

In light of this, I now turn to the servant's role in this soteriological narrative, to explore how they can transform the wilderness into the "blisfull kyngdom" Julian describes in subsequent chapters. First and foremost, this recovery of homeliness on earth depends on the servant's own recovery from their fall into the ditch and the pains which follow. The fall has afflicted the servant with complaints of various kinds: he suffers "vii grete peynes" (seven great pains), the first of which is of a bodily kind—"sore brosyng" (sore bruising)—which is called a "felable peyne" (sensate pain); the second is "hevynes of his body" (heaviness of his body); the third "febilnes folowyng of these two" (weakness following these two); the fourth, the blinding of his "reason"—he is "stonyed in his mend" (astonished in his mind) to such an extent that he has almost "forgotten his owne luf" (forgotten his own love); the fifth, the pain that "he myte not rysen" (he might not rise); the sixth, the pain that he "lay alone;" and finally, that the place which he lay on was "lang, herd and grevous" (long, hard and grievous).[33] Like Julian's own sickness, these types of tribulation can be glossed phenomenologically for the ways they disrupt the servant's being-in-the-world. Their afflictions broadly correspond to the disruption of a number of existential characteristics in the Heideggerian model. First, the servant has lost *homelike attunement*—"faylyng of comforte" (failing of comfort)—and second, his *understanding*, or the way he can project himself into the world: "he ne may rysen ne helpyn hymself" (he may not rise nor help himself).[34] Third, he is unable to articulate himself discursively—he is "stonyed in his mend"—and finally, he has lost the use of his lived body: he has "hevynes of his body."[35] Such a critical unsettling of these existentials renders the servant entirely consumed by his incapacitation, the intensity of which not only discloses but constitutes the very first human experience of homelessness. Nevertheless, in Julian's optimistic schema, this picture is colored by the promise of recovery, as the servant's fall is followed by another image: that of their cultivation of the earth. This double-layering of imagery ties together the servant's suffering with their recovery, in a complicated causal tangle of fall and redemption.

The cultivation of the earth is depicted in the showing as hard work, but it holds the promise of a flourishing world to come: the servant is meant to "delvyn and dykyn, swinkin and swetyn, and turne the earth upsodowne, and sekyn the depnes, and wattir the plants in tyme" (delve and dig, toil and sweat, and turn the earth upside-down, and seek the deepness, and water the plants in time).[36] This "travel" (work) will soon make "swete flods to rennen, and noble and plenteous fruits to springen" (sweet floods to run, and noble and plenteous fruits to spring forth) to bring before God, whose love "grounds" this agrarian enterprise.[37] Again, a semantic doubling here renders this agricultural labor as twofold: first, as a cultivation of the earth in the external world, and, second, as a cultivation of the internal landscape of the soul. This second level of meaning relies on the metonym of earth for human, which Julian invokes in her description of the human body as made from the "slyppe of erth" (mud of earth), a creation story which encloses *soul* in *soil*, and draws on the possible derivation of "Adam" from *adamah*, "earth."[38] Baker has commented on the echoes of Genesis in this agricultural passage, which she reads as potentially alluding to two events: "God's bestowal on the newly created Adam of dominion over the earth (Gen. 2:19–20) and his curse on the ground to punish the disobedient Adam (Gen. 3:17–19)."[39] While both of these tasks require hard physical labor—the "gretest labor and herdest travel that is" (the greatest labor and hardest work there is)—Baker remarks that Julian transforms the punitive implications of this story with her description of "the earth's bounty and the lord's pleasure," making it "about creation rather than transgression."[40]

Instead of the fall transforming the earth into a tool for punishment, then, Julian's exegesis glosses the soil as the means of redemptive *re-creation*. This redemption is fulfilled by the next layer of the showing's double allegory, in which the servant can be read as Christ or second Adam. Great labor is also required in this stage of the narrative, where the plants (humanity) are watered by the flood of Christ's blood shed at the passion, which provides nourishment (food and drink, as in the Eucharist). In this emphasis on growth and maturation, Margaret Ann Palliser reads echoes of Paul (Ephesians 4:4–16) and the early Christian tradition exemplified in the writings of Irenaeus of Lyons, for whom Adam was not endowed with supernatural perfection in his creation, but rather with a childlike aptitude for growth toward perfection that had to be developed.[41] Palliser subsequently describes Julian's understanding of sin as "not unlike a debilitating illness or an immaturity that evokes pity, not wrath, from God."[42] The sin of the servant-as-Adam absolutely invokes the kinds of disruption that have been shown to affect a person in illness: lying in the ditch, the servant is unaware of—closed off from—the world, unable to see the world before him. And, as is characteristic of Julian's compassionate theodicy, he is not blamed for his affliction; the lord's focus is on the *intention* of the servant rather than on the failure of his action.

As such, I read Julian's earthy imagery as a further expression of her ecological poetics of recovery: she engages the natural world as another metaphor-beyond-metaphor, putting into words the homely dwelling of humanity on earth and God in the soul. In so doing, she draws on various scriptural precedents that similarly frame the soul as a garden to be tended with loving care. Richard Rolle's *Incendium Amoris* (before 1343), for instance, describes the soul as blooming with virtues, seemingly punning on the similarity of the Latin terms "ortus" (birth) and "hortus" (garden) in his description of the soul as like the birth of Christ.[43] Walter Hilton (d. 1396) meanwhile uses a similarly horticultural vocabulary in his *Scale of Perfection*, describing the ground of the soul—as in the *bottom* of the soul—as the place where the image of vain self-love is found. For Hilton, growth depends on the individual blocking the bottom of the well, which is in the garden of the soul and from which the stinking water of sin flows, otherwise "it wole corrumpe alle the floures of the gardyn of thi soule" (it will corrupt all the flowers of the garden of your soul).[44] Hilton's contemplative, too, must dig deep to search for this kind of spiritual treasure: "Thee bihoveth for to delve deepe in thyn herte" (It requires you to delve deep into your heart).[45] This allegory can be traced to the *Somme le Roi* tradition—a moral treatise written in 1279 for Philip III (d. 1285) of France by his confessor, the Dominican friar Laurent d'Orléans. In this text, the soul reaches for the spade of penance to dig its ground and remove that which prevents it from witnessing God, who appears as a gardener, paralleling Julian's own rendering of the servant as Christ, who "shuld ben a gardiner" (should be [also: should have been] a gardener).[46] In Julian's soul-as-garden configuration, as in her representation of the soul as the "cite" from the sixteenth showing, this spatial construction is defined by its suitability—its *capacity*—for habitation or dwelling. The capacity of the ecological soul for receiving God is the locus of its "tresor" (treasure), which must be dug and planted and watered over time.[47] To realize this flourishing, the servant must do the work of beseking; they must be willing to "stirtith and rynnith in grete haste for love to don his lords will" (leap up and run in great haste for love to do his lord's will), even if they happen to "fallith in a slade and takith ful grete sore" (fall in a ditch and sustain a great injury).[48]

Julian's description of the soul as earth therefore also sets up the participatory emphasis of her theology, as she finds yet another homely image to depict the practice of beseking and the preparation of the soul for God. Two final comparisons will shed more light on this ecological design, providing a helpful theological backdrop for understanding beseking as an act of willed cultivation. The first is another Rhinelandish parallel, found in Eckhart's commentary on Luke 14:21–32, the parable of the Great Supper, in which the lord tells his servant to "go out into the highways and hedges, and compel [the people] to come in, that my house may be filled."[49] In his sermon on this verse, Eckhart reads the land as the soul, with the hedgerows signifying its hedged-in powers: "the more the soul is collected, the narrower she is, and the narrower, the wider."[50] For Eckhart, the servant is the "spark of the soul" (*vunkelin der sele*), like the *scintilla*, the "spark of conscience," which ignites the soul into union with God—as with Julian's "godly will," the part of the soul that only intends toward good. The image of the "highways and hedges" thus indicates the soul as *capax Dei*, which is expanded by the labor of the will in service of the lord.

The second parallel is in passus 18 of the *Piers Plowman* C-text, when Will is shown the way to the Tree by Liberum Arbitrium (Free Will), who replaces Piers in tending to the Tree within the human heart.[51] Will's journey across this "contre" (country) is the culmination of his spiritual pilgrimage. He has already traversed the "lond of longyng" (land of longing), the *regio dissimilitudinis* or land of unlikeness; this is the moral and psychological realm where Will sees himself in the "myrrour" (mirror), as does Julian in her own Godforsaken moment: "Here may you sene what I am of myselfe" (Here you may see what I am of myself).[52] Then, in Will's first interaction with this character in passus 16, he asks: "Whareof serue ȝe . . . sire *Liberum Arbitrium*?" (How do you serve . . . sir Liberum Arbitrium [Free Will])—an inquiry which serves to establish the role of Free Will.[53] But the line also inverts the oft-quoted speech by Reason in passus 5, when Reason questions Will, "can thow seruen . . . or syngen in a churche" (can you serve . . . or sing in church), going on to list other tasks he might be able to perform in service: "Heggen or harwen, or swyn or gees dryue / Or eny other kynes craft þat þe comune nedeth" (Hedge or harrow, or drive hogs or geese / Or any other skill that serves the community).[54] Will answers affirmatively, "sertes!" (certainly!), but perhaps not with the "kynes craft" prescribed by Reason: he claims to contribute by creating verse and praying for others.[55] He is subsequently impelled to repent by Conscience, who convinces him that he must be *productive* in his labor, like the apostles. Will's later interaction with Liberum Arbitrium at the Tree reiterates this theme, stressing the need for works of charity as well as clerical teaching. Will's service, he learns, must be performed as a *willed labor* of "heggen and harwen," cultivating the hedgerows and harrowing the soil of the soul.

For Langland, then, the search for salvation is a *doing*, or a series of doings—*Dowel, Dobet, Dobest*—which ascends the epistemological ladder, only to land on the "synthetic self-knowing" that Eleanor Johnson calls "participatory contemplation," a practice which breaks down the boundary between the active and the contemplative life.[56] Similarly, Julian's beseking is an active, not passive, pursuit, a labor which *brings things forth*—a "craft" as Langland's Reason (and later, Heidegger, in his use of the term *technē*) understands it. In this way, beseking also defies any separation between the inward-facing practice of prayer, as an act of attentive receptivity, and the outward-facing cultivation of oneself in relation to others, as a responsibility to give back to one's community. It is a practice of both giving and receiving—present participles that reflect its processual nature—which promises to fulfill the statement that "al shal be wele," where being well is also a *doing* well. By committing to this work, the laborer or servant practises nonresistance to the falls, hurts, and sins that delay their task, moving through the land of longing, the region of unlikeness, without judgment or blame. And, in doing so, they recognize their ability to cultivate this wilderness and transform it into a home. This does not mean disengaging from its barrenness and waste, but rather choosing to persist, choosing to see the goodness and love within that place, and choosing to abide in it. As phenomenologist Norman Wirzba writes, "Care-ful work introduces us to the sanctity of the world or, as Henry Bugbee would put it, the wilderness that everywhere surrounds us: 'The more we experience things in depth, the more we participate in a mystery intelligible to us only as such; and the more we understand our world to be an unknown world. *Our true home is wilderness, even the world of everyday.*' "[57] Julian's ecological poetic constructs a vision of this care-ful work, showing how divine grace and human response come together to catalyze redemption and recovery.

HOME IS AT HAND

Julian's theology of spiritual growth and cultivation has been read so far as a recovery narrative in which the human connection to God enables them to choose him, and so to work toward reunifying the soul. This is a superficially temporal timeline, with the task of "digging and delving" following the fall, as in the lord and the servant parable and in Langland's sequential *Dowel*, *Dobet*, *Dobest* triad. But Julian's revelation is also predicated upon God's eschatological perspective, wherein past, present, and future are held together in eternal atemporality: as she puts it in the *Revelations*, God "made," "restorid" (restored), and "kepith us in his blissid love" (sustains us in his blessed love).[58] From this angle, human salvation is always in the process of being fulfilled. Julian has witnessed something of this complex temporality in the realm of visionary beholding, which suspends her for a moment in God-time. But this glimpse of God's omniscient (and omnipotent) perspective raises important questions about the nature of free will, and so, too, the possibility of human participation in their own recovery. As I show above, Julian offers beseking as a voluntary way of being-in-the-world that relies on the "godly will" of the individual, which can only ever tend toward God. This will must then be reunified with the lower aspect of the soul, which is prone to veering off the path of righteousness and toward sin. Again, this is a voluntary act, or series of acts, whereby prayer must be willingly performed, penance willingly suffered, and confession willingly given. Nevertheless, as I explained in chapter 4, Julian's system of the wills is not Pelagian; she does not hold that humans can perfect themselves through their free will. Instead, she grounds her soteriology in Christ, whose death provides the remedy for the soul's fragmentariness—just as the fall provides the fault for which his death atoned. But with creation, fall, incarnation, and redemption occurring in one instant in God's view, the causality of these events is complicated. Linear temporality is disrupted, and human agency must be reconfigured against the backdrop of God's divine plan.

In this section, I consider how Julian tackles this problem of a participatory theology that is governed by divine predetermination. To navigate this apparent paradox, my discussion turns once again to Julian's ontology, now thinking through her metaphysics of creation and its relationship to time. This throws up further disagreements between Julian's theology and Heidegger's phenomenology: though both thinkers reject a scholastic metaphysics of creation, emphasizing the processual nature of human *being*, their diverging temporal grounds set up differently their answers to the possibility of recovery. These divergences will become clearer as the discussion unfolds, but first I want to examine their similarly processual accounts of human ontology. On an initial glance, a reader might be forgiven for interpreting Julian's writing on the soul as formal rather than performative, materialist rather than metaphysical. Humankind is *made*—the body molded from the mucky earth—in the likeness of God: a product, crafted and realized in relation to the prefactical form of the creator. Heidegger challenges the medieval scholastic metaphysics of creation on the grounds of this very distinction, arguing that it eclipsed the active constitution of the human being. He traces this creator/created dichotomy to the Greek terms *eidos* (literally "form" for Plato) and *ousia* ("substance" for Aristotle), writing that the former equated to *essentia* (the "whatness" of a thing), the model or image by which the thing is crafted or made, its quiddity, and the latter to *existentia* (the "thatness" of the thing), its ontic properties or haecceity.[59] From the Heideggerian perspective, the moment of creation or production realizes the eidos of a thing, releasing it into an existence independent of its creator or its perfect model. It thereby becomes ousia, a thing with ontic properties. Sean J. McGrath even notes that "the prephilosophical meaning of *ousia* is property, that which is present-at-hand in a household, that which, at any given moment is available for use and over which I have right of disposal."[60] Ousia, in Heidegger's understanding, is akin to that which is present-at-hand, "the objective presence corresponding to *eidos*."[61]

In his study of Heidegger and medieval philosophy, however, McGrath outlines a number of difficulties with Heidegger's critique of medieval scholasticism, a discussion that in turn sheds light on Julian's own representation of causality and human action.[62] In Heidegger's view, the scholastic reduction of being to a causal nexus obscures the spontaneous emergence of being present in *phusis*, the energetic presencing of a thing into being. As I mentioned in chapter 4, in classical philosophy *phusis* was set against the immovability of God, while the scholastic approach translated its catalyzing *energeia* into the Latin *actualitas*, which has a causal point of reference. In the Greek model, being emerges spontaneously from nothing; in the creator/created model, the presencing of being is temporal, awaiting completion. According to Heidegger, this scholastic objectification of being covers over this productive capacity of the product: as McGrath puts it, "When Christianity appropriates Greek ontology in a theology of creation, all being becomes product in relation to the Creator. The producer, God, is a nonfactical being, a being outside of time. The nonproduct character of Dasein is forgotten."[63] This precludes, then, the dynamic being of human being: "the being that we ourselves are, the Dasein, cannot at all be *interrogated* as such by the question *What* is this? We gain access to this being only if we ask: *Who* is it? The Dasein is not constituted by whatness but—if we may coin the expression—by *whoness.* The answer does not give a thing but an I, you, we."[64] Heidegger's critique is that if human being is just another product, they can no longer be considered participants in the production of their world. He thereby rejects the conceptual paradigm of humanity and world as product in relation to producer.

This critique presses into a tension between the prefactical and the factical as well as the infinite and the temporal. Heidegger's argument is a refusal of the infinite potentiality of a higher power, implicating not only medieval scholasticism but also, as McGrath points out, all ontologies that invoke a creator: "Heidegger's life project is to think the finitude of being without referencing the infinite."[65] And so, my discussion once again arrives at the crucial distinction between the secular philosophy of Heidegger and the eschatological metaphysics of Julian's *Revelations.* Rather than Heidegger's "nothing" of death, Julian frames God as both creative producer and the teleological end of beseking, an end toward which the soul is continually self-projecting. Yet McGrath also points out that "Heidegger shows no signs of ever having truly understood the radical break with Greek ontology in [Thomas] Aquinas's notion of being," which underwent a transformation, conceiving of being as *esse*, the act signified by the verb "to be."[66] *Essentia*, McGrath writes, "is a limitation of *esse*, a contraction of the act of being to determinate structure. *Substantia* is a further contraction of *esse* to a particular *this* . . . In its concretization and finitization in the thing, *esse* is released from God and channeled into determinate thinghood."[67] Put another way, *esse* frees Aquinas's notion of being from the constrictions of formal, temporal categories. Heidegger's rejection of the doctrine of creation on account of its causal nexus seems not to account for this active understanding of being as a *verbal* concept.

My reading of Julian can therefore be triangulated between Heidegger and the scholastic ontotheology he criticizes. In Julian's theology of mutual indwelling, the soul is "a creature in god," made of substance but from nothing made, while the body is made from the created earth. So she recognizes the presence of the creator within the subject, meaning that the soul transcends a state of simply creature, as in created product. Humanity is already "oned" to God in substance, a fact which is obscured by the fragmentariness of the soul. Christ's sacrifice then redeems the divinity of human creatureliness, providing a path through the dark night of the postlapsarian soul to its true home, fully whole and "oned" with God. This wholeness (as it stands from the human, penultimate perspective in the eschatological timeline) is achieved through action, always available and realized through the process of beseking, an existential enterprise enacted through worldly living. Human being is therefore *participatory* in the re-productive, re-creative reunification of its wholeness or essential nature—its ontology. This lapsarian principle allows Julian to speak of the soul not only as product but also as a necessary actor within the salvation narrative. The sense is that the lifelong performance of beseking restores the soul's porosity and homely relation to God, thereby redeeming the feeling of homelessness that has pervaded the earthly experience. This requires agency on the part of the seeker, who must work and strive toward self-understanding—the self-unfolding or flourishing of spiritual growth—so as to cultivate their soul as an appropriate dwelling for God. In this way, just as the phenomenological model understands human existence as a transcending-returning projection within a referential web of meaning-structures—a *whoness*, not a whatness—Julian's understanding is, similarly, of human nature as a constant process of reunification and fulfillment. But while for Heidegger the creator/created distinction eclipses the dynamic constitution of human being, Julian works out a complex solution to the question of the human capacity for action and production independent of a producer. She does so through her theology of mutual indwelling, wherein the soul is both "oned" to God as its creator *and* as the likeness of humanity's ontological wholeness to which it is beseking.

Aquinas makes a similar argument in his own writing on predestination in the *Summa*, which also illuminates the temporal mechanics of Julian's theology. He quotes Paul's description of predestination as a "call" to glorification: "And whom he predestinated, them he also called. And whom he called, them he also justified. And whom he justified, them he also glorified" (Romans 8:30). The act of predestination remains in the "doer," like the immanent activities of "understanding" and "willing," which Aquinas compares to transitive actions like "heating or cutting . . . those that produce a reaction in outside material."[68] Predestination, he argues, "does not *put anything into the predestined*," but its execution "reaches out into external things and produces an effect there."[69] This is an act contingent on grace, "which is temporal," and must therefore be in "the person predestined," since God is eternal. As such, predestination is defined as "*a preparation for grace in the present, and for glory in the future*."[70] Aquinas concludes this article by stating that grace is "not included in the definition of predestination as though it were an essential element, but because predestination implies a relationship to grace, namely a relationship of cause to effect, and *of act to objective*. Hence it does not follow that predestination is temporal."[71] The phrase "*of act to objective*" is key here, and Thomas Gilby expounds its meaning in a footnote to his edition of the *Summa*, writing that it implies a relationship of glory to grace "beyond the 'mechanics' of causality": "The specific significance of grace is that it is a sharing in God's life by friendship, the exemplar of which is in heaven. The distinction between them is not just that between different historical periods, one now, the other hereafter. In one sense the Kingdom is at hand, in another it is already present."[72]

This excerpt speaks to my reading of Julian's *Revelations* as promoting a theology wherein a degree of homeliness or wholeness is available now as well as in heaven. Aquinas is arguing that God's predestined plan produces an *effect* in the predestined soul (rather than putting something into it directly), which correlates directly to its preparedness to receive the grace of God. Similarly, Julian's anthropology leaves room for human action as essential to the fulfillment of the soul's fundamental identity. Denys Turner summarizes this well, writing that Julian's theology "is wholly resistant to that picture of the divine providence and governance of human affairs according to which God causes the overall drama of human history, as it were micromanaging the general lines of the salvific plot, leaving human agents to exercise their freedom of action within the plot, but free only insofar as they are free *from* the providential causality."[73] Indeed, the idea of the kingdom as both at hand and already present is communicated via Julian's theology of indwelling, where Christ finds his "homliest home" in the "blisfull kyngdom" of the heart. This is a dwelling which, as I explore above, dissolves the boundary between heaven and earth, and is available to humanity not only after death but also in part *within* themselves. In an argument of reciprocity akin to that which grounds this doctrine of indwelling, Aquinas refers to this necessary "preparedness" as twofold: preparedness "of the thing acted on" (i.e., the making ready of one's own soul) and preparedness of the agent, God, who "has already conceived the idea of how a work is to be done."[74] God is already prepared in the eschatological plan; humankind is then required to uphold their side of the bargain. God's predestination is therefore an immanent action, effecting the human receptivity to his grace, but the human cultivation of this receptivity is transitive in form: he has created the capacity for grace, but humans do the transfiguring, or "produce the reaction" through beseking. God is the object of this transitive action, but the action itself also becomes objective: "*our besekyng*."[75] With this grammatical doubling, Julian thus expresses the lively activity of the soul—its dynamism—as a realization of its essential capacity.

In this reading, Julian's theology of recovery is *ontological* as much as it is teleological. This statement is by no means an attempt, however, to hem Julian in as a scholastic theologian. As I have demonstrated, her theology is itself an ecology of thought, its roots brushing up against a knotted rhizome of scholastic, monastic, and vernacular texts. But unlike Aquinas and other scholastic theologians of her time, Julian's focus is not so much on the abstract conceptual understanding of ontology; it lies, instead, on the lived practice that is both a constituent and a consequence of this ontology, a practice which will see her (and her "even cristen") through the "hidouse and dredfull, swete and lovely" (hideous and frightening, sweet and lovely) spectrum of worldly experience.[76] In this sense, Julian is drawing on Boethian and pseudo-Dionysian traditions as much as those of the schools. This is most evident in her writing on sin, the final aspect of her theology to be addressed in this discussion. Figuratively speaking, Julian's attitude is of sin as a great wound that, gifted to humanity, will be turned to honors upon God's judgment. She determines that the pains and tribulation of human living stem from an ontological separation from God, rather than moral defect. In Nicholas Watson's words, "In this system not only is divine lack merely an aspect of the divine fullness, a manifestation of God's need to pour himself out; human lack, properly understood, is essentially no different."[77] For Julian, then, the ontological fact of human separation from God is the foundation for their lapse into sin (the soul's dynamism directed wrongfully; action in the wrong direction), but it is also the foundation for human fulfillment: both facts are mutually coexistent in the creation/fall/redemption timeline. Sin and suffering are thus configured as part of the very essence of existence and, moreover, part of the process of reunification which defines the existence of "all mankinde that shall be savid."[78] It is on account of this that Julian can say, "Synne is behovabil" (Sin is necessary): sin is befitting, appropriate, an ontological fact of human existence.[79]

It follows that the performative action required in Julian's ontotheology is one of both preparedness *and* fulfillment. The future home in heaven is brought to hand, as it were, by Christ's redemption of earthly existence. This was prophesied by John the Baptist who, preaching in the wilderness of Judea, declared "the kingdom of heaven is at hand" (Matthew 3:2). He advised the people to repent, calling for the "way" to be prepared for the lord, for paths to be "made straight:" "*uox* clamantis *in* [*deserto*] *p*arate *u*iam domini *r*ectas *f*acite semitas *e*jus" (a voice crying in [the desert], prepare the way of the lord, make his paths straight), glossed as "makeð þe lou*er*des weies. *and* rihteð his peðes" (make the lord's ways, and make right his paths) in one thirteenth-century homily.[80] "At hand" in this verse is a translation of *appropinquavit* in the Vulgate, indicating a drawing near, from adverbial *prope* (near, nigh, close), related to *propinquity* (nearness, kindred), *proper*, and *appropriate*—as in Julian's "behovabil," which also indicates a sense of *appropriateness* or expediency in the existence of sin. Turner offers a similar translation of "behovabil" as the Latin *conveniens*, "in the sense that Anselm, Hugh of St. Victor, Thomas Aquinas, and Bonaventure would have understood it, which is . . . that it 'fits,' it is 'just so.'"[81] But Julian goes further than this reading allows: sin is not only "behovabil" as in convenient or fitting; it is beneficial, in fact it is necessary. Sin is the gift that is better for the servant than his own health—"a geft that be better to hym and more worshipfull than his own hole shuld have ben" (a gift that is better for him and more beneficial than his own wholeness would have been)—because this wholeness would never have exposed him to his ontological condition of separation, and so to its fulfillment.[82] The awareness or knowledge of this lack rests on the disclosure of human existence to the self, or the self-understanding described above. It is in this way that Julian's model of recovery can be understood, at its heart, as a hermeneutic project. For Julian, her sickness and subsequent beholding of Christ discloses to her this state, but she will spend the rest of her life seeking the understanding of it. For her "even cristen," meanwhile, they must begin with the will, seeking into themselves and so also into the divine.

One further etymological twist concludes my close reading of this difficult theological idea and its phenomenological character. The above nexus of *appropriateness*, *nearness*, or *at-handness* also includes *property*, as in the Greek *ousia*; that which is objectively present-at-hand in a household, available at any given moment for use. As I have shown, present-at-handedness in Heideggerian terms denotes a sense of availability (literally "being-before-the-hand"), a theoretical determination of a thing's essence, defined as such by the thing's showing itself apart from its web of relation. McGrath reiterates that this emerges out of ready-to-handedness, a condition of homelike attunement or inauthenticity, whereby the thing functions transparently within a referential whole. When a person ceases to *use* the thing or when they move to define it, it becomes present-at-hand; it becomes objective, removed from its situational context and so disclosed in its thingliness. This phenomenological principle can also be applied to the soteriological story outlined above, where the kingdom is brought to hand by Christ's incarnation, the coming of the prophet-son who embodies God's Word, the disclosive act par excellence. Of course, the kingdom has not been disclosed as broken (unready-to-hand), as in Heidegger's famous example of the hammer. Rather, via the *mene* of the incarnation, humanity is given *disposal over* that which is at-hand: the kingdom of heaven, "our homliest home," is brought to hand by the incarnation, like the existential realization of humanity by the creative hand of God. Humankind's ontological fulfillment or homlyhede is in this way also made present-at-hand, made available, by both the creation and incarnation, events which are equally and simultaneously contingent for their redemption.

To conclude this discussion of salvation and time, I want to reiterate that both Heideggerian phenomenology and Julian's theology understand human existence as always in a state of production or fulfillment. The "almost-thereness" implied by John the Baptist's use of *appropinquavit* captures the penultimacy of this state, which is also borne out in Julian's discussion of beseking. Like Heidegger's Dasein, Julian positions humanity in the "being-between," a continuous projection of the self into the unknown. But where for Heidegger this projection occurs against a background of nothingness, Julian understands the human soul as always connected to God in substance. And so, her theology is framed by an infinite horizon absent in Heideggerian philosophy. For Julian, things being well, or homlyhede, is *made available* by God at any given moment; the human task is to prepare for the realization of this potential through the act of seeking. Put another way: Julian writes of the soul as already in a sense at home in God, and him in the soul. This homeliness is realized, fulfilled, or simply disclosed by the incarnation of Christ, which reveals to humanity the goodness and love of God. As such, the recovery process I have been glossing as *coming home* or *performing homlyhede* can also be understood as an inner journey of fulfillment which parallels the topography expressed in Matthew 3:2 and Luke 14:23; a making straight of the paths in the soul, an expanding of the hedges, or a cultivating of the land. Christ leads humanity on this pathway home, he *is* the pathway home, and all the while the human soul is already at home in God, because God is at home in it, in his seat in the wilderness. Just as Christ comes into the Judean desert as the path through this postlapsarian wilderness, suffering on the cross to lead his subjects onward, Julian theorizes the human recovery project as one of loving labor, of cultivating the soul such that its capacity—its highways and hedges—is expanded enough to allow the journey.

CHRISTUS MEDICUS

This reading of temporality in Julian's *Revelations* has shown how her theory of redemption relies on both divine and human actors: on the grace of God and the human will to choose him. In this sense, her theology can also be understood as an intersubjective project, though a rather more complicated kind of intersubjectivity than that between two human beings. In this final discussion of the chapter, I refer once more to recent phenomenologies of well-being to consider the therapeutic component of the God-human relationship as Julian describes it—which I read as a subtle rendering of the medieval *Christus medicus* topos. In staging this final comparison between Julian's theology and phenomenological approaches to well-being, I aim to reiterate the Christological crux of the *Revelations*, highlighting how Julian positions Christ as the healer of human ills and the facilitator of human redemption. Phenomenological theories of the physician-patient encounter help to gloss the precise dynamics of this relationship, stressing in particular the need for trust and reciprocity between the two actors. In turn, this enriches my earlier reading of the willed cultivation of the soul, and the world as a home, by considering in relationship the two actors of Julian's lord and the servant parable: the human (Adam) and the divine (Christ). By examining this final feature of Julian's contemplative work, I therefore conclude my reading of her recovery theology as a joint hermeneutic project: the communal task of the corporate body of humankind and God, which is enacted through mutual understanding, compassion, and everlasting love.

The notion of *Christus medicus* (Christ the physician) or Christ as *medicus animae* (physician of the soul) can be found in Christian texts as early as the second century.[83] Through the work of prominent theologians such as Augustine and Aelred of Rievaulx, the idea then made its way into a wide range of vernacular devotional texts—such as the fifteenth-century treatise, *A Deuout Treatyse Called The Tree & XII. Frutes of The Holy Goost*, which proclaims: "I go now to receyue it. as a sike body to a leche.þat þi blissid gostly medicyne mow make my seke soule hole The sikker þat I am lord ih*es*u.þe more me nedith to come to þe" (I go now to receive it, as a sick body to a physician, that by your blessed spiritual medicine may make my sick soul whole. The sicker I am, lord Jesus, the more I need to come to you).[84] Elsewhere, I have identified particular resonances between the *Revelations* and a vernacular medical imaginary rooted in humoral theory.[85] Specifically, I stressed the ways that Julian combines both humoral and surgical elements to construct a hybrid "Man of Sorrows" who hurts and heals, suffers on the cross and remedies the sins of humanity. Extending this work, I here turn from the medieval medical features of Julian's rendering of Christ to consider how her medical hermeneutic can be better understood alongside phenomenologies of the physician-patient encounter. My focus remains on Julian's medical hermeneutic (the way she understands the showings with and through medical ideas), but I now address the significance of understanding itself as a key to her representation of Christ the physician.

In his writing on the clinical setting, phenomenologist Fredrik Svenaeus theorizes the medical meeting between physician and patient as a hermeneutic encounter, contingent upon the mutual understanding of these two actors. Such a view departs from the psychoanalytic framework, which typically frames the clinical goal as the transformation of the patient's self-understanding—as in Sigmund Freud's hermeneutics of suspicion, defined as such by Paul Ricoeur, which uncovers unconscious desires and resistances beneath the patient's symptoms.[86] In the psychoanalytic meeting, "the only possibility of healing goes through the *patient*'s, and not the analyst's, understanding."[87] This is quite different, Svenaeus writes, to what he calls the *medical* encounter, wherein the patient's self-understanding "does not guarantee restored health." Instead, the clinician must "understand the patient as an understanding person, through projecting himself into the patient's understanding and vice versa."[88] Which is to say, while the psychoanalyst seeks to change the patient's understanding of themselves, the clinician works with the patient in a joint project of reciprocal understanding. To explain this theory further, Svenaeus quotes from the work of Thomas S. Szasz and Marc H. Hollender, who together describe the physician-patient encounter: "This relationship, characterized by a high degree of empathy, has elements often associated with the notions of friendship and partnership and the imparting of expert advice. The physician may be said to help the patient to help himself.

The physician's gratification cannot stem from power or from the control over someone else. His satisfactions are derived from more abstract kinds of mastery, which are as yet poorly understood."[89] So, this meeting is asymmetrical in that the physician is regarded as the therapeutic authority in the partnership, a higher power or causal component. But this account also makes room for the productive capacity of the subject or patient, who must work with the physician to increase their own self-understanding; the physician *helps them to help themselves*. Szasz and Hollender's "high degree of empathy" might therefore be redefined as a high degree of compassion: as I suggested in chapter 4 of this book, compassion foregrounds the *person*-in-pain rather than the pain itself, performing an act of *co*-feeling, not *in*-feeling with the ill person. Just so, Szasz and Hollender's physician sees the person-in-pain and prioritizes the development of mutual understanding.

Svenaeus calls this approach *clinical hermeneutics*, which he explains with the help of phenomenologist Hans-Georg Gadamer's model of textual interpretation.[90] Gadamer held that the reader must understand a text as authoritative, posing to it a question that can only be answered by their meeting with it. When applied to the clinical scenario, the doctor remains the "reader" or "interpreter" of the patient-text, but since the meeting is dialogic this is a mutual process of questions and answers. This dialogue serves to hone the "lifeworld horizons" of clinician and patient, bringing them closer together until they touch each other. In contrast to the psychoanalytic hermeneutics of suspicion, then, this phenomenological model is action-oriented: the doctor does not adopt the basic paranoid assumption that the patient's account is hidden or distorted, to be mistrusted. Rather, they understand the patient's account as simply incomplete, "in the sense that the patient himself is often unaware of the ways in which a particular disease can make life unhomelike."[91] It becomes the mutual project of clinician and patient to take the necessary actions to make life as homelike as possible, even in the face of illness or dying. As such, this phenomenological approach also stresses the intersubjectivity of the recovery project and the necessity for action: that recovery may be work, but work that does not need to be undertaken alone.

This two-way exchange between physician and patient is somewhat complicated by the Christian story, wherein God and humankind are not equals but exist in a relationship of creator to created. Earlier in this chapter, I investigated the ways Julian negotiates this dynamic: how she manages to sustain the notion of free will even in the context of God's omnipotence. In this participatory theology, Julian frames the soul as not only *creature* as in created product, but as active participant or *producer* in the redemptive project. So it is that Svenaeus's model of clinical reciprocity can be mapped onto Julian's writing of Christ as healer, despite the various paradoxical dynamics that inhere in the salvation narrative—such as Christ acting as both physician (healer of humanity's ills) and patient (sufferer whom humanity must seek to understand in turn). These dynamics are fleshed out further below, but here I focus on one particular property which Julian identifies as central to this therapeutic relationship, which is also borne out in phenomenological writings on the clinical encounter: the condition of *trust*.[92] By examining Julian's writing on trust, I extend my reading above of beseking as a cultivation of the soul to consider this as a project of mutual understanding, instigated and fueled by love.

Julian identifies "sekir troste" (certain trust) as a condition which grounds prayer in her account of the fourteenth showing, which begins in chapter 41 of the long text.[93] In Julian's view, if prayer is the direction of the intention toward God then trust is the acknowledgment that the intention may not be enough to reach him in beholding. This principle of epistemological concession undergirds all apophatic contemplation—as articulated by Proverbs 3:5–6, which in the King James Version reads: "Trust in the Lord with all thine heart; and lean not unto thine own understanding. In all thy ways acknowledge him, and he shall direct thy paths."[94] The translation of "gressus" as "paths" recalls the making straight of paths of Matthew 3:2, which I already described above as a topographical parallel to Julian's act of beseking. The Douay-Rheims version meanwhile reads: "Have confidence in the Lord with all thy heart, and lean not upon thy own prudence. In all thy ways think on him, and he will direct thy steps." Both are valid translations of the Vulgate's "habe fiduciam," "fiduciam" from *fidere*, to trust or have confidence in.[95] Douay-Rheims' "prudence" is, however, closer to the Vulgate's "prudentiae." As I noted in chapter 3, prudence or *prudentia* is the cardinal virtue which governs the ability to project oneself forward, to direct one's intention as is required in prayer. But trust requires the subject to abandon this perceived wisdom, this intellectual capacity of directed intention, instead submitting to the wisdom of God.

Trust, in Julian's hermeneutic, is therefore a property predicated upon *activity* or *process*—one created and developed through participation. This aligns with modern studies of affect and behavioral psychology, which have theorized trust as an intersubjective condition of vulnerability.[96] These studies suggest that trust must be a total and complete commitment to be effective—"sekir" trust, as Julian puts it—or else it is automatically negated, becoming *dis*trust: as the philosopher Knud Eljer Løgstrup writes, "the least interruption, the least calculation, the least dilution of it in the service of something else destroys it entirely, indeed turns it into the opposite of what it is."[97] Julian describes such an experience in chapter 41, when she writes that "oftentymes our troste is not full, for we arn not sekir that God herith us" (oftentimes our trust is not full, for we are not certain that God hears us).[98] The result is that the supplicant is left "as barren and dry" after their prayers as they were before. In this instance, they did not trust, not only because they were afraid that God would not hear, but that he would not be listening; that if they truly laid themselves at his mercy, they would find themselves abandoned and alone. By choosing to trust *fully*, a person acknowledges and "overpasses" (again, to use Julian's word) this potential for Godforsakenness.

This example echoes the catch-22 of the shame cycle I described in chapter 3, where an individual feels unworthy, leading them to act in ways which prevent them from rebuilding a sense of worth. Just so, in Julian's understanding, a person's lack of trust prevents them from seeking connection, which in turn corroborates their feelings of abandonment and distrust. And, as with shame, breaking out of the distrust cycle requires the person to remember their innate union with God, which secures their sense of homeliness even if they feel alone—a requirement of *faith*. According to Julian, this is a different condition entirely to trust: she configures faith as a specific condition of the ontological mutual indwelling of the soul in God. It is situated in the soul, fulfilling its capacity for receiving God—"we faith*fully* pray"—and is also a spatial zone in which the soul dwells—"stedfastly hold me *in the faith*," Julian writes.[99] Trust, meanwhile, discloses this indwelling through the choice to turn toward God. In this way, trust might be understood as *faith-in-action*; the leap in a "leap of faith," or perhaps more accurately, the continuous and dynamic series of leaps which constitute beseking.[100] As in the Anselmian model of *fides quaerens intellectum*, first comes faith, then comes the act of seeking understanding. This definition in turn highlights the vulnerability necessary in the act of beseking: that in seeking him, a person chooses to put themselves in the hands of God without certain knowledge of his workings.

This relationship of trust is not, however, predicated upon belief without proof, or without disclosure on the part of God as is faith. It is, as the phenomenological model of mutual participation defines it, a *reciprocal* act. In the theological context, the incarnation discloses God's dealings with humanity, functioning as God's own "willed, kenotic leaping of love," as Cristina Maria Cervone writes: the *leap* which provided humanity with the opportunity to seek salvation.[101] God then sacrificed his son for this same purpose in the ultimate and eternal act of trust: as Julian puts it in chapter 52, "Be Criste we are stedfastly kept, and be his grace touchyng we are reysid into sekir troste of salvation" (We are steadfastly kept by Christ, and by the touchings of his grace we are raised into certain trust of salvation).[102] The Greek term *therápōn*, meaning "earthly attendant" or "servant," captures the essence of Christ's role as physician within this narrative, closely related as it is to the modern borrowing, *therapy*.[103] The term is used once in the Greek Testament of the King James Version, in Hebrews 3:5, when Jesus is described as worthy of greater honor than even Moses, who was "faithful in all his house, as a servant [Greek: *therápōn*];" Christ is to Moses as "he who hath builded the house" is to the house itself. Christ, however, is double in nature: he is divine *and* human, creator *and* created. So, he embodies both the builder of the house (God) and the house God built (humanity). In this sense, Christ is the lord God's *therápōn* and the lord himself, serving and engaging humanity in service of the same project—their therapy. He does so by *changing the way they figure things out*, to return to Maggie Ross's definition of transfiguration: as his earthly attendant,

Christ reveals God's home-building project, disclosing to humankind the present-at-handedness of heaven on earth.[104] But the human actors still have to perform the "figuring out:" to keep up the building and rebuilding of the house within the soul, which is God's "homliest home;" to engage "faithfully and trostily" (faithfully and trustily) in beseking.[105]

Julian's anthropology therefore anticipates Svenaeus's requirement for the physician to "[project] himself into the patient's understanding," whereby the incarnation of Christ on earth allows God to take on human form and so also human understanding. In this, Julian configures a comparable model to the phenomenological account of clinical reciprocity outlined above. Certainly, Christ-the-physician's "gratifications" or "satisfactions" do not stem from a desire for control or power, as Szasz and Hollender put it, but neither are they "derived from more abstract kinds of mastery, which are as yet poorly understood." Indeed, Julian's *Revelations* are very clear as to where the satisfactions of the physician derive from, and how they manifest in the therapeutic encounter: "Wete it wele: love was his mening. Who shewid it the? Love. What shewid he the? Love. Wherfore shewid it he? For love" (Know it well: love was his meaning. Who showed it to you? Love. What did he show you? Love. Why did he show it to you? For love).[106] God's love is the motivating force of humanity's recovery, which can be felt when the soul is in tune with its divine aspect, or at least seeking toward it in beseking. Julian therefore revises the traditional satisfaction theory of Anselm, which conceives of Christ's death as satisfying the debt humanity has failed to pay.[107] In a striking inversion of this economy, Christ instead asks *Julian* if she is satisfied—"Art thou wele payd that I suffrid for thee?" (Are you satisfied enough that I suffered for you?)—and places Julian's satisfaction ahead of his own, in a claim to total reciprocity: "If thou art payde, I am payde" (If you are satisfied, I am satisfied).[108]

In light of this emphasis on shared understanding, I read the therapeutic relationship in Julian's *Revelations* as one of both compassion and empathy, co-feeling *and* in-feeling. As Julian understands it, the incarnation occurred because it was necessary for God to live and die as a human, to take on humanity's suffering—to feel into their pain. But the fulfillment of this redemptive arc then depends upon the compassion of humanity, who must seek into their own understanding of God's will in turn. This is a joint hermeneutic exercise, wherein God seeks to understand humanity through Christ, providing a patient-text—Christ's suffering body—for humanity to then interpret. Julian exemplifies this project in her ongoing interpretation of her revelation, a lifelong process of reading the book of Christ: *lectio Domini*. For as the eighth showing reveals, the physical suffering of Christ is only the outward expression of this act; there are meanwhile less accessible, inner expressions of joy and "chere" that persist behind and beyond his pain. To access these, Julian—and her reader—must in turn seek into the text of his passion, and with this seeking realize its therapeutic purpose. It is because of this hermeneutic that Julian can finally state, at the start of chapter 82 of the long text, that Christ is "our medicyne" (our medicine), both therapeutic object and healing subject for humanity's well-being.[109]

In this way, Julian engages the *Christus medicus* topos as at once a linguistic expression, an ontological fact, and the hermeneutic disclosure of her entire recovery theology. The image of Christ's side-wound is a perfect example of this multiplicity, functioning as both a literal and figurative expression of the nexus of suffering and healing. She describes her encounter with the side-wound in chapter 24, in her account of the tenth revelation: "Than with a glad chere our Lord loked into his syde and beheld, enjoyand; and with his swete lokyng he led forth the understondyng of his creture be the same wound into his syde withinne" (Then with a glad expression our Lord looked into his side and beheld, enjoying; and with his sweet looking he led forth the understanding of this creature by the same wound into his side within).[110] In this passage, Christ beholds his own body with gladness, a gaze which allows Julian to enter into this "faire delectabil place" (fair delightful place)—to dwell a while in this enclosure, long enough for her own understanding and comfort to be born.[111] With this, Julian enters Christ's body as God has entered humanity's, resolving recovery once more through the union of human and divine. But this kind of wholeness does not depend upon the cohesion of the physician and patient's "lifeworlds" as in the phenomenological model described above. Instead, Julian envisages a hermeneutic and ontological form of togetherness, realized through a continuous turning and re-turning of attentive understanding and love. It is through this joint work—the coming together of Christ's passion and humanity's compassionate participation—that the performance of homlyhede can finally be fulfilled: that which was always present, and which is now at hand.

CONCLUSION

Not Yet Performed: Julian in Time

I confess to you, O Lord, that I still do not know what time is, and moreover I confess to you, Lord, that I know I am saying these things in time.

—Augustine, *Confessions*

What does it mean to be well? In what ways do illness and well-being relate to each other? Is recovery possible—of health, but also of the past? These are the questions that have animated this book and to which I return here for its concluding discussion. In particular, I wish to draw out the final query, pressing into the entanglements of past and present that I theorized in the book's introduction as *paramodern*: that is, "a premodern existing not before the modern, but alongside it and within it as a trace," as Louise D'Arcens puts it.[1] Andrew Cole and D. Vance Smith also argue that the modern "as we know it" cannot be thought without the medieval. These two periods exist "as necessary anachronisms," wherein the medieval "exists in a world that does not fully contain us; yet it remains a world that presupposes our awareness of it."[2] This chiastic frame—of the medieval existing for the scholar as analogy to modernity, and modernity existing only as it relates to the medieval—has a good deal in common with the theological concept of mutual indwelling that Julian of Norwich takes as her central anthropological theme in her *Revelations of Divine Love*: the notion that the soul dwells in God, while God also dwells in the soul. There is an irony, however, in invoking Julian to shed light on this historiographical project: a modernizing move of translating a theological concept for a secular project. This is precisely the focus of *Impossible Recovery*'s final word: the question of whether the temporal multiplicity identified by so many medievalist scholars can also permit multiple versions of the medieval text, existing alongside and within the modern perspective. Put another way, this conclusion dwells with the paradoxes of recovery that the book has identified, to ask how they can be reconciled by the historian, or how they might take recovery's impossibility as a "productive category."[3]

Julian exists as a "shadowy figure," as Elisabeth Dutton calls her, a silhouetted persona who remains always presently absent, or absently present, beneath and beyond her *Revelations*.[4] It is perhaps this very absence that invites modernizing readings of her texts, which locate in Julian a figure of comfort for the reader's personal concerns and the concerns of modern society. Evidence of this can be found in Julian's continued presence in popular spirituality, for Christians and non-Christians alike.[5] She has garnered new attention in recent years, when global events have pulled focus on narratives of illness and recovery, especially those written in isolation or enclosure: for many around the world, the COVID-19 pandemic demonstrated the disruptive power of sickness, on both an individual and a societal level. Particularly striking was the way that the pandemic changed people's experiences of time: medievalist scholar Eric Weiskott writes powerfully of this "Coronavirus Time Warp," relating the feeling of simultaneous standstill and acceleration to the boundlessness of Augustine's present moment—"But how is the future diminished or consumed, when it does not yet exist? Or how does the past increase, when it no longer exists?"[6] This might conceivably be understood as a collective experience of the "stagnating present" described by S. Kay Toombs in her phenomenological account of illness.[7] Certainly, in some ways these events can be seen to have incurred similar disruptions to Julian's own sickness, and so have invited questions as to how the medieval can help make sense of the pandemic and its attendant traumas. For many, Julian's own dark night of the soul and her subsequent enclosure in the anchorhold have become a model for theorizing their own experiences with sickness and loss.[8]

Rather than investigating how Julian's works can inform present-day discourses around illness, however, the following discussion is more concerned with the ways her theology can—or cannot—inform historiography, because as this book argues, one depends on the other. The book has reiterated throughout its dialogue between Julian's mysticism and Heideggerian phenomenology that the divine horizon of the former precludes its full recovery in the latter, secular context, despite both models offering a picture of human being as an enactive, participatory project of self-understanding. I have sought to demonstrate how post-Heideggerian phenomenologies of illness and health are greatly enriched by the analogy of the medieval, by profiling their likeness against the divine horizon of theology, which was obscured by Heidegger's own rejection of religion. But I have also highlighted the problems with the detheologized philosophy of Heidegger's work. By resituating understanding and meaning in the time of the present, I have shown how Heidegger's modernized eschatology attempts to borrow claims to ontological possibility from a model that is bound by the paradox of recovery's impossibility. In other words, the capaciousness of Julian's theology makes room for homeliness on earth even while it is always in fulfillment, but this paradox is forestalled for Heidegger, whose eschatology claims only what it can achieve on earth and in the present. Even while the phenomenologist understands human being as a constant dynamic process, then, its time-boundedness and nihilistic background render Dasein's recovery project a mere echo of the promise made by Christian theology. This irreconcilability means that Heideggerian phenomenology cannot reproduce the impossible possibility that underwrites Julian's recovery theology, and so the recovery of the medieval for modernity is precluded in turn.

This internesting of ontological and temporal concerns highlights once more the deeply secularized investments of Heidegger's medievalism. Despite the dynamism of being in Heidegger's phenomenology, his certainty as to the lack of eschaton beyond the world means that Dasein's transcendence is always earthbound, and so humans are responsible for their own realization. Such a relocation of power emphasizes human being itself as deliverance: the presencing of being as parousia, replacing that of the second coming of Christ. As Hans Ruin writes of Heidegger's later turn to the phenomenology of religion, "Heidegger orients himself towards what he takes to be the basic existential meaning of the Pauline discourse, as characterized by a temporal horizon of the coming of Christ, of the Parousia, not primarily understood in the context of a theological-metaphysical dogma but as an open horizon of lived meaning."[9] Indeed, in his 1920–1921 lectures on religion (published as *The Phenomenology of Religious Life*) Heidegger identifies the early Christian experience in the New Testament as historical: "Factical life experience is historical. Christian religiosity lives temporality as such."[10] *Historical* for Heidegger here does not mean history-as-object, but rather a historical situation of living in an expectation of the parousia, oriented toward Christ's second coming. When Heidegger transforms the expectation of parousia into being-toward-death, however, he argues that he is reinvigorating an earlier, pre-Christian philosophical tradition: as he states, "The meaning of this temporality is also fundamental for factical life experience, as well as for problems such as that of the eternity of God. In the medieval period these problems were no longer grasped originally, following the penetration of Platonic-Aristotelian philosophy into Christianity."[11] Heidegger sees the Christian understanding of this temporality as only one possibility of orientation, and with his renewed focus on factical life—the personal temporality of Dasein—as the emergent condition of its own existence, he resituates the possibility of its realization away from the Christian model. Xin Leng articulates this departure, writing that "Heidegger believes that the primordial Christian experience is that people exist towards God to escape from the mundanity of the world, and the significance of their factical life is constant insecurity. The non-Christians indulge in the peace and security of factical life, attach to the world, and immerse themselves in what life brings to them."[12]

With this theory of being in time, Heidegger lays the groundwork for a secular ideology of transformation, wherein a utopia—a final home—can be achieved through apocalyptic means, deliverance from the trials of existence through a parousiastic presencing-into-being. Apocalypse and utopia therefore exist, for Heidegger, as a coincidence of opposites, where the eschatological expectation both defines and realizes the fulfilled ontological existence of humanity. Eric Voegelin identifies in this philosophy the roots of Heidegger's avowal of Nazism, arguing that instead of turning away from all ideological constructs, Heidegger simply replaces them: "Gone are the ludicrous images of positivist, socialist, and super man. In their place Heidegger puts being itself, emptied of all content, to whose approaching power we must submit . . . the power of being replaces the power of God and the parousia of being, the Parousia of Christ."[13] It must be reiterated that Heidegger's notion of being as always being fulfilled defers the possibility of parousia, and so this submission is not a state of arrival—a revelation never fully revealed. But despite this, it would seem that Heidegger himself could not reconcile this paradox: that parousia is the unsurpassable structure of existence, even while it has already begun. Instead, his focus on the power of presencing—on its beginning, rather than its ending—leads Heidegger to a certainty about historical reality and the role of politics in realizing this vision.

In the context of his turn to Nazism, Heidegger's early phenomenology can be read as an expression of the secular ideology described by Bruno Latour: as akin to religious fundamentalism, where transcendence is immanentized within a totalizing frame of knowledge about reality. In a *Le Monde* article following the Charlie Hebdo massacres in Paris of January 2015, Latour paraphrases Voegelin's claim that "modernity begins in earnest when religion loses its uncertainty and becomes the realization on earth of that which should be kept for the beyond."[14] The modernizer, Latour continues, is "convinced that he can achieve the goals of religion by means of politics," a politics that then "[claims] for itself the absolute certainty borrowed from a religion that did not possess it." Just so for Heidegger: the phenomenological deferral of becoming—Dasein's constant being-*toward*—would appear to sustain the uncertainty of the eschatological vision, but Heidegger's turn to the apocalypse of Nazism forecloses this openness. Returning to Julian and her own temporal framing, this closure becomes all the more stark: set against Julian's insistence that her own revelation is "begunne . . . but it is not yet performid" (begun . . . but it is not yet complete), the claims of Heidegger's hermeneutic project and its subsequent ideological expression are disclosed as a totalizing vision.[15] In his overstepping of the medieval, Heidegger abandons the temporal possibilities of Christian theology, the origins of which he claimed to find in Plato and Aristotle, and instead locates revelation in the time of the present.

What are the implications of this secularizing project then for a modern reading of Julian's *Revelations*? Heidegger's implicit reappropriation of the medieval offers, I think, a cautionary tale or anti-exemplum for the historian, because he cannot sustain the nonclosure his own philosophy demands of him. With this in mind, I tentatively propose that the very transcendent horizon of Julian's texts may still offer the historian a model for their own hermeneutic projects. This statement demands some further unpacking, however, for how can a claim be made for Julian's eschatology as a historiographical model without enacting the same secularization as Heidegger does? A potential answer lies in the very impossibility of Julian's own framework: the paradox that a degree of revelation—a degree of homeliness—can be accessed even while remaining penultimate to its full realization. As both Latour and Voegelin suggest, this religious attitude is one of *un*certainty, an acknowledgment that paradise cannot be realized on earth, but an acknowledgment, too, that this does not preclude trying. For the premodern theologian, this paradox is held in tension by the all-encompassing force of faith. For the potentially secular modern, meanwhile, the question becomes how to sustain the uncertainty of recovery in their own readings of the historical text, in their own approaches to the past. To return to Cole and Smith's argument quoted above, the past "does not fully contain us; yet it remains a world that presupposes our awareness of it." Put in the terms of Julian's own project, the historian must therefore be able to accept that the past will remain elusive—that it can never be a home for modernity, nor can modernity make a home for it—despite the necessary supposition that it already exists as a precondition of knowledge, or homeliness, in the present.

The logic of this statement only works if, like in Julian's eschatological vision, multiple temporal frames are engaged at once. Paul Zumthor's work helps to ground this possibility: "The time in which the reception of the text takes place is an extension of a past in which all truth has its roots, yet it produces an accumulation of knowledge, generating science and a sense of right that belong as a whole to the future. At one and the same time the mind valorizes both memory and prediction, resulting in the collapse of the sense of time, the integration of the past into the present."[16] Cole and Smith call this Zumthor's "circular, turning-and-returning image," which recalls in turn Julian's hermeneutic circle, or the pseudo-Dionysian spiral, which never returns to the same place, with each rotation moving further inward. But for Zumthor, Cole and Smith write, "a symmetrical return is possible— . . . a future can be generated from the past."[17] This is, in fact, not so different from Julian's recovery model, since she understands the recovery of homely well-being as a move forward into a new existential condition and also as always grounded in the eternal substance of God. To accept Zumthor's claim, then, the historian must accept the contingency of multiple time frames, as well as the penultimacy of knowledge, since this future will only be recognized, as Cole and Smith put it, "at a time and place not yet known."[18] Zumthor's claim works under analogous conditions of temporality as the eschatological frame of Julian's anthropology, where the past is both already created and always in creation.

This framing also justifies, to some degree, the existence of multiple Julians to multiple readers. In Zumthor's view, self-recognition is a facet of medieval imaginings of the future as much as modern imaginings of the past: as Cole and Smith write, "Medieval memory and modern recognition are, for Zumthor, consanguine temporal modes that defy the strictures and thematizations of their own epochs."[19] Recognition does not, therefore, necessarily elide the past—quite the opposite: self-recognition is contingent upon the past for moderns just as it is contingent on the future for premoderns. Finally, then, I want to suggest, as this book's own project has sought to exemplify, that modern readings of Julian need not be modern*izing*; they need not sublimate the irrecoverable elements of her text. Instead, by approaching the text with the openness she herself theorizes as the condition of being, the reader may in fact allow Julian's voice to resonate in and through the present. This requires a sustained acknowledgment of the multiplicity of the text and its more shadowy moments: of the text's alterity as well as its more recognizable facets. This is not a "hard-edged alterity" that would identify a rigid distance between the medieval and the modern, but rather a relationality based on the continued present absence, or absent presence of the paramodern.[20] The negative space of this condition is as crucial as the positive, as Julian's mystical poetic has also shown, and it is only when positivist claims to certainty ignore this underbelly that modernizing presentism takes hold. While Julian directs her text to her medieval "even cristen" reader, then, instructing them to engage their own hermeneutic capabilities in the interpretation of her revelation, her modern reader, too, might heed her call to joint interpretation and intersubjectivity. For despite the inaccessibility of the former perspective, it is this very openness to uncertainty (and to seeking further understanding) that makes room for the impossible possibility of revelation—and so also for recovery.

NOTES

INTRODUCTION: THEN AND NOW—RECOVERING JULIAN OF NORWICH

1. I here avoid the common distinction drawn between Hoccleve the author and the poet-narrator, often called "Thomas," since my reading depends, as Julie Orlemanski puts it, "on the unstable overlap between these categories as they constantly implicate each other"; Orlemanski, *Symptomatic Subjects: Bodies, Medicine, and Causation in the Literature of Late Medieval England* (Philadelphia: University of Pennsylvania Press, 2019), 218.
2. Thomas Hoccleve, "*Complaint*: Edited Text," in *Thomas Hoccleve's Complaint and Dialogue*, ed. J. A. Burrow, EETS o.s. 313 (Oxford: Oxford University Press, 1999), 3–33 (5, line 40). Translations are taken from Jenni Nuttall, trans., "Hoccleve's 'Complaint': An Open-Access Prose Translation," Hoccleve Society.org, accessed January 9, 2024, https://hocclevesociety.org/texts-and-resources/hoccleves-complaint/.
3. Hoccleve, "*Complaint*," 5, line 42.
4. Hoccleve, 15, lines 176–82.
5. Hoccleve, 9, lines 85, 92–93.
6. Hoccleve, 33, line 408.
7. For more on this complicated tangle of illness, autobiography, and (mis)interpretation, see Laurie Atkinson, "'Why þat yee meeued been / can I nat knowe': Autobiography, Convention, and Discerning *Doublenesse* in Thomas Hoccleve's *The Series*," *Neophilologus* 101 (2017): 479–94; Marion Turner, "Illness Narratives in the Later Middle Ages: Arderne, Chaucer, and Hoccleve," *Journal of Medieval and Early Modern Studies* 46, no. 1 (2016): 61–87; Karen Smyth, "Reading Misreadings in Thomas Hoccleve's *Series*," *English Studies* 87, no. 1 (2006): 3–22.

8. See appendix B to Nicholas Watson and Jacqueline Jenkins's edition: Julian of Norwich, *The Writings of Julian of Norwich: A Vision Showed to a Devout Woman and A Revelation of Love*, ed. Nicholas Watson and Jacqueline Jenkins (Turnhout, Belgium: Brepols, 2006), 431–35. See also Norman P. Tanner, "Popular Religion in Norwich with Special Reference to the Evidence of Wills, 1370–1532" (DPhil diss., University of Oxford, 1974), 334–40.
9. For a full account of the divergences between these two versions, see Julian of Norwich, *Julian of Norwich: Revelations of Divine Love: The Short Text and the Long Text*, ed. Barry Windeatt (Oxford: Oxford University Press, 2016), ix–xv.
10. *Revelations of Divine Love*, lxv. Barry Windeatt "places a high value on presenting a text as near to Julian's original language as the complicated history of her work's survival allows" and therefore chooses Sloane MS 2499 as "the preferred choice as the base-text . . . because of the precious testimony in S1's [Sloane MS 2499's] retention, in its northern form of East Anglian language, of a text that is presumably nearer to the Norfolk language of Julian's working copy of her text" (lxvii).
11. Andrew Cole and D. Vance Smith, "Introduction: Outside Modernity," in *The Legitimacy of the Middle Ages: On the Unwritten History of Theory*, ed. Cole and Smith (Durham, NC: Duke University Press, 2010), 1. See also Andrew Cole, *The Birth of Theory* (Chicago: University of Chicago Press, 2014). For examples of such a critical turn in Julian scholarship, see Nancy Coiner, "The 'Homely' and the *Heimliche*: The Hidden, Doubled Self in Julian of Norwich's Showings," *Exemplaria* 5, no. 2 (1993): 305–23; Michael Raby, "The Phenomenology of Attention in Julian of Norwich's *A Revelation of Love*," *Exemplaria* 26, no. 4 (2014): 347–67; Louise Nelstrop, "Nakedness and Anthropology in Julian of Norwich and Maurice Merleau-Ponty: Conversation Partners or Dangerous Liaisons?" *Medieval Mystical Theology* 25, no. 1 (2016): 69–85; Daniel Theodore Fishley, "A Revelation of Weakness: Julian of Norwich, John Caputo, and the Event of Hospitality," *Medieval Mystical Theology* 31, no. 2 (2022): 67–79.
12. Cole and Smith, "Introduction," 2.
13. Cole and Smith, 24. See also Bruno Latour, *We Have Never Been Modern*, trans. Catherine Porter (Cambridge, MA: Harvard University Press, 1993).
14. For one such study, see Jason Ā. Josephson-Storm, *The Myth of Disenchantment: Magic, Modernity, and the Birth of the Human Sciences* (Chicago: University of Chicago Press, 2017). For more work on secularism, see Gil Anidjar, "Secularism," *Critical Inquiry* 33, no. 1 (2006): 52–77; Rajeev Bhargava, *Secularism and Its Critics* (Oxford: Oxford University Press, 1999); Kathleen Davis, "The Sense of An Epoch: Periodization, Sovereignty, and

the Limits of Secularization," in *The Legitimacy of the Middle Ages*, 39–69; Anuradha Dingwaney Needham and Rajeswari Sunder Rajan, eds. *The Crisis of Secularism in India* (Durham, NC: Duke University Press, 2007); Gauri Viswanathan, *Masks of Conquest: Literary Study and British Rule in India* (Oxford: Oxford University Press, 1989); Hent de Vries and Lawrence E. Sullivan, eds., *Political Theologies: Public Religions in a Post-Secular World* (New York: Fordham University Press, 2006).

15. Talal Asad, *Formations of the Secular: Christianity, Islam, Modernity* (Stanford, CA: Stanford University Press, 2003), 191, emphasis in original.
16. Asad, *Formations of the Secular*, 1.
17. Charles Taylor, *A Secular Age* (Cambridge, MA: Harvard University Press, 2007), 3.
18. Taylor, *Secular Age*, 30.
19. For more on these two thinkers, see Joseph A. Camilleri, "Postsecularist Discourse in an 'Age of Transition,'" *Review of International Studies* 38, no. 5 (2012): 1019–39.
20. Cole and Smith, "Introduction," 4, emphasis in original.
21. Cole and Smith, 9.
22. Cole and Smith cite the term "hard-edged alterity" in their discussion of Paul Zumthor against the "New Medievalism" promoted by Stephen G. Nichols; "Introduction," 18. See also Kathleen Biddick, *The Shock of Medievalism* (Durham, NC: Duke University Press, 1998), 4; Howard R. Bloch and Stephen G. Nichols, *Medievalism and the Modernist Temper* (Baltimore: Johns Hopkins University Press, 1996), 49; Marina S. Brownlee, Kevin Brownlee, and Stephen G. Nichols, eds., *The New Medievalism* (Baltimore: Johns Hopkins University Press, 1991), 12.
23. Cole and Smith, "Introduction," 18–19; Paul Zumthor, *Toward a Medieval Poetics*, trans. Philip Bennett (Minneapolis: University of Minnesota Press, 1992), 39.
24. Zumthor, *Toward a Medieval Poetics*, 11; Cole and Smith, "Introduction," 17.
25. Cole and Smith, 24.
26. Cole and Smith, 28.
27. Cole and Smith, 22. For example, Jeffrey Jerome Cohen, *Medieval Identity Machines* (Minneapolis: University of Minnesota Press, 2003), 1–34, esp. 8.
28. Dipesh Chakrabarty, *Provincializing Europe: Postcolonial Thought and Historical Difference* (Princeton, NJ: Princeton University Press, 2000).
29. See Carolyn Dinshaw, *How Soon Is Now? Medieval Texts, Amateur Readers, and the Queerness of Time* (Durham, NC: Duke University Press, 2012). Chakrabarty is also cited as an influence on Dinshaw's work. For Cole and Smith on Dinshaw, see "Introduction," 35, note 94.

30. Louise D'Arcens, "From 'Eccentric Affiliation' to 'Corrective Medievalism': Bruce Holsinger's *The Premodern Condition*," *postmedieval* 1 (2010): 304.
31. D'Arcens, "From 'Eccentric Affiliation,'" 304.
32. Bruce Holsinger, *The Premodern Condition: Medievalism and the Making of Theory* (Chicago: University of Chicago Press, 2005), 5.
33. See Richard Wolin, *The Heidegger Controversy: A Critical Reader* (Cambridge, MA: MIT Press, 1993) and *Heidegger in Ruins: Between Philosophy and Ideology* (New Haven, CT: Yale University Press, 2023), which through an examination of Heidegger's letters and "Black Notebooks" proves that Heidegger was a card-carrying member of the Nazi Party and that his philosophy cannot be separated from this ideology. For a discussion of whether this should affect readings of his work, see Patricia Cohen, "An Ethical Question: Does a Nazi Deserve a Place Among Philosophers?," *New York Times*, November 9, 2009, https://www.nytimes.com/2009/11/09/books/09philosophy.html?smid=tw-share.
34. For another essay on this topic, see Ethan Knapp, "Medieval Studies, Historicity, and Heidegger's Early Phenomenology," in *The Legitimacy of the Middle Ages*, 159–93.
35. Cole and Smith, "Introduction," 7.
36. In one revealing example of this lexis, Richard Wolin quotes Heidegger's reading of a study on the philosophy of a German-Jewish scholar, which he described as "so grotesque one can only laugh. One wonders whether from this contamination we will ever return to the primordial freshness and rootedness of life"; Wolin, *Heidegger in Ruins*, 182.
37. Jennifer Schuessler, "Medieval Scholars Joust with White Nationalists. And One Another." *New York Times*, May 5, 2019, https://www.nytimes.com/2019/05/05/arts/the-battle-for-medieval-studies-white-supremacy.html. For more on the appeal of medievalism to the far right, see Vanessa Jaeger, "Eating Up the Enemy: Teaching Richard Coer de Lyon and the Misrepresentation of Crusader Ideology in White Nationalist Agendas," *New Chaucer Studies: Pedagogy and Profession* 2, no. 2 (2021): 39–48; Dorothy Kim, "Teaching Medieval Studies in a Time of White Supremacy," In the Middle, August 28, 2017, https://www.inthemedievalmiddle.com/2017/08/teaching-medieval-studies-in-time-of.html; Dorothy Kim, "The Alt-Right and Medieval Religions," Berkley Forum, Berkley Center for Religion, Peace & World Affairs, Georgetown University, November 5, 2018, https://berkleycenter.georgetown.edu/responses/the-alt-right-and-medieval-religions; Rachel Moss, "Teaching Medieval Chivalry in an Age of White Supremacy," *New Chaucer Studies: Pedagogy and Profession* 3, no. 2 (2022): 6–18; Cord J. Whitaker, "The Problem of Alt-Right Medievalist White Supremacy, and Its Black Medievalist

Answer," in *Far-Right Revisionism and the End of History*, ed. Louie Dean Valencia-García (New York: Routledge, 2020), 159–76.

38. Françoise Meltzer, *For Fear of the Fire: Joan of Arc and the Limits of Subjectivity* (Chicago: University of Chicago Press, 2001), 9, 34, 44.
39. Meltzer, *For Fear of the Fire*, 44, 32.
40. Holsinger, *Premodern Condition*, 6. Richard Wolin also highlights the significance of Heidegger's "conversion" to Protestantism c. 1917 to the development of his philosophy; Wolin, *Heidegger in Ruins*, xi–xii.
41. Ryan Coyne, *Heidegger's Confessions: The Remains of Saint Augustine in* Being and Time *and Beyond* (Chicago: University of Chicago Press, 2015), 3. See also Helmuth Vetter, ed., *Heidegger und das Mittelalter* (Frankfurt: Peter Lang, 1999).
42. Martin Heidegger, "Mein Bisheriger Weg (1937/38)," in *Gesamtausgabe*, vol. 66: *Besinnung*, ed. Friedrich-Wilhelm von Herrmann (Frankfurt: Vittorio Klostermann, 1997), 415. Translation taken from Judith Wolfe, *Heidegger and Theology* (London: Bloomsbury, 2014), 136, emphasis in original. See also Martin Heidegger, "My Pathway Hitherto," in *Mindfulness*, trans. Parvis Emad and Thomas Kalary (1997; London: Bloomsbury, 2016), 352–57.
43. Wolfe, *Heidegger and Theology*, 62.
44. Many theologians (and philosophers of theology) have taken up Heidegger's work, including Gerhard Ebeling, Eberhard Jüngel, J. B. Lotz, Annemarie Gethmann-Siefert, and Jean-Luc Nancy, to name a few. For more on Heidegger's theology, see Jean-Yves Lacoste, "Heidegger Among the Theologians," *Journal for Continental Philosophy of Religion* 2, no. 2 (2020): 159–74.
45. Laurence Paul Hemming, *Heidegger's Atheism: The Refusal of a Theological Voice* (Notre Dame, IN: University of Notre Dame Press, 2002).
46. Sean J. McGrath, *The Early Heidegger and Medieval Philosophy: Phenomenology for the Godforsaken* (Washington, DC: Catholic University of America Press, 2006), xiii, second emphasis added.
47. For studies of some of the other mystical elements of Heidegger's work, see John D. Caputo, "Meister Eckhart and the Later Heidegger: The Mystical Element in Heidegger's Thought: Part One," *Journal of the History of Philosophy* 12, no. 4 (1974): 479–94; Sonya Sikka, "Transcendence in Death: A Heideggerian Approach to *Via Negativa* in *The Cloud of Unknowing*," in *The Medieval Mystical Tradition in England V, Papers Read at The Devon Centre, Dartington Hall, July 1992*, ed. Marion Glasscoe (Cambridge: Brewer, 1992), 179–92; Sonya Sikka, *Forms of Transcendence: Heidegger and Medieval Mystical Theology* (Albany: State University of New York Press, 1997).
48. Judith Wolfe, *Heidegger's Eschatology: Theological Horizons in Martin Heidegger's Early Work* (Oxford: Oxford University Press, 2013), 2.

49. Wolfe, *Heidegger and Theology*, 101.
50. Wolfe, *Heidegger and Theology*, 101, emphasis added. For an additional reading of the recently published "Black Notebooks," see Judith Wolfe, "The Black Notebooks: Caught in the Trap of His Own Metaphysics," *Standpoint Magazine*, May 29, 2014, available at https://research-repository.st-andrews.ac.uk/bitstream/handle/10023/4872/Caught_in_the_Trap_of_His_Own_Ideas.pdf?sequence=1&isAllowed=y.
51. Wolin, *Heidegger in Ruins*, 104.
52. It is worth noting that following Fredrik Svenaeus's and Havi Carel's respective philosophies, my discussion of Heidegger is broadly limited to his early work. For more on Heidegger's later work and its theological elements, see Daniel J. Martino, "The Later Heidegger and Contemporary Theology of God" (PhD diss., Duquesne University, 2004).
53. Barbara Newman, "New Seeds, New Harvests: Thirty Years of Tilling the Mystic Field," *Traditio* 72 (2017): 13.
54. Caroline Walker Bynum, *Holy Feast and Holy Fast: The Religious Significance of Food to Medieval Women* (Berkeley: University of California Press, 1987); Alexandra Barratt, "'In the Lowest Part of Our Need': Julian and Medieval Gynaecological Writing," in *Julian of Norwich: A Book of Essays*, ed. Sandra J. McEntire (New York: Garland, 1998), 239–56; Grace M. Jantzen, *Power, Gender, and Christian Mysticism* (Cambridge: Cambridge University Press, 1995); Grace M. Jantzen, *Julian of Norwich: Mystic and Theologian* (London: SPCK, 2000); Barbara Newman, *From Virile Woman to WomanChrist* (Philadelphia: University of Pennsylvania Press, 1995); Elizabeth Robertson, "Medieval Medical Views of Women and Female Spirituality in the *Ancrene Wisse* and Julian of Norwich's *Showings*," in *Feminist Approaches to the Body in Medieval Literature*, ed. Linda Lomperis and Sarah Stanbury (Philadelphia: University of Pennsylvania Press, 1993), 142–67.
55. Liz Herbert McAvoy, "'Flourish Like a Garden': Pain, Purgatory and Salvation in the Writing of Medieval Religious Women," *Medieval Feminist Forum: A Journal of Gender and Sexuality* 50, no. 1 (2015): 33–60. See also Liz Herbert McAvoy, *Authority and the Female Body in the Writings of Julian of Norwich and Margery Kempe* (Cambridge: Brewer, 2004).
56. Jantzen, *Julian of Norwich*, xiv.
57. A. S. Lazikani, "Encompassment in Love: Rabi'a of Basra in Dialogue with Julian of Norwich," *Journal of Medieval Religious Cultures* 46, no. 2 (2020): 115–36; Liz Herbert McAvoy, "Tears, Mediation, and Literary Entanglement: The Writings of Medieval Visionary Women," in *Women and Medieval Literary Culture: From the Early Middle Ages to the Fifteenth Century*, ed. Corinne Saunders and Diane Watt (Cambridge: Cambridge University

Press, 2023), 269–84; Laura Saetveit Miles, "Queer Touch Between Holy Women: Julian of Norwich, Margery Kempe, Birgitta of Sweden, and the Visitation," in *Touching, Devotional Practices, and Visionary Experience in the Late Middle Ages*, ed. David Carrillo-Rangel, Delfi I. Nieto-Isabel, and Pablo Acosta-García (New York: Palgrave, 2019), 203–35; Godelinde Gertrude Perk, "In Loving Memory? Indecent Forgetting of the Dead in Continental Sister-Books and Julian of Norwich's *Revelation of Love*," *Religions* 14, no. 922 (2023), doi:10.3390/rel14070922; Alexandra Verini and Abir Bazaz, eds., *Gender and Medieval Mysticism from India to Europe* (London: Routledge, 2023).

58. Sandra Lee Bartky, *Femininity and Domination: Studies in the Phenomenology of Oppression* (New York: Routledge, 1990).
59. Jean Graybeal, *Language and "the Feminine" in Nietzsche and Heidegger* (Bloomington: Indiana University Press, 1990); Patricia J. Huntington, *Ecstatic Subjects, Utopia, and Recognition: Kristeva, Heidegger, Irigaray* (Albany: State University of New York Press, 1998). More recently, the volume of essays edited by Nancy J. Holland and Patricia Huntington has illuminated a diversity of opportunities for feminist approaches to Heidegger: Holland and Huntington, eds., *Feminist Interpretations of Martin Heidegger* (Philadelphia: Penn State University Press, 2001).
60. Graybeal, *Language and "the Feminine,"* 25.
61. Huntington, *Ecstatic Subjects*, xvii, 5–6.
62. Huntington, xvii.
63. Huntington, 142.
64. Huntington, 142.
65. Jantzen takes her cue from Rosemary Radford Ruether here; see Grace M. Jantzen, *Becoming Divine: Towards a Feminist Philosophy of Religion* (Manchester: Manchester University Press, 1998), 102; Ruether, *Sexism and God-Talk: Towards a Feminist Theology* (London: SCM Press, 1983), 19.
66. Kenneth Leech, "Hazelnut Theology: Its Potential and Perils," in *Julian Reconsidered*, ed. Kenneth Leech and Benedicta Ward (Oxford: SLG Press, 1988), 1.
67. Leech, "Hazelnut Theology," 6.
68. Leech, 7.
69. Leech, 7–8.
70. Leech, 9.
71. John Welwood, "Human Nature, Buddha Nature: On Spiritual Bypassing, Relationship, and the Dharma: An Interview with John Welwood by Tina Fossella," accessed January 9, 2024, https://www.johnwelwood.com/articles/TRIC_interview_uncut.pdf. See also Gabriela Piccioto, Jesse Fox, and Félix

Neto, "A Phenomenology of Spiritual Bypass: Causes, Consequences, and Implications," *Journal of Spirituality in Mental Health* 20, no. 4 (2018): 333–54.

72. *Revelations of Divine Love*, L.1.14, 15.rubric, 19.15, 52.rubric, 52.7, 68.20.
73. Maggie Ross, *Silence: A User's Guide*, vol. 1: *Process* (Eugene: Cascade, 2018), 31.
74. *Revelations of Divine Love*, L.86.1.
75. Philip Sheldrake, *Julian of Norwich: In God's Sight, Her Theology in Context* (Hoboken, NJ: John Wiley, 2019), 4.
75. Cole and Smith, "Introduction," 19–20, emphasis added.

1. MAPPING THE JOURNEY HOME: A PHENOMENOLOGY OF WELL-BEING

1. Geoffrey Chaucer, "The House of Fame," in *The Riverside Chaucer*, ed. Larry Dean Benson and F. N. Robinson, 3rd ed. (Oxford: Oxford University Press, 2008), 360, lines 1021–22.
2. "The Life of St. Julian the Hospitaller: Introduction," in *Saints' Lives in Middle English Collections*, ed. E. Gordon Whatley, Anne B. Thompson, and Robert K. Upchurch, TEAMS Middle English Texts (Kalamazoo, MI: Medieval Institute Publications, 2004), available at https://d.lib.rochester.edu/teams/publication/whatley-saints-lives-in-middle-english-collections.
3. *The South English Legendary*, vol. 1: *Text*, ed. Charlotte D'Evelyn and Anna Jean Mill, EETS o.s. 235 (London: Oxford University Press, 1956), 35, line 101.
4. "Sir Gawain and the Green Knight," in *The Poems of the Pearl Manuscript:* Pearl, Cleanness, Patience, Sir Gawain and the Green Knight, ed. Malcolm Andrew and Ronald Waldron, 5th ed. (Liverpool: Liverpool University Press, 2007), 237, lines 774–76.
5. *MED*, s.v. "yēten," *v.* (2).
6. *Ancrene Wisse*, ed. Robert Hasenfratz, TEAMS Middle English Texts (Kalamazoo, MI: Medieval Institute Publications, 2000), available at https://d.lib.rochester.edu/teams/publication/hasenfratz-ancrene-wisse, part 6, lines 33–34.
7. Hasenfratz, *Ancrene Wisse*, part 6, lines 23–25.
8. "Sir Gawain and the Green Knight," 299, line 2504.
9. Julian of Norwich, *The Writings of Julian of Norwich: A Vision Showed to a Devout Woman* and *A Revelation of Love*, ed. Nicholas Watson and Jacqueline Jenkins (Turnhout, Belgium: Brepols, 2006), 6, note 12. Robert Flood suggests the alternative of St. Juliana of Nicomedia in *A Description of St Julian's Church, Norwich and an Account of Dame Julian's Connection with It* (Norwich: Wherry Press, 1936), 9.

10. Julian of Norwich, *Julian of Norwich: Revelations of Divine Love: The Short Text and the Long Text*, ed. Barry Windeatt (Oxford: Oxford University Press, 2016), L.27.8–9.
11. *MED*, s.v. "schulen," *v.* (1).
12. *Revelations of Divine Love*, L.31.2–3.
13. For more on Julian's grammar, see Eleanor Johnson, *Staging Contemplation: Participatory Theology in Middle English Prose, Verse, and Drama* (Chicago: University of Chicago Press, 2018), esp. 62–63, 69.
14. *Revelations of Divine Love*, L.10.57–73.
15. *Revelations of Divine Love*, L.86.4.
16. *Revelations of Divine Love*, L.5.2.
17. Martin Heidegger, "Letter on Humanism," in *Martin Heidegger: Basic Writings: From* Being and Time *(1927) to* The Task of Thinking *(1964)*, ed. David Farrell Krell, rev. ed. (1947; San Francisco: HarperCollins, 1993), 217.
18. Martin Heidegger, *Being and Time*, trans. Joan Stambaugh, rev. and with a foreword by Dennis J. Schmidt (1927; Albany: State University of New York Press, 2010), §166.
19. Described as a strategy that "will help give your language impressiveness"; Aristotle, *Rhetoric and Poetics*, trans. W. Rhys Roberts and Ingram Bywater with an introduction by Edward P. J. Corbett (New York: Modern Library, 1984), 176, 1407b, lines 26–27.
20. "Geoffrey of Vinsauf, *Poetria nova*, ca. 1208–1213," in *Medieval Grammar and Rhetoric: Language Arts and Literary Theory, AD 300–1475*, ed. and trans. Rita Copeland and Ineke Sluiter (Oxford: Oxford University Press, 2009), 594–606.
21. Copeland and Sluiter, "Geoffrey of Vinsauf," 596.
22. Friedrich Nietzsche, "On Truth and Lie in an Extra-Moral Sense," in *The Continental Aesthetics Reader*, ed. Clive Cazeaux (1873; London: Routledge, 2000), 53–62; Hans-Georg Gadamer, *Truth and Method*, trans. and rev. Joel Weinsheimer and Donald G. Marshall, 2nd ed. (1960; London: Continuum, 2004), 431. See also Clive Cazeaux, "Conflicting Perspectives: Epistemology and Ontology in Nietzsche's Will to Power," in *Metaphor and Continental Philosophy: From Kant to Derrida* (New York: Routledge, 2007), 103–32.
23. Paul Ricoeur, *The Rule of Metaphor: The Creation of Meaning in Language*, trans. Robert Czerny with Kathleen McLaughlin and John Costello (1975; London: Routledge, 2003).
24. I. A. Richards, *The Philosophy of Rhetoric* (1936; New York: Galaxy, 1965), 92–93.
25. For example, Theodor W. Adorno, *The Jargon of Authenticity*, trans. Knut Tarnowski and Frederic Will (London: Routledge and Kegan Paul, 1973).

26. Heidegger, *Being and Time*, §220, emphasis in original. The mysticism claim is invoked once more by Eric Voegelin, who would later blame "linguistic delirium" as the cause for Heidegger's being swayed by Nazism: "In a state of alliterative ecstasy now, many may lose sight of the reality of being . . . When thousands of voices are raised in an alliterative *Heil Hitler!* those shouting may believe, lost in the operatic language, that the scales have fallen from their eyes"; Voegelin, *The Collected Works of Eric Voegelin*, vol. 12: *Published Essays, 1966–1985*, ed. Ellis Sandoz (Baton Rouge: Louisiana State University Press, 1966; repr. 1990), 9.
27. *MED*, s.v. "mistik(e)," *adj.*
28. Giuseppe Stellardi, *Heidegger and Derrida on Philosophy and Metaphor: Imperfect Thought* (Amherst, NY: Humanity Books, 2000), 137, 140.
29. David Nowell Smith, *Sounding/Silence: Martin Heidegger at the Limits of Poetics* (New York: Fordham University Press, 2013), 108, emphasis in original.
30. Jacques Derrida, "The *Retrait* of Metaphor," in *The Derrida Reader: Writing Performances*, ed. Julian Wolfreys (Edinburgh: Edinburgh University Press, 1998), 119, 120.
31. Martin Heidegger, *Unterwegs zur Sprache*, 3rd ed. (1959; Pfullingen: Neske, 1965), 121. Quoted in Smith, *Sounding/Silence*, 109.
32. Smith, *Sounding/Silence*, 109.
33. Anita Wohlmann, *Metaphor in Illness Writing: Fight and Battle Reused* (Edinburgh: Edinburgh University Press, 2022).
34. Susan Sontag, *Illness as Metaphor* and *AIDS and Its Metaphors* (London: Penguin, 1991), 3.
35. Sontag, *Illness as Metaphor*, 3, emphasis added.
36. Wohlmann, *Metaphor in Illness Writing*, 58.
37. Havi Carel, *Phenomenology of Illness* (Oxford: Oxford University Press, 2016), 3. This study is Carel's successor to *Illness* (Durham, UK: Acumen Publishing, 2008).
38. Carel, *Phenomenology of Illness*, 17.
39. S. Kay Toombs, *The Meaning of Illness: A Phenomenological Account of the Different Perspectives of Physician and Patient* (Boston: Kluwer, 1992), 28.
40. Sontag, *Illness as Metaphor*, 3. See also Fredrik Svenaeus, *The Hermeneutics of Medicine and the Phenomenology of Health: Steps Towards a Philosophy of Medical Practice* (Dordrecht, The Netherlands: Kluwer, 2000) and Kevin Aho and James Aho, *Body Matters: A Phenomenology of Sickness, Disease, and Illness* (Lanham, MD: Lexington Books, 2008).
41. Aho and Aho, *Body Matters*, 69.
42. Svenaeus, *Hermeneutics of Medicine*, 112. See also Fredrik Svenaeus, "The Phenomenology of Health and Illness," in *Handbook of Phenomenology and*

Medicine, ed. S. Kay Toombs (Dordrecht, The Netherlands: Kluwer, 2001), 87–108.

43. See E. Lindsey, "Health Within Illness: Experiences of Chronically Ill/Disabled People," *Journal of Advanced Nursing* 24, no. 3 (1996): 465–72; Susan Diemert Moch, "Health Within Illness: Conceptual Evolution and Practice Possibilities," *Advances in Nursing Science* 11, no. 4 (1989): 23–31.
44. Carel, *Phenomenology of Illness*, 140.
45. Carel, 132.
46. Sonja Lyubomirsky, *The How of Happiness* (London: Penguin, 2007), 47. Cited in Carel, *Phenomenology of Illness*, 135.
47. Carel, *Phenomenology of Illness*, 133.
48. Martin Heidegger, *Zollikon Seminars: Protocols, Conversations, Letters*, ed. Medard Boss and trans. Franz Mayr and Richard Askay (Evanston, IL: Northwestern University Press 2001), 63.
49. Hans-Georg Gadamer, *Über die Verborgenheit der Gesundheit. Aufsätze und Vorträge* (Frankfurt: Suhrkamp Verlag, 1993), 143–44. Quoted and trans. in Svenaeus, *Hermeneutics of Medicine*, 80.
50. Gadamer, *Über die Verborgenheit*, quoted in Svenaeus, *Hermeneutics of Medicine*, 80.
51. Plato, *Republic*, IV.444d, quoted in Niall Keane, "On the Origins of Illness and the Hiddenness of Health: A Hermeneutic Approach to the History of a Problem," in *Medicine and Society: New Perspectives in Continental Philosophy*, ed. Darian Meacham (Dordrecht, The Netherlands: Springer, 2015), 63.
52. See Noga Arikha, *Passions and Tempers: A History of the Humours* (New York: HarperCollins, 2007).
53. Carel, *Phenomenology of Illness*, 71.
54. Maurice Merleau-Ponty, *Phenomenology of Perception*, trans. Colin Smith (1945; London: Routledge, 1962; repr. 2002).
55. See Taylor Carman, "The Body in Husserl and Merleau-Ponty," *Philosophical Topics* 27, no. 2 (1999): 205–26.
56. Merleau-Ponty, *Phenomenology of Perception*, 157.
57. Fredrik Svenaeus, "Das Unheimliche—Towards a Phenomenology of Illness," *Medicine, Health Care and Philosophy* 3 (2000): 3.
58. Sigmund Freud, "The Uncanny," in *The Standard Edition of the Complete Psychological Works of Sigmund Freud*, vol. 17: *An Infantile Neurosis and Other Works, 1917–1919*, trans. and gen. ed. James Strachey and Anna Freud, asst. Alix Strachey and Alan Tyson (1919; London: Hogarth Press and The Institute of Psycho-Analysis, 1971), 237.
59. E.T.A. Hoffman, *Der Sandmann/The Sandman*, trans. John Oxenford, German-English edition (1816; Berlin: Michael Holzinger, 2015), 4–5.

60. Freud, "The Uncanny," 230. See also Paul Ricoeur, *Freud and Philosophy: An Essay in Interpretation*, trans. Denis Savage (New Haven, CT: Yale University Press, 1970), 515–16.
61. Fredrik Svenaeus, "Freud's Philosophy of the Uncanny," *Scandinavian Psychoanalytic Review* 22, no. 2 (1999): 242–43, emphasis in original.
62. Marc Falkenberg, *Rethinking the Uncanny in Hoffman and Tieck* (Bern, Switzerland: Peter Lang, 2005), 56.
63. Heidegger, *Being and Time*, §189, emphases in original.
64. Svenaeus, "Das Unheimliche," 8, emphasis in original.
65. Heidegger, *Being and Time*, §189, emphasis in original.
66. Svenaeus, *Hermeneutics of Medicine*, 113.
67. Svenaeus, 113.
68. Svenaeus, 129.
69. Havi Carel, "Can I Be Ill and Happy?" *Philosophia* 35, no. 2 (2007): 103. Carel here cites Lindsey, "Health Within Illness," 467.
70. Carel, *Phenomenology of Illness*, 83, emphasis added. See also Havi Carel, "'I Am Well, Apart from the Fact That I Have Cancer': Explaining Well-being Within Illness," in *Philosophy and Happiness*, ed. L. Bortolotti (Basingstoke, UK: Palgrave, 2009), 82–99.
71. Carel, *Phenomenology of Illness*, 80.
72. Carel, 81.
73. Carel, 81.
74. Carel, 84.
75. Frank Buckley, "An Approach to a Phenomenology of At-Homeness," in *Duquesne Studies in Phenomenological Psychology*, vol. 1, ed. Amedeo Giorgi, William Frank Fischer, and Rolf Von Eckartsberg (Pittsburgh: Duquesne University Press, 1971), 198–211.
76. Buckley, "Approach to a Phenomenology," 198, emphasis in original.
77. Buckley, 198.
78. Martha C. Nussbaum, "Human Capabilities, Female Human Beings," in *Women, Culture, and Development: A Study of Human Capabilities*, ed. Martha C. Nussbaum and Jonathan Glover (New York: Oxford University Press, 1995), 76.
79. Merleau-Ponty, *Phenomenology of Perception*, 162.
80. Merleau-Ponty, xxii.
81. Svenaeus, *Hermeneutics of Medicine*, 94.
82. David Seamon, *A Geography of the Lifeworld: Movement, Rest, and Encounter* (New York: St. Martin's, 1979), 80.
83. Seamon, *Geography of the Lifeworld*, 79.

84. Neil Smith and Cindi Katz, "Grounding Metaphor: Towards a Spatialized Politics," in *Place and the Politics of Identity*, ed. Michael Keith and Steve Pile (London: Routledge, 1993), 68, emphasis added.
85. For more on this relationship, see Josep Maria Bech, "Merleau-Ponty's Many-Layered Presence in Bourdieu's Thought," *Cosmos and History: The Journal of Natural and Social Philosophy* 17, no. 1 (2021): 243–64.
86. Henri Lefebvre, *The Production of Space*, trans. Donald Nicholson-Smith (Oxford: Blackwell, 1991), 423.
87. Sara Ahmed, *Queer Phenomenology: Orientations, Objects, Others* (Durham, NC: Duke University Press, 2006), 9.
88. Ahmed, *Queer Phenomenology*, 9, emphasis added.
89. Ahmed, 9.
90. Ahmed, 11.
91. Aho and Aho, *Body Matters*, 120, emphasis in original. See also Toombs, *Meaning of Illness*, 68–70.
92. Thomas Fuchs, "Corporealized and Disembodied Minds: A Phenomenological View of the Body in Melancholia and Schizophrenia," *Philosophy, Psychiatry, and Psychology* 12, no. 2 (2005): 99; Thomas Fuchs, "The Phenomenology of Shame, Guilt and the Body in Body Dysmorphic Disorder and Depression," *Journal of Phenomenological Psychiatry* 33, no. 2 (2003): 237.
93. Thomas Fuchs, "Corporealized and Disembodied Minds," 100.
94. Aho and Aho, *Body Matters*, 118; Ahmed, *Queer Phenomenology*, 9.
95. Aho and Aho, *Body Matters*, 118.
96. Gaston Bachelard, *The Poetics of Space*, with a foreword by Mark Z. Danielewski and introduction by Richard Kearney (1958; New York: Penguin, 2014), 125.
97. Bachelard, *Poetics of Space*, 26.
98. Bachelard, 127.
99. Toombs, *Meaning of Illness*, 88.
100. Seamon, *Geography of the Lifeworld*, 80.
101. Seamon, 81.
102. Otto F. Bollnow, "Lived-space," *Philosophy Today* 5, no. 1 (1961): 34.
103. Martin Heidegger, "Building Dwelling Thinking," in *Poetry, Language, Thought*, trans. and with an introduction by Albert Hofstadter (1954; New York: Harper and Row, 1975), 147.
104. Heidegger, "Building Dwelling Thinking," 147.
105. Bollnow, "Lived-space," 35.
106. Bollnow, 32.
107. Anne Winning, "Homesickness," *Phenomenology + Pedagogy* 8 (1990): 251.

108. Gabriel Marcel, *Homo Viator: Introduction to the Metaphysic of Hope*, trans. Emma Crauford (New York: Harper and Row, 1962).
109. Wim Dekkers, "On the Notion of Home and the Goals of Palliative Care," *Theoretical Medicine and Bioethics* 30, no. 5 (2009): 345.

2. LEARNING TO LIVE: JULIAN'S ILLNESS AND THE CRAFT OF DYING

This chapter's epigraph is from Oliver Sacks, "My Own Life," *New York Times*, February 19, 2015, https://www.nytimes.com/2015/02/19/opinion/oliver-sacks-on-learning-he-has-terminal-cancer.html.

1. Susan Sontag, *Illness as Metaphor* and *AIDS and Its Metaphors* (London: Penguin, 1991), 3; Sacks, "My Own Life."
2. David Hume, "The life of David Hume, Esq: Written by himself. To which is added, a letter from Adam Smith, LL.D. to William Strahan, Esq.," *Eighteenth Century Collections Online*, available at https://name.umdl.umich.edu/004854280.0001.000, p. 13.
3. Martin Heidegger, *The Question Concerning Technology and Other Essays*, trans. and with an introduction by William Lovitt (1954; New York: Garland, 1977), 13. Quoted in Kevin Aho and James Aho, eds., *Body Matters: A Phenomenology of Sickness, Disease, and Illness* (Lanham, MD: Lexington Books, 2008), 145, emphasis added.
4. Aho and Aho, *Body Matters*, 145.
5. Julian of Norwich, *Julian of Norwich: Revelations of Divine Love: The Short Text and the Long Text*, ed. Barry Windeatt (Oxford: Oxford University Press, 2016), L.3.1–2, 3.13.
6. For example, Robert H. Thouless, *The Lady Julian: A Psychological Study* (London: SPCK, 1924), 25; Conrad Pepler, *English Religious Heritage* (London: Blackfriars, 1958), 312.
7. For studies on this *discretio* discourse as it relates to Julian, see Anna Kelner, "Trusting Women's Visions: The Discernment of Spirits in Julian of Norwich's *Revelation of Love*," *Journal of Medieval and Early Modern Studies* 51, no. 2 (2021): 193–214; Juliette Vuille, "'Maybe I'm Crazy?' Diagnosis and Contextualisation of Medieval Female Mystics," in *Medicine, Religion, and Gender in Medieval Culture*, ed. Naoë Kukita Yoshikawa (Cambridge: Brewer, 2015), 103–20.
8. Paul Molinari, *Julian of Norwich: The Teaching of a 14th Century English Mystic* (London: Longmans, Green, 1958).
9. James T. McIlwain, "'The bodelye syeknes' of Julian of Norwich," *Journal of Medical History* 10 (1984): 167–80.

10. For more recent studies of Julian's illness that avoid such problems, see Gillian Adler, "Visionary Metaphors: Sight, Sickness, and Space in Boethius's *Consolation of Philosophy* and Julian of Norwich's *Showings*," *Journal of Medieval Religious Cultures* 46, no. 1 (2020): 53–70; Vincent Gillespie, "Seek, Suffer, and Trust: 'Ese' and 'Disese' in Julian of Norwich," *Studies in the Age of Chaucer* 39 (2017): 129–58; Cathinka D. Hambro, "Pain and Epiphany: Julian of Norwich's *Revelations of Divine Love* as Pathography," *Tidsskrift for Forskning i Sygdom og Samfund* 31 (2019): 27–43; S. Kyle Johnson, "Love Amidst Fear: Julian of Norwich, Affect, and Orthopathy," *Spiritus: A Journal of Christian Spirituality* 21, no. 2 (2021): 282–301; Maria R. Lichtmann, "'I desyrede a bodylye syght': Julian of Norwich and the Body," *Mystics Quarterly* 17, no. 1 (1991): 12–19; Anna Minore, "Julian of Norwich and Catherine of Siena: Pain and the Way of Salvation," *Journal of Medieval Religious Cultures* 40, no. 1 (2014): 44–74.
11. *Revelations of Divine Love*, L.3.15–18.
12. *Revelations of Divine Love*, S.2.19.
13. Amy Appleford, *Learning to Die in London, 1380–1540* (Philadelphia: University of Pennsylvania Press, 2014), 31. For Appleford's reading of Julian in this context, see Amy Appleford, "The 'Comene Course of Prayers': Julian of Norwich and Late Medieval Death Culture," *The Journal of English and Germanic Philology* 107, no. 2 (2008): 190–214.
14. Appleford, *Learning to Die*, 31.
15. See Mary Catharine O'Connor, *The Art of Dying Well: The Development of the Ars Moriendi* (New York: Columbia University Press, 1942); Ashby Kinch, *Imago Mortis: Mediating Images of Death in Late Medieval Culture* (Leiden and Boston: Brill, 2013), esp. chapters 5 and 6.
16. For more on this text and its place in English and Continental piety, see Amy Appleford, "Wounded Texts and Worried Readers: The Book of the Craft of Dying," in *Learning to Die*, 137–80; Nancy Lee Beaty, *The Craft of Dying: A Study in the Literary Tradition of the "Ars Moriendi" in England* (New Haven, CT: Yale University Press, 1970); Paul Binski, *Medieval Death: Ritual and Representation* (London: British Museum Press, 1996); T.S.R. Boase, *Death in the Middle Ages: Mortality, Judgment and Remembrance* (London: Thames and Hudson, 1972); Caroline Walker Bynum and Paul H. Freedman, *Last Things: Death and the Apocalypse in the Middle Ages* (Philadelphia: University of Pennsylvania Press, 2000).
17. Appleford, *Learning to Die*, 140.
18. Appleford, 146.
19. G. R. Morgan, "A Critical Edition of Caxton's *The Art and Craft to Know Well to Die* and *Ars moriendi* Together with the Antecedent Manuscript Material,"

2 vols. (DPhil diss., University of Oxford, 1972), 2:53. Quoted in Appleford, *Learning to Die*, 147.

20. Appleford, *Learning to Die*, 140.
21. D. Vance Smith, *Arts of Dying: Literature and Finitude in Medieval England* (Chicago: University of Chicago Press, 2020), 1.
22. Johan Huizinga, *Herfsttij der Middeleeuwen: Studie over levens-en gedachtenvormen der veertiende en vijftiende eeuw in Frankrijk en de Nederlanden* (Haarlem: H. D. Tjeenk Willink, 1919), translated by Rodney J. Payton and Ulrich Mammitzsch as *The Autumn of the Middle Ages* (Chicago: University of Chicago Press, 1996). Quoted in Appleford, *Learning to Die*, 3.
23. Havi Carel, *Phenomenology of Illness* (Oxford: Oxford University Press, 2016), 12.
24. Carel, *Phenomenology of Illness*, 13.
25. Martin Heidegger, "What Is Metaphysics?," in *Martin Heidegger: Basic Writings: From* Being and Time *(1927) to* The Task of Thinking *(1964)*, ed. David Farrell Krell, rev. ed. (1967; San Francisco: HarperCollins, 1993), 103, emphasis added.
26. Martin Heidegger, *Pathmarks*, ed. William McNeill (1919–1961; Cambridge: Cambridge University Press, 1998), 91.
27. Martin Heidegger, *Being and Time*, trans. Joan Stambaugh, rev. and with a foreword by Dennis J. Schmidt (1927; Albany: State University of New York Press, 2010), §187, emphases in original.
28. Carel, *Phenomenology of Illness*, 98.
29. Carel, 94.
30. Carel, 96, emphasis added.
31. Heidegger, *Being and Time*, §186, emphasis added.
32. Carel, *Phenomenology of Illness*, 94.
33. Carel, 98.
34. Carel, 99.
35. Heidegger, *Being and Time*, §186.
36. Taylor Carman, "Authenticity," in *A Companion to Heidegger*, ed. Hubert L. Dreyfus and Mark A. Wrathall (Oxford: Blackwell, 2005), 285. Authenticity has been interpreted and analyzed extensively, particularly in existentialist philosophy and in Adorno's *Jargon of Authenticity*. Carel retains the translation of authenticity "while bearing in mind the inflated resonance of the English term" in *Phenomenology of Illness*, 152, note 4.
37. Carman, "Authenticity," 285.
38. Heidegger, *Being and Time*, §175–76.
39. Heidegger, §175.
40. Heidegger, §176.

41. Rudi Visker, for example, views authenticity as momentary and writes that in order to have basic continuous existence humans must therefore be inauthentic: "Dropping—The 'Subject' of Authenticity: *Being and Time* on Disappearing Existentials and True Friendship with Being," in *Deconstructive Subjectivities*, ed. Simon Critchley and Peter Dews (Albany: State University of New York Press, 1996), 80. See also Michael Lewis, *Heidegger and the Place of Ethics* (London: Continuum, 2005), 35.
42. Fredrik Svenaeus, *The Hermeneutics of Medicine and the Phenomenology of Health: Steps Towards a Philosophy of Medical Practice* (Dordrecht, The Netherlands: Kluwer, 2000), 107.
43. Carel, *Phenomenology of Illness*, 173.
44. Carel, 178.
45. Carel, 174.
46. Carel, 174.
47. Heidegger, *Being and Time*, §297.
48. Carman, "Authenticity," 291.
49. Carman, 291.
50. Heidegger, *Being and Time*, §146, emphasis in original.
51. Heidegger, §247, emphasis in original.
52. Heidegger, §247, emphasis in original.
53. Carman, "Authenticity," 290.
54. Martin Heidegger, *The History of the Concept of Time: Prolegomena*, trans. Theodore Kisiel (1979; Bloomington: Indiana University Press, 1985), 318.
55. William Blattner, "The Concept of Death in Heidegger's *Being and Time*," *Man and World* 27 (1994): 49–70.
56. Carel, *Phenomenology of Illness*, 170.
57. Heidegger, *Being and Time*, §373.
58. Heidegger, §254, emphasis in original.
59. Heidegger, §266, emphasis in original.
60. Heidegger, §240, emphasis in original.
61. Carel, *Phenomenology of Illness*, 177.
62. Heidegger, *Being and Time*, §298.
63. Bruce Campbell, *The Great Transition: Climate, Disease and Society in the Late-Medieval World* (Cambridge: Cambridge University Press, 2016), 307.
64. Smith, *Arts of Dying*, 9.
65. Smith, 87.
66. Smith, 86.
67. *Revelations of Divine Love*, S.6.34–35.
68. Sarah McNamer, *Affective Meditation and the Invention of Medieval Compassion* (Philadelphia: University of Pennsylvania Press, 2010), 12.

69. *Revelations of Divine Love*, L.3.11.
70. Svenaeus, *Hermeneutics of Medicine*, 86.
71. *Revelations of Divine Love*, L.3.18.
72. *Revelations of Divine Love*, L.3.4.
73. *Revelations of Divine Love*, L.2.19–20.
74. *Revelations of Divine Love*, S.1.35–37. See Susan K. Hagen, "St. Cecilia and St. John of Beverley: Julian of Norwich's Early Model and Late Affirmation," in *Julian of Norwich: A Book of Essays*, ed. Sandra J. McEntire (New York: Garland, 1998), 91–114.
75. *Revelations of Divine Love*, S.2.5–10.
76. *Revelations of Divine Love*, L.3.6.
77. *Revelations of Divine Love*, L.3.19.
78. *MED*, s.v. "wēle," *n.* (1).
79. Blattner, "Concept of Death," 55.
80. Blattner, 55.
81. *Revelations of Divine Love*, L.3.13–14.
82. Maurice Merleau-Ponty, *Phenomenology of Perception*, trans. Colin Smith (1954; London: Routledge, 1962; repr. 2002), 105.
83. Herbert Plügge, "Man and His Body," in *The Philosophy of the Body: Rejections of Cartesian Dualism*, ed. Stuart F. Spicker (Chicago: Quadrangle Books, 1970), 296.
84. Toombs, *Meaning of Illness*, 135, note 84.
85. Toombs, 135. For a discussion of Edmund Husserl's analysis of the role of kinesthetic sensation in the constitution of lived body, see H. T. Engelhardt Jr., "Husserl and the Mind-Body Relation," in *Interdisciplinary Phenomenology*, ed. Don Ihde and Richard Zaner (The Hague: Martinus Nijhoff, 1977), 51–70.
86. Yochai Ataria, *Body Disownership in Complex Posttraumatic Stress Disorder* (New York: Palgrave Macmillan, 2018), 59.
87. Ataria, *Body Disownership*, 59.
88. Ataria, 29, 53, 60. Example taken from R. Cogliano, C. Crisci, M. Conson, D. Grossi, and L. Trojano, "Chronic Somatoparaphrenia: A Follow-Up Study on Two Clinical Cases," *Cortex* 48, no. 6 (2012): 765.
89. Ataria, *Body Disownership*, 60, emphasis in original.
90. Yochai Ataria makes further distinctions between the mismatch between a sense of bodily ownership (SBO) and a sense of agency (SA) at the body-schema level, and then between body-schema and body-image; Ataria, *Body Disownership*, 71–75.
91. *Revelations of Divine Love*, L.3.14–15. The short text adds "lenande with clothes to my heede."

92. *Revelations of Divine Love*, L.3.15.
93. James T. McIlwain writes that Julian "struggles to breathe if the diaphragm and thoracic muscles are severely affected"; McIlwain, "'The bodelye syeknes' of Julian of Norwich," 176. Richard Lawes also remarks that Julian's "urge to sit upright suggests breathlessness": "Psychological Disorder and the Autobiographical Impulse in Julian of Norwich, Margery Kempe and Thomas Hoccleve," in *Writing Religious Women: Female Spiritual and Textual Practices in Late Medieval England*, ed. Christiania Whitehead and Denis Renevey (Toronto: University of Toronto Press, 2000), 235.
94. Erwin W. Straus, "The Upright Posture," *Psychiatric Quarterly* 26, no. 4 (1952): 534–35.
95. Straus, "Upright Posture," 536.
96. *Revelations of Divine Love*, L.3.22–27.
97. *Revelations of Divine Love*, S.2.32–34.
98. M. Herigstad, A. Hayen, K. Wiech, and K.T.S. Pattinson, "Dyspnoea and the Brain," *Respiratory Medicine* 105, no. 6 (2011): 809–17. Cited in Carel, *Phenomenology of Illness*, 107.
99. Carel, *Phenomenology of Illness*, 107.
100. *Revelations of Divine Love*, L.3.26.
101. *Revelations of Divine Love*, L.3.25.
102. For another reading of the *(un)heimlich* in Julian's *Revelations*, see Nancy Coiner, "The 'Homely' and the *Heimliche*: The Hidden, Doubled Self in Julian of Norwich's Showings," *Exemplaria* 5, no. 2 (1993): 305–23.
103. Augustine of Hippo, *Confessions*, vol. 1: *Books 1–8*, ed. and trans. Carolyn J. B. Hammond, Loeb Classical Library 26 (Cambridge, MA: Harvard University Press, 2014), 329, vii.10. See also Augustine of Hippo, *The Works of Saint Augustine: A Translation for the 21st Century*, part 1, vol. 1: *The Confessions*, trans. with introduction and notes by Maria Boulding, ed. John E. Rotelle (New York: New City Press, 1997), 173, vii.10, note 72: "The formula is from Plotinus, *Enn.* 1.8.13, who derived it from Plato's 'bottomess sea of unlikeness,' *Politicus* 273 D6–E1. But Lk 15:13 is perhaps equally in Augustine's mind. In his *Expositions of the Psalms* 99, 5 Augustine says, 'In your unlikeness to God you have gone far from him; as you become like him you draw near.'"
104. *Revelations of Divine Love*, L.3.28–30.
105. *Revelations of Divine Love*, L.3.33–35, emphasis added.
106. Vincent Gillespie and Maggie Ross, "The Apophatic Image: The Poetics of Effacement in Julian of Norwich," in *The Medieval Mystical Tradition in England V, Papers Read at The Devon Centre, Dartington Hall, July 1992*, ed. Marion Glasscoe (Cambridge: Brewer, 1992), 60.
107. *Revelations of Divine Love*, L.4.1.

3. BEARING WITNESS: REVELATION, SUFFERING, AND THE FIEND

This chapter's epigraph is from T. S. Eliot, "East Coker," from *Four Quartets*, from *The Poems of T.S. Eliot* © Estate of T.S. Eliot. Reprinted by permission of Faber and Faber Ltd.

1. Donald Weinstein and Rudolph Bell, *Saints and Society: The Two Worlds of Western Christendom, 1000–1700* (Chicago: University of Chicago Press, 1982), 220, 234. See also Caroline Walker Bynum, *Fragmentation and Redemption: Essays on Gender and the Human Body in Medieval Religion* (New York: Zone Books, 1991), 54, 131–32, 145–56.
2. Nicholas Love, *The Mirror of the Blessed Life of Jesus Christ: A Full Critical Edition*, ed. Michael G. Sargent (Exeter: Exeter University Press, 2005); Sarah McNamer, *Affective Meditation and the Invention of Medieval Compassion* (Philadelphia: University of Pennsylvania Press, 2010), 12.
3. Julian of Norwich, *Julian of Norwich: Revelations of Divine Love: The Short Text and the Long Text*, ed. Barry Windeatt (Oxford: Oxford University Press, 2016), L.55.1; "I harde a man telle of halye kyrke of the storye of Saynte Cecylle, in the whilke schewynge I undyrstode that sche hadde thre woundys with a swerde in the nekke, with the whilke sche pynede to the dede" (I heard a man tell of holy church's story of Saint Cecilia, from which I understood that she had three wounds with a sword in the neck, with which she suffered until death, S.1.35–37).
4. Laura Saetveit Miles, *The Virgin Mary's Book at the Annunciation* (Cambridge: Brewer, 2020), 116. For the full discussion, see 115–74.
5. *Revelations of Divine Love*, L.3.29.
6. Maggie Ross, "Behold Not the Cloud of Experience," in *The Medieval Mystical Tradition in England VIII, Papers Read at Charney Manor, July 2011*, ed. E. A. Jones (Woodbridge: Brewer, 2013), 33.
7. S. Kay Toombs, *The Meaning of Illness: A Phenomenological Account of the Different Perspectives of Physician and Patient* (Boston: Kluwer, 1992), 15.
8. Toombs, *Meaning of Illness*, 15.
9. John B. Brough, "Temporality and Illness: A Phenomenological Perspective," in *Handbook of Phenomenology and Medicine*, ed. S. Kay Toombs (Dordrecht, The Netherlands: Kluwer, 2001), 41. See also T. J. Murray, "Personal Time: The Patient's Experience," *Annals of Internal Medicine* 132.1 (2000): 62: "When patients become ill, they may begin to see time running backward as well as forward, with life spread out as on a landscape" (quoted in Brough, "Temporality and Illness," 41).

10. Vincent Gillespie, "Seek, Suffer, and Trust: 'Ese' and 'Disese' in Julian of Norwich," *Studies in the Age of Chaucer* 39 (2017): 138.
11. *Revelations of Divine Love*, L.3.34.
12. *Revelations of Divine Love*, S.2.32–34.
13. Paris has "hole" while Sloane has "hele"; *Revelations of Divine Love*, L.3.28.
14. *Revelations of Divine Love*, L.8.18–19.
15. *MED*, s.v. "abīden," *v.* and "abōd," *n.*
16. Liz Herbert McAvoy, *Authority and the Female Body in the Writings of Julian of Norwich and Margery Kempe* (Cambridge: Brewer, 2004), 64.
17. Laura Saetveit Miles, "Space and Enclosure in Julian of Norwich's *A Revelation of Love*," in *A Companion to Julian of Norwich*, ed. Liz Herbert McAvoy (Cambridge: Brewer, 2008), 156.
18. Miles, "Space and Enclosure," 156.
19. *Revelations of Divine Love*, L.74.17.
20. G. R. Morgan, "A Critical Edition of Caxton's *The Art and Craft to Know Well to Die* and *Ars moriendi* Together with the Antecedent Manuscript Material," 2 vols. (DPhil diss., University of Oxford, 1972), 2:33.
21. Daniel McCann, *Soul-Health: Therapeutic Reading in Later Medieval England* (Cardiff: University of Wales Press, 2018), 28.
22. *Revelations of Divine Love*, L.74.16.
23. *Revelations of Divine Love*, L.8.1–2.
24. Jennifer Bryan, *Looking Inward: Devotional Reading and the Private Self in Late Medieval England* (Philadelphia: University of Pennsylvania Press, 2008), 155. Corinne Saunders meanwhile identifies the expression as part of the conversation of voices in the text: "'A Lowde Voys Cleping': Voice-Hearing, Revelation, and Imagination," in *Literature and the Senses*, ed. Annette Kern-Stähler and Elizabeth Robertson (Oxford: Oxford University Press, 2023), 118. For more on this conversational quality of Julian's text, see Christopher C. H. Cook, *Hearing Voices: Medieval Mystics, Meaning and Psychiatry* (London: T&T Clark, 2023), 43–70.
25. *Revelations of Divine Love*, L.8.21.
26. *Revelations of Divine Love*, L.8.23.
27. *Revelations of Divine Love*, L.8.25–26.
28. *Revelations of Divine Love*, L.8.32–33.
29. Carel, *Phenomenology of Illness*, 177.
30. *Revelations of Divine Love*, L.8.21, 8.29. The other instances of "myn even-Cristen" are at 9.7–8, 13.20, 28.3, 37.4, twice at 37.9–10, and at 68.15. "Our even-Cristen" is at 40.35, 40.37, 49.28, 52.16–17.
31. *Revelations of Divine Love*, L.9.2–8, emphasis added.

32. *Revelations of Divine Love*, L.15.18.
33. *MED*, s.v. "sekir," *adj* and "sǐken," *v.*(1).
34. *Revelations of Divine Love*, L.17.36–38, emphasis added. Barry Windeatt notes: "*he suffryd but onys*: see Hebrews 10:10. Julian here acknowledges that she observes not the Passion itself but a representation, 'as he would reveal it to me and fill me with awareness' (37)." See also Hebrews 10:10: "In the which will, we are sanctified by the oblation of the body of Jesus Christ once."
35. *Revelations of Divine Love*, L.17.39. Evoking Christ's words: "You know not what you ask. Can you drink the chalice that I shall drink?" (Matthew 20:22).
36. *Revelations of Divine Love*, L.17.41.
37. *Revelations of Divine Love*, L.17.41–43.
38. *Revelations of Divine Love*, S.10.33, emphases added.
39. *Revelations of Divine Love*, L.73.6–7.
40. For more on Julian, anchoritism, and acedia, see A. S. Lazikani, "The Vagabond Mind: Depression and the Medieval Anchorite," *Journal of Medieval Monastic Studies* 6 (2017): 141–168; Godelinde Gertrude Perk, "'Idleness Breeds Disgust for the Cell': Circumscribing Sloth, Acedia and Health in Anchoritic Literature," *Nordic Journal of English Studies* 21, no. 2 (2022): 8–31; Spencer Strub, "The Anchorite as Analysand: Depression and the Uses of Analogy," *Exemplaria* 35, no. 1 (2023): 48–65.
41. John Cassian, "The Foundations of the Cenobitic Life," in *The Nature of Melancholy: From Aristotle to Kristeva*, ed. Jennifer Radden (Oxford: Oxford University Press, 2000), 71.
42. On acedia, distraction, and religious practice, see Irina Dumitrescu and Caleb Smith, "The Demon of Distraction," *Critical Inquiry* 47, no. S2, special issue: "Posts from the Pandemic," ed. Hank Scotch (2021): S77–S81.
43. *Revelations of Divine Love*, L.73.25.
44. *Revelations of Divine Love*, L.73.28–29.
45. *Revelations of Divine Love*, L.15.5–7.
46. *Revelations of Divine Love*, L.15.9.
47. *Revelations of Divine Love*, S.9.20.
48. *Revelations of Divine Love*, L.15.13–15.
49. *Revelations of Divine Love*, L.47.30–34.
50. *Revelations of Divine Love*, L.47.11–14. For "overcummyng" Paris has "vnkunnyng."
51. *Revelations of Divine Love*, L.64.28–29, 37.1.
52. *Revelations of Divine Love*, L.15.16–17.
53. *Revelations of Divine Love*, L.15.18.
54. *Revelations of Divine Love*, L.15.22–24.
55. *Revelations of Divine Love*, L.15.24–26.

56. *Revelations of Divine Love*, L.65.22–24.
57. *Revelations of Divine Love*, L.65.21–22.
58. Edmund Husserl, *Logical Investigations*, trans. J. N. Findlay (1900/01; London: Routledge, 1973). For more on Husserl and intentionality, see Hubert L. Dreyfus and Harrison Hall, *Husserl, Intentionality, and Cognitive Science* (Cambridge, MA: MIT Press, 1982); Fredrik Svenaeus, *The Hermeneutics of Medicine and the Phenomenology of Health: Steps Towards a Philosophy of Medical Practice* (Dordrecht, The Netherlands: Kluwer, 2000), 75–78.
59. Thomas Aquinas, *Summa Theologiae*, vol. 5: *God's Will and Providence: 1a. 19–26*, ed. and trans. Thomas Gilby (London: Blackfriars in conjunction with Eyre & Spottiswoode, 1964), 1aq37a1. Quoted in Michael Raby, "The Phenomenology of Attention in Julian of Norwich's *A Revelation of Love*," *Exemplaria* 26, no. 4 (2014): 360.
60. Augustine, "De Genesi ad litteram Libri XII," in *Opera Omnia*, ed. Jacques-Paul Migne, 245–484 (Patrologia Latina 34. Paris: Migne, 1841), 12.49. Quoted in Raby, "Phenomenology of Attention," 360.
61. *Revelations of Divine Love*, L.66.6–10. For "morned and hevyd," Sloane has "moned," Paris has "mornyd hevyly," and BL MS Add. 37790 has "hevyed and mourned."
62. *Revelations of Divine Love*, L.66.5.
63. *Revelations of Divine Love*, L.47.30, emphasis added.
64. Julian of Norwich, *The Writings of Julian of Norwich: A Vision Showed to a Devout Woman and A Revelation of Love*, ed. Nicholas Watson and Jacqueline Jenkins (Turnhout, Belgium: Brepols, 2006), 108, note to line 6.
65. *Revelations of Divine Love*, L.66.11–13. Windeatt notes that for "inderly" Paris has "inwardly" while BL MS Add. 37790 has "enterlye," and "this has troubled copyists before; see 41/32–3."
66. *Revelations of Divine Love*, L.66.14.
67. *MED*, s.v. "rẹ̄chelẹ̄s," *adj.* (1).a. See also "The Parson's Tale," in *The Riverside Chaucer*, ed. Larry Dean Benson and F. N. Robinson, 3rd ed. (Oxford: Oxford University Press, 2008), 312, line 709, where "reccheleesnesse" is equivalent to "necligence"; and William Langland, *Piers Plowman: An Edition of the C-Text*, ed. Derek Pearsall (Berkeley: University of California Press, 1978), 203, note to line 196: "One of the major innovations in C is the extension of the role of Rechelesnesse . . . [who] is an aspect of the dreamer's consciousness."
68. Anicius Manlius Severinus Boethius, *Theological Tractates: The Consolation of Philosophy*, trans. H. F. Stewart, E. J. Rand, and S. J. Tester, Loeb Classical Library 74 (Cambridge: Harvard University Press, 1973), 179, II.1.

69. "A Tretis of Discrescyon of Spirites," in *Deonise Hid Diuinite and other treatises on Contemplative Prayer related to* The Cloud of Unknowing, ed. Phyllis Hodgson, EETS o.s. 231 (London: Oxford University Press, 1955), 90, line 22. Attributed to "the author of *The Cloud of Unknowing*" in Raby, "Phenomenology of Attention," 353.
70. Karma Lochrie, *Margery Kempe and Translations of the Flesh* (Philadelphia: University of Pennsylvania Press, 1991), 72.
71. *Revelations of Divine Love*, L.66.20–22. Barry Windeatt notes that for "left" Paris and BL MS Add. 37790 have "lost," suggesting that the Sloane reading "may derive from confusion of *f* and long *s*."
72. *Revelations of Divine Love*, L.66.17, 66.14.
73. Patricia A. DeYoung, *Understanding and Treating Chronic Shame: A Relational/Neurobiological Approach* (New York: Routledge, 2015), xii.
74. DeYoung, *Understanding and Treating Chronic Shame*, 18.
75. Norbert Elias, *The Civilizing Process*, trans. Edmund Jephcott, 3 vols. (1939; London: Blackwell, 1978–1983); James Gilligan, *Violence: Reflections on a National Epidemic* (New York: Vintage Books, 1997), 110–11; Thomas J. Scheff, "A Retrospective Look at Emotions," in *Handbook of the Sociology of Emotions*, vol. 2, ed. Jan E. Stets and Jonathan H. Turner (Dordrecht, The Netherlands: Springer, 2014), 245–66.
76. Peter N. Stearns, *Shame: A Brief History* (Springfield: University of Illinois Press, 2017), 37.
77. Stearns, *Shame*, 37.
78. *Revelations of Divine Love*, L.39.3–4.
79. *Revelations of Divine Love*, L.39.7–8, emphasis added.
80. *Revelations of Divine Love*, L.39.5–6, 39.8, emphasis added. Barry Windeatt notes: for "underfongyth" Sloane has "underforgeth" and Paris has "vndertakyth."
81. Nicholas Watson, "The Trinitarian Hermeneutic in Julian of Norwich's *Revelation of Love*," in *The Medieval Mystical Tradition in England V, Papers Read at The Devon Centre, Dartington Hall, July 1992*, ed. Marion Glasscoe (Cambridge: Brewer, 1992), 79–100.
82. *Revelations of Divine Love*, L.48.1–3.
83. *Revelations of Divine Love*, L.55.13–15, emphasis added.
84. *Revelations of Divine Love*, L.66.18. Paris adds: "when I by seaying I ravid I shewed myselfe nott to believe" (by saying I raved I showed myself not to believe).
85. *MED*, s.v. "astŏned, astŏuned," *ppl.*
86. *Revelations of Divine Love*, L.66.23.

87. For a further reading of these visitations and their parallels to the experiences of German women visionaries, see David F. Tinsley, "Julian's Diabology," in *Julian of Norwich: A Book of Essays*, ed. Sandra J. McEntire (New York: Garland, 1998), 207–37.
88. *Revelations of Divine Love*, L.66.25–40.
89. *Revelations of Divine Love*, L.66.42.
90. *Revelations of Divine Love*, L.66.42–44, emphasis added.
91. *Revelations of Divine Love*, L.66.35–36.
92. *Revelations of Divine Love*, L.68.9–11.
93. *Revelations of Divine Love*, L.69.rubric.
94. *Revelations of Divine Love*, L.69.1.
95. *MED*, s.v. "bisī," *adj.*
96. *Revelations of Divine Love*, L.33.25–27, emphasis added.
97. *Revelations of Divine Love*, L.11.4.
98. *Revelations of Divine Love*, L.11.4, 11.38–41.
99. Augustine of Hippo, "Sermon CXVII," in *Opera Omnia*, ed. Jacques-Paul Migne, Patrologia Latina 38 (Paris: Migne, 1865), 663.
100. *Revelations of Divine Love*, L.11.43. For more on the hermeneutics of reverent dread and love in Julian's *Revelations*, see Raphaela Sophia Rohrhofer, "The Potentiality of 'Nought': Julian of Norwich's Understanding of the Deity and the Self Through the Apophatic Matrices of Love and Dread" (DPhil diss., University of Oxford, 2021).
101. Geoffrey Chaucer, "Troilus and Criseyde," in *The Riverside Chaucer*, ed. Larry Dean Benson and F. N. Robinson, 3rd ed. (Oxford: Oxford University Press, 2008), 559, line 1645; John Lydgate, *Lydgate's Troy Book*, vol. 2, ed. H. Bergen, EETS e.s. 103 (London: Kegan Paul, Trench, Trübner and Oxford University Press for the Early English Text Society, 1906), book 3, line 189: "pensifhed and inward besy drede" (melancholy and inward busy dread).
102. *Revelations of Divine Love*, L.69.4.
103. *Revelations of Divine Love*, L.69.5.
104. *Revelations of Divine Love*, L.69.9–10.
105. *Revelations of Divine Love*, L.13.16–17, emphasis added.
106. *Revelations of Divine Love*, L.69.12–13.
107. *Revelations of Divine Love*, L.69.14–16.
108. *Revelations of Divine Love*, L.69.18, 10.66.
109. Taylor Carman, "Authenticity," in *A Companion to Heidegger*, ed. Hubert L. Dreyfus and Mark A. Wrathall (Oxford: Blackwell, 2005), 291.
110. Lynn Staley, *Margery Kempe's Dissenting Fictions* (University Park: Pennsylvania State University Press, 1994), esp. 3.

111. *The Book of Margery Kempe*, ed. Lynn Staley, TEAMS Middle English Texts (Kalamazoo, MI: Medieval Institute Publications, 1996), https://d.lib.rochester.edu/teams/publication/staley-the-book-of-margery-kempe, chapter 18, line 955. For more on this connection, see Laura Saetveit Miles, "Queer Touch Between Holy Women: Julian of Norwich, Margery Kempe, Birgitta of Sweden, and the Visitation," in *Touching, Devotional Practices, and Visionary Experience in the Late Middle Ages*, ed. David Carrillo-Rangel, Delfi I. Nieto-Isabel, and Pablo Acosta-García (New York: Palgrave, 2019), 203–35.
112. For the performance of Margery Kempe's religious identity, see Hannah Lucas, "'Clad in flesch and blood': The Sartorial Body and Female Self-Fashioning in *The Book of Margery Kempe*," *Journal of Medieval Religious Cultures* 45, no. 1 (2019): 29–60; Laura Varnam, "The Crucifix, The Pietà, and the Female Mystic: Devotional Objects and Performative Identity in *The Book of Margery Kempe*," *Journal of Medieval Religious Cultures* 41, no. 2 (2015): 208–37.
113. *Revelations of Divine Love*, S.6.1–6.
114. *Revelations of Divine Love*, L.9.6–8.
115. Liz Herbert McAvoy, "Introduction," in *A Companion to Julian of Norwich*, 2.
116. Vincent Gillespie, "'[S]he do the police in different voices': Pastiche, Ventriloquism and Parody in Julian of Norwich," in *A Companion to Julian of Norwich*, 196.
117. Liz Herbert McAvoy and Mari Hughes-Edwards, eds., *Anchorites, Wombs and Tombs: Intersections of Gender and Enclosure in the Middle Ages* (Cardiff: University of Wales Press, 2005; repr. 2010), 18.
118. McAvoy and Hughes-Edwards, *Anchorites, Wombs and Tombs*, 19; Gillespie, "[S]he do the police," 197. See also Justin M. Byron-Davies, *Revelation and the Apocalypse in Late Medieval Literature: The Writings of Julian of Norwich and William Langland* (Cardiff: University of Wales Press, 2020), 10, 50–51.
119. Mikhail Bakhtin, *The Dialogic Imagination: Four Essays*, ed. Michael Holquist (Austin: University of Texas Press, 1981), 324, emphases in original.
120. *Revelations of Divine Love*, S.10.26–29.
121. *Writings of Julian of Norwich*, 82, note to lines 26–28.
122. Benedicta Ward, "Julian the Solitary," in *Julian Reconsidered*, ed. Kenneth Leech and Benedicta Ward (Oxford: SLG Press, 1988), 24; McAvoy, *Authority and the Female Body*, 76.
123. McAvoy, *Authority and the Female Body*, 76, 77.
124. Ross, "Behold Not the Cloud," 29.
125. *Revelations of Divine Love*, L.4.24. For a recent discussion of this chain of hermeneutic beholding, see Laura Saetveit Miles, *The Virgin Mary's Book at the Annunciation* (Cambridge: Brewer, 2020), 150–51.

126. For the Heideggerian substitution of being-toward-God with being-toward-death, see Matheson Russell, "Phenomenology and Theology: Situating Heidegger's Philosophy of Religion," *Sophia* 50, no. 4 (2011): 641–55.
127. For an example of one of these services, see Luke Ayers and Victoria Bahr, "A Twelfth-Century Service for Enclosing an Anchorite or Anchoress: Introduction, Latin Text, and Translation," *Expositor: A Journal of Undergraduate Research in the Humanities* 14 (2019): 1–12.
128. *Ancrene Wisse*, ed. Robert Hasenfratz, TEAMS Middle English Texts (Kalamazoo, MI: Medieval Institute Publications, 2000), https://d.lib.rochester.edu/teams/publication/hasenfratz-ancrene-wisse, part 2, lines 815–16.
129. *OED*, s.v. "anchorite," *n.* and *adj.*, etymology.
130. *Revelations of Divine Love*, L.14.3–5.
131. *Revelations of Divine Love*, L.14.5–7.
132. *Revelations of Divine Love*, L.64.10–12.
133. *Revelations of Divine Love*, L.14.14.
134. Martin Heidegger, "Was ist Metaphysik? (1929)," in *Gesamtausgabe*, vol. 9: *Wegmarken*, ed. Friedrich-Wilhelm von Herrmann (1967; Frankfurt: Vittorio Klostermann, 1976), 115, §12. Quoted and trans. in Sean J. McGrath, *The Early Heidegger and Medieval Philosophy: Phenomenology for the Godforsaken* (Washington, DC: Catholic University of America Press, 2006), 133.
135. Martin Heidegger, *Being and Time*, trans. Joan Stambaugh, rev. and with a foreword by Dennis J. Schmidt (1937; Albany: State University of New York Press, 2010), §266, emphasis in original.
136. Heidegger, *Being and Time*, §266, emphasis in original.
137. Carel, *Phenomenology of Illness*, 159.
138. Judith Wolfe, *Heidegger's Eschatology: Theological Horizons in Martin Heidegger's Early Work* (Oxford: Oxford University Press, 2013), 2.
139. Wolfe, *Heidegger's Eschatology*, 7.
140. Heidegger, *Being and Time*, §262, emphasis in original.
141. *Revelations of Divine Love*, L.2.19–20, emphasis added.
142. McGrath, *Early Heidegger*, 134.
143. *Revelations of Divine Love*, L.63.16.

4. SEEKING UNDERSTANDING: JULIAN'S MYSTICAL TEXT

1. René Descartes, *Principles of Philosophy*, trans. V. R. Miller and R. P. Miller (Dordrecht, The Netherlands: Reidel, 1983), xxiv.

2. Barbara Newman, "What Did It Mean to Say 'I Saw'? The Clash Between Theory and Practice in Medieval Visionary Culture," *Speculum* 80, no. 1 (2005): 1–43.
3. Ioannis Duns Scoti, *Opera Omnia*, vol. 18: *Lectura* II, dist. 1–6, ed. L. Modrić, S. Bušelić, B. Hechich, I. Jurić, I. Percan, R. Rosini, S. Ruiz de Loizaga, and C. Saco Alarcón (Vatican City: Typis Polyglottis Vaticanis, 1982), dist. 3a, Q.IV.9; Bernard of Clairvaux, *Sancti Bernardi Opera*, vols. 1–2: *Sermones super Cantica Canticorum*, ed. Jean Leclercq, C. H. Talbot, and H. M. Rochais (Rome: Editiones Cistercienses, 1957–1958), sermon 51.2.3. This *expertus/inexpertus* distinction was later utilized in nominalist circles to justify their insistence on *cognitio intuitiva*. See, for example, Sebastian Day, *Intuitive Cognition: A Key to the Significance of the Later Scholastics* (St. Bonaventure: Franciscan Institute, 1947); C. K. Brampton, "Scotus, Ockham, and the Theory of Intuitive Cognition," *Antonianum* 40 (1965): 449–66; Gyula Klima and Alexander W. Hall, eds., *The Demonic Temptations of Medieval Nominalism*, Proceedings of the Society for Medieval Logic and Metaphysics 9 (Newcastle-upon-Tyne, UK: Cambridge Scholars, 2011).
4. Sabetai Unguru, "Experiment in Medieval Optics," in *Physics, Cosmology and Astronomy, 1300–1700: Tension and Accommodation*, ed. Sabetai Unguru, Boston Studies in the Philosophy of Science 126 (Dordrecht, The Netherlands: Springer, 1991), 163.
5. Unguru, "Experiment in Medieval Optics," 163.
6. Heiko A. Oberman, quoted in Brian Stock, "Experience, Praxis, Work and Planning in Bernard of Clairvaux: Observations on the *Sermones in Cantica*," in *The Cultural Context of Medieval Learning: Proceedings of the First International Colloquium on Philosophy, Science, and Theology in the Middle Ages—September 1973*, ed. John Emery Murdoch and Edith Dudley Sylla (Dordrecht, The Netherlands: Reidel, 1973), 267.
7. Aristotle, *Metaphysics*, vol. 1: *Books 1–9*, trans. Hugh Tredennick, Loeb Classical Library 271 (Cambridge, MA: Harvard University Press, 1933), I.I.981a.11, 981a.13, emphasis in original. For an interesting discussion of the ways medieval philosophers drew on Aristotle for theories of subjectivity, especially how they theorized the relation to other people as inessential, see Juhuna Toivanen, "Beasts, Human Beings, or Gods? Human Subjectivity in Medieval Political Philosophy," in *Subjectivity and Selfhood in Medieval and Early Modern Philosophy*, ed. Jari Kaukua and Tomas Ekenberg, Studies in the History of Philosophy of Mind 16 (Dordrecht, The Netherlands: Springer, 2016), 181–97.
8. Aristotle, *Metaphysics*, I.I.981b.10–12, emphasis in original.
9. Rosemary Ann Lees, *The Negative Language of the Dionysian School of Mystical Theology: An Approach to the* Cloud of Unknowing, Analecta Cartusiana

107, 2 vols. (Salzburg: Institut für Anglistik und Amerikanistik, Universität Salzburg, 1983), 1:279, 286.

10. *The Cloud of Unknowing*, ed. Patrick J. Gallacher, TEAMS Middle English Texts (Kalamazoo, MI: Medieval Institute Publications, 1997), https://d.lib.rochester.edu/teams/publication/gallacher-the-cloud-of-unknowing.
11. Hugh of Balma, *Viae Sion Lugent*, quoted in Peter Tyler, *The Return to the Mystical: Ludwig Wittgenstein, Teresa of Avila, and the Christian Mystical Tradition* (London: Continuum, 2011), 96, emphasis added.
12. For a history of *lectio divina* in the Latin West, see Jean Leclercq, *L'amour des lettres et le désir de dieu: initiation aux auteurs monastiques du moyen age* (Paris: Éditions du Cerf, 1957). Translated as *The Love of Learning and the Desire for God: A Study of Monastic Culture*, 3rd ed. (New York: Fordham University Press, 1982). For an overview of Leclercq's work, see Duncan Robertson, *Lectio Divina: The Medieval Experience of Reading*, Cistercian Studies 238 (Collegeville, MN: Cistercian Publications/Liturgical Press, 2011), 4–11.
13. "Meditatio vero est studiosa mentis intentio circa aliquid investigandum diligenter insistens": Richardi a Sancto Victore, "De gratia contemplationis libri quinque occasione accepta ab arca Moysis et o beam rem hactenus dictum Benjamin Maior," in *Opera Omnia*, ed. Jacques-Paul Migne, Patrologia Latina 196 (Paris: Migne, 1855), col. 67.
14. Karl Baier, "Meditation and Contemplation in High to Late Medieval Europe," in *Yogic Perception, Meditation and Altered States of Consciousness*, ed. Eli Franco (Vienna: Verlag der Österreichischen Akademie der Wissenschaften, 2009), 328.
15. Aristotle, *Metaphysics*, I.II.982b.9, emphasis added.
16. Aristotle, I.II.982b.10.
17. Mary-Jane Rubenstein, *Strange Wonder: The Closure of Metaphysics and the Opening of Awe* (New York: Columbia University Press, 2008), 12–13, emphasis in original.
18. Rubenstein, *Strange Wonder*, 8.
19. Rubenstein, 8, emphasis added.
20. Rubenstein, 23.
21. Julian of Norwich, *Julian of Norwich: Revelations of Divine Love: The Short Text and the Long Text*, ed. Barry Windeatt (Oxford: Oxford University Press, 2016), L.11.6, 11.9. 47.13, 52.21, 72.rubric, 73.12, 85.2.
22. *Revelations of Divine Love*, L.86.1.
23. Maggie Ross, "Behold Not the Cloud of Experience," in *The Medieval Mystical Tradition in England VIII, Papers Read at Charney Manor July 2011*, ed. E. A. Jones (Cambridge: Brewer, 2013), 34–35.
24. Ross, "Behold Not the Cloud," 33, note 13.
25. Ross, 29–30.

26. René Tixier, trans. with Victoria Hobson, "'Good Gamesumli Pley': Games of Love in *The Cloud of Unknowing*," *Downside Review* 108, no 373 (1990): 244.
27. Ross, "Behold Not the Cloud," 39.
28. Ross, 38, 39, emphases in original.
29. Ross, 41.
30. Ross, 34.
31. Jessica Barr reads this combination of approaches to knowledge as superseding the gendered implications of ways of visionary knowing; Barr, *Willing to Know God: Dreamers and Visionaries in the Later Middle Ages* (Columbus: Ohio State University Press, 2010), 96–121.
32. *Revelations of Divine Love*, L.11.4.
33. *Revelations of Divine Love*, L.11.4–6.
34. *Revelations of Divine Love*, L.11.6, 12. David Aers has also noted Julian's "vernacular version of a scholastic discourse, a reasoning inquiry with carefully articulated questions and answers deploying pointedly abstract terms": Aers and Lynn Staley, *The Powers of the Holy: Religion, Politics, and Gender in Late Medieval English Culture* (University Park: Pennsylvania State University Press, 1996), 83–84.
35. See also Bernardo Bazán, John Wippel, Gérard Fransen, and Danielle Jacquart, eds., *Les Questions Disputées et Les Questions Quodlibétiques dans les Facultés de Théologie, de Droit et de Médecine* (Turnhout, Belgium: Brepols, 1985), 40.
36. *Revelations of Divine Love*, L.50.7, 10–11.
37. *Revelations of Divine Love*, L.50.12.
38. *Revelations of Divine Love*, L.50.13, 51.22.
39. *Revelations of Divine Love*, L.35.1–2.
40. *Revelations of Divine Love*, L.35.2, 35.5–6.
41. *Revelations of Divine Love*, L.10.63–64.
42. *Revelations of Divine Love*, L.10.57. The Paris and Westminster MSS here read "seke into the beholdyng," while Sloane 2499 reads "seke him to the beholdyng." While Barry Windeatt's note to this line claims that "the PW agreement suggests S1's less clear reading is an error," seeking *into* beholding seems to refer to the contemplative journey inward, but is also a contradiction in terms in Julian's schema, in which beholding is a state that precludes the self-conscious process of seeking. Sloane's seeking him *to* the beholding is the less theologically schematic of the two phrases, and so seems closer to Julian's epistemology. I am grateful to Vincent Gillespie for pointing out this distinction.
43. Denys Turner, *Julian of Norwich, Theologian* (New Haven, CT: Yale University Press, 2011), 141.
44. Turner, *Julian of Norwich*, 141.
45. *Revelations of Divine Love*, L.11.1–2.

46. This is the translation given by Elizabeth Spearing, who notes that "poynte" can mean "a point of space or of time." Julian of Norwich, *Revelations of Divine Love*, trans. Elizabeth Spearing, with introduction and notes by A. C. Spearing (London: Penguin, 1998), 181. For more on the "poynte" as a moment in time, see Amy Laura Hall, *Laughing at the Devil: Seeing the World with Julian of Norwich* (Durham, NC: Duke University Press, 2018), 19–39.
47. Anna Maria Reynolds, "Some Literary Influences in the *Revelations* of Julian of Norwich (c. 1342–post-1416)," *Leeds Studies in English and Kindred Languages* 7–8 (1952): 24. See also Cynthea Masson, "The Point of Coincidence: Rhetoric and the Apophatic in Julian of Norwich's *Showings*," in *Julian of Norwich: A Book of Essays*, ed. Sandra J. McEntire (New York: Garland, 1998), 153–81.
48. Wolfgang Riehle, *The Middle English Mystics*, trans. Bernard Standring (London: Routledge & Kegan Paul, 1981), 83.
49. *Revelations of Divine Love*, L.10.12–13.
50. Philologist Friedrich Ast wrote of this as "the foundational law of all understanding and knowledge"; Ast, *Grundlinien der Grammatik, Hermeneutik und Kritik* (Landshut, Germany: Jos. Thomann, Buchdrucker und Buchhändler, 1808), 178.
51. Martin Heidegger, *Being and Time*, trans. Joan Stambaugh, rev. and with a foreword by Dennis J. Schmidt (1927; Albany: State University of New York Press, 2010), §153, emphasis in original.
52. Judith N. Shklar, "Squaring the Hermeneutic Circle", *Social Research* 71, no. 3 (2004): 657 (originally published in 1986). Heidegger determines what is "pre-known" in terms of "fore-having" (*Vorhabe*), "fore-sight" (*Vorsicht*), and "fore-conception" (*Vorgriff*), but these a priori categories do not have the fixed or formal character of theoretical *knowledge*: they are, instead, precognitive presuppositions. For more on Heidegger's epistemology, see Merold Westphal, "Hermeneutics as Epistemology," in *Overcoming Onto-Theology: Towards a Postmodern Christian Faith* (New York: Fordham University Press, 2001), 47–74.
53. Shklar, "Squaring the Hermeneutic Circle," 657–58.
54. *Revelations of Divine Love*, L.10.57–58.
55. *Revelations of Divine Love*, L.10.56, emphasis added.
56. Aristotle, *On the Soul. Parva Naturalia. On Breath*, trans. Walter Stanley Hett, rev. ed., Loeb Classical Library 288 (Cambridge, MA: Harvard University Press, 1957), 412a20–413a11.
57. Edmund Husserl, *Logical Investigations*, trans. J. N. Findlay (1900/01; London: Routledge, 1973). Quoted in Fredrik Svenaeus, *The Hermeneutics of Medicine and the Phenomenology of Health: Steps Towards a Philosophy of Medical Practice* (Dordrecht, The Netherlands: Kluwer, 2000), 75–78. For more on

Husserl and intentionality, see Hubert L. Dreyfus and Harrison Hall, *Husserl, Intentionality, and Cognitive Science* (Cambridge, MA: MIT Press, 1982).

58. *Revelations of Divine Love*, L.6.26–27. See also Alexandra Barratt, "'In the Lowest Part of Our Need': Julian and Medieval Gynaecological Writing," in *Julian of Norwich: A Book of Essays*, 253.
59. Cristina Maria Cervone, "The 'Soule' Crux in Julian of Norwich's *A Revelation of Love*," *Review of English Studies* 55, no. 219 (2004): 151–56.
60. Cervone, "'Soule' Crux," 151.
61. Julian of Norwich, *The Writings of Julian of Norwich: A Vision Showed to a Devout Woman and A Revelation of Love*, ed. Nicholas Watson and Jacqueline Jenkins (Turnhout, Belgium: Brepols, 2006), 142, note to lines 29–31. For another reading of this passage, see Liz Herbert McAvoy, "'. . . a purse fulle feyer': Feminising the Body in Julian of Norwich's *A Revelation of Love*," *Leeds Studies in English* n.s. 33 (2002): 99–113.
62. *Revelations of Divine Love*, L.6.26n; Isidore of Seville, *The* Etymologies *of Isidore of Seville*, trans. and ed. Stephen A. Barney, W. J. Lewis, J. A. Beach, and Oliver Berghof, collab. with Muriel Hall (Cambridge: Cambridge University Press, 2006), 231. See also *Ancrene Wisse*: "Thi flesch—hwet frut bereth hit in all his openunges? Amid te menske of thi neb—thet is the fehereste deal—bitweonen muthes smech ant neases smeal, ne berest tu as twa prive thurles?" (What fruit does your body produce from all its orifices? Amidst the beauty of your fair face—which is the fairest part of the body—between the taste of the mouth and the smell of the nose, do you not have, as it were, two privy-holes?): *Ancrene Wisse*, ed. Robert Hasenfratz, TEAMS Middle English Texts (Kalamazoo, MI: Medieval Institute Publications, 2000), https://d.lib.rochester.edu/teams/publication/hasenfratz-ancrene-wisse, part 4, lines 1201–3.
63. *Revelations of Divine Love*, L.64.21–22.
64. *Revelations of Divine Love*, L.64.23, 64.25, emphasis added.
65. Cervone, "'Soule' Crux," 155.
66. *Revelations of Divine Love*, L.64.29.
67. *Revelations of Divine Love*, L.6.23–24.
68. Katie L. Walter has also observed this in *Middle English Mouths: Late Medieval Medical, Religious and Literary Traditions* (Cambridge: Cambridge University Press, 2018), 55–56.
69. Michael Raby, "The Phenomenology of Attention in Julian of Norwich's *A Revelation of Love*," *Exemplaria* 26, no. 4 (2014): 353.
70. Augustine of Hippo, *The Works of Saint Augustine: A Translation for the 21st Century*, part 3, vol. 14: *Homilies on the First Epistle of John* (Tractatus in Epistolam Joannis ad Parthos), trans. with an introduction and notes by

Boniface Ramsey, ed. Daniel E. Doyle and Thomas Martin (New York: New City Press, 2008), 70, XXIX.6. Cf. Phil. 3:12–14. As the editors note, Augustine's Latin for this passage pairs the verb *extend* and the noun *intentio*, which are related. Quoted in Raby, "Phenomenology of Attention," 353.

71. *Revelations of Divine Love*, L.43.22.
72. Simon Tugwell, *Ways of Imperfection: An Exploration of Christian Spirituality* (London: Templegate, 1985), 201, emphases in original.
73. *Revelations of Divine Love*, L.56.1–4.
74. *Revelations of Divine Love*, L.46.7–8.
75. *Revelations of Divine Love*, L.46.5–7.
76. *Revelations of Divine Love*, L.73.25.
77. Heidegger, *Being and Time*, §175–76.
78. *Revelations of Divine Love*, L.45.1–4.
79. *Revelations of Divine Love*, L.58.18.
80. *Revelations of Divine Love*, L.55.12, 53.15.
81. *Revelations of Divine Love*, L.57.5–6.
82. *Revelations of Divine Love*, L.55.37–39.
83. *Revelations of Divine Love*, L.56.9–11.
84. *Revelations of Divine Love*, L.67.1–2.
85. *Revelations of Divine Love*, L.67.11.
86. *Revelations of Divine Love*, L.54.15–16.
87. 1 John 4:15, quoted in James Walsh, "God's Homely Loving: St. John and Julian of Norwich on the Divine Indwelling," *Month* 205, n.s. 19 (1958): 167. For more on this connection, see Justin M. Byron-Davies, *Revelation and the Apocalypse in Late Medieval Literature: The Writings of Julian of Norwich and William Langland* (Cardiff: University of Wales Press, 2020), 11–12.
88. Grace M. Jantzen, *Julian of Norwich: Mystic and Theologian* (London: SPCK, 2000), 140.
89. *Revelations of Divine Love*, L.54.17–19.
90. Wolfgang Riehle, *The Secret Within: Hermits, Recluses, and Spiritual Outsiders in Medieval England*, trans. Charity Scott-Stokes (2011; Ithaca, NY: Cornell University Press, 2014), 222.
91. Riehle, *Secret Within*, 222.
92. See also Judith Lang, "'The Godly Wylle' in Julian of Norwich," *Downside Review* 102, no. 348 (1984): 163–73.
93. *Revelations of Divine Love*, L.37.11–13.
94. Denise N. Baker, *Julian of Norwich's Showings: From Vision to Book* (Princeton, NJ: Princeton University Press, 1994), 75; see also Denise N. Baker, "The Structure of the Soul and the 'Godly Wylle' in Julian of Norwich's *Showings*," in *The Medieval Mystical Tradition in England VII, Papers Read at*

Charney Manor, July 2004, ed. E. A. Jones (Cambridge: Brewer, 2004), 37–49.

95. Baker, *Julian of Norwich's Showings*, 76–79. For a recent discussion of Baker's work and Julian's theodicy, see Davis Aers, "'What is synne?': Exploring Julian of Norwich's Question," in *New Directions in Medieval Mystical and Devotional Literature: Essays in Honor of Denise N. Baker*, ed. Amy N. Vines and Lee Templeton (Lanham, MD: Rowman and Littlefield, 2023), 11–28.
96. Baker, *Julian of Norwich's Showings*, 116. Quote from Bernard McGinn, "The Human Person as Image of God, II. Western Christianity," in *Christian Spirituality: Origins to the Twelfth Century*, ed. Bernard McGinn and John Meyendorff in collaboration with Jean Leclercq (New York: Crossroad, 1985; repr. 2000), 325.
97. Baker, *Julian of Norwich's Showings*, 116, emphasis in original. For the comparison with Julian, see 117.
98. Bernard of Clairvaux, *The Works of Bernard of Clairvaux*, vol. 7: *Treatises III: On Grace and Free Choice*, trans. Daniel O'Donovan with an introduction by Bernard McGinn, Cistercian Studies 19 (Kalamazoo, MI: Cistercian Publications, 1977), 85, 9.29. Quoted in Baker, *Julian of Norwich's Showings*, 117.
99. Baker, *Julian of Norwich's Showings*, 118. Quote from Bernard McGinn, "Love, Knowledge and *Unio Mystica* in the Western Christian Tradition," in *Mystical Union and Monotheistic Faith: An Ecumenical Dialogue*, ed. Moshe Idel and Bernard McGinn (New York: Macmillan, 1989), 63, 71.
100. *Revelations of Divine Love*, L.43.1–2, emphases added.
101. *Revelations of Divine Love*, L.54.12, 56.41.
102. *Revelations of Divine Love*, L.54.12–14.
103. *Revelations of Divine Love*, L.53.34.
104. *Revelations of Divine Love*, L.53.30–33.
105. Ross, "Behold Not the Cloud," 36.
106. *Revelations of Divine Love*, L.50.25, emphasis added.
107. *Revelations of Divine Love*, L.83.7, emphasis added.
108. *Revelations of Divine Love*, L.80.4, 80.2, 32.10.
109. *Revelations of Divine Love*, L.47.11n. This could indicate the Paris scribe's allegiance to the short text.
110. *MED*, s.v. "cŏnning," *ppl.* See also entries for "kennen" and "connan."
111. Genesis 3:1 describes the serpent in Eden as the most cunning—"more subtle [Latin: 'calliador,' also 'cunning']"—of all the animals on earth.
112. Sigmund Freud, "The Uncanny," in *The Standard Edition of the Complete Psychological Works of Sigmund Freud*, vol. 17: *An Infantile Neurosis and Other Works, 1917–1919*, trans. and gen. ed. James Strachey and Anna Freud, asst. Alix Strachey and Alan Tyson (1919; London: Hogarth Press and The Institute of Psycho-Analysis, 1971), 237.

113. *Revelations of Divine Love*, L.47.11.
114. *MED*, s.v. "overcŏmen," *v.*
115. *Revelations of Divine Love*, L.10.4, 47.12, emphases added.
116. *Revelations of Divine Love*, L.68.10–11.
117. Søren Kierkegaard, *Concluding Unscientific Postscript to* Philosophical Fragments, ed. and trans. Howard V. Hong and Edna H. Hong (Princeton, NJ: Princeton University Press, 1992), 130, 216.
118. *Revelations of Divine Love*, L.63.5, where Paris has "vnmade"—see Barry Windeatt's note to this line: "P's reading 'unmade kind' alters the balance of the sentence with what may be a scribal recollection of 53/34"; L.56.30.
119. *MED*, s.v. "kinde," *n.*
120. Alfred Kentigern Siewers, "Earth: A Wandering," *postmedieval* 4, no. 1: *Ecomaterialism* (2013): 9, emphases in original.
121. Rebecca M. Douglass, "Ecocriticism and Middle English Literature," *Studies in Medievalism* 10 (1998): 145; Neil Evernden, *The Social Creation of Nature* (Baltimore: John Hopkins University Press, 1992), 41.
122. Evernden, *Social Creation of Nature*, 20.
123. Douglass, "Ecocriticism and Middle English Literature," 145.
124. *Revelations of Divine Love*, L.10.36, 57.12.
125. Gerald Bonner, "Pelagius (fl. c. 390–418), theologian," *Oxford Dictionary of National Biography* (Oxford: Oxford University Press, 2014), doi:10.1093/ref:odnb/21784. For more on Julian and Pelagianism, see Baker, *Julian of Norwich's Showings*, 74.
126. *Pore Caitif: A Middle English Manual of Religion and Devotion*, ed. Karine Moreau-Guibert (Turnhout, Belgium: Brepols, 2019), 124, line 437, emphasis added.
127. *Revelations of Divine Love*, L.53.16–17.
128. *Revelations of Divine Love*, L.22.3, emphasis added.
129. Michelle Karnes, "Will's Imagination in *Piers Plowman*," *Journal of English and Germanic Philology* 108, no. 1 (2009): 27–58; Nicolette Zeeman, Piers Plowman *and the Medieval Discourse of Desire* (Cambridge: Cambridge University Press, 2006), 3, 7, 20. See also Michelle Karnes, *Imagination, Meditation, and Cognition in the Middle Ages* (Chicago: University of Chicago Press, 2011).
130. Mary Clemente Davlin, "*Kynde Knowyng* as a Middle English Equivalent for 'Wisdom' in *Piers Plowman* B," *Medium Ævum* 50 (1981): 8.
131. Zeeman, Piers Plowman, 157.
132. D. Vance Smith, "Negative Langland," *Yearbook of Langland Studies* 23 (2009): 56. Rebecca Davis advances a more positive reading of "Kynde," suggesting that "it signals the magnitude of the poem's investment in the positive value

of nature and its spiritual meaning for human life": Davis, *Piers Plowman and the Books of Nature* (Oxford: Oxford University Press, 2016), 3.

133. William Langland, *Piers Plowman: The B Version*, ed. George Kane and E. Talbot Donaldson, 2nd ed. (London: Athlone Press, 1988), passus 1, line 138.
134. Kane and Donaldson, *Piers Plowman*, passus 16, line 74. See also James Simpson, *Piers Plowman: An Introduction to the B-Text* (London: Longman, 1990), 190.
135. James Simpson, "From Reason to Affective Knowledge: Modes of Thought and Poetic Form in *Piers Plowman*," *Medium Ævum* 55, no. 1 (1986): 1–23. An alternative reading is offered by Edward Vasta, who interprets this journey as a mystical ascent, assigning linear categories of contemplation to Will's quest for "knowyng." Vasta defines Langland's *kynde knowyng* as the contemplative point at which the soul is deified by the Holy Spirit, identifying the term as a kind of revelation predicated upon love rather than knowledge: Vasta, *The Spiritual Basis of Piers Plowman*, Studies in English 18 (New York: Humanities Press, 1965), 92.
136. Hugh White, *Nature and Salvation in Piers Plowman* (Cambridge: Brewer, 1988), 48, emphasis added.
137. White, *Nature and Salvation*, 45. Responding to Davlin, "*Kynde Knowyng*," 15.
138. See Robert Adams, "Langland's Theology," in *A Companion to Piers Plowman*, ed. John A. Alford (Berkeley: University of California Press, 1988), 88.
139. White, *Nature and Salvation*, 58.
140. White, 58.
141. Kane and Donaldson, *Piers Plowman*, passus 5, line 542. See also Denise N. Baker, "From Plowing to Penitence: Piers Plowman and Fourteenth-Century Theology," *Speculum* 55, no. 4 (1980): 721.
142. Davlin, "*Kynde Knowing*," 14.
143. *Revelations of Divine Love*, L.51.152. While it is not my objective to ascertain direct influence between Julian and Langland, it is worth pointing out, as Barbara Newman and Nicolette Zeeman have each done, that (and I quote from Newman) "by the time of her final revisions, she [Julian] could have had an opportunity to read Langland in either the B or C text": Barbara Newman, "Redeeming the Time: Langland, Julian, and the Art of Lifelong Revision," *Yearbook of Langland Studies* 23 (2009): 23; Nicolette Zeeman, "Julian Reads Langland," *Chaucer Review* 58, nos. 3–4 (2023): 468–80.
144. Martin Heidegger, *The Phenomenology of Religious Life*, trans. Matthias Fritsch and Jennifer Anna Gosetti-Ferencei (1995; Bloomington: Indiana University Press, 2010), 40, §12.
145. Heidegger, *Being and Time*, §236, emphasis in original.

146. René Tixier, "'Þis louely blinde werk': Contemplation in *The Cloud of Unknowing* and Related Treatises," in *Mysticism and Spirituality in Medieval England*, ed. William F. Pollard and Robert Boenig (Woodbridge: Brewer, 1997), 120; *Revelations of Divine Love*, L.86.1.
147. Newman, "Redeeming the Time," 2, emphasis in original. In *Piers Plowman*, the terms "visio" and "vita" are used to divide the principal vision of society as a whole (passus 1–7) from the life of Will (passus 8–20), or more accurately, the ideal life which serves as an education of his soul.
148. Newman, "Redeeming the Time," 3.
149. See Vincent Gillespie, "Postcards from the Edge: Interpreting the Ineffable in the Middle English Mystics," in *Looking Into Holy Books: Essays on Late Medieval Religious Writing in England* (1993; Turnhout, Belgium: Brepols, 2011), 335, note 57: "The notion of wounded language derives from the work of Michel de Certeau." For more on this, see A. Lion, "Le Discours blessé: Sur le langage mystique selon Michel de Certeau," *Révue des sciences philosophies et théologiques* 71 (1987): 405–20.
150. *Revelations of Divine Love*, L.7.13.
151. *Revelations of Divine Love*, S.6.34.
152. D. Vance Smith, *Arts of Dying: Literature and Finitude in Medieval England* (Chicago: University of Chicago Press, 2020), 1–10.
153. Havi Carel, *Phenomenology of Illness* (Oxford: Oxford University Press, 2016), 178, emphasis added.
154. A. S. Lazikani, *Cultivating the Heart: Feeling and Emotion in Twelfth- and Thirteenth-Century Religious Texts* (Cardiff: Cardiff University Press, 2015), 74.
155. Charles R. Figley, ed., *Treating Compassion Fatigue* (New York: Brunner-Routledge, 2002).
156. J. S. Felton, "Burnout as a Clinical Entity: Its Importance in Health Care Workers," *Occupational Medicine*, 48, no. 4 (1998): 237–50.
157. Olga M. Klimecki, Susanne Leiberg, Matthieu Ricard, and Tania Singer, "Differential Pattern of Functional Brain Plasticity After Compassion and Empathy Training," *Social Cognitive and Affective Neuroscience* 9, no. 6 (2014): 873–79.
158. Sarah McNamer, *Affective Meditation and the Invention of Medieval Compassion* (Philadelphia: University of Pennsylvania Press, 2010), 12.
159. McNamer, *Affective Meditation*, 11.
160. Lazikani, *Cultivating the Heart*, 74.
161. *Revelations of Divine Love*, L.9.1–2.
162. Joanna Raczaszek-Leonardi, Agnieszka Debska, and Adam Sochanowicz, "Pooling the Ground: Understanding and Coordination in Collective

Sense-Making," in *Towards an Embodied Science of Intersubjectivity: Widening the Scope of Social Understanding Research*, ed. E. Di Paolo and H. De Jaegher (Lausanne, Switzerland: Frontiers Media, 2015), 353. See also Leonhard Schilbach, Bert Timmermans, Vasudevi Reddy, and Alan Costall, "Towards a Second-Person Neuroscience," *Behavioral and Brain Sciences* 36 (2013): 393–462.

163. Claire Gilbert, "Restoring Porosity and the Ecological Crisis: A Post-Ricoeurian Reading of the Julian of Norwich Texts" (PhD diss., King's College London, 2018), 74. Dissertation published as *Julian of Norwich and the Ecological Crisis: Restoring Porosity* (London: Routledge, 2024).
164. Gilbert, "Restoring Porosity," 76.
165. William Langland, *Piers Plowman: A New Translation of the B-Text*, ed. and trans. A. V. C. Schmidt (Oxford: Oxford University Press, 1992), 302, note 126.
166. Ross, "Behold Not the Cloud," 34.
167. *Revelations of Divine Love*, L.10.57, emphasis added. See note 39 in this chapter for my discussion of the manuscript variations of this phrase.
168. *Revelations of Divine Love*, L.10.56.
169. See Gillespie, "Postcards from the Edge," 311.
170. Vincent Gillespie and Maggie Ross, "The Apophatic Image: The Poetics of Effacement in Julian of Norwich," in *The Medieval Mystical Tradition in England V, Papers Read at The Devon Centre, Dartington Hall, July 1992*, ed. Marion Glasscoe (Cambridge: Brewer, 1992), 53. With "play of signification," they refer to Jacques Derrida, "Structure, Sign and Play in the Discourse of the Human Sciences," in *Writing and Difference*, trans. Alan Bass (1967; London: Routledge, 1978), 278–93.
171. Martin Heidegger, "Letter on Humanism," in *Martin Heidegger: Basic Writings: From* Being and Time *(1927) to The* Task of Thinking *(1964)*, ed. David Farrell Krell, rev. ed. (1947; San Francisco: HarperCollins, 1993), 217.
172. Riehle, *Middle English Mystics*, 104.
173. Riehle, 104.
174. Cervone, *Poetics of the Incarnation*, 33, emphasis in original.
175. Heidegger, *Being and Time*, §161, emphasis in original.
176. Heidegger, §161, emphasis in original.
177. Heidegger, §161, emphasis added.
178. Heidegger, §166.
179. Heidegger, §166, emphasis in original.
180. Heidegger, §166.
181. Heidegger, §168.
182. Matthew King, "Heidegger's Etymological Method: Discovering Being by Recovering the Richness of the Word," *Philosophy Today* 51, no. 3 (2007): 282.

183. For more on Heidegger and language, see Duane Williams, *Language and Being: Heidegger's Linguistics* (London: Bloomsbury Publishing, 2017); Jeffrey Powell, ed., *Heidegger and Language* (Bloomington: Indiana University Press, 2013).
184. Heidegger, *Being and Time*, §68.
185. Heidegger, §35.
186. Heidegger, §161, emphasis in original.
187. Heidegger, §165.
188. Heidegger, §165. To this he adds the footnote, "*and what calls for saying [*das Zu-sagende*]? (being) [*Seyn*]."
189. Maggie Ross, *Silence: A User's Guide*, vol. 1: *Process* (Eugene, OR: Cascade, 2018), 66.
190. Ross, *Silence*, 66, emphasis added.
191. Liz Herbert McAvoy also spoke to the theme of threads in Julian's writing in her plenary presentation at the "New Visions of Julian of Norwich" conference in Oxford, July 15–16, 2022. A version of this talk is forthcoming in the conference special issue of *Medieval Feminist Forum: A Journal of Gender and Sexuality*.
192. Ross, *Silence*, 66.
193. Pseudo-Dionysius, "The Divine Names," in *Pseudo-Dionysius: The Complete Works*, trans. Colm Luibheid, with foreword, notes, and translation collaboration by Paul Rorem, preface by René Roques, and introductions by Jaroslav Pelikan, Jean Leclercq, and Karlfried Froehlich (New York: Paulist Press, 1987), 588C.2, 596A.6, 597A.7.
194. Augustine of Hippo, "On Christian Doctrine," in *Nicene and Post-Nicene Fathers of the Christian Church*, series I, volume 2, ed. Philip Schaff and trans. J. F. Shaw. Christian Classics Ethereal Library (Grand Rapids, MI: Eerdmans), https://www.ccel.org/ccel/schaff/npnf102, 524, I.6, emphasis added. Echoes of this "avoidance by silence" can be found in Wittgenstein's "whereof one cannot speak thereof one must be silent": Ludwig Wittgenstein, *Tractatus Logico-Philosophicus*, trans. C. K. Ogden with an introduction by Bertrand Russell (1921; New York: Routledge, 2005), 27, 189. For more on this connection, see James K. A. Smith, "Between Predication and Silence: Augustine on How (Not) to Speak of God," *Heythrop Journal* 41, no. 1 (2000): 66–86.
195. *Revelations of Divine Love*, L.17.35.
196. Gillespie and Ross, "Apophatic Image," 58.
197. Cervone, *Poetics of the Incarnation*, 5.
198. Cervone, 26.
199. Cervone, 26, 7, emphasis added.
200. Cervone, 6, emphasis added.

201. Cervone, 6.
202. For Cervone's reading of Julian's term *hame* to describe the veronica and its associated meanings of enwrapment and clothing, see Cristina Maria Cervone, "Julian of Norwich and John Capgrave: *Foule Black Dede Hame / Hame of Blyndnes*," *Journal of English and Germanic Philology* 114, no. 1 (2015): 88–96.
203. Cervone, *Poetics of the Incarnation*, 5, emphasis added.
204. Cervone, 57.
205. Turner, *Julian of Norwich*, 4.
206. Turner, 4.
207. *Revelations of Divine Love*, L.10.12–13.
208. Martin Heidegger, *An Introduction to Metaphysics*, trans. Ralph Mannheim (1953; New Haven, CT: Yale University Press, 1959), 93–206.
209. Heidegger, *Introduction to Metaphysics*, 156, emphasis added.
210. Heidegger, 157–58.
211. Heidegger, 158, emphasis in original.
212. Jacques Derrida, "Semiology and Grammatology: An Interview with Julia Kristeva" [1968], in *The Routledge Language and Cultural Theory Reader*, ed. Lucy Burle, Tony Crowley, and Alan Girvin (1968; London: Routledge, 2000), 241–48.

5. THE CONTEMPLATIVE WAY: THE PERFORMANCE OF PRAYER AND *HOMLYHEDE*

The epigraph of this chapter is from Clarissa Pinkola Estés, *Women Who Run With the Wolves* (London: Rider, 2008).

1. Clarissa Pinkola Estés, *Women Who Run with The Wolves: Contacting the Power of the Wild Woman* (London: Rider, 1992; repr. 2008), 281.
2. Martin Heidegger, "Letter on Humanism," in *Martin Heidegger: Basic Writings: From* Being and Time *(1927) to* The Task of Thinking *(1964)*, ed. David Farrell Krell, rev. ed. (1947; San Francisco: HarperCollins, 1993), 217.
3. Philip Sheldrake, *Julian of Norwich: In God's Sight, Her Theology in Context* (Hoboken, NJ: John Wiley, 2019), 157.
4. For discussions of Julian's literacy, see Felicity Riddy, "'Women Talking About the Things of God': A Late Medieval Sub-Culture," in *Women and Literature in Britain, 1150–1500*, ed. Carol M. Meale, Cambridge Studies in Medieval Literature 17, 2nd ed. (Cambridge: Cambridge University Press, 1996), 104–27. For Julian's oral literacy, see Jennifer Rebecca Rytting, "'Hearing the Word': Julian of Norwich and the Middle English Sermon Tradition" (PhD diss., Arizona State University, 2005).

5. Vincent Gillespie, "Vernacular Theology," in *Middle English: Oxford Twenty-First Century Approaches to Literature*, ed. Paul Strohm (Oxford: Oxford University Press, 2007), 403. See also Vincent Gillespie, "'[S]he do the police in different voices': Pastiche, Ventriloquism and Parody in Julian of Norwich," in *A Companion to Julian of Norwich*, ed. Liz Herbert McAvoy (Cambridge: Brewer, 2008), 195.
6. *OED*, s.v. "vernacular," *adj.*, etymology.
7. Richard Ullerston, quoted in Nicholas Watson, "Censorship and Cultural Change in Late-Medieval England: Vernacular Theology, the Oxford Translation Debate, and Arundel's Constitutions of 1409," *Speculum* 70, no .4 (1995): 843.
8. Watson, "Censorship and Cultural Change," 850–51.
9. Justin M. Byron-Davies, *Revelation and the Apocalypse in Late Medieval Literature: The Writings of Julian of Norwich and William Langland* (Cardiff: University of Wales Press, 2020), 83.
10. Julian of Norwich, *XVI. Revelations of Divine Love, Made to a Devout Servant of Our Lord, Called Mother Juliana, An Anchorite of Norwich, Who Lived in the Days of King Edward the Third*, ed. Serenus Cressy and repr. with a preface by George Hargreaves Parker (1670; London: S. Clarke, 1843), vi. Quoted in Nancy Bradley Warren, "Julian of Norwich: Lives and Afterlives," in *New Directions in Medieval Mystical and Devotional Literature: Essays in Honor of Denise N. Baker*, ed. Amy N. Vines and Lee Templeton (Lanham, MD: Rowman and Littlefield, 2023), 151.
11. Julian of Norwich, *Julian of Norwich: Revelations of Divine Love: The Short Text and the Long Text*, ed. Barry Windeatt (Oxford: Oxford University Press, 2016), L.9.8.
12. Sheldrake, *Julian of Norwich*, 56.
13. Denys Turner, *Julian of Norwich, Theologian* (New Haven, CT: Yale University Press, 2011), 14.
14. Sarah Stanbury, "Vernacular Nostalgia and *The Cambridge History of Medieval English Literature*," *Texas Studies in Literature and Language* 44, no. 1 (2002): 95.
15. *The Cloud of Unknowing*, ed. Patrick J. Gallacher, TEAMS Middle English Texts (Kalamazoo, MI: Medieval Institute Publications, 1997), https://d.lib.rochester.edu/teams/publication/gallacher-the-cloud-of-unknowing, lines 500–4.
16. Eleanor Johnson, "Feeling Time, Will, and Words: Vernacular Devotion in the *Cloud of Unknowing*," *Journal of Medieval and Early Modern Studies* 41, no. 2 (2011): 361.
17. Johnson, "Feeling Time," 361. Johnson here draws on the work of Charles Lock, who also suggests that the *Cloud*-author chose English for its distinct linguistic and etymological features; Lock, "*The Cloud of Unknowing*:

Apophatic Discourse and Vernacular Anxieties," in *Text and Voice: The Rhetoric of Authority in the Middle Ages*, ed. Marianne Børch (Odense: University of Southern Denmark Press, 2004), 207–33.

18. *Revelations of Divine Love*, L.86.12–13.
19. *MED*, s.v. "hōmlī," *adj*, emphases in original.
20. *The English Text of the Ancrene Riwle: Magdalene College Cambridge MS Pepys 2498*, ed. A. Zettersten, EETS o.s. 274 (London: Oxford University Press, 1976), quoted in *MED*, s.v. "hōmlī," *adj.* (1).a.
21. *Pearl*, ed. Sarah Stanbury, TEAMS Middle English Texts (Kalamazoo, MI: Medieval Institute Publications, 2001), https://d.lib.rochester.edu/teams/text/stanbury-pearl, line 1211; *The Chastising of God's Children, And the Treatise of Perfection of the Sons of God*, ed. Joyce Bazire and Eric Colledge (Oxford: Basil Blackwell, 1957), 198, lines 9–10.
22. Thomas Hoccleve, "*Complaint*: Edited Text," in *Thomas Hoccleve's Complaint and Dialogue*, ed. J. A. Burrow, EETS o.s. 313 (Oxford: Oxford University Press, 1999), 7, line 64.
23. See John Wycliffe, *The English Works of Wyclif Hitherto Unprinted*, ed. F. D. Matthew, EETS o.s. 74 (1880; London: Trübner, 1973), 219, 435, 462, 468, 477.
24. *The Holy Bible Containing the Old and New Testaments with the Apocryphal Books in the Earliest English Versions Made from the Latin Vulgate by John Wycliffe and His Followers*, ed. J. Forshall and F. Madden, 4 vols. (Oxford: Oxford University Press, 1850), 1:64.
25. Julian of Norwich, *The Shewings of Julian of Norwich*, ed. Georgia Ronan Crampton, TEAMS Middle English Texts (Kalamazoo, MI: Medieval Institute Publications, 1994), https://d.lib.rochester.edu/teams/publication/crampton-shewings-of-julian-norwich, part 1, note to lines 574–76.
26. Edmund Colledge and James Walsh, "Editing Julian of Norwich's *Revelations*: A Progress Report," *Medieval Studies* 38 (1976): 404–27. Cited in *Shewings*, part 1, note to lines 574–76.
27. Annie Sutherland, "'Oure Feyth Is Groundyd in Goddes Worde'—Julian of Norwich and the Bible," in *The Medieval Mystical Tradition in England VII, Papers Read at Charney Manor, July 2004*, ed. E. A. Jones (Cambridge: Brewer, 2004), 6, emphasis in original.
28. *Ancrene Wisse*, ed. Robert Hasenfratz, TEAMS Middle English Texts (Kalamazoo, MI: Medieval Institute Publications, 2000), https://d.lib.rochester.edu/teams/publication/hasenfratz-ancrene-wisse, part 6, lines 12–15.
29. *Ancrene Wisse*, part 6, lines 33–34.
30. Rosanne Gasse, "Dowel, Dobet, and Dobest in Middle English Literature," *Florilegium* 14, no. 1 (1995–1996): 177.

31. John A. Alford, "Design of the Poem," in *A Companion to Piers Plowman*, ed. John A. Alford (Berkeley: University of California Press, 1988), 46.
32. Alford, "Design of the Poem," 46.
33. Alford, 46.
34. Alford, 47.
35. Alford, 47.
36. Alford, 47.
37. Ralph Hanna, *London Literature, 1300–1380* (Cambridge: Cambridge University Press, 2005), 275.
38. *Revelations of Divine Love*, L.5.1–2, 6.34, 67.11, emphases added.
39. *Revelations of Divine Love*, L.4.14, emphasis added.
40. *Revelations of Divine Love*, L.5.1–2, 5.6.
41. *Revelations of Divine Love*, S.4.39–40.
42. *Revelations of Divine Love*, L.5.7–8, 5.10.
43. *Revelations of Divine Love*, L.5.12–13, 5.14–16.
44. *Revelations of Divine Love*, L.5.21, 5.23–24.
45. *Revelations of Divine Love*, L.5.25–26, emphasis added.
46. Cristina Maria Cervone, *Poetics of the Incarnation: Middle English Writing and the Leap of Love* (Philadelphia: University of Pennsylvania Press, 2012), 5.
47. *Revelations of Divine Love*, L.5.6–7.
48. *Revelations of Divine Love*, L.5.6–7, 5.2, 5.3–4.
49. *Revelations of Divine Love*, L.17.22.
50. *Revelations of Divine Love*, L.6.23–24.
51. *Revelations of Divine Love*, L.6.24–25, 6.32–35.
52. *Revelations of Divine Love*, L.67.2, 67.11.
53. *Revelations of Divine Love*, L.67.1–3.
54. *Revelations of Divine Love*, L.67.24–25.
55. *Revelations of Divine Love*, L.67.5, 67.20.
56. *Revelations of Divine Love*, L.67.27–29.
57. *Revelations of Divine Love*, L.67.11.
58. Julian of Norwich, *The Writings of Julian of Norwich: A Vision Showed to a Devout Woman* and *A Revelation of Love*, ed. Nicholas Watson and Jacqueline Jenkins (Turnhout, Belgium: Brepols, 2006), 335, note to lines 1–4.
59. *Writings of Julian of Norwich*, 335, note to line 5.
60. *Revelations of Divine Love*, L.12.11, emphasis added.
61. *Revelations of Divine Love*, L.12.9–13.
62. *Writings of Julian of Norwich*, 167, 77, emphasis added; *Revelations of Divine Love*, L.12.11n.
63. *Writings of Julian of Norwich*, 166, note to lines 9–14, emphasis added.

64. *Revelations of Divine Love*, L.14.7, emphasis added.
65. *Revelations of Divine Love*, L.67.32–33.
66. Wolfgang Riehle, *The Middle English Mystics*, trans. Bernard Standring (London: Routledge & Kegan Paul, 1981), 97.
67. Walter Hilton, "Eight Chapters on Perfection," in *English Mystics of the Middle Ages*, ed. Barry Windeatt (Cambridge: Cambridge University Press, 1994), 145.
68. Gabriel Marcel, *Homo Viator: Introduction to the Metaphysic of Hope*, trans. Emma Crauford (New York: Harper & Row, 1962).
69. Ranulf Higden, *Polychronicon Ranulphi Higden, Monachi Cestrensis; Together with the English Translations of John Trevisa and of an Unknown Writer of the Fifteenth Century*, ed. Churchill Babington, vol. 2 (London: Longmans, Green, 1869), 219–21.
70. Meister Eckhart, quoted and translated in Riehle, *Middle English Mystics*, 154.
71. This is, as Louise Nelstrop has noted, a complex model of deification, wherein "deification is inseparable from Christ's Incarnation yet, in this life at least, it is not automatic"; Nelstrop, *On Deification and Sacred Eloquence: Richard Rolle and Julian of Norwich* (London: Routledge, 2020), 127.
72. *Writings of Julian of Norwich*, 36.
73. Julian of Norwich, *XVI revelations of divine love shewed to a devout servant of our Lord called Mother Juliana, an anchorete of Norwich, who lived in the dayes of King Edward the Third*, ed. Serenus Cressy (orig. pub. London: n.p., 1670), Early English Books Online (Ann Arbor: Text Creation Partnership, 2014), http://name.umdl.umich.edu/B20816.0001.001, 10.
74. *Writings of Julian of Norwich*, 30.
75. The short text, the Amherst manuscript, and the Westminster manuscript also retain the *-hede* suffix in most of the text, confirming this reading via convergence. A survey using the *Linguistic Atlas of Late Medieval English* also throws up a significant distribution of the *-hede* suffix to the north of England, most heavily grouped in the northeast, disclosing the inclusion of the term as a feature specific to northern—and most importantly for present concerns, Norfolk—dialect; *An Electronic Version of A Linguistic Atlas of Late Mediaeval English*, ed. M. Benskin, M. Laing, V. Karaiskos, and K. Williamson (Edinburgh: University of Edinburgh, 2013), accessed January 9, 2024, http://www.lel.ed.ac.uk/ihd/elalme/elalme.html.
76. *MED*, s.v. "-nes(se," *suf.*
77. *Polychronicon Ranulphi Higden*, 219–21.
78. *OED*, s.v. "-ness," *suf.*
79. *MED*, s.v. "-hēd(e," *suf.*
80. *OED*, s.v. "-hood," *suf.*

81. Gregory of Nyssa, "An Answer to Ablabius: That We Should Not Think of Saying That There Are Three Gods," in *Christology of the Later Fathers*, ed. Edward Rochie Hardy in collaboration with Cyril C. Richardson, Library of Christian Classics 3 (Philadelphia: Westminster Press, 1954), 259, emphasis added. For original Latin, see "Ad Ablabium: Quod non sint tres dei," in *Gregorii Nysseni opera*, ed. W. Jaeger, vol. 3, part 1: *Gregorii Nysseni opera dogmatica minora*, ed. F. Mueller (Leiden: E. J. Brill, 1958), 42–43.
82. See R. Kendall Soulen, *Divine Names and the Holy Trinity*, vol. 1: *Distinguishing the Voices* (Louisville, KY: Westminster John Knox Press, 2011).
83. *Revelations of Divine Love*, L.7.10, emphasis added.
84. *Revelations of Divine Love*, L.7.18, 7.16–17.
85. *Revelations of Divine Love*, L.7.21–22, 7.24.
86. *OED*, s.v. "beseech," *v.* (1).a–b.
87. Benskin et al., *Electronic Version*, marker 236: "SEEK, *pres.*"
88. *MED*, s.v "bi-," *pref.* (2).
89. *OED*, s.v. "be-," *pref.*
90. *MED*, s.v. "bisẹchinge," *ger.*, emphasis in original.
91. *Revelations of Divine Love*, L.41.15, 41.12, 41.18, emphasis added.
92. *Revelations of Divine Love*, L.43.22.
93. Paul Molinari, *Julian of Norwich: The Teaching of a 14th Century English Mystic* (London: Longmans, Green, 1958), 75, emphasis added; Sheldrake, *Julian of Norwich*, 142.
94. Sheldrake, *Julian of Norwich*, 142.
95. *Revelations of Divine Love*, L.41.18–19, 41.8.
96. Molinari, *Julian of Norwich*, 94.
97. Molinari, 96.
98. *Revelations of Divine Love*, L.41.8–10.
99. *Revelations of Divine Love*, L.41.23–24.
100. *Revelations of Divine Love*, L.42.5–6.
101. Martin Heidegger, *The Phenomenology of Religious Life*, trans. Matthias Fritsch and Jennifer Anna Gosetti-Ferencei (1995; Bloomington: Indiana University Press, 2010), 66, §25, emphasis in original.
102. *Revelations of Divine Love*, L.41.32, emphasis added.
103. *Revelations of Divine Love*, L.39.11, 39.19–20.
104. Molinari, *Julian of Norwich*, 76.
105. Bernard of Clairvaux, "An Apologia to Abbot William," in *The Works of Bernard of Clairvaux*, vol. 1: *Treatises 1*, ed. M. Basil Pennington and trans. Michael Casey (Spencer, MA: Cistercian Publications, 1970), 50. For original Latin, see Bernard of Clairvaux, "Apologia ad Guillelmum abbatem,"

in *Sancti Bernardi Opera*, vol. 3, ed. Jean Leclercq, C. H. Talbot, and H. M. Rochais (Rome: Editiones Cistercienses, 1963), 93.

106. For example, Shinzen Young, *Break Through Pain: A Step-by-Step Mindfulness Meditation Program for Transforming Chronic and Acute Pain* (Boulder, CO: Sounds True, 2004). Nonresistance has also been investigated in a 2014 study by University College London, which found higher levels of reported happiness in those with lower expectations (i.e., lower resistance to the potential actuality of the situation); Robb B. Rutledge, Nikolina Skandali, Peter Dayan, and Raymond J. Dolan, "A Computational and Neural Model of Momentary Subjective Well-Being," *Proceedings of the National Academy of Sciences* 11, no. 33 (2014): 12252–57.
107. *Revelations of Divine Love*, L.17.41, 15.23.
108. Thomas Aquinas, *Opera Omnia*, vol. 22.3: *Quaestiones disputatae de veritate*, ed. A. Dondaine (Rome: Leonine Commission/Editori di San Tommaso, 1975–1976), q26a8. See also Thomas Aquinas, *Sancti Thomae de Aquino Summa Theologiae* (Rome: Editiones Paulinae, 1962), 3q15a4.
109. See also Paul Gondreau, *The Passions of Christ's Soul in the Theology of St. Thomas Aquinas* (Scranton, NJ: University of Scranton Press, 2009), esp. 67–70, 366–72.
110. Aquinas, *Summa Theologiae*, 3q46a7–8.
111. Nicholas Kahm, *Aquinas: On Emotion's Participation in Reason* (Washington, DC: Catholic University of America Press, 2019), 252.
112. *Revelations of Divine Love*, L.21.4–5.
113. *Revelations of Divine Love*, L.21.8.
114. For more on this "dying-but-not-death," see my discussion in Lucas, "Passion and Melancholy: Julian of Norwich's Medical Hermeneutic," *Review of English Studies* 72, no. 303 (2020): 15–18. See also Marion Glasscoe, "Changing Chere and Changing Text in the Eighth Revelation of Julian of Norwich," *Medium Ævum* 66, no. 1 (1997): 115–21.
115. Benjamin Crowe, "Heidegger and the Prospect of a Phenomenology of Prayer," in *The Phenomenology of Prayer*, ed. Bruce Ellis Benson and Norman Wirzba (New York: Fordham University Press, 2005), 128.
116. Crowe, "Heidegger and the Prospect," 128, emphasis in original.
117. Crowe, "Heidegger and the Prospect," 129, 129–30, emphasis in original.
118. *Revelations of Divine Love*, L.6.26–28.
119. Merold Westphal, "Prayer as the Posture of the Decentered Self," in *The Phenomenology of Prayer*, 30.
120. Westphal, "Prayer as the Posture," 31, emphasis added.
121. See *MED*, s.v. "sparren," *v.* (1).

122. Martin Heidegger, *Zollikon Seminars*, ed. Medard Boss and trans. Franz Mayr and Richard Askay (1959–1969; Evanston, IL: Northwestern University Press, 2001), 90–91 (original 118). Hence Fredrik Svenaeus's inclusion of the lived body (*Leib*) as a fourth existential; Svenaeus, *The Hermeneutics of Medicine and the Phenomenology of Health: Steps Towards a Philosophy of Medical Practice* (Dordrecht, The Netherlands: Kluwer, 2000), 110.
123. Erwin W. Straus, "The Upright Posture," *Psychiatric Quarterly* 26, no. 4 (1952): 536.
124. Straus, "Upright Posture," 535.
125. Straus, 536.
126. Straus, 536–37, emphasis added.
127. *MED*, s.v. "stōnden," *v.* (1), emphasis added; MED, s.v. "rǫte," *n.* (4).
128. Straus, "Upright Posture," 537.
129. *Revelations of Divine Love*, L.64.28–29.
130. *Revelations of Divine Love*, L.6.27–29.
131. *Revelations of Divine Love*, L.37.12, 55.38.
132. J. A. Burrow, *Gestures and Looks in Medieval Narrative* (Cambridge: Cambridge University Press, 2002), 17. See, for example, Peter the Chanter, *The Christian at Prayer: An Illustrated Prayer Manual Attributed to Peter the Chanter (d. 1197)*, ed. Richard C. Trexler (Binghamton: Medieval & Renaissance Texts & Studies, State University of New York, 1987), esp. 194.
133. William Langland, *Piers Plowman: The B Version*, ed. George Kane and E. Talbot Donaldson, 2nd ed. (London: Athlone Press, 1988), passus 5, lines 62–63. Quoted in Burrow, *Gestures and Looks*, 18. See also Mary Clemente Davlin, "Devotional Postures in 'Piers Plowman' B, with an Appendix on Divine Postures," *The Chaucer Review* 42, no. 2 (2007), 164.
134. John Mirk, *John Mirk's Instructions for Parish Priests*, ed. Gillis Kristensson, Lund Studies in English 49 (Lund, Denmark: Gleerup, 1974), 82–83, lines 283–86.
135. Ignatius of Loyola, *The Spiritual Exercises of St Ignatius of Loyola*, trans. John Morris (London: Burns and Oates, 1880), 29.
136. Denise N. Baker, "The Structure of the Soul and the 'Godly Wylle' in Julian of Norwich's *Showings*," in *The Medieval Mystical Tradition in England VII, Papers Read at Charney Manor, July 2004*, ed. E. A. Jones (Cambridge: Brewer, 2004), 42.
137. Denys Turner, *The Darkness of God: Negativity in Christian Mysticism* (Cambridge: Cambridge University Press, 1995), 99. Quoted in Baker, "Structure of the Soul," 42.
138. Straus, "Upright Posture," 539, emphasis added.

139. Trexler, *Christian at Prayer*, 39.
140. See Walter Simons, "Reading a Saint's Body: Rapture and Bodily Movement in the *Vitae* of Thirteenth-Century Beguines," in *Framing Medieval Bodies*, ed. Sarah Kay and Miri Rubin (Manchester: Manchester University Press, 1997), 10–23; Mary A. Suydam, "Visionaries in the Public Eye: Beguine Literature as Performance," in *The Texture of Society: Medieval Women in the Southern Low Countries*, ed. Ellen E. Kittell and Mary A. Suydam (New York: Palgrave Macmillan, 2004), 131–52.
141. Edmund Husserl, *Die Krisis der europäischen Wissenschaften und die transzendentale Phänomenologie. Eine Einleitung in die phänomenologische Philosophie*, ed. W. Biemel, Husserliana VI (1954; The Hague: Martinus Nijhoff, 1962), §47. Translated by David Carr as *The Crisis of European Sciences and Transcendental Phenomenology. An Introduction to Phenomenological Philosophy* (1954; Evanston, IL: Northwestern University Press, 1970), 161.
142. Dorion Cairns, *The Philosophy of Edmund Husserl*, ed. Lester Embree (Dordrecht, The Netherlands: Springer, 2013), 157, note 14.
143. *Revelations of Divine Love*, L.10.56.

6. MAKE STRAIGHT THE PATHS: CHRIST, PROVIDENCE, AND SALVATION

The epigraph for this chapter is taken from Norman Fischer, *Sailing Home: Homer's Odyssey to Navigate Life's Perils and Pitfalls* (Berkeley, CA: North Atlantic Books, 2008). © Norman Fischer. Reprinted with the permission of Atria Books, an imprint of Simon & Schuster LLC. All rights reserved.

1. Julian of Norwich, *The Writings of Julian of Norwich: A Vision Showed to a Devout Woman and A Revelation of Love*, ed. Nicholas Watson and Jacqueline Jenkins (Turnhout, Belgium: Brepols, 2006), 33–34, 112, note to lines 23–31; Nicholas Watson, "The Composition of Julian of Norwich's *Revelation of Love*," *Speculum* 68, no. 3 (1993): 669, note 77. For Watson's most recent work on the composition of the showings and the "Amen par charite" moment, see "'Sixteen Shewinges': The Composition of Julian of Norwich's *Revelation of Love* Revisited," in *Mystics, Goddesses, Lovers, and Teachers: Medieval Visions and the Modern Legacies: Studies in Honour of Barbara Newman*, ed. Stephen Rozenski, Joshua Byron Smith, and Claire M. Waters (Turnhout, Belgium: Brepols, 2023), 131–54 (esp. 140).
2. Watson, "Composition," 669.
3. Cristina Maria Cervone, *Poetics of the Incarnation: Middle English Writing and the Leap of Love* (Philadelphia: University of Pennsylvania Press, 2012), 3–5.

4. Barry Commoner, *The Closing Circle: Nature, Man and Technology* (New York: Bantam, 1974), 29.
5. For more on the interaction of porosity and ecological thinking in Julian, see Claire Gilbert, "Restoring Porosity and the Ecological Crisis: A Post-Ricoeurian Reading of the Julian of Norwich Texts" (PhD diss., King's College London, 2018). Dissertation published as *Julian of Norwich and the Ecological Crisis: Restoring Porosity* (London: Routledge, 2024).
6. Julian of Norwich, *Julian of Norwich: Revelations of Divine Love: The Short Text and the Long Text*, ed. Barry Windeatt (Oxford: Oxford University Press, 2016), L.67.11.
7. Denise N. Baker, "The Structure of the Soul and the 'Godly Wylle' in Julian of Norwich's *Showings*," in *The Medieval Mystical Tradition in England VII, Papers Read at Charney Manor, July 2004*, ed. E. A. Jones (Cambridge: Brewer, 2004), 38.
8. Baker, "Structure of the Soul," 41. See also David N. Bell, *The Image and Likeness: The Augustinian Spirituality of William of St. Thierry*, Cistercian Studies 78 (Kalamazoo, MI: Cistercian Publications 1984), 23.
9. *Revelations of Divine Love*, L.57.12.
10. Cervone, *Poetics of the Incarnation*, 44.
11. Denys Turner, *The Darkness of God: Negativity in Christian Mysticism* (Cambridge: Cambridge University Press, 1995), 99.
12. See Evelyn Underhill, *Mysticism: A Study in the Nature and Development of Man's Spiritual Consciousness* (1911; London: University Paperbacks Edition, 1960), 54.
13. Wolfgang Riehle, *The Middle English Mystics*, trans. Bernard Standring (London: Routledge & Kegan Paul, 1981), 156. See also J. B. Dalgairns, ed., *The Scale (or Ladder) of Perfection: Written by Walter Hilton: With an Essay on the Spiritual Life of Medieval England* (London: Art and Book, 1870, repr. 1901), xix; Evelyn Underhill, *The Essentials of Mysticism* (1920; New York: Cosimo, 2007), 192; Anna Maria Reynolds, "Some Literary Influences in the *Revelations* of Julian of Norwich (c. 1342–post-1416)," *Leeds Studies in English and Kindred Languages* 7–8 (1952): 26.
14. Cervone, *Poetics of the Incarnation*, 47.
15. Grace M. Jantzen also writes "whether there was actual historical influence from Bernard and Eckhart [on Julian] cannot be established, although it is certainly possible, given the spread of Cistercian monasteries in England, on the one hand, and the flourishing trade between East Anglia and the Rhineland on the other"; Jantzen, *Julian of Norwich: Mystic and Theologian* (London: SPCK, 2000), 159.
16. *OED*, s.v. "ground," *n.* I.(1).a–b.

17. *Revelations of Divine Love*, L.10.15–16. Barry Windeatt comments that *wrekke* is "probably seaweed, but possibly debris. *Promptorum Parvulorum*, a Latin dictionary for English schoolboys, glosses: 'Wreke of the se: *Alga* [seaweed]' (Mayhew 1908: 535). The river valley east of Carrow Priory, with its marshes and low-lying meadows, was subject to widespread tidal inundations, especially at spring tides (Flood 1937: 36–8)."
18. *Revelations of Divine Love*, L.10.17, 10.19–20.
19. Juliana Dresvina, "What Julian Saw: The Embodied Showings and the Items for Private Devotion," *Religions* 10, no. 245 (2019): 13; *Writings of Julian of Norwich*, 158. Grace M. Jantzen writes that Julian "takes delight in the creation of God, the beauty of the sea valley and the hazelnut and the intricacy of herring scales," and Amy Appleford argues for the passage as a reiteration of the Office of the Dead, underlining "the limits of natural human physicality in this life"; see, respectively, Jantzen, *Julian of Norwich*, 216, and Appleford, "The Sea Ground and the London Street: The Ascetic Self in Julian of Norwich and Thomas Hoccleve," *Chaucer Review* 51, no. 1 (2016): 58.
20. For this triad, see Vincent Gillespie, "Seek, Suffer, and Trust: 'Ese' and 'Disese' in Julian of Norwich," *Studies in the Age of Chaucer* 39 (2017): 129–58.
21. Appleford, "Sea Ground and the London Street," 57.
22. *Revelations of Divine Love*, L.51.152–54.
23. *Revelations of Divine Love*, L.51.110.
24. Cervone, *Poetics of the Incarnation*, 32–39.
25. Turner, *Darkness of God*, 162.
26. Plato, "Timaeus," in *Timaeus. Critias. Cleitophon. Menexenus. Epistles*, trans. R. G. Bury, Loeb Classical Library 234 (Cambridge, MA: Harvard University Press, 1929), 245.
27. Johann Peter Hebel, quoted in Martin Heidegger, "Memorial Address," in *Discourse on Thinking: A Translation of* Gelassenheit, trans. John M. Anderson and E. Hans Freund with an introduction by John M. Anderson (New York: Harper & Row, 1966), 47.
28. Heidegger, "Memorial Address," 47.
29. Michael Marder, *Plant-Thinking: A Philosophy of Vegetal Life* (New York: Columbia University Press, 2013), 57.
30. *Revelations of Divine Love*, L.51.163, 51.96.
31. "Sir Gawain and the Green Knight," in *The Poems of the Pearl Manuscript:* Pearl, Cleanness, Patience, Sir Gawain and the Green Knight, ed. Malcolm Andrew and Ronald Waldron, 5th ed. (Liverpool: Liverpool University Press, 2007), 234, lines 701–2. The *Oxford English Dictionary* quotes this line in definition (1).b of "wilderness," supporting this historical (c. 1400) definition of wilderness as "a wild or uncultivated region or tract of land, uninhabited, or

inhabited only by wild animals; a 'tract of solitude and savageness' (Johnson)"; *OED*, s.v. "wilderness," *n.* (1).b. See also Gillian Rudd, "'The Wilderness of Wirral' in 'Sir Gawain and the Green Knight,'" *Arthuriana* 23, no. 1 (2013): 52–65.

32. Rebecca M. Douglass, "Ecocriticism and Middle English Literature," *Studies in Medievalism* 10 (1998): 148–49.
33. *Revelations of Divine Love*, L.51.17–27.
34. *Revelations of Divine Love*, L.51.14, 51.12–13. "Comforte" denoting support, steadfastness, the ability to *withstand*: *MED*, s.v. "cŏmfort," *n.* (5–6).
35. I include the lived body (*Leib*) as a fourth existential following Fredrik Svenaeus; Svenaeus, *The Hermeneutics of Medicine and the Phenomenology of Health: Steps Towards a Philosophy of Medical Practice* (Dordrecht, The Netherlands: Kluwer, 2000), 110.
36. *Revelations of Divine Love*, L.51.151–53.
37. *Revelations of Divine Love*, L.51.153–54.
38. *Revelations of Divine Love*, L.53.31–32. A semiotic parallelism taken up, for example, by the medieval lyric "erthe toc of erthe" from London, BL MS Harley 2253, in Neil R. Ker, ed., *Facsimile of British Museum MS. Harley 2253*, EETS o.s. 255 (London: Oxford University Press, 1965), f. 59[v]. Quoted in Gillian Rudd, *Greenery: Ecocritical Readings of Late Medieval English Literature* (Manchester: Manchester University Press, 2007), 21.
39. Denise N. Baker, *Julian of Norwich's Showings: From Vision to Book* (Princeton, NJ: Princeton University Press, 1994), 93.
40. *Revelations of Divine Love*, L.51.150–51; Baker, *Julian of Norwich's Showings*, 93.
41. Margaret Ann Palliser, *Christ, Our Mother of Mercy: Divine Mercy and Compassion in the Theology of the* Shewings *of Julian of Norwich* (Berlin: Walter de Gruyter, 1992), 65.
42. Palliser, *Christ, Our Mother of Mercy*, 65.
43. "Anima namque que et suauis est per nitorem consciencie, et decora per caritatem dileccionis eterne, ortus Christi potest dici; quia a uiciis purgata, uirtutibus floret, et suauitate cantus iubilei, quasi concentu auium gaudet." Richard Rolle, *The Incendium Amoris of Richard Rolle of Hampole*, ed. Margaret Deanesly (Manchester: Manchester University Press, 1915), 227, f. 43*b*. Wolfgang Riehle also gives the example of the *Epistle of Prayer*, which uses the tree image to describe the garden of the soul; Riehle, *Middle English Mystics*, 161.
44. Walter Hilton, *Scale of Perfection*, ed. Thomas H. Bestul, TEAMS Middle English Texts (Kalamazoo, MI: Medieval Institute Publications, 2000), https://d.lib.rochester.edu/teams/publication/bestul-hilton-scale-of-perfection, book 1, lines 1577–78.

45. Bestul, *Scale of Perfection*, book 1, lines 1379–80.
46. See *Two Middle English Translations of Friar Laurent's "Somme le roi": Critical Edition*, ed. Emmanuelle Roux, Textes vernaculaires du moyen âge 8 (Turnhout, Belgium: Brepols, 2010), 61–62, lines 2161–220; *Revelations of Divine Love*, L.51.151.
47. *Revelations of Divine Love*, L.51.145.
48. *Revelations of Divine Love*, L.51.10–12.
49. Luke 14:23, quoted in Meister Eckhart, "Sermon Thirty-Two (b)," in *The Complete Mystical Works of Meister Eckhart*, trans. and ed. Maurice O'C. Walshe, rev. with a foreword by Bernard McGinn (New York: Crossroad, 2009), 199. The verse is also quoted by David Aers in his reading of Augustine and Langland; Aers, *Salvation and Sin: Augustine, Langland and Fourteenth-Century Theology* (Notre Dame: University of Notre Dame Press, 2009), 23. See also David Blamires, "Eckhart and Tauler: A Comparison of Their Sermons on 'Homo quidam fecit cenam magnam' (Luke XIV.16)," *Modern Language Review* 66, no. 3 (1971): 608–27.
50. Eckhart, "Sermon Thirty-Two (b)," 199.
51. William Langland, *Piers Plowman: An Edition of the C-Text*, ed. Derek Pearsall (Berkeley: University of California Press, 1978), passus 18.
52. Pearsall, *Piers Plowman*, passus 11, line 170; *Revelations of Divine Love*, L.66.23.
53. Pearsall, *Piers Plowman*, passus 16, line 173.
54. Pearsall, *Piers Plowman*, passus 5, lines 12–21.
55. Pearsall, *Piers Plowman*, passus 5, lines 5, 48, 84–85. For a discussion of service in Langland and Julian, see Jim Knowles, "Can You Serve? The Theology of Service from Langland to Luther," *Journal of Medieval and Early Modern Studies* 40, no. 3 (2010): 527–57.
56. Eleanor Johnson, *Staging Contemplation: Participatory Theology in Middle English Prose, Verse, and Drama* (Chicago: University of Chicago Press, 2018), 81, 76.
57. Norman Wirzba, "Attention and Responsibility: The Work of Prayer," in *The Phenomenology of Prayer*, ed. Bruce Ellis Benson and Norman Wirzba (New York: Fordham University Press, 2005), 99, emphasis added.
58. *Revelations of Love*, L.5.34–35.
59. See Sean J. McGrath, *The Early Heidegger and Medieval Philosophy: Phenomenology for the Godforsaken* (Washington, DC: Catholic University of America Press, 2006), 210–28.
60. McGrath, *Early Heidegger*, 213.
61. McGrath, 213.
62. McGrath, 208–42.

63. McGrath, 214.
64. Martin Heidegger, *Gesamtausgabe*, vol. 24: *Die Grundprobleme der Phänomenologie*, ed. Friedrich-Wilhelm von Herrmann (Frankfurt: Vittorio Klostermann, 1997), 169, §12.(c). Translated in Albert Hofstadter, *The Basic Problems of Phenomenology*, rev. ed. (Bloomington: Indiana University Press, 1982), 120, emphases in original.
65. McGrath, *Early Heidegger*, 217.
66. McGrath, 225. See also Étienne Gilson, *History of Christian Philosophy in the Middle Ages* (Toronto: Pontifical Institute of Mediaeval Studies, 1955), 368.
67. McGrath, *Early Heidegger*, 225, emphases in original. See also John D. Caputo, *Heidegger and Aquinas: An Essay on Overcoming Metaphysics* (New York: Fordham University Press, 1982).
68. Thomas Aquinas, *Summa Theologiae*, vol. 5: *God's Will and Providence: 1a. 19–26*, ed. and trans. Thomas Gilby (London: Blackfriars in conjunction with Eyre & Spottiswoode, 1964), 1aq23a2ad1. For a discussion of the Augustinianism of this approach, see Matthew Barnett, *The Reformation as Renewal: Retrieving the One, Holy, Catholic and Apostolic Church* (Grand Rapids, MI: Zondervan, 2023), 144–45.
69. Aquinas, *Summae Theologiae*, 1aq23a2ad1, emphasis added.
70. Aquinas, 1aq23a2, emphasis in original.
71. Aquinas, 1aq23a2ad4, emphasis added.
72. Aquinas, 1aq23a2ad4, note h.
73. Denys Turner, *Julian of Norwich, Theologian* (New Haven, CT: Yale University Press, 2011), 53–54, emphasis in original.
74. Aquinas, *Summa Theologiae*, 1aq23a3.
75. *Revelations of Divine Love*, L.41.18, emphasis added.
76. *Revelations of Divine Love*, L.7.21–22.
77. Nicholas Watson, "Conceptions of the Word: The Mother Tongue and the Incarnation of God," *New Medieval Literatures* 1 (1997): 121.
78. *Revelations of Divine Love*, L.9.8.
79. *Revelations of Divine Love*, L.27.8.
80. *Old English Homilies of the Twelfth Century: From the Unique MS. B.14.52. in the Library of Trinity College, Cambridge: Second Series, with Three Thirteenth Century Hymns from MS. 54 D.4.14 in Corpus Christi College*, ed. and trans. Richard Morris, EETS o.s. 53 (London: Trübner, 1873), 129.
81. Turner, *Julian of Norwich*, 38.
82. *Revelations of Divine Love*, L.51.42–43. Sloane has "hole," but Paris has "hele," and Windeatt comments that "P's reading 'hele' (health, well-being) is plausible, but 'hole' (entirety) may be the harder reading if the Lord's gift is to surpass it."

83. The first mention of the trope occurred in a letter to the Ephesians ascribed to Bishop Ignatius of Antioch, who died a martyr in Rome in 107 CE. Quoted in Philip Schaff, ed., *Ante-Nicene Fathers*, vol. 1: *The Apostolic Fathers with Justin Martyr and Irenaeus*, Christian Classics Ethereal Library (Grand Rapids, MI: Eerdmans, 2001), https://www.ccel.org/ccel/schaff/anf01.html, 76. See also Rudolf Arbesmann, "The Concept of 'Christus Medicus' in St Augustine," *Traditio* 10 (1954): 1–28.
84. *A Deuout Treatyse Called The Tree & XII. Frutes of The Holy Goost*, ed. Johannes Joseph Vaissier (Groningen, The Netherlands: J. B. Walters, 1960), 24–25, f. 110ᵛ; Johannes Joseph Vaissier points out that interest in physicians can frequently be found elsewhere, such as in Walter Hilton's writings.
85. Hannah Lucas, "Passion and Melancholy: Julian of Norwich's Medical Hermeneutic," *Review of English Studies* 72, no. 303 (2020): 1–18. For another "paramodern" reading of Julian's *Christus medicus* and the therapeutic power of his blood, see Eleanor Myerson, "Derek Jarman's Medieval Blood: Queer Devotion, Affective Medicine, and the AIDS Crisis," *postmedieval* 14, no. 1 (2023): 61–88.
86. Paul Ricoeur, *Freud and Philosophy: An Essay on Interpretation*, trans. Denis Savage (New Haven, CT: Yale University Press, 1970).
87. Svenaeus, *Hermeneutics of Medicine*, 145, emphasis in original.
88. Svenaeus, *Hermeneutics of Medicine*, 147.
89. Thomas S. Szasz and Marc H. Hollender, "Contribution to the Philosophy of Medicine: The Basic Models of the Doctor-Patient Relationship," *American Medical Association—Archives of Internal Medicine* 97, no. 5 (1956): 588. Quoted in Svenaeus, *Hermeneutics of Medicine*, 43.
90. Svenaeus, *Hermeneutics of Medicine*, 148–49. Citing Hans-Georg Gadamer, *Über die Verborgenheit der Gesundheit* (Frankfurt: Suhrkamp Verlag, 1993).
91. Svenaeus, *Hermeneutics of Medicine*, 150.
92. Svenaeus, *Hermeneutics of Medicine*, 147–48.
93. *Revelations of Divine Love*, L.41.2.
94. Latin Vulgate: "Habe fiduciam in Domino ex toto corde tuo, et ne innitaris prudentiae tuae. In omnibus viis tuis cogita illum, et ipse diriget gressus tuos."
95. *DMLBS*, s.v. "fidere."
96. Most famously articulated by Annette Baier, "Trust and Antitrust," *Ethics* 96, no. 2 (1986): 231–60. For more on trust as process, see Guido Möllering, "Process Views of Trusting and Crises," in *Handbook of Advances in Trust Research*, ed. R. Bachmann and A. Zaheer (Cheltenham, UK: Edward Elgar, 2013), 285–305.
97. Knud Eljer Løgstrup, *Beyond the Ethical Demand*, with an introduction by Kees van Kooten Niekerk (Notre Dame: University of Notre Dame Press,

2007), 85. Løgstrup refers here to the destruction of mercy, but he says the same of trust.

98. *Revelations of Divine Love*, L.41.3.
99. *Revelations of Divine Love*, L.6.4, 32.39, emphases added.
100. For more on this "leap," see Guido Möllering, "The Nature of Trust: From Georg Simmel to a Theory of Expectation, Interpretation and Suspension," *Sociology* 35, no. 2 (2001): 403–20.
101. Cervone, *Poetics of the Incarnation*, 6.
102. *Revelations of Divine Love*, L.52.8–9.
103. James Strong, *A Concise Dictionary of the Words in The Greek Testament* (New York: Abingdon Press, 1890), Archive.org, accessed January 9, 2024, https://archive.org/details/StrongsGreekAndHebrewDictionaries1890, s.v. "θεράπων" (therápōn) [#G2324].
104. Maggie Ross, *Silence: A User's Guide*, vol. 1: *Process* (Eugene, OR: Cascade, 2018), 31.
105. *Revelations of Divine Love*, L.32.13.
106. *Revelations of Divine Love*, L.86.12–13.
107. For more on this, see Giles E. M. Gasper, "Anselm of Canterbury," in *Christian Theologies of Salvation: A Comparative Introduction*, ed. Justin S. Holcomb (New York: New York University Press, 2017), 124–42. See also Kerrie Hide, "Julian of Norwich," in the same volume, 160–79.
108. *Revelations of Divine Love*, L.22.1–3. For a reading of the hermeneutics of this passage, see Daniel Theodore Fishley, "A Revelation of Weakness: Julian of Norwich, John Caputo, and the Event of Hospitality," *Medieval Mystical Theology* 31, no. 2 (2022): 67–79. For more on how the passage configures satisfaction, see Jill Mann, "Satisfaction and Payment in Middle English Literature," *Studies in the Age of Chaucer* 5, no. 1 (1983): 44–45.
109. *Revelations of Divine Love*, L.82.rubric.
110. *Revelations of Divine Love*, L.24.1–3.
111. *Revelations of Divine Love*, L.24.3.

CONCLUSION: NOT YET PERFORMED—JULIAN IN TIME

1. Louise D'Arcens, "From 'Eccentric Affiliation' to 'Corrective Medievalism': Bruce Holsinger's *The Premodern Condition*," *postmedieval* 1 (2010): 304.
2. Andrew Cole and D. Vance Smith, "Introduction: Outside Modernity," in *The Legitimacy of the Middle Ages: On the Unwritten History of Theory*, ed. Cole and Smith (Durham, NC: Duke University Press, 2010), 24, 9.
3. Cole and Smith, "Introduction," 19.

4. Elisabeth Dutton, *Julian of Norwich: The Influence of Late-Medieval Devotional Compilations* (Cambridge: Brewer, 2008), 2.
5. See, for example, the "Friends of Julian of Norwich" society, which describes its community as including "men and women, ordained and lay, in the Church and outside of it, people who identify as Christians and those who don't," who come together with the intention of "exploring and celebrating what her experiences may mean for us today." "Becoming a Friend of Julian," www.julianofnorwich.org, accessed January 9, 2024, https://julianofnorwich.org/pages/friends-of-julian-becoming-a-friend-of-julian. See also Sarah Law, "In the Centre: Spiritual and Cultural Representations of Julian of Norwich in the Julian Centre," in *Julian of Norwich's Legacy: Medieval Mysticism and Post-Medieval Reception*, ed. Sarah Salih and Denise N. Baker (New York: Palgrave Macmillan, 2009), 173–89.
6. Quoted in Eric Weiskott, "The Coronavirus Time Warp: Reading Medieval Literature in the Midst of a Pandemic," Public Seminar, April 10, 2020, https://publicseminar.org/2020/04/the-coronavirus-time-warp/.
7. S. Kay Toombs, *The Meaning of Illness: A Phenomenological Account of the Different Perspectives of Physician and Patient* (Boston: Kluwer, 1992), 15.
8. For publications of this kind, see Matthew Fox, *Julian of Norwich: Wisdom in a Time of Pandemic—and Beyond*, with a foreword by Mirabai Starr (Bloomington, IN: iUniverse, 2020); Lisa Fullam, "Julian of Norwich: The Socially-Distanced Saint," *Spiritus: A Journal of Christian Spirituality* 21, no. 1 (2021): 59–68. For news items referring to Julian, see Kim Kaschor, "When to Be Still, When to Be Stirred: What Mystics Can Teach Us About Patience During COVID-19," CBC Radio, February 12, 2021, https://www.cbc.ca/radio/tapestry/when-to-be-still-when-to-be-stirred-what-mystics-can-teach-us-about-patience-during-covid-19-1.5911991; Nic Rigby, "Coronavirus: Mystic's 'Relevance' to Self-Isolating World," BBC News, March 30, 2020, https://www.bbc.co.uk/news/uk-england-norfolk-52020227.
9. Hans Ruin, "In the Spirit of Paul: Thinking the Hebraic Inheritance (Heidegger, Bultmann, Jonas)," in *Heidegger's Black Notebooks and the Future of Theology*, ed. Mårten Björk and Jayne Svenungsson (New York: Palgrave Macmillan, 2017), 53.
10. Martin Heidegger, *The Phenomenology of Religious Life*, trans. Matthias Fritsch and Jennifer Anna Gosetti-Ferencei (1995; Bloomington: Indiana University Press, 2010), 55, §19.
11. Heidegger, *Phenomenology of Religious Life*, 73, §26.
12. Xin Leng, "Martin Heidegger on Primordial Christian Life Experience: A Phenomenological Theological Perspective," *Religions* 13, no. 1082 (2022), doi:10.3390/rel13111082.

13. Eric Voegelin, *The Collected Works of Eric Voegelin*, vol. 5: *Modernity without Restraint*, ed. Manfred Henningsen (Columbia: University of Missouri Press, 2000), 276.
14. Bruno Latour, "La vraie sagesse de l'imam," *Le Monde*, January 16, 2015, https://www.lemonde.fr/idees/article/2015/01/19/la-vraie-sagesse-de-l-imam_4558988_3232.html. Available as a translation by Tim Howles, "Two Lessons from an Old Imam," at http://www.bruno-latour.fr/sites/default/files/downloads/15-1-IMAM-LEMONDE-GB.pdf, and accessed January 9, 2024.
15. Julian of Norwich, *Julian of Norwich: Revelations of Divine Love: The Short Text and the Long Text*, ed. Barry Windeatt (Oxford: Oxford University Press, 2016), L.86.1.
16. Paul Zumthor, *Toward a Medieval Poetics*, trans. Philip Bennett (Minneapolis: University of Minnesota Press, 1992), 16.
17. Cole and Smith, "Introduction," 19.
18. Cole and Smith, 19.
19. Cole and Smith, 20.
20. Kathleen Biddick, *The Shock of Medievalism* (Durham, NC: Duke University Press, 1998), 4, quoting Howard R. Bloch and Stephen G. Nichols, *Medievalism and the Modernist Temper* (Baltimore: Johns Hopkins University Press, 1996), 49. See also Marina S. Brownlee, Kevin Brownlee, and Stephen G. Nichols, eds., *The New Medievalism* (Baltimore: Johns Hopkins University Press, 1991), 12; Cole and Smith, "Introduction," 18.

BIBLIOGRAPHY

PRIMARY TEXTS

Aquinas, Thomas. *Opera Omnia*. Vol. 22.3: *Quaestiones disputatae de Veritate*. Ed. A. Dondaine. Rome: Leonine Commission/Editori di San Tommaso, 1975–1976.

——. *Sancti Thomae de Aquino Summa Theologiae*. Rome: Editiones Paulinae, 1962.

——. *Summa Theologiae*. Vol. 5: *God's Will and Providence: 1a. 19–26*. Ed. and trans. Thomas Gilby. London: Blackfriars in conjunction with Eyre & Spottiswoode, 1964.

Aristotle. *Metaphysics*. Vol. 1: *Books 1–9*. Trans. Hugh Tredennick. Loeb Classical Library 271. Cambridge, MA: Harvard University Press, 1933.

——. *On the Soul. Parva Naturalia. On Breath*. Rev. ed. Trans. Walter Stanley Hett. Cambridge, MA: Harvard University Press, 1957.

——. *Rhetoric and Poetics*. Trans. W. Rhys Roberts and Ingram Bywater with an introduction by Edward P. J. Corbett. New York: Modern Library, 1984.

Augustine of Hippo. *Confessions*. Vol. 1: *Books 1–8*. Ed. and trans. Carolyn J. B. Hammond. Loeb Classical Library 26. Cambridge, MA: Harvard University Press, 2014.

——. "De Genesi ad litteram Libri XII." In *Opera Omnia*, ed. Jacques-Paul Migne, 245–484. Patrologia Latina 34. Paris: Migne, 1841.

——. "On Christian Doctrine." In *Nicene and Post-Nicene Fathers of the Christian Church*, ser. 1, vol. 2, ed. Philip Schaff, trans. J. F. Shaw [orig. pub. Buffalo: Christian Literature, 1887]. Christian Classics Ethereal Library. Grand Rapids, MI: Eerdmans, 2001. https://www.ccel.org/ccel/schaff/npnf102.

——. "Sermon CXVII." In *Opera Omnia*, ed. Jacques-Paul Migne, 661–71. Patrologia Latina 38. Paris: Migne, 1865.

——. *The Works of Saint Augustine: A Translation for the 21st Century.* Part 1, vol 1: *The Confessions.* Ed. John E. Rotelle. Trans. with introduction and notes by Maria Boulding. New York: New City Press, 1997.

——. *The Works of Saint Augustine: A Translation for the 21st Century.* Part 3, vol. 14: *Homilies on the First Epistle of John* (Tractatus in Epistolam Joannis ad Parthos). Trans. with introduction and notes by Boniface Ramsey, ed. Daniel E. Doyle and Thomas Martin. New York: New City Press, 2008.

Bazire, Joyce, and Eric College, eds. *The Chastising of God's Children, And the Treatise of Perfection of the Sons of God.* Oxford: Basil Blackwell, 1957.

Benson, Larry Dean, and F. N. Robinson, eds. *The Riverside Chaucer.* 3rd ed. Oxford: Oxford University Press, 2008.

Bernard of Clairvaux. "An Apologia to Abbot William." In *The Works of Bernard of Clairvaux*, vol. 1: *Treatises 1*, ed. M. Basil Pennington and trans. Michael Casey, 33–72. Spencer, MA: Cistercian Publications, 1970.

——. "Apologia ad Guillelmum abbatem." In *Sancti Bernardi Opera*, vol. 3, ed. Jean Leclercq, C. H. Talbot, and H. M. Rochais, 81–108. Rome: Editiones Cistercienses, 1963.

——. *Sancti Bernardi Opera.* Vols. 1–2: *Sermones super Cantica Canticorum.* Ed. Jean Leclercq, C. H. Talbot, and H. M. Rochais. Rome: Editiones Cistercienses, 1957–1958.

——. *The Works of Bernard of Clairvaux.* Vol. 7: *Treatises III: On Grace and Free Choice.* Trans. Daniel O'Donovan with an introduction by Bernard McGinn. Cistercian Studies 19. Kalamazoo, MI: Cistercian Publications, 1977.

Boethius, Anicius Manlius Severinus. *Theological Tractates: The Consolation of Philosophy.* Trans. H. F. Stewart, E. J. Rand, and S. J. Tester. Cambridge, MA: Harvard University Press, 1973.

Chaucer, Geoffrey. "The House of Fame." In Benson and Robinson, *The Riverside Chaucer*, 347–74.

——. "The Parson's Tale." In Benson and Robinson, *The Riverside Chaucer*, 288–328.

——. "Troilus and Criseyde." In Benson and Robinson, *The Riverside Chaucer*, 471–585.

D'Evelyn, Charlotte, and Anna Jean Mill, eds. *The South English Legendary.* Vol 1: *Text.* EETS o.s. 235. London: Oxford University Press, 1956.

Meister Eckhart. *The Complete Mystical Works of Meister Eckhart.* Trans. and ed. Maurice O'C. Walshe, rev. with a foreword by Bernard McGinn. New York: Crossroad, 2009.

Gallacher, Patrick J., ed. *The Cloud of Unknowing.* TEAMS Middle English Texts. Kalamazoo, MI: Medieval Institute Publications, 1997. https://d.lib.rochester.edu/teams/publication/gallacher-the-cloud-of-unknowing.

Geoffrey of Vinsauf. "Geoffrey of Vinsauf, *Poetria nova*, ca. 1208–1213." In *Medieval Grammar and Rhetoric: Language Arts and Literary Theory, AD 300–1475*, ed. and trans. Rita Copeland and Ineke Sluiter, 594–606. Oxford: Oxford University Press, 2009.

Gregory of Nyssa. "An Answer to Ablabius: That We Should Not Think of Saying That There Are Three Gods." In *Christology of the Later Fathers*, ed. Edward Rochie Hardy in collaboration with Cyril C. Richardson, 256–67. Philadelphia: Westminster Press, 1954.

——. *Gregorii Nysseni opera*. Ed. W. Jaeger. Vol. 3, part 1: *Gregorii Nysseni opera dogmatica minora*. Ed. F. Mueller. Leiden: E. J. Brill, 1958.

Hasenfratz, Robert, ed. *Ancrene Wisse*. TEAMS Middle English Texts. Kalamazoo, MI: Medieval Institute Publications, 2000. https://d.lib.rochester.edu/teams/publication/hasenfratz-ancrene-wisse.

Higden, Ranulf. *Polychronicon Ranulphi Higden, Monachi Cestrensis; Together with the English Translations of John Trevisa and of an Unknown Writer of the Fifteenth Century*. Ed. Churchill Babington. Vol. 2. London: Longmans, Green, 1869.

Hilton, Walter. "Eight Chapters on Perfection." In *English Mystics of the Middle Ages*, ed. Barry Windeatt, 137–48. Cambridge: Cambridge University Press, 1994.

——. *Scale of Perfection*. Ed. Thomas H. Bestul. TEAMS Middle English Texts. Kalamazoo, MI: Medieval Institute Publications, 2000. https://d.lib.rochester.edu/teams/publication/bestul-hilton-scale-of-perfection.

Hoccleve, Thomas. *Thomas Hoccleve's Complaint and Dialogue*. Ed. J. A. Burrow. EETS o.s. 313. Oxford: Oxford University Press, 1999.

Hume, David. "The life of David Hume, Esq: Written by himself. To which is added, a letter from Adam Smith, LL.D. to William Strahan, Esq." *Eighteenth Century Collections Online*, available at https://name.umdl.umich.edu/004854280.0001.000.

Ignatius of Loyola. *The Spiritual Exercises of St Ignatius of Loyola*. Trans. John Morris. London: Burns and Oates, 1880.

Ioannis Duns Scoti. *Opera Omnia*. Vol. 18: *Lectura* 2, dist. 1–6. Ed. L. Modrić, S. Bušelić, B. Hechich, I. Jurić, I. Percan, R. Rosini, S. Ruiz de Loizaga, and C. Saco Alarcón. Vatican City: Typis Polyglottis Vaticanis, 1982.

Isidore of Seville. *The* Etymologies *of Isidore of Seville*. Trans. and ed. Stephen A. Barney, W. J. Lewis, J. A. Beach, and Oliver Berghof, in collaboration with Muriel Hall. Cambridge: Cambridge University Press, 2006.

Julian of Norwich. *A Book of Showings to the Anchoress Julian of Norwich*. Ed. Edmund Colledge and James Walsh. 2 vols. Toronto: Pontifical Institute of Medieval Studies, 1978.

——. *Julian of Norwich: Revelations of Divine Love: The Short Text and the Long Text*. Ed. Barry Windeatt. Oxford: Oxford University Press, 2016.

——. *Revelations of Divine Love*. Trans. Elizabeth Spearing with introduction and notes by A. C. Spearing. London: Penguin, 1998.

——. *The Shewings of Julian of Norwich*. Ed. Georgia Ronan Crampton. TEAMS Middle English Texts. Kalamazoo, MI: Medieval Institute Publications, 1994. https://d.lib.rochester.edu/teams/publication/crampton-shewings-of-julian-norwich.

——. *The Writings of Julian of Norwich: A Vision Showed to a Devout Woman* and *A Revelation of Love*. Ed. Nicholas Watson and Jacqueline Jenkins. Turnhout, Belgium: Brepols, 2006.

——. *XVI revelations of divine love shewed to a devout servant of our Lord called Mother Juliana, an anchorete of Norwich, who lived in the dayes of King Edward the Third*. Ed. Serenus Cressy [orig. pub. London: n.p., 1670]. Early English Books Online. Ann Arbor and Oxford: Text Creation Partnership, 2014. http://name.umdl.umich.edu/B20816.0001.001.

——. *XVI. Revelations of Divine Love, Made to a Devout Servant of Our Lord, Called Mother Juliana, An Anchorite of Norwich, Who Lived in the Days of King Edward the Third*. Ed. Serenus Cressy and repr. with a preface by George Hargreaves Parker [orig. pub. London: n.p., 1670]. London: S. Clarke, 1843.

Langland, William. *Piers Plowman: The B Version*. Ed. George Kane and E. Talbot Donaldson. 2nd ed. London: Athlone Press, 1988.

——. *Piers Plowman: An Edition of the C-Text*. Ed. Derek Pearsall. Berkeley: University of California Press, 1978.

——. *Piers Plowman: A New Translation of the B-Text*. Ed. and trans. A. V. C. Schmidt. Oxford: Oxford University Press, 1992.

Kempe, Margery. *The Book of Margery Kempe*. Ed. Lynn Staley. TEAMS Middle English Texts. Kalamazoo, MI: Medieval Institute Publications, 1996. https://d.lib.rochester.edu/teams/publication/staley-the-book-of-margery-kempe.

Love, Nicholas. *The Mirror of the Blessed Life of Jesus Christ: A Full Critical Edition*. Ed. Michael G. Sargent. Exeter, UK: Exeter University Press, 2005.

Lydgate, John. *Lydgate's Troy Book*. Vol. 2. Ed. H. Bergen. EETS e.s. 103. London: Kegan Paul, Trench, Trübner and Oxford University Press for the Early English Text Society, 1906.

Mirk, John. *John Mirk's Instructions for Parish Priests*. Ed. Gillis Kristensson. Lund Studies in English 49. Lund, Denmark: Gleerup, 1974.

Nuttall, Jenni, trans. "Hoccleve's 'Complaint': An Open-Access Prose Translation." Hoccleve Society.org. Accessed January 9, 2024. https://hocclevesociety.org/texts-and-resources/hoccleves-complaint/.

Moreau-Guibert, Karine, ed. *Pore Caitif: A Middle English Manual of Religion and Devotion*. Turnhout, Belgium: Brepols, 2019.

Morris, Richard, ed. and trans. *Old English Homilies of the Twelfth Century: From the Unique MS. B.14.52. in the Library of Trinity College, Cambridge: Second Series, with Three Thirteenth Century Hymns from MS. 54 D.4.14 in Corpus Christi College*. EETS o.s. 53. London: Trübner, 1873.

Peter the Chanter. *The Christian at Prayer: An Illustrated Prayer Manual Attributed to Peter the Chanter (d. 1197)*. Ed. Richard C. Trexler. Binghamton: Medieval & Renaissance Texts & Studies, State University of New York, 1987.

Plato. "Timaeus." In *Timaeus. Critias. Cleitophon. Menexenus. Epistles*, trans. R. G. Bury, 1–254. Cambridge, MA: Harvard University Press, 1929.

Pseudo-Dionysius. "The Divine Names." In *Pseudo-Dionysius: The Complete Works*, trans. Colm Luibheid, with foreword, notes, and translation collaboration by Paul Rorem, preface by René Roques, and introductions by Jaroslav Pelikan, Jean Leclercq, and Karlfried Froehlich, 43–131. New York: Paulist Press, 1987.

Richardi a Sancto Victore. "De gratia contemplationis libri quinque occasione accepta ab arca Moysis et o beam rem hactenus dictum Benjamin Maior." In *Opera Omnia*, ed. Jacques-Paul Migne, 64–192. Patrologia Latina 196. Paris: Migne, 1855.

Rolle, Richard. *The Incendium Amoris of Richard Rolle of Hampole*. Ed. Margaret Deanesly. Manchester: Manchester University Press, 1915.

Roux, Emmanuelle, ed. *Two Middle English Translations of Friar Laurent's "Somme le roi": Critical Edition*. Textes vernaculaires du moyen âge 8. Turnhout, Belgium: Brepols, 2010.

Schaff, Philip, ed. *Ante-Nicene Fathers*. Vol. 1: *The Apostolic Fathers with Justin Martyr and Irenaeus* [orig. pub. New York: Christian Literature, 1885]. Christian Classics Ethereal Library. Grand Rapids, MI: Eerdmans, 2001. https://www.ccel.org/ccel/schaff/anf01.html.

"Sir Gawain and the Green Knight." In *The Poems of the Pearl Manuscript:* Pearl, Cleanness, Patience, Sir Gawain and the Green Knight, 5th ed., ed. Malcolm Andrew and Ronald Waldron, 207–300. Liverpool: Liverpool University Press, 2007.

Stanbury, Sarah, ed. *Pearl*. TEAMS Middle English Texts. Kalamazoo, MI: Medieval Institute Publications, 2001. https://d.lib.rochester.edu/teams/text/stanbury-pearl.

"A Tretis of Discrescyon of Spirites." In *Deonise Hid Diuinite and other treatises on Contemplative Prayer related to* The Cloud of Unknowing, ed. Phyllis Hodgson, 93–94. EETS o.s. 231. London: Oxford University Press, 1955.

Vaissier, Johannes Joseph, ed. *A Deuout Treatyse Called The Tree & XII. Frutes of The Holy Goost*. Groningen, The Netherlands: J. B. Walters, 1960.

Whatley, Gordon, Anne B. Thompson, and Robert K. Upchurch, eds. "The Life of St. Julian the Hospitaller: Introduction." In *Saints' Lives in Middle English Collections*. TEAMS Middle English Texts. Kalamazoo, MI: Medieval Institute Publications, 2004. https://d.lib.rochester.edu/teams/publication/whatley-saints-lives-in-middle-english-collections.

Wycliffe, John. *The English Works of Wyclif Hitherto Unprinted*. Ed. F. D. Matthew. EETS o.s. 74. London: Trübner, 1973. Orig. pub. 1880.

——. *The Holy Bible Containing the Old and New Testaments with the Apocryphal Books in the Earliest English Versions Made from the Latin Vulgate by John Wycliffe and His Followers*. Ed. J. Forshall and F. Madden. 4 vols. Oxford: Oxford University Press, 1850.

Zettersten, A., ed. *The English Text of the Ancrene Riwle: Magdalene College Cambridge MS Pepys 2498*. EETS o.s. 274. London: Oxford University Press, 1976.

SECONDARY TEXTS

Adams, Robert. "Langland's Theology." In *A Companion to* Piers Plowman, ed. John A. Alford, 87–114. Berkeley: University of California Press, 1988.

Adler, Gillian. "Visionary Metaphors: Sight, Sickness, and Space in Boethius's *Consolation of Philosophy* and Julian of Norwich's *Showings*." *Journal of Medieval Religious Cultures* 46, no. 1 (2020): 53–70.

Adorno, Theodor W. *The Jargon of Authenticity*. Trans. Knut Tarnowski and Frederic Will. London: Routledge & Kegan Paul, 1973.

Aers, David. *Salvation and Sin: Augustine, Langland and Fourteenth-Century Theology*. Notre Dame: University of Notre Dame Press, 2009.

——. "'What is synne?': Exploring Julian of Norwich's Question." In *New Directions in Medieval Mystical and Devotional Literature: Essays in Honor of Denise N. Baker*, ed. Amy N. Vines and Lee Templeton, 11–28. Lanham, MD: Rowman and Littlefield, 2023.

Aers, David, and Lynn Staley. *The Powers of the Holy: Religion, Politics, and Gender in Late Medieval English Culture*. University Park: Pennsylvania State University Press, 1996.

Ahmed, Sara. *Queer Phenomenology: Orientations, Objects, Others*. Durham, NC: Duke University Press, 2006.

Aho, Kevin, and James Aho, eds. *Body Matters: A Phenomenology of Sickness, Disease, and Illness*. Lanham, MD: Lexington Books, 2008.

Alford, John A. "Design of the Poem." In *A Companion to* Piers Plowman, ed. John A. Alford, 29–65. Berkeley: University of California Press, 1988.

Anidjar, Gil. "Secularism." *Critical Inquiry* 33, no. 1 (2006): 52–77.

Appleford, Amy. "The 'Comene Course of Prayers': Julian of Norwich and Late Medieval Death Culture." *Journal of English and Germanic Philology* 107, no. 2 (2008): 190–214.

——. *Learning to Die in London, 1380–1540*. Philadelphia: University of Pennsylvania Press, 2014.

——. "The Sea Ground and the London Street: The Ascetic Self in Julian of Norwich and Thomas Hoccleve." *Chaucer Review* 51, no. 1 (2016): 49–67.

Arbesmann, Rudolf. "The Concept of 'Christus Medicus' in St Augustine." *Traditio* 10 (1954): 1–28.

Arikha, Noga. *Passions and Tempers: A History of the Humours*. New York: HarperCollins, 2007.

Asad, Talal. *Formations of the Secular: Christianity, Islam, Modernity*. Stanford, CA: Stanford University Press, 2003.

Ashdowne, R. K., D. R. Howlett, and R. E. Latham, eds. *Dictionary of Medieval Latin from British Sources*. Oxford: British Academy, 2018. Accessed January 9, 2024. http://www.dmlbs.ox.ac.uk/web.

Ast, Friedrich. *Grundlinien der Grammatik, Hermeneutik und Kritik*. Landshut, Germany: Jos. Thomann, Buchdrucker und Buchhändler, 1808.

Ataria, Yochai. *Body Disownership in Complex Posttraumatic Stress Disorder*. New York: Palgrave Macmillan, 2018.

Atkinson, Laurie. "'Why þat yee meeued been / can I nat knowe': Autobiography, Convention, and Discerning *Doublenesse* in Thomas Hoccleve's *The Series*." *Neophilologus* 101 (2017): 479–94.

Ayers, Luke, and Victoria Bahr. "A Twelfth-Century Service for Enclosing an Anchorite or Anchoress: Introduction, Latin Text, and Translation." *Expositor: A Journal of Undergraduate Research in the Humanities* 14 (2019): 1–12.

Bachelard, Gaston. *The Poetics of Space*, with a foreword by Mark Z. Danielewski and introduction by Richard Kearney. New York: Penguin, 2014. Orig. pub. 1958.

Baier, Annette. "Trust and Antitrust." *Ethics* 96, no. 2 (1986): 231–60.

Baier, Karl. "Meditation and Contemplation in High to Late Medieval Europe." In *Yogic Perception, Meditation and Altered States of Consciousness*, ed. Eli Franco, 325–49. Vienna: Verlag der Österreichischen Akademie der Wissenschaften, 2009.

Baker, Denise N. "From Plowing to Penitence: *Piers Plowman* and Fourteenth-Century Theology." *Speculum* 55, no. 4 (1980): 715–25.

——. *Julian of Norwich's Showings: From Vision to Book*. Princeton, NJ: Princeton University Press, 1994.

——. "The Structure of the Soul and the 'Godly Wylle' in Julian of Norwich's *Showings*." In Jones, *Medieval Mystical Tradition in England VII*, 37–49.

Barnett, Matthew. *The Reformation as Renewal: Retrieving the One, Holy, Catholic and Apostolic Church*. Grand Rapids, MI: Zondervan, 2023.

Barr, Jessica. *Willing to Know God: Dreamers and Visionaries in the Later Middle Ages*. Columbus: Ohio State University Press, 2010.

Barratt, Alexandra. "'In the Lowest Part of Our Need': Julian and Medieval Gynaecological Writing." In McEntire, *Julian of Norwich*, 239–56.

Bartky, Sandra Lee. *Femininity and Domination: Studies in the Phenomenology of Oppression*. New York: Routledge, 1990.

Bazán, Bernardo, John Wippel, Gérard Fransen, and Danielle Jacquart, eds. *Les Questions Disputées et Les Questions Quodlibétiques dans les Facultés de Théologie, de Droit et de Médecine*. Turnhout, Belgium: Brepols, 1985.

Beaty, Nancy Lee. *The Craft of Dying: A Study in the Literary Tradition of the "Ars Moriendi" in England*. New Haven, CT: Yale University Press, 1970.

Bech, Josep Maria. "Merleau-Ponty's Many-Layered Presence in Bourdieu's Thought." *Cosmos and History: The Journal of Natural and Social Philosophy* 17, no. 1 (2021): 243–64.

Bell, David N. *The Image and Likeness: The Augustinian Spirituality of William of St. Thierry*. Cistercian Studies 78. Kalamazoo, MI: Cistercian Publications, 1984.

Benskin, M., M. Laing, V. Karaiskos, and K. Williamson, eds. *An Electronic Version of A Linguistic Atlas of Late Mediaeval English*. Edinburgh: University of Edinburgh, 2013. Accessed January 9, 2024. http://www.lel.ed.ac.uk/ihd/elalme/elalme.html.

Benson, Bruce Ellis, and Norman Wirzba, eds. *The Phenomenology of Prayer*. New York: Fordham University Press, 2005.

Bhargava, Rajeev. *Secularism and Its Critics*. Oxford: Oxford University Press, 1999.

Biddick, Kathleen. *The Shock of Medievalism*. Durham, NC: Duke University Press, 1998.

Binski, Paul. *Medieval Death: Ritual and Representation*. London: British Museum Press, 1996.

Blamires, David. "Eckhart and Tauler: A Comparison of Their Sermons on 'Homo quidam fecit cenam magnam' (Luke XIV.16)." *Modern Language Review* 66, no. 3 (1971): 608–27.

Blattner, William. "The Concept of Death in Heidegger's *Being and Time*." *Man and World* 27 (1994): 49–70.

Bloch, Howard R., and Stephen G. Nichols. *Medievalism and the Modernist Temper*. Baltimore: Johns Hopkins University Press, 1996.

Boase, T.S.R., *Death in the Middle Ages: Mortality, Judgment and Remembrance*. London: Thames and Hudson, 1972.

Bollnow, Otto F. "Lived-space." *Philosophy Today* 5, no. 1 (1961): 31–39.

Bonner, Gerald. "Pelagius (fl. c.390–418), theologian." *Oxford Dictionary of National Biography*. Oxford: Oxford University Press, 2014. Accessed January 9, 2024. doi:10.1093/ref:odnb/21784.

Brampton, C. K. "Scotus, Ockham, and the Theory of Intuitive Cognition." *Antonianum* 40 (1965): 449–66.

Brough, John B. "Temporality and Illness: A Phenomenological Perspective." In *Handbook of Phenomenology and Medicine*, ed. S. Kay Toombs, 29–46. Dordrecht, The Netherlands: Kluwer, 2001.

Brownlee, Marina S., Kevin Brownlee, and Stephen G. Nichols, eds. *The New Medievalism*. Baltimore: Johns Hopkins University Press, 1991.

Bryan, Jennifer. *Looking Inward: Devotional Reading and the Private Self in Late Medieval England*. Philadelphia: University of Pennsylvania Press, 2008.

Buckley, Frank. "An Approach to a Phenomenology of At-Homeness." In *Duquesne Studies in Phenomenological Psychology*, vol. 1, ed. Amedeo Giorgi, William Frank Fischer, and Rolf Von Eckartsberg, 198–211. Pittsburgh: Duquesne University Press, 1971.

Burrow, J. A. *Gestures and Looks in Medieval Narrative*. Cambridge: Cambridge University Press, 2002.

Bynum, Caroline Walker. *Holy Feast and Holy Fast: The Religious Significance of Food to Medieval Women*. Berkeley: University of California Press, 1987.

——. *Fragmentation and Redemption: Essays on Gender and the Human Body in Medieval Religion*. New York: Zone Books, 1991.

Bynum, Caroline Walker, and Paul H. Freedman. *Last Things: Death and the Apocalypse in the Middle Ages*. Philadelphia: University of Pennsylvania Press, 2000.

Byron-Davies, Justin M. *Revelation and the Apocalypse in Late Medieval Literature: The Writings of Julian of Norwich and William Langland*. Cardiff: University of Wales Press, 2020.

Cairns, Dorion. *The Philosophy of Edmund Husserl*. Ed. Lester Embree. Dordrecht, The Netherlands: Springer, 2013.

Camilleri, Joseph A. "Postsecularist Discourse in an 'Age of Transition.' " *Review of International Studies* 38, no. 5 (2012): 1019–39.

Campbell, Bruce. *The Great Transition: Climate, Disease and Society in the Late-Medieval World*. Cambridge: Cambridge University Press, 2016.

Caputo, John D. *Heidegger and Aquinas: An Essay on Overcoming Metaphysics*. New York: Fordham University Press, 1982.

——. "Heidegger and Theology." In *The Cambridge Companion to Heidegger*, ed. Charles B. Guignon, 270–88. Cambridge: Cambridge University Press, 1993.

——. "Meister Eckhart and the Later Heidegger: The Mystical Element in Heidegger's Thought: Part One." *Journal of the History of Philosophy* 12, no. 4 (1974): 479–94.

Carel, Havi. "Can I Be Ill and Happy?" *Philosophia* 35, no. 2 (2007): 95–110.

——. " 'I Am Well, Apart from the Fact That I Have Cancer': Explaining Well-being Within Illness." In *Philosophy and Happiness*, ed. L. Bortolotti, 82–99. Basingstoke, UK: Palgrave, 2009.

——. *Illness*. Durham, UK: Acumen Publishing, 2008.

——. *Phenomenology of Illness*. Oxford: Oxford University Press, 2016.

Carman, Taylor. "Authenticity." In *A Companion to Heidegger*, ed. Hubert L. Dreyfus and Mark A. Wrathall, 285–96. Oxford: Blackwell, 2005.

——. "The Body in Husserl and Merleau-Ponty." *Philosophical Topics* 27, no. 2 (1999): 205–26.

Cassian, John. "The Foundations of the Cenobitic Life." In *The Nature of Melancholy: From Aristotle to Kristeva*, ed. Jennifer Radden, 71–74. Oxford: Oxford University Press, 2000.

Cervone, Cristina Maria. "Julian of Norwich and John Capgrave: *Foule Black Dede Hame / Hame of Blyndnes*." *Journal of English and Germanic Philology* 114, no. 1 (2015): 88–96.

——. *Poetics of the Incarnation: Middle English Writing and the Leap of Love*. Philadelphia: University of Pennsylvania Press, 2012.

——. "The 'Soule' Crux in Julian of Norwich's *A Revelation of Love*." *Review of English Studies* 55, no. 219 (2004): 151–56.

Cogliano, R., C. Crisci, M. Conson, D. Grossi, and L. Trojano. "Chronic Somatoparaphrenia: A Follow-Up Study on Two Clinical Cases." *Cortex* 48, no. 6 (2012): 758–67.

Cohen, Jeffrey Jerome. *Medieval Identity Machines*. Minneapolis: University of Minnesota Press, 2003.

Cohen, Patricia. "An Ethical Question: Does a Nazi Deserve a Place Among Philosophers?" *New York Times*, November 9, 2009, https://www.nytimes.com/2009/11/09/books/09philosophy.html?smid=tw-share.

Coiner, Nancy. "The 'Homely' and the *Heimliche*: The Hidden, Doubled Self in Julian of Norwich's Showings." *Exemplaria* 5, no. 2 (1993): 305–23.

Cole, Andrew. *The Birth of Theory*. Chicago: University of Chicago Press, 2014.

Cole, Andrew, and D. Vance Smith. "Introduction: Outside Modernity." In Cole and Smith, *The Legitimacy of the Middle Ages*, 1–36.

—— eds. *The Legitimacy of the Middle Ages: On the Unwritten History of Theory*. Durham, NC: Duke University Press, 2010.

Colledge, Edmund, and James Walsh. "Editing Julian of Norwich's *Revelations*: A Progress Report." *Medieval Studies* 38 (1976): 404–27.

Commoner, Barry. *The Closing Circle: Nature, Man and Technology*. New York: Bantam, 1974.

Cook, Christopher C. H. *Hearing Voices: Medieval Mystics, Meaning and Psychiatry*. London: T&T Clark, 2023.

Coyne, Ryan. *Heidegger's Confessions: The Remains of Saint Augustine in "Being and Time" and Beyond*. Chicago: University of Chicago Press, 2015.

Crowe, Benjamin. "Heidegger and the Prospect of a Phenomenology of Prayer." In Benson and Wirzba, *Phenomenology of Prayer*, 119–33.

D'Arcens, Louise. "From 'Eccentric Affiliation' to 'Corrective Medievalism': Bruce Holsinger's *The Premodern Condition*." *postmedieval* 1 (2010): 299–308.

Dalgairns, J. B., ed. *The Scale (or Ladder) of Perfection: Written by Walter Hilton: With an Essay on the Spiritual Life of Medieval England*. London: Art and Book, 1870, repr. 1901.

Davies, Oliver. "Transformational Processes in the Work of Julian of Norwich and Mechtild of Magdeburg." In Glasscoe, *Medieval Mystical Tradition in England V*, 39–52.

Davis, Kathleen. "The Sense of An Epoch: Periodization, Sovereignty, and the Limits of Secularization." In *The Legitimacy of the Middle Ages*, 39–69.

Davis, Rebecca. Piers Plowman *and the Books of Nature*. Oxford: Oxford University Press, 2016.

Davlin, Mary Clemente. "Devotional Postures in 'Piers Plowman' B, with an Appendix on Divine Postures." *Chaucer Review* 42, no. 2 (2007): 161–79.

——. "*Kynde Knowyng* as a Major Theme in *Piers Plowman* B." *Review of English Studies* 22, no. 85 (1971): 1–19.

——. "*Kynde Knowyng* as a Middle English Equivalent for 'Wisdom' in *Piers Plowman* B." *Medium Ævum* 50 (1981): 5–17.

Day, Sebastian. *Intuitive Cognition: A Key to the Significance of the Later Scholastics*. St. Bonaventure, NY: Franciscan Institute, 1947.

Dekkers, Wim. "On the Notion of Home and the Goals of Palliative Care." *Theoretical Medicine and Bioethics* 30, no. 5 (2009): 335–49.

Derrida, Jacques. "The *Retrait* of Metaphor." In *The Derrida Reader: Writing Performances*, ed. Julian Wolfreys, 102–30. Edinburgh: Edinburgh University Press, 1998.

——. "Semiology and Grammatology: An Interview with Julia Kristeva [1968]." In *The Routledge Language and Cultural Theory Reader*, ed. Lucy Burle, Tony Crowley, and Alan Girvin, 241–48. London: Routledge, 2000.

——. "Structure, Sign and Play in the Discourse of the Human Sciences." In *Writing and Difference*, trans. Alan Bass, 278–93. London: Routledge, 1978. Orig. pub. 1967.

Descartes, René. *Principles of Philosophy*. Trans. V. R. Miller and R. P. Miller. Dordrecht, The Netherlands: Reidel, 1983.

DeYoung, Patricia A. *Understanding and Treating Chronic Shame: A Relational/Neurobiological Approach*. New York: Routledge, 2015.

Dinshaw, Carolyn. *How Soon Is Now? Medieval Texts, Amateur Readers, and the Queerness of Time*. Durham, NC: Duke University Press, 2012.

Douglass, Rebecca M. "Ecocriticism and Middle English Literature." *Studies in Medievalism* 10 (1998): 136–63.

Dresvina, Juliana. "What Julian Saw: The Embodied Showings and the Items for Private Devotion." *Religions* 10, no. 245 (2019): 1–20.

Dreyfus, Hubert L., and Harrison Hall. *Husserl, Intentionality, and Cognitive Science*. Cambridge, MA: MIT Press, 1982.

Dumitrescu, Irina, and Caleb Smith. "The Demon of Distraction." *Critical Inquiry* 47, no. S2, special issue: "Posts from the Pandemic," ed. Hank Scotch (2021): S77–S81.

Dutton, Elisabeth. *Julian of Norwich: The Influence of Late-Medieval Devotional Compilations.* Cambridge: Brewer, 2008.

Eliot, T. S. "Four Quartets." In *The Poems of T. S. Eliot*, vol. 1: *Collected and Uncollected Poems*, ed. Christopher Ricks and Jim McCue, 177–210. London: Faber & Faber, 2015.

Elias, Norbert. *The Civilizing Process.* Trans. Edmund Jephcott. 3 vols. London: Blackwell, 1978–1983. Orig. pub. 1939.

Engelhardt Jr., H. T. "Husserl and the Mind-Body Relation." In *Interdisciplinary Phenomenology*, ed. Don Ihde and Richard Zaner, 51–70. The Hague: Martinus Nijhoff, 1977.

Estés, Clarissa Pinkola. *Women Who Run with The Wolves: Contacting the Power of the Wild Woman.* London: Penguin, 1992; repr. 2008.

Evernden, Neil. *The Social Creation of Nature.* Baltimore: John Hopkins University Press, 1992.

Falkenberg, Marc. *Rethinking the Uncanny in Hoffman and Tieck.* Bern, Switzerland: Peter Lang, 2005.

Felton, J. S. "Burnout as a Clinical Entity: Its Importance in Health Care Workers." *Occupational Medicine*, 48, no. 4 (1998): 237–50.

Figley, Charles R., ed. *Treating Compassion Fatigue.* New York: Brunner-Routledge, 2002.

Fischer, Norman. *Sailing Home: Using the Wisdom of Homer's* Odyssey *to Navigate Life's Perils and Pitfalls.* Berkeley: North Atlantic Books, 2008.

Fishley, Daniel Theodore. "A Revelation of Weakness: Julian of Norwich, John Caputo, and the Event of Hospitality." *Medieval Mystical Theology* 31, no. 2 (2022): 67–79.

Flood, Robert. *A Description of St Julian's Church, Norwich and an Account of Dame Julian's Connection with It.* Norwich: Wherry Press, 1936.

Fox, Matthew. *Julian of Norwich: Wisdom in a Time of Pandemic—and Beyond.* Foreword by Mirabai Starr. Bloomington, IN: iUniverse, 2020.

Freud, Sigmund. "The Uncanny." In *The Standard Edition of the Complete Psychological Works of Sigmund Freud*, vol. 17: *An Infantile Neurosis and Other Works, 1917–1919*, trans. and ed. James Strachey and Anna Freud, assisted by Alix Strachey and Alan Tyson, 218–253. London: Hogarth Press and the Institute of Psycho-Analysis, 1971. Orig. pub. 1919.

Fuchs, Thomas. "Corporealized and Disembodied Minds: A Phenomenological View of the Body in Melancholia and Schizophrenia." *Philosophy, Psychiatry, and Psychology* 12, no. 2 (2005): 95–107.

——. "The Phenomenology of Shame, Guilt and the Body in Body Dysmorphic Disorder and Depression." *Journal of Phenomenological Psychiatry* 33, no. 2 (2003): 223–43.

Fullam, Lisa. "Julian of Norwich: The Socially-Distanced Saint." *Spiritus: A Journal of Christian Spirituality* 21, no. 1 (2021): 59–68.

Gadamer, Hans-Georg. *Truth and Method.* 2nd ed. Trans. and revised by Joel Weinsheimer and Donald G. Marshall. London: Continuum, 2004. Orig. pub. 1960.

——. *Über die Verborgenheit der Gesundheit.* Frankfurt: Suhrkamp Verlag, 1993.

Gasper, Giles E. M. "Anselm of Canterbury." In *Christian Theologies of Salvation: A Comparative Introduction*, ed. Justin S. Holcomb, 124–42. New York: New York University Press, 2017.

Gasse, Rosanne. "Dowel, Dobet, and Dobest in Middle English Literature." *Florilegium* 14, no. 1 (1995–1996): 171–95.

Gilbert, Claire. *Julian of Norwich and the Ecological Crisis: Restoring Porosity.* London: Routledge, 2024.

——. "Restoring Porosity and the Ecological Crisis: A Post-Ricoeurian Reading of the Julian of Norwich Texts." PhD diss., King's College London, 2018.

Gillespie, Vincent. "The Colours of Contemplation: Less Light on Julian of Norwich." In Jones, *Medieval Mystical Tradition in England VIII*, 7–28.

——. "Postcards from the Edge: Interpreting the Ineffable in the Middle English Mystics." In *Looking Into Holy Books: Essays on Late Medieval Religious Writing in England*, 307–38. Turnhout, Belgium: Brepols, 2011. Orig. pub. 1993.

——."Seek, Suffer, and Trust: 'Ese' and 'Disese' in Julian of Norwich." *Studies in the Age of Chaucer* 39 (2017): 129–58.

——." '[S]he do the police in different voices': Pastiche, Ventriloquism and Parody in Julian of Norwich." In McAvoy, *Companion to Julian of Norwich*, 192–207.

——. "Vernacular Theology." In *Middle English: Oxford Twenty-First Century Approaches to Literature*, ed. Paul Strohm, 401–20. Oxford: Oxford University Press, 2007.

Gillespie, Vincent, and Maggie Ross. "The Apophatic Image: The Poetics of Effacement in Julian of Norwich." In Glasscoe, *Medieval Mystical Tradition in England V*, 53–77.

——. " 'With Mekeness Aske Perserverantly': On Reading Julian of Norwich." *Mystics Quarterly* 30, nos. 3–4 (2004): 126–41.

Gilligan, James. *Violence: Reflections on a National Epidemic.* New York: Vintage Books, 1997.

Gilson, Étienne. *History of Christian Philosophy in the Middle Ages.* Toronto: Pontifical Institute of Mediaeval Studies, 1955.

Glasscoe, Marion. "Changing Chere and Changing Text in the Eighth Revelation of Julian of Norwich." *Medium Ævum* 66, no. 1 (1997): 115–21.

——, ed. *The Medieval Mystical Tradition in England V, Papers Read at The Devon Centre, Dartington Hall, July 1992*. Cambridge: Brewer, 1992.

——. "Visions and Revisions: A Further Look at the Manuscripts of Julian of Norwich." *Studies in Bibliography* 42 (1989): 103–20.

Gondreau, Paul. *The Passions of Christ's Soul in the Theology of St. Thomas Aquinas*. Scranton, NJ: University of Scranton Press, 2009.

Graybeal, Jean. *Language and "the Feminine" in Nietzsche and Heidegger*. Bloomington: Indiana University Press, 1990.

Hagen, Susan K. "St. Cecilia and St. John of Beverley: Julian of Norwich's Early Model and Late Affirmation." In McEntire, *Julian of Norwich*, 91–114.

Hall, Amy Laura. *Laughing at the Devil: Seeing the World with Julian of Norwich*. Durham, NC: Duke University Press, 2018.

Hambro, Cathinka D. "Pain and Epiphany: Julian of Norwich's *Revelations of Divine Love* as Pathography." *Tidsskrift for Forskning i Sygdom og Samfund* 31 (2019): 27–43.

Hanna, Ralph. *London Literature, 1300–1380*. Cambridge: Cambridge University Press, 2005.

Heidegger, Martin. *The Basic Problems of Phenomenology*. Trans. Albert Hofstadter. Rev. ed. Bloomington: Indiana University Press, 1982. Orig. pub. 1927.

——. *Being and Time*. Trans. Joan Stambaugh, revised and with a foreword by Dennis J. Schmidt. Albany: State University of New York Press, 2010. Orig. pub. 1927.

——. "Building Dwelling Thinking." In *Poetry, Language, Thought*. Trans. and with an introduction by Albert Hofstadter, 145–61. New York: Harper & Row, 1975. Orig. pub. 1954.

——. *Gesamtausgabe*. Vol. 24: *Die Grundprobleme der Phänomenologie*. Ed. Friedrich-Wilhelm von Herrmann. Frankfurt: Vittorio Klostermann, 1997.

——. *The History of the Concept of Time: Prolegomena*. Trans. Theodore Kisiel. Bloomington: Indiana University Press, 1985. Orig. pub. 1979.

——. *An Introduction to Metaphysics*. Trans. Ralph Mannheim. New Haven, CT: Yale University Press, 1959. Orig. pub. 1953.

——. "Letter on Humanism." In *Martin Heidegger: Basic Writings: From* Being and Time *(1927) to* The Task of Thinking *(1964)*, rev. ed., ed. David Farrell Krell, 215–66. San Francisco: HarperCollins, 1993. Orig. pub. 1947.

——. "Mein Bisheriger Weg (1937/38)." In *Gesamtausgabe*, vol. 66: *Besinnung*, ed. Friedrich-Wilhelm von Herrmann, 411–18. Frankfurt: Vittorio Klostermann, 1997.

——. "Memorial Address." In *Discourse on Thinking: A Translation of* Gelassenheit, trans. John M. Anderson and E. Hans Freund with an introduction by John M. Anderson, 43–57. New York: Harper & Row, 1966.

——. "My Pathway Hitherto." In *Mindfulness*, trans. Parvis Emad and Thomas Kalary, 352–57. London: Bloomsbury, 2016. Orig. pub. 1997.

——. *Pathmarks*. Ed. William McNeill. Cambridge: Cambridge University Press, 1998. Orig. pub. 1919–1961.

——. *The Phenomenology of Religious Life*.Trans. Matthias Fritsch and Jennifer Anna Gosetti-Ferencei. Bloomington: Indiana University Press, 2010. Orig. pub. 1995.

——. *The Question Concerning Technology and Other Essays*. Trans. and with an introduction by William Lovitt. New York: Garland, 1977. Orig. pub. 1954.

——. *Sein und Zeit*. 17th ed. Niemeyer: Tübingen, 1993. Orig. pub. 1927.

——. "Was ist Metaphysik? (1929)." In *Gesamtausgabe*, vol. 9: *Wegmarken*, ed. Friedrich-Wilhelm von Herrmann, 103–22. Frankfurt: Vittorio Klostermann, 1976. Orig. pub. 1967.

——. "What Is Metaphysics?" In *Martin Heidegger: Basic Writings: From* Being and Time *(1927) to* The Task of Thinking *(1964)*, rev. ed., ed. David Farrell Krell, 89–110. San Francisco: HarperCollins, 1993. Orig. pub. 1967.

——. *Unterwegs zur Sprache*. 3rd ed. Pfullingen: Neske, 1965. Orig. pub. 1959.

——. *Zollikon Seminars: Protocols, Conversations, Letters*. Ed. Medard Boss. Trans. Franz Mayr and Richard Askay. Evanston, IL: Northwestern University Press, 2001. Orig. pub. 1959–1969.

Hemming, Laurence Paul. *Heidegger's Atheism: The Refusal of a Theological Voice*. Notre Dame: University of Notre Dame Press, 2002.

Herigstad, M., A. Hayen, K. Wiech, and K.T.S. Pattinson. "Dyspnoea and the Brain." *Respiratory Medicine* 105, no. 6 (2011): 809–17.

Hide, Kerrie. "Julian of Norwich." In *Christian Theologies of Salvation: A Comparative Introduction*, ed. Justin S. Holcomb, 160–79. New York: New York University Press, 2017.

Hoffman, E.T.A. *Der Sandmann/The Sandman*. German-English edition. Trans. John Oxenford. Berlin: Michael Holzinger, 2015. Orig. pub. 1816.

Holland, Nancy J., and Patricia Huntington, eds. *Feminist Interpretations of Martin Heidegger*. Philadelphia: Penn State University Press, 2001.

Holsinger, Bruce. *The Premodern Condition: Medievalism and the Making of Theory*. Chicago: University of Chicago Press, 2005.

Huizinga, Johan. *The Autumn of the Middle Ages*. Trans. Rodney J. Payton and Ulrich Mammitzsch. Chicago: University of Chicago Press, 1996.

——. *Herfsttij der Middeleeuwen: Studie over levens-en gedachtenvormen der veertiende en vijftiende eeuw in Frankrijk en de Nederlanden.* Haarlem, The Netherlands: H. D. Tjeenk Willink, 1919.

Huntington, Patricia J. *Ecstatic Subjects, Utopia, and Recognition: Kristeva, Heidegger, Irigaray.* Albany: State University of New York Press, 1998.

Husserl, Edmund. *The Crisis of European Sciences and Transcendental Phenomenology: An Introduction to Phenomenological Philosophy.* Trans. David Carr. Evanston, IL: Northwestern University Press, 1970. Orig. pub. 1954.

——. *Die Krisis der europäischen Wissenschaften und die transzendentale Phänomenologie. Eine Einleitung in die phänomenologische Philosophie.* Ed. W. Biemel. Husserliana VI. The Hague: Martinus Nijhoff, 1962. Orig. pub. 1954.

——. *Logical Investigations.* Trans. J. N. Findlay. London: Routledge, 1973. Orig. pub. 1900/01.

Jaeger, Vanessa. "Eating Up the Enemy: Teaching Richard Coer de Lyon and the Misrepresentation of Crusader Ideology in White Nationalist Agendas." *New Chaucer Studies: Pedagogy and Profession* 2, no. 2 (2021): 39–48.

Jantzen, Grace M., *Becoming Divine: Towards a Feminist Philosophy of Religion.* Manchester: Manchester University Press, 1998.

——. *Julian of Norwich: Mystic and Theologian.* London: SPCK, 2000.

——. *Power, Gender, and Christian Mysticism.* Cambridge: Cambridge University Press, 1995.

Johnson, Eleanor. "Feeling Time, Will, and Words: Vernacular Devotion in the *Cloud of Unknowing.*" *Journal of Medieval and Early Modern Studies* 41, no. 2 (2011): 345–68.

——. *Staging Contemplation: Participatory Theology in Middle English Prose, Verse, and Drama.* Chicago: University of Chicago Press, 2018.

Johnson, S. Kyle. "Love Amidst Fear: Julian of Norwich, Affect, and Orthopathy." *Spiritus: A Journal of Christian Spirituality* 21, no. 2 (2021): 282–301.

Jones, E. A., ed. *The Medieval Mystical Tradition in England VII, Papers Read at Charney Manor, July 2004.* Cambridge: Brewer, 2004.

——, ed. *The Medieval Mystical Tradition in England VIII, Papers Read at Charney Manor July 2011.* Cambridge: Brewer, 2013.

Josephson-Storm, Jason Ā. *The Myth of Disenchantment: Magic, Modernity, and the Birth of the Human Sciences.* Chicago: University of Chicago Press, 2017.

Kahm, Nicholas. *Aquinas: On Emotion's Participation in Reason.* Washington, DC: Catholic University of America Press, 2019.

Karnes, Michelle. *Imagination, Meditation, and Cognition in the Middle Ages.* Chicago: University of Chicago Press, 2011.

——. "Will's Imagination in *Piers Plowman.*" *Journal of English and Germanic Philology* 108, no. 1 (2009): 27–58.

Kaschor, Kim. "When to Be Still, When to Be Stirred: What Mystics Can Teach Us About Patience During COVID-19." CBC Radio, February 12, 2021. https://www.cbc.ca/radio/tapestry/when-to-be-still-when-to-be-stirred-what-mystics-can-teach-us-about-patience-during-covid-19-1.5911991.

Keane, Niall. "On the Origins of Illness and the Hiddenness of Health: A Hermeneutic Approach to the History of a Problem." In *Medicine and Society: New Perspectives in Continental Philosophy*, ed. Darian Meacham, 57–72. Dordrecht, The Netherlands: Springer, 2015.

Kelner, Anna. "Trusting Women's Visions: The Discernment of Spirits in Julian of Norwich's *Revelation of Love*." *Journal of Medieval and Early Modern Studies* 51, no. 2 (2021): 193–214.

Ker, Neil R., ed. *Facsimile of British Museum MS. Harley 2253*. EETS o.s. 255. London: Oxford University Press, 1965.

Kierkegaard, Søren. *Concluding Unscientific Postscript to* Philosophical Fragments. Ed. and trans. Howard V. Hong and Edna H. Hong. Princeton, NJ: Princeton University Press, 1992.

Kim, Dorothy. "The Alt-Right and Medieval Religions." Berkley Forum, Berkley Center for Religion, Peace & World Affairs, Georgetown University November 5, 2018. https://berkleycenter.georgetown.edu/responses/the-alt-right-and-medieval-religions.

——. "Teaching Medieval Studies in a Time of White Supremacy." In the Middle. August 28, 2017. https://www.inthemedievalmiddle.com/2017/08/teaching-medieval-studies-in-time-of.html.

King, Matthew. "Heidegger's Etymological Method: Discovering Being By Recovering the Richness of the Word." *Philosophy Today* 51, no. 3 (2007): 278–89.

Klima, Gyula, and Alexander W. Hall, eds. *The Demonic Temptations of Medieval Nominalism*. Proceedings of the Society for Medieval Logic and Metaphysics 9. Newcastle-upon-Tyne, UK: Cambridge Scholars, 2011.

Klimecki, Olga M., Susanne Leiberg, Matthieu Ricard, and Tania Singer. "Differential Pattern of Functional Brain Plasticity After Compassion and Empathy Training." *Social Cognitive and Affective Neuroscience* 9, no. 6 (2014): 873–79.

Knapp, Ethan. "Medieval Studies, Historicity, and Heidegger's Early Phenomenology." In *The Legitimacy of the Middle Ages*, 159–93.

Knowles, Jim. "Can You Serve? The Theology of Service from Langland to Luther." *Journal of Medieval and Early Modern Studies* 40, no. 3 (2010): 527–57.

Lacoste, Jean-Yves. "Heidegger Among the Theologians." *Journal for Continental Philosophy of Religion* 2, no. 2 (2020): 159–74.

Lafont, Cristina. "Hermeneutics." In *A Companion to Heidegger*, ed. Hubert L. Dreyfus and Mark A. Wrathall, 265–84. Oxford: Blackwell, 2005.

Lang, Judith. "'The Godly Wylle' in Julian of Norwich." *Downside Review* 102, no. 348 (1984): 163–73.

Latour, Bruno. "La vraie sagesse de l'imam," *Le Monde*, January 16, 2015, https://www.lemonde.fr/idees/article/2015/01/19/la-vraie-sagesse-de-l-imam_4558988_3232.html. Available in translation by Tim Howles, "Two Lessons from an Old Imam," at http://www.bruno-latour.fr/sites/default/files/downloads/15-1-IMAM-LEMONDE-GB.pdf, and accessed January 9, 2024.

——. *We Have Never Been Modern*. Trans. Catherine Porter. Cambridge, MA: Harvard University Press, 1993.

Law, Sarah. "In the Centre: Spiritual and Cultural Representations of Julian of Norwich in the Julian Centre." In *Julian of Norwich's Legacy: Medieval Mysticism and Post-Medieval Reception*, ed. Sarah Salih and Denise N. Baker, 173–89. New York: Palgrave Macmillan, 2009.

Lawes, Richard. "Psychological Disorder and the Autobiographical Impulse in Julian of Norwich, Margery Kempe and Thomas Hoccleve." In *Writing Religious Women: Female Spiritual and Textual Practices in Late Medieval England*, ed. Christiania Whitehead and Denis Renevey, 217–44. Toronto: University of Toronto Press, 2000.

Lazikani, A. S. *Cultivating the Heart: Feeling and Emotion in Twelfth- and Thirteenth-Century Religious Texts*. Cardiff: Cardiff University Press, 2015.

——. "Encompassment in Love: Rabi'a of Basra in Dialogue with Julian of Norwich." *Journal of Medieval Religious Cultures* 46, no. 2 (2020): 115–36.

——. "The Vagabond Mind: Depression and the Medieval Anchorite." *Journal of Medieval Monastic Studies* 6 (2017): 141–68.

Leech, Kenneth. "Hazelnut Theology: Its Potential and Perils." In *Julian Reconsidered*, ed. Kenneth Leech and Benedicta Ward, 1–10. Oxford: SLG Press, 1988.

Lees, Rosemary Ann. *The Negative Language of the Dionysian School of Mystical Theology: An Approach to the* Cloud of Unknowing. Analecta Cartusiana 107. 2 vols. Salzburg: Institut für Anglistik und Amerikanistik, Universität Salzburg, 1983.

Leclercq, Jean. *L'amour des lettres et le désir de dieu: initiation aux auteurs monastiques du moyen age*. Paris: Éditions du Cerf, 1957. Translated as *The Love of Learning and the Desire for God: A Study of Monastic Culture*, 3rd ed. New York: Fordham University Press, 1982.

Lefebvre, Henri. *The Production of Space*. Trans. Donald Nicholson-Smith. Oxford: Blackwell, 1991.

Leget, Carlo. "Retrieving the *Ars moriendi* Tradition." *Medicine, Health Care and Philosophy* 10 (2007): 313–19.

Leng, Xin. "Martin Heidegger on Primordial Christian Life Experience: A Phenomenological Theological Perspective." *Religions* 13, no. 1082 (2022). doi:10.3390/rel13111082.

Lewis, Michael. *Heidegger and the Place of Ethics*. London: Continuum, 2005.

Lichtmann, Maria R. "'I desyrede a bodylye syght': Julian of Norwich and the Body." *Mystics Quarterly* 17, no. 1 (1991): 12–19.

Lindsey, E. "Health Within Illness: Experiences of Chronically Ill/Disabled People." *Journal of Advanced Nursing* 24, no. 3 (1996): 465–72.

Lion, A. "Le Discours blessé: sur le langage mystique selon Michel de Certeau." *Révue des sciences philosophies et théologiques* 71 (1987): 405–20.

Lochrie, Karma. *Margery Kempe and Translations of the Flesh*. Philadelphia: University of Pennsylvania Press, 1991.

Lock, Charles. "*The Cloud of Unknowing*: Apophatic Discourse and Vernacular Anxieties." In *Text and Voice: The Rhetoric of Authority in the Middle Ages*, ed. Marianne Børch, 207–33. Odense: University of Southern Denmark Press, 2004.

Løgstrup, Knud Eljer. *Beyond the Ethical Demand*, with an introduction by Kees van Kooten Niekerk. Notre Dame: University of Notre Dame Press, 2007.

Lucas, Hannah. "'Clad in flesch and blood': The Sartorial Body and Female Self-Fashioning in *The Book of Margery Kempe*." *Journal of Medieval Religious Cultures* 45, no. 1 (2019): 29–60.

——. "Passion and Melancholy: Julian of Norwich's Medical Hermeneutic." *Review of English Studies* 72, no. 303 (2020): 1–18.

Lyubomirsky, Sonja. *The How of Happiness*. London: Penguin, 2007.

Mann, Jill. "Satisfaction and Payment in Middle English Literature." *Studies in the Age of Chaucer* 5, no. 1 (1983): 17–48.

Marcel, Gabriel. *Homo Viator: Introduction to the Metaphysic of Hope*. Trans. Emma Crauford. New York: Harper & Row, 1962.

Marder, Michael. *Plant-Thinking: A Philosophy of Vegetal Life*. New York: Columbia University Press, 2013.

Martino, Daniel J. "The Later Heidegger and Contemporary Theology of God." PhD diss., Duquesne University, 2004.

Masson, Cynthea. "The Point of Coincidence: Rhetoric and the Apophatic in Julian of Norwich's *Showings*." In McEntire, *Julian of Norwich*, 153–81.

McAvoy, Liz Herbert, ed. *A Companion to Julian of Norwich*. Cambridge: Brewer, 2008.

——. "'. . . a purse fulle feyer': Feminising the Body in Julian of Norwich's *A Revelation of Love*." *Leeds Studies in English*, n.s. 33 (2002): 99–113.

——. *Authority and the Female Body in the Writings of Julian of Norwich and Margery Kempe*. Cambridge: Brewer, 2004.

——. "'Flourish Like a Garden': Pain, Purgatory and Salvation in the Writing of Medieval Religious Women." *Medieval Feminist Forum: A Journal of Gender and Sexuality* 50, no. 1 (2015): 33–60.

——. "Introduction." In McAvoy, *Companion to Julian of Norwich*, 1–16.

——, ed. *Rhetoric of the Anchorhold: Space, Place and Body Within the Discourses of the Enclosure*. Cardiff: University of Wales Press, 2008.

——. "Tears, Mediation, and Literary Entanglement: The Writings of Medieval Visionary Women." In *Women and Medieval Literary Culture: From the Early Middle Ages to the Fifteenth Century*, ed. Corinne Saunders and Diane Watt, 269–84. Cambridge: Cambridge University Press, 2023.

McAvoy, Liz Herbert, and Mari Hughes-Edwards, eds. *Anchorites, Wombs and Tombs: Intersections of Gender and Enclosure in the Middle Ages*. Cardiff: University of Wales Press, 2005; repr. 2010.

McCann, Daniel. *Soul-Health: Therapeutic Reading in Later Medieval England*. Cardiff: University of Wales Press, 2018.

McEntire, Sandra J., ed. *Julian of Norwich: A Book of Essays*. New York: Garland, 1998.

McGinn, Bernard. "The Human Person as Image of God, II. Western Christianity." In *Christian Spirituality: Origins to the Twelfth Century*, ed. Bernard McGinn and John Meyendorff in collaboration with Jean Leclercq, 312–30. New York: Crossroad, 1985; repr. 2000.

——. "Love, Knowledge and *Unio Mystica* in the Western Christian Tradition." In *Mystical Union and Monotheistic Faith: An Ecumenical Dialogue*, ed. Moshe Idel and Bernard McGinn, 59–86. New York: Macmillan, 1989.

McGrath, Sean J. *The Early Heidegger and Medieval Philosophy: Phenomenology for the Godforsaken*. Washington, DC: Catholic University of America Press, 2006.

McIlwain, James T. "'The bodelye syeknes' of Julian of Norwich." *Journal of Medical History* 10 (1984): 167–80.

McNamer, Sarah. *Affective Meditation and the Invention of Medieval Compassion*. Philadelphia: University of Pennsylvania Press, 2010.

Meltzer, Françoise. *For Fear of the Fire: Joan of Arc and the Limits of Subjectivity*. Chicago: University of Chicago Press, 2001.

Merleau-Ponty, Maurice. *Phenomenology of Perception*. Trans. Colin Smith. London: Routledge, 1962; repr. 2002. Orig. pub. 1945.

Middle English Dictionary. Edited by Robert E. Lewis et al. Ann Arbor: University of Michigan Press, 1952–2001. *Online Edition in Middle English Compendium*. Edited by Frances McSparran et al. Ann Arbor: University of Michigan Library, 2000–2018. Accessed January 9, 2024. http://quod.lib.umich.edu/m/middle-english-dictionary/.

Miles, Laura Saetveit. "Queer Touch Between Holy Women: Julian of Norwich, Margery Kempe, Birgitta of Sweden, and the Visitation." In *Touching,*

Devotional Practices, and Visionary Experience in the Late Middle Ages, ed. David Carrillo-Rangel, Delfi I. Nieto-Isabel, and Pablo Acosta-García, 203–35. New York: Palgrave, 2019.

——. "Space and Enclosure in Julian of Norwich's *A Revelation of Love*." In McAvoy, *Companion to Julian of Norwich*, 154–65.

——. *The Virgin Mary's Book at the Annunciation*. Cambridge: Brewer, 2020.

Minore, Anna. "Julian of Norwich and Catherine of Siena: Pain and the Way of Salvation." *Journal of Medieval Religious Cultures* 40, no. 1 (2014): 44–74.

Moch, Susan Diemert. "Health Within Illness: Conceptual Evolution and Practice Possibilities." *Advances in Nursing Science* 11, no. 4 (1989): 23–31.

Molinari, Paul. *Julian of Norwich: The Teaching of a 14th Century English Mystic*. London: Longmans, Green, 1958.

Möllering, Guido. "The Nature of Trust: From Georg Simmel to a Theory of Expectation, Interpretation and Suspension." *Sociology* 35, no. 2 (2001): 403–20.

——. "Process Views of Trusting and Crises." In *Handbook of Advances in Trust Research*, ed. R. Bachmann and A. Zaheer, 285–305. Cheltenham, UK: Edward Elgar, 2013.

Morgan, G. R. "A Critical Edition of Caxton's *The Art and Craft to Know Well to Die* and *Ars moriendi* Together with the Antecedent Manuscript Material." 2 vols. DPhil diss., University of Oxford, 1972.

Moss, Rachel. "Teaching Medieval Chivalry in an Age of White Supremacy." *New Chaucer Studies: Pedagogy and Profession* 3, no. 2 (2022): 6–18.

Murray, T. J. "Personal Time: The Patient's Experience." *Annals of Internal Medicine* 132, no. 1 (2000): 58–62.

Myerson, Eleanor. "Derek Jarman's Medieval Blood: Queer Devotion, Affective Medicine, and the AIDS Crisis." *postmedieval* 14, no. 1 (2023): 61–88.

Needham, Anuradha Dingwaney, and Rajeswari Sunder Rajan, eds. *The Crisis of Secularism in India*. Durham, NC: Duke University Press, 2007.

Nelstrop, Louise. "Nakedness and Anthropology in Julian of Norwich and Maurice Merleau-Ponty: Conversation Partners or Dangerous Liaisons?" *Medieval Mystical Theology* 25, no. 1 (2016): 69–85.

——. *On Deification and Sacred Eloquence: Richard Rolle and Julian of Norwich*. London: Routledge, 2020.

Newman, Barbara. *From Virile Woman to WomanChrist*. Philadelphia: University of Pennsylvania Press, 1995.

——. "Redeeming the Time: Langland, Julian, and the Art of Lifelong Revision." *Yearbook of Langland Studies* 23 (2009): 1–32.

——. "'What Did It Mean to Say 'I Saw'? The Clash between Theory and Practice in Medieval Visionary Culture." *Speculum* 80, no. 1 (2005): 1–43.

Nussbaum, Martha C. "Human Capabilities, Female Human Beings." In *Women, Culture, and Development: A Study of Human Capabilities*, ed. Martha C. Nussbaum and Jonathan Glover, 61–104. New York: Oxford University Press, 1995.

O'Connor, Mary Catharine. *The Art of Dying Well: The Development of the Ars Moriendi*. New York: Columbia University Press, 1942.

Orlemanski, Julie. *Symptomatic Subjects: Bodies, Medicine, and Causation in the Literature of Late Medieval England*. Philadelphia: University of Pennsylvania Press, 2019.

Oxford English Dictionary Online. Oxford: Oxford University Press, 2021. Accessed January 9, 2024. www.oed.com.

Palliser, Margaret Ann. *Christ, Our Mother of Mercy: Divine Mercy and Compassion in the Theology of the* Shewings *of Julian of Norwich*. Berlin: Walter de Gruyter, 1992.

Pepler, Conrad. *English Religious Heritage*. London: Blackfriars, 1958.

Perk, Godelinde Gertrude. "'Idleness Breeds Disgust for the Cell': Circumscribing Sloth, Acedia and Health in Anchoritic Literature." *Nordic Journal of English Studies* 21, no. 2 (2022): 8–31.

——. "In Loving Memory? Indecent Forgetting of the Dead in Continental Sister-Books and Julian of Norwich's *Revelation of Love*." *Religions* 14, no. 922 (2023). doi:10.3390/rel14070922.

Piccioto, Gabriela, Jesse Fox, and Félix Neto. "A Phenomenology of Spiritual Bypass: Causes, Consequences, and Implications." *Journal of Spirituality in Mental Health* 20, no. 4 (2018): 333–54.

Plügge, Herbert. "Man and His Body." In *The Philosophy of the Body: Rejections of Cartesian Dualism*, ed. Stuart F. Spicker, 293–311. Chicago: Quadrangle Books, 1970.

Powell, Jeffrey, ed. *Heidegger and Language*. Bloomington: Indiana University Press, 2013.

Raby, Michael. "The Phenomenology of Attention in Julian of Norwich's *A Revelation of Love*." *Exemplaria* 26, no. 4 (2014): 347–67.

Raczaszek-Leonardi, Joanna, Agnieszka Debska, and Adam Sochanowicz. "Pooling the Ground: Understanding and Coordination in Collective Sense-Making." In *Towards an Embodied Science of Intersubjectivity: Widening the Scope of Social Understanding Research*, ed. E. Di Paolo and H. De Jaegher, 352–65. Lausanne, Switzerland: Frontiers Media, 2015.

Reynolds, Anna Maria. "Some Literary Influences in the *Revelations* of Julian of Norwich (c. 1342–post-1416)." *Leeds Studies in English and Kindred Languages* 7–8 (1952): 18–28.

Richards, I. A. *The Philosophy of Rhetoric*. New York: Galaxy, 1965. Orig. pub. 1936.

Ricoeur, Paul. *Freud and Philosophy: An Essay in Interpretation*. Trans. Denis Savage. New Haven, CT: Yale University Press, 1970.

——. *The Rule of Metaphor: The Creation of Meaning in Language*. Trans. Robert Czerny with Kathleen McLaughlin and John Costello. London: Routledge, 2003. Orig. pub. 1975.

Riddy, Felicity. "'Women Talking About the Things of God': A Late Medieval Sub-Culture." In *Women and Literature in Britain, 1150–1500*, 2nd ed., ed. Carol M. Meale, 104–27. Cambridge: Cambridge University Press, 1996.

Rigby, Nic. "Coronavirus: Mystic's 'Relevance' to Self-Isolating World." BBC News, March 30, 2020, https://www.bbc.co.uk/news/uk-england-norfolk-52020227.

Riehle, Wolfgang. *The Middle English Mystics*. Trans. Bernard Standring. London: Routledge & Kegan Paul, 1981.

——. *The Secret Within: Hermits, Recluses, and Spiritual Outsiders in Medieval England*. Trans. Charity Scott-Stokes. Ithaca, NY: Cornell University Press, 2014. Orig. pub. 2011.

Robertson, Duncan. *Lectio Divina: The Medieval Experience of Reading*. Cistercian Studies 238. Collegeville, MN: Cistercian Publications/Liturgical Press, 2011.

Robertson, Elizabeth. "Medieval Medical Views of Women and Female Spirituality in the *Ancrene Wisse* and Julian of Norwich's *Showings*." In *Feminist Approaches to the Body in Medieval Literature*, ed. Linda Lomperis and Sarah Stanbury, 142–67. Philadelphia: University of Pennsylvania Press, 1993.

Rohrhofer, Raphaela Sophia. "The Potentiality of 'Nought': Julian of Norwich's Understanding of the Deity and the Self Through the Apophatic Matrices of Love and Dread." DPhil diss., University of Oxford, 2021.

Ross, Maggie. "Behold Not the Cloud of Experience." In Jones, *Medieval Mystical Tradition in England VIII*, 29–50.

——. *Silence: A User's Guide*. Vol. 1: *Process*. Eugene, OR: Cascade, 2018.

Rubenstein, Mary-Jane. *Strange Wonder: The Closure of Metaphysics and the Opening of Awe*. New York: Columbia University Press, 2008.

Rudd, Gillian. *Greenery: Ecocritical Readings of Late Medieval English Literature*. Manchester: Manchester University Press, 2007.

——. "'The Wilderness of Wirral' in 'Sir Gawain and the Green Knight.'" *Arthuriana* 23, no. 1 (2013): 52–65.

Ruether, Rosemary Radford. *Sexism and God-Talk: Towards a Feminist Theology*. London: SCM Press, 1983.

Ruin, Hans. "In the Spirit of Paul: Thinking the Hebraic Inheritance (Heidegger, Bultmann, Jonas)." In *Heidegger's Black Notebooks and the Future of Theology*, ed. Mårten Björk and Jayne Svenungsson, 49–76. New York: Palgrave Macmillan, 2017.

Russell, Matheson. "Phenomenology and Theology: Situating Heidegger's Philosophy of Religion." *Sophia* 50, no. 4 (2011): 641–55.

Rutledge, Robb B., Nikolina Skandali, Peter Dayan, and Raymond J. Dolan. "A Computational and Neural Model of Momentary Subjective Well-Being." *Proceedings of the National Academy of Sciences* 11, no. 33 (2014): 12252–57.

Rytting, Jennifer Rebecca. "'Hearing the Word': Julian of Norwich and the Middle English Sermon Tradition." PhD diss., Arizona State University, 2005.

Sacks, Oliver. "My Own Life." *New York Times*, February 19, 2015. https://www.nytimes.com/2015/02/19/opinion/oliver-sacks-on-learning-he-has-terminal-cancer.html?_r=0.

Saunders, Corinne. "'A Lowde Voys Cleping': Voice-Hearing, Revelation, and Imagination." In *Literature and the Senses*, ed. Annette Kern-Stähler and Elizabeth Robertson, 107–24. Oxford: Oxford University Press, 2023.

Scheff, Thomas J. "A Retrospective Look at Emotions." In *Handbook of the Sociology of Emotions*, vol. 2, ed. Jan E. Stets and Jonathan H. Turner, 245–66. Dordrecht, The Netherlands: Springer, 2014.

Schilbach, Leonhard, Bert Timmermans, Vasudevi Reddy, and Alan Costall. "Towards a Second-Person Neuroscience." *Behavioral and Brain Sciences* 36 (2013): 393–462.

Schuessler, Jennifer. "Medieval Scholars Joust with White Nationalists. And One Another." *New York Times*, May 5, 2019. https://www.nytimes.com/2019/05/05/arts/the-battle-for-medieval-studies-white-supremacy.html.

Seamon, David. *A Geography of the Lifeworld: Movement, Rest, and Encounter*. New York: St. Martins, 1979.

Sheldrake, Philip. *Julian of Norwich: In God's Sight, Her Theology in Context*. Hoboken, NJ: John Wiley, 2019.

Shklar, Judith N. "Squaring the Hermeneutic Circle." *Social Research* 71, no. 3 (2004): 655–78. Orig. pub. 1986.

Siewers, Alfred Kentigern. "Earth: A Wandering." *postmedieval* 4, no. 1: *Ecomaterialism* (2013): 6–17.

Sikka, Sonya. *Forms of Transcendence: Heidegger and Medieval Mystical Theology*. Albany: State University of New York Press, 1997.

——. "Transcendence in Death: A Heideggerian Approach to *Via Negativa* in *The Cloud of Unknowing*." In Glasscoe, *Medieval Mystical Tradition V*, 179–92.

Simons, Walter. "Reading a Saint's Body: Rapture and Bodily Movement in the *Vitae* of Thirteenth-Century Beguines." In *Framing Medieval Bodies*, ed. Sarah Kay and Miri Rubin, 10–23. Manchester: Manchester University Press, 1997.

Simpson, James. "From Reason to Affective Knowledge: Modes of Thought and Poetic Form in *Piers Plowman*." *Medium Ævum* 55, no. 1 (1986): 1–23.

——. *Piers Plowman: An Introduction to the B-Text*. London: Longman, 1990.

Smith, D. Vance. *Arts of Dying: Literature and Finitude in Medieval England*. Chicago: University of Chicago Press, 2020.

——. "Negative Langland." *Yearbook of Langland Studies* 23 (2009): 33–59.

Smith, David Nowell. *Sounding/Silence: Martin Heidegger at the Limits of Poetics.* New York: Fordham University Press, 2013.

Smith, James K. A. "Between Predication and Silence: Augustine on How (Not) to Speak of God." *Heythrop Journal* 41, no. 1 (2000): 66–86.

Smith, Neil, and Cindi Katz. "Grounding Metaphor: Towards a Spatialized Politics." In *Place and the Politics of Identity*, ed. Michael Keith and Steve Pile, 66–81. London: Routledge, 1993.

Smyth, Karen. "Reading Misreadings in Thomas Hoccleve's *Series.*" *English Studies* 87, no. 1 (2006): 3–22.

Sontag, Susan. *Illness as Metaphor* and *AIDS and Its Metaphors.* London: Penguin, 1991.

Soulen, R. Kendall. *Divine Names and the Holy Trinity.* Vol. 1: *Distinguishing the Voices.* Louisville, KY: Westminster John Knox Press, 2011.

Staley, Lynn. *Margery Kempe's Dissenting Fictions.* University Park: Pennsylvania State University Press, 1994.

Stanbury, Sarah. "Vernacular Nostalgia and *The Cambridge History of Medieval English Literature.*" *Texas Studies in Literature and Language* 44, no. 1 (2002): 92–107.

Stearns, Peter N. *Shame: A Brief History.* Springfield: University of Illinois Press, 2017.

Stellardi, Giuseppe. *Heidegger and Derrida on Philosophy and Metaphor: Imperfect Thought.* Amherst, NY: Humanity Books, 2000.

Stock, Brian. "Experience, Praxis, Work and Planning in Bernard of Clairvaux: Observations on the *Sermones in Cantica.*" In *The Cultural Context of Medieval Learning: Proceedings of the First International Colloquium on Philosophy, Science, and Theology in the Middle Ages—September 1973*, ed. John Emery Murdoch and Edith Dudley Sylla, 219–61. Dordrecht, The Netherlands: D. Reidel, 1973.

Straus, Erwin W. "The Upright Posture." *Psychiatric Quarterly* 26, no. 4 (1952): 529–61.

Strohm, Paul. *Theory and the Premodern Text.* Minneapolis: University of Minnesota Press, 2000.

Strong, James. *A Concise Dictionary of the Words in The Greek Testament.* New York: Abingdon Press, 1890. Archive.org. Accessed January 9, 2024. https://archive.org/details/StrongsGreekAndHebrewDictionaries1890.

Strub, Spencer. "The Anchorite as Analysand: Depression and the Uses of Analogy." *Exemplaria* 35, no. 1 (2023): 48–65.

Sutherland, Annie. "'Oure Feyth is Groundyd in Goddes Worde'—Julian of Norwich and the Bible." In Jones, *Medieval Mystical Tradition in England VII*, 1–20.

Suydam, Mary A. "Visionaries in the Public Eye: Beguine Literature as Performance." In *The Texture of Society: Medieval Women in the Southern Low Countries*, ed. Ellen E. Kittell and Mary A. Suydam, 131–52. New York: Palgrave Macmillan, 2004.

Svenaeus, Fredrik. "Freud's Philosophy of the Uncanny." *Scandinavian Psychoanalytic Review* 22, no. 2 (1999): 239–54.

——. *The Hermeneutics of Medicine and the Phenomenology of Health: Steps Towards a Philosophy of Medical Practice.* Dordrecht, The Netherlands: Kluwer, 2000.

——. "The Phenomenology of Health and Illness." In *Handbook of Phenomenology and Medicine*, ed. S. Kay Toombs, 87–108. Dordrecht, The Netherlands: Kluwer, 2001.

——. "Das Unheimliche—Towards a Phenomenology of Illness." *Medicine, Health Care and Philosophy* 3 (2000): 3–16.

Szasz, Thomas S. and Marc H. Hollender. "Contribution to the Philosophy of Medicine: The Basic Models of the Doctor-Patient Relationship." *American Medical Association—Archives of Internal Medicine* 97, no. 5 (1956): 585–92.

Tanner, Norman P. "Popular Religion in Norwich with Special Reference to the Evidence of Wills, 1370–1532." DPhil diss., University of Oxford, 1974.

Taylor, Charles. *A Secular Age.* Cambridge, MA: Harvard University Press, 2007.

Thouless, Robert H. *The Lady Julian: A Psychological Study.* London: SPCK, 1924.

Tinsley, David F. "Julian's Diabology." In McEntire, *Julian of Norwich*, 207–37.

Tixier, René. "'Good Gamesumli Pley': Games of Love in *The Cloud of Unknowing.*" Trans. with Victoria Hobson. *Downside Review* 108, no. 373 (1990): 235–53.

——. "'Þis louely blinde werk': Contemplation in *The Cloud of Unknowing* and Related Treatises." In *Mysticism and Spirituality in Medieval England*, ed. William F. Pollard and Robert Boenig, 107–37. Woodbridge: Brewer, 1997.

Toombs, S. Kay. *The Meaning of Illness: A Phenomenological Account of the Different Perspectives of Physician and Patient.* Boston: Kluwer, 1992.

Toivanen, Juhuna. "Beasts, Human Beings, or Gods? Human Subjectivity in Medieval Political Philosophy." In *Subjectivity and Selfhood in Medieval and Early Modern Philosophy*, ed. Jari Kaukua and Tomas Ekenberg, 181–97. Studies in the History of Philosophy of Mind 16. Dordrecht, The Netherlands: Springer, 2016.

Tugwell, Simon. *Ways of Imperfection: An Exploration of Christian Spirituality.* London: Templegate, 1985.

Turner, Denys. *The Darkness of God: Negativity in Christian Mysticism.* Cambridge: Cambridge University Press, 1995.

——. *Julian of Norwich, Theologian.* New Haven, CT: Yale University Press, 2011.

Turner, Marion. "Illness Narratives in the Later Middle Ages: Arderne, Chaucer, and Hoccleve." *Journal of Medieval and Early Modern Studies* 46, no. 1 (2016): 61–87.

Tyler, Peter. *The Return to the Mystical: Ludwig Wittgenstein, Teresa of Avila, and the Christian Mystical Tradition.* London: Continuum, 2011.

Underhill, Evelyn. *The Essentials of Mysticism.* New York: Cosimo, 2007. Orig. pub. 1920.

——. *Mysticism: A Study in the Nature and Development of Man's Spiritual Consciousness.* London: University Paperbacks Edition, 1960. Orig. pub. 1911.

Unguru, Sabetai. "Experiment in Medieval Optics." In *Physics, Cosmology and Astronomy, 1300–1700: Tension and Accommodation*, ed. Sabetai Unguru, 163–81. Dordrecht, The Netherlands: Springer, 1991.

Varnam, Laura. "The Crucifix, The Pietà, and the Female Mystic: Devotional Objects and Performative Identity in *The Book of Margery Kempe.*" *Journal of Medieval Religious Cultures* 41, no. 2 (2015): 208–37.

Vasta, Edward. *The Spiritual Basis of* Piers Plowman. New York: Humanities Press, 1965.

Verini, Alexandra and Abir Bazaz, eds. *Gender and Medieval Mysticism from India to Europe.* London: Routledge, 2023.

Vetter, Helmuth, ed. *Heidegger und das Mittelalter.* Frankfurt: Peter Lang, 1999.

Visker, Rudi. "Dropping—The 'Subject' of Authenticity: *Being and Time* on Disappearing Existentials and True Friendship with Being." In *Deconstructive Subjectivities*, ed. Simon Critchley and Peter Dews, 59–83. Albany: State University of New York Press, 1996.

Viswanathan, Gauri. *Masks of Conquest: Literary Study and British Rule in India.* Oxford: Oxford University Press, 1989.

Voegelin, Eric. *The Collected Wodrks of Eric Voegelin.* Vol. 5: *Modernity Without Restraint.* Ed. Manfred Henningsen. Columbia: University of Missouri Press, 2000.

——. *The Collected Works of Eric Voegelin.* Vol. 12: *Published Essays, 1966–1985.* Ed. Ellis Sandoz. Baton Rouge: Louisiana State University Press, 1966; repr. 1990.

Vries, Hent de, and Lawrence E. Sullivan, eds. *Political Theologies: Public Religions in a Post-Secular World.* New York: Fordham University Press, 2006.

Vuille, Juliette. "'Maybe I'm Crazy?' Diagnosis and Contextualisation of Medieval Female Mystics." In *Medicine, Religion, and Gender in Medieval Culture*, ed. Naoë Kukita Yoshikawa, 103–20. Cambridge: Brewer, 2015.

Walsh, James. "God's Homely Loving: St. John and Julian of Norwich on the Divine Indwelling." *Month* 205, n.s. 19 (1958): 164–72.

Walter, Katie L. *Middle English Mouths: Late Medieval Medical, Religious and Literary Traditions.* Cambridge: Cambridge University Press, 2018.

Ward, Benedicta. "Julian the Solitary." In *Julian Reconsidered*, ed. Kenneth Leech and Benedicta Ward, 11–35. Oxford: SLG Press, 1988.

Warren, Nancy Bradley. "Julian of Norwich: Lives and Afterlives." In *New Directions in Medieval Mystical and Devotional Literature: Essays in Honor of Denise N.*

Baker, ed. Amy N. Vines and Lee Templeton, 145–62. Lanham, MD: Rowman and Littlefield, 2023.

Watson, Nicholas. "The Composition of Julian of Norwich's *Revelation of Love*." *Speculum* 68, no. 3 (1993): 637–83.

——. "Conceptions of the Word: The Mother Tongue and the Incarnation of God." *New Medieval Literatures* 1 (1997): 85–124.

——. "Censorship and Cultural Change in Late-Medieval England: Vernacular Theology, the Oxford Translation Debate, and Arundel's Constitutions of 1409." *Speculum* 70, no. 4 (1995): 822–64.

——. "'Sixteen Shewinges': The Composition of Julian of Norwich's *Revelation of Love* Revisited." in *Mystics, Goddesses, Lovers, and Teachers: Medieval Visions and the Modern Legacies. Studies in Honour of Barbara Newman*, ed. Stephen Rozenski, Joshua Byron Smith, and Claire M. Waters, 131–54. Turnhout, Belgium: Brepols, 2023.

——. "The Trinitarian Hermeneutic in Julian of Norwich's *Revelation of Love*." In Glasscoe, *Medieval Mystical Tradition in England V*, 79–100.

——. "Visions of Inclusion: Universal Salvation and Vernacular Theology in Pre-Reformation England." *Journal of Medieval and Early Modern Studies* 27 (1997): 145–87.

Weinstein, Donald, and Rudolph Bell. *Saints and Society: The Two Worlds of Western Christendom, 1000–1700*. Chicago: University of Chicago Press, 1982.

Weiskott, Eric. "The Coronavirus Time Warp: Reading Medieval Literature in the Midst of a Pandemic." Public Seminar, April 10, 2020. https://publicseminar.org/2020/04/the-coronavirus-time-warp/.

Welwood, John, "Human Nature, Buddha Nature: On Spiritual Bypassing, Relationship, and the Dharma: An Interview with John Welwood by Tina Fossella." Accessed January 9, 2024. https://www.johnwelwood.com/articles/TRIC_interview_uncut.pdf.

Westphal, Merold. "Hermeneutics as Epistemology." In *Overcoming Onto-Theology: Towards a Postmodern Christian Faith*, 47–74. New York: Fordham University Press, 2001.

——. "Prayer as the Posture of the Decentered Self." In Benson and Wirzba, *Phenomenology of Prayer*, 13–31.

Whitaker, Cord J. "The Problem of Alt-Right Medievalist White Supremacy, and Its Black Medievalist Answer." In *Far-Right Revisionism and the End of History*, ed. Louie Dean Valencia-García, 159–76. New York: Routledge, 2020.

White, Hugh. *Nature and Salvation in* Piers Plowman. Cambridge: Brewer, 1988.

Williams, Duane. *Language and Being: Heidegger's Linguistics*. London: Bloomsbury, 2017.

Winning, Anne. "Homesickness." *Phenomenology + Pedagogy* 8 (1990): 245–58.

Wirzba, Norman. "Attention and Responsibility: The Work of Prayer." In Benson and Wirzba, *Phenomenology of Prayer*, 88–100.

Wittgenstein, Ludwig. *Tractatus Logico-Philosophicus*. Trans. C. K. Ogden with an introduction by Bertrand Russell. New York: Routledge, 2005. Orig. pub. 1921.

Wohlmann, Anita. *Metaphor in Illness Writing: Fight and Battle Reused*. Edinburgh: Edinburgh University Press, 2022.

Wolfe, Judith. "The Black Notebooks: Caught in the Trap of His Own Metaphysics." *Standpoint Magazine*, May 29, 2014. https://research-repository.st-andrews.ac.uk/bitstream/handle/10023/4872/Caught_in_the_Trap_of_His_Own_Ideas.pdf?sequence=1&isAllowed=y.

——. *Heidegger and Theology*. London: Bloomsbury, 2014.

——. *Heidegger's Eschatology: Theological Horizons in Martin Heidegger's Early Work*. Oxford: Oxford University Press, 2013.

Wolin, Richard, ed. *The Heidegger Controversy: A Critical Reader*. Cambridge, MA: MIT Press, 1993.

——. *Heidegger in Ruins: Between Philosophy and Ideology*. New Haven, CT: Yale University Press, 2023.

Young, Shinzen. *Break Through Pain: A Step-by-Step Mindfulness Meditation Program for Transforming Chronic and Acute Pain*. Boulder, CO: Sounds True, 2004.

Zeeman, Nicolette. Piers Plowman *and the Medieval Discourse of Desire*. Cambridge: Cambridge University Press, 2006.

——. "Julian Reads Langland." *Chaucer Review* 58, nos. 3–4 (2023): 468–80.

Zumthor, Paul. *Toward a Medieval Poetics*. Trans. Philip Bennett. Minneapolis: University of Minnesota Press, 1992.

INDEX